THE

DEAN OF LISMORE'S BOOK

A SELECTION OF

ANCIENT GAELIC POETRY

FROM A MANUSCRIPT COLLECTION MADE BY SIR JAMES M'GREGOR,
DEAN OF LISMORE, IN THE BEGINNING OF THE
SIXTEENTH CENTURY.

EDITED WITH A TRANSLATION AND NOTES

BY THE REV. THOMAS M'LAUCHLAN

AND

AN INTRODUCTION AND ADDITIONAL NOTES

BY WILLIAM F. SKENE Esq.

EDINBURGH
EDMONSTON AND DOUGLAS
1862.

CONTENTS.

INTRODUCTION.

In the heart of the Perthshire Highlands, and not far from the northern shore of Loch Tay, there lies a secluded vale of about six miles long. The river Lyon, which issues from the long and narrow valley of Glenlyon through the pass of Chesthill, hardly less beautiful than the celebrated pass of Killichranky, meanders through it. On the east bank of a small stream which falls into the Lyon about the centre of the vale, is the Clachan or Kirkton of Fortingall, anciently called Fothergill, from which it takes its name; and on the west or opposite bank is the mansion of Glenlyon House, anciently called Tullichmullin.

A stranger stationed at the clachan or little village of Fortingall, would almost fancy that there was neither egress from nor ingress to this little district, so secluded and shut in among the surrounding mountains does it appear to be. It is a spot where one could well suppose that the traditions of former times, and the remains of a forgotten oral literature, might still linger in the memories of its inhabitants; while the local names of the mountains and streams about it are redolent of the mythic times of the Feine. On the west is the glen of Glenlyon, the ancient Cromgleann nan Clach or Crooked Glen of the Stones, associated with many a tradition of the Feine, and where the remains of those rude forts, termed Caistealan na Feine, crown many a rocky summit; and the vale is bounded on the south and east by the ridge of Druimfhionn or Finn's Ridge.

In the latter part of the fifteenth and beginning of the sixteenth centuries, there dwelt here a family of the name of Macgregor. They were descended from a vicar of Fortingall, who, at the time when, during the century preceding the Reformation, the Catholic Church was breaking up, and their benefices passing into the hands of laymen, secured for himself and his descendants the vicarage of Fortingall and a lease of the church lands.

Of the history of this family we know somewhat from an obituary commenced by one of his descendants, and continued to the year 1579 by the Curate of Fothergill, which is still preserved.

His son, whether legitimate or illegitimate we know not, was Ian Rewych, or John the Grizzled, termed Makgewykar or son of the Vicar.[1]

His grandson was Dougall Maol, or Dougall the Bald or Tonsured, called patronymically Dougall Johnson, or the son of John.

This Dougall Johnson appears in 1511 as a notary-

[1] Obitus Katherine neyn Ayn Weyll Sponsse Johannis M'Ayn Rawych Macgewykar apud Aychly in Mense Decembris anno Domini M v c xlij —Chron. Fort.

public,[1] and dwelt at Tullichmullin, where his wife Katherine, daughter of Donald M'Clawe, *alias* Grant, died in 1512.[2] He is twice mentioned in the obituary or Chronicle of Fortingall; in 1526, as repairing the cross in Inchadin, or the old church of Kenmore, situated on the north bank of the river Tay, nearly opposite Taymouth Castle; and in 1529, as placing a stone cross in Larkmonemerkyth, the name of a pass among the hills which leads from Inchadin to the south.[3]

Of Dougall the Bald, the son of John the Grizzled, we have no further mention; but of his family we know of two sons, James and Duncan.

James was a Churchman. He appears as a notary-public, an office then held by ecclesiastics, along with his father, in the year 1511, and he early attained to honour and influence, through what channel is unknown; for, in 1514, we find him Dean of Lismore,[4] an island in Argyllshire, lying between the districts of Lorn and Morvern, which was at that time the Episcopal seat of the Bishops of Argyll. He was, besides, Vicar of Fortingall and Firmarius or tenant of the church lands; and died possessed of these benefices in the year 1551, and

1 Charter Robert Menzies of that ilk to Sir Duncan Campbell of Glenurchy, dated at the Isle of Loch Tay, 18th September 1511. Inter test. Dugallo Johneson Notario et domino Jacobo M'Gregour notario-publico.—Reg. Mag. Sig. xvii. 69.

2 Obitus Catherine neyn Donyll M'Clawe alias Grant uxoris Dougalli Johnson apud Tullychmolliu xxij. die Julij anno domini M°V°xj.

3 Memorandum solium crucis in Inchadin compositum fuit per Dougallum Johnson. Anno domini M°V°xxvj°. Crux lapidea fuit posita in Larkmonemerkyth in magno lapide qui alio nomine vocatur clachur . . . per Dougallum Johnson primo Octobris anno domini, etc., V°xxix.—Chron. Fort.

4 Origines Parochiales, vol. ii. pt. i. p. 161.

was buried in the choir of the old church of Inchadin.[1]

In 1552, a year after his death, Gregor Macgregor, son of the deceased Sir James Macgregor, Dean of Lismore, as became the head of a small but independent sept of the Macgregors, and with a due regard to its safety, bound himself to Colin Campbell of Glenurchy and his heirs, "taking him for his chief, in place of the Laird of Macgregor, and giving him his calp." [2]

In 1557 Gregor and Dougall Macgregors, natural sons of Sir James Macgregor, receive letters of legitimation;[3] and, in 1574, Dougall Macgregor appears as Chancellor of Lismore.[4]

It is unnecessary for our purpose to follow the history of this family any further; suffice it to say, that the two brothers, James and Duncan,[5] members of a clan which, though under the ban of the Government, and exposed to the grasping aggression of their powerful neighbours, the Campbells of Glenurchy, considered themselves as peculiarly Highland, and had high pretensions, as descended from the old Celtic monarchs of Scotland—connected with the Church, and as such, possessing some

[1] Obitus honorabilis viri ac egregii Viri Domini Jacobi (M'Gregor) filii Dougalli Johnson ac decani Lesmorensis Vicarii de Fortyrgill et Firmarii dicte ecclesie . . . bone memorie in nocte Sancte Lucie virginis hora . . . post meridiem et sepultus in die Lucie videlicet . . . Anno Domini M V^c lj^o. in choro de Inchadin.—Chron. Fort.

[2] Black Book of Taymouth, p. 196.

[3] Precept of Legitimation in favour of Gregor and Dougal MacGregors, natural sons of Sir James MacGregor.—Privy Seal, xxix. 46.

[4] Charter by Dougall Macgregor, Chancellor of Lismoir, with consent of Sir Colin Campbell of Glenurchy, of the lands of Auchnacroftie, dated at Balloch, 25th December 1574.

[5] Duncan mcCowle voil vic Eoyne Reawych.—MS., p. 223.

cultivation of mind and such literary taste as Churchmen at that time had, yet born and reared in the farm-house of Tullichmullin, in the secluded vale of Fortingall, and imbued with that love of old Highland story and cherished fondness for Highland song, which manifests itself in so many a quiet country Highlander, and which the scenery and associations around them were so well calculated to foster—the one, from his high position in the Church of Argyll, having peculiar facilities for collecting the poetry current in the West Highlands—the other, though his brother, yet, as was not uncommon in those days, his servitor or amanuensis, and himself a poet—and both natives of the Perthshire Highlands—collected and transcribed into a commonplace book Gaelic poetry obtained from all quarters.

This collection has fortunately been preserved. It is, unquestionably, a native compilation made in the central Highlands, upwards of three hundred years ago. It contains the remains of an otherwise lost literature. In it we find all that we can now recover of native compositions current in the Highlands prior to the sixteenth century, as well as the means of ascertaining the extent to which the Highlanders were familiar with the works of Irish poets.

It is a quarto volume of some 311 pages, and is written in the current Roman hand of the period. Though much injured by time, the leaves in part worn away, and the ink faint, it is still possible to read the greater part of its contents.

With the exception of a short Latin obituary, and one or two other short pieces, it consists entirely of a collection of Gaelic poetry made by the two brothers.

At the bottom of the 27th page appears the following note in Latin:—Liber Dni Jacobi Macgregor Decani Lismoren.

At page 78, there is a chronological list of Scottish kings written in the Scottish language, which ends thus:—"James the Fyfte reignis now in great felicitie." He reigned from 1513 to 1542; and, on page 144, there is a genealogy of the Macgregors, written by the brother Duncan, deducing their descent from the old Scottish kings, and he adds a docquet in Gaelic, which may be thus translated:—Duncan the Servitor, the son of Dougall, who was son of John the Grizzled, wrote this from the Book of the History of the Kings, and it was done in the year 1512.[1]

There can be no question, therefore, that this collection was formed during the lifetime of the Dean of Lismore, and a great part of it as early as the year 1512. How it was preserved through that and the succeeding century is unknown. In the last century it passed into the possession of the Highland Society of London, by whom it was transferred to the custody of the Highland Society of Scotland, when a committee of that Society was engaged in an inquiry into the authenticity of the Poems of Ossian, published by Macpherson. It has now been deposited, along

[1] Agis Duncha Deyr oclych mcDowle vec oyne Reywich di Skreyve so a loywrow Shenchych nyn reig agis ros zenyt Anno Domini 1512.—MS., p. 144. Deyroclych is Daoroglach, and is the Gaelic rendering of Servitor.

with other Gaelic MSS. in the possession of that Society, in the Library of the Faculty of Advocates, and forms part of that collection of Gaelic MSS. which have been brought together within the last few years, and contain nearly all the Gaelic MSS. which are known still to exist.[1]

The Dean's MS. differs from all the other MSS. in that collection in two essential particulars. It is not, like the other MSS., written in what is called the Irish character, but in the current Roman character of the early part of the sixteenth century; and the language is not written in the orthography used in writing Irish, and now universally employed in writing Scotch Gaelic, but in a peculiar kind of phonetic orthography, which aims at presenting the words in English orthography as they are pronounced.

The peculiar orthography employed is, however, evidently not the mere attempt of a person ignorant of the

1 This collection has been formed within the last few years mainly through the instrumentality of the writer. When he commenced, the Faculty of Advocates possessed four Gaelic MSS. The collection now consists of sixty-five.

The writer formed the plan of collecting the remains of the MS. Gaelic literature of Scotland, which was rapidly disappearing, into one place, where they could be preserved, by inducing the possessors of Gaelic MSS. to deposit them in some public library for preservation; and as the Faculty of Advocates were already in the possession of some MSS., their library was evidently the most appropriate depository for this purpose. The valuable MSS. belonging to the Highland Society of Scotland formed the basis of the collection; the directors, and their secretary, John Hall Maxwell, Esq., C.B., having at once responded to the call, and the fortunate discovery of the Kilbride collection, which its possessor likewise agreed to deposit, added a large number. The remainder consists of MSS. deposited by individual possessors, and the collection now embraces nearly all the MSS. known or believed still to exist.

It is hoped that, if any Gaelic MSS. still remain in the hands of individual possessors, they will add to the value of this collection by making them known, and depositing them in the Advocates' Library for preservation.

The MSS. are preserved in a locked cabinet, and a general catalogue of the whole has been prepared by the writer.

proper orthography to write the words in English letters in an arbitrary manner, so as to present, as nearly as possible, the sound of the words as they struck his ear when repeated to him, but bears evident marks of having been a regular and known system of orthography, which, although we have few specimens of it left, may not the less have once prevailed in that part of the Highlands more removed from the influence of Irish teaching.

It is a peculiarity of all the Celtic dialects, that the consonants suffer a change in the beginning of words, from the influence of the preceding words, or in forming the oblique cases, and likewise change their sound in the middle of words by being aspirated.

In the Irish orthography, the original consonant is invariably preserved; and the change is indicated by prefixing another consonant when the sound is affected by eclipsis, or the influence of the preceding word, or by adding the letter *h*, when it is changed by aspiration.

In the Welsh dialects, however, and in the Manx, which is a dialect of the Gaelic division of the Celtic languages, a different system of orthography has always prevailed. Instead of retaining the original letter, and indicating the change in the sound by prefixing or adding another, a different letter expressing simply the new sound, is substituted for the original letter; and hence the orthography bears more of a phonetic and less of an etymologic character.

Both systems have their advantages and disadvantages. In the one, the original form of the word is preserved, and the primary sounds of the letters are retained. The alteration in their sound in inflection is marked by prefixing another letter, or adding the letter *h*. It is by the application of grammatical rules that the pronunciation of the word is ascertained, and that pronunciation may deviate from time to time to a greater degree from the original standard, while the orthography, always remaining the same, fails to chronicle it.

In the other, a new letter is substituted for the original letter, when the sound is changed by inflection, or by the position of the word in a sentence, and the orthography employed expresses the pronunciation of the word in its inflected, without reference to its original form.

The one presents the language in its etymologic form, without reference to its pronunciation, and is of value in preserving the original form of the written speech.

The other stereotypes its sounds as spoken at the time; it is committed to writing without reference to the original form or primary shape of the words; and is of value in exhibiting the living dialects as spoken by the people.

An apt illustration of this is afforded by the English language and its dialects.

The English orthography exhibits the language as it once was, but from which it has greatly deviated in pronunciation; and it is hardly possible to frame rules by applying which, to the orthography, the present pronunciation can be deduced. It is obvious that if the words, which are differently pronounced in the Scotch dialect, were spelt according to the English orthography, no clue would be afforded to its peculiarities. On the other hand, when the Scotch dialect is spelt phonetically, as is done, for instance, by Sir Walter Scott in his Scotch romances, the peculiarities in the pronunciation of a living dialect are vividly presented, and these elements of the original language, which may have been preserved in this dialect, are made available for philological purposes.

The collection of Gaelic poetry made by the Dean of Lismore and his brother is thus written in an orthography of this latter class. It attracted some notice when the Highland Society was engaged in its inquiry into the authenticity of Ossian's Poems, from its including among its contents some poems attributed to Ossian. Three of these are printed in the report, though incorrectly and imperfectly, but little was known of the other contents of the MS.

A transcript was made of the MS. for the Highland Society by the late Mr. Ewen M'Lachlan, an accomplished Gaelic scholar, who was employed to examine their MS. It, however, passed into the possession of the Rev. J. Macintyre of Kilmanievaig, who allowed it to be examined for a short time by the editors, but no full or correct account was given of the MS. till the Rev. T. M'Lauchlan, one of the editors of this work, read an account of it to the Society of Scottish Antiquaries in the year 1856, which is printed in their proceedings.[1] This account attracted considerable notice to the MS., and led to its value being more appreciated.

[1] Vol ii pt i. p. 35.

The present publication has, in consequence, been undertaken.

The Dean's MS. has a double value, philological and literary, and is calculated to throw light both on the language and the literature of the Highlands of Scotland. It has a philological value, because its peculiar orthography presents the language at the time in its aspect and character as a spoken language, and enables us to ascertain whether many of the peculiarities which now distinguish it were in existence three hundred years ago; and it has a literary value, because it contains poems attributed to Ossian, and to other poets prior to the sixteenth century, which are not to be found elsewhere; and thus presents to us specimens of the traditionary poetry current in the Highlands prior to that period, which are above suspicion, having been collected upwards of three hundred years ago, and before any controversy on the subject had arisen.

It has been found impossible to present so large a collection entire, but the selection has been made with reference to these two objects. Each poem selected for publication has been presented entire. There is a literal translation of the poem made by the Rev. T. M'Lauchlan, and appended is the original Gaelic text of the poem in the Dean's orthography, exactly as it appears in the MS.; and, on the opposite page, the same Gaelic has been transferred by Mr. M'Lauchlan into the modern orthography of the Scotch Gaelic, which is nearly the same as that of the Irish, so as to afford the means of comparing the one orthography with the other, and the modern spoken dialect in the Highlands with the language of the poems collected by the Dean upwards of three hundred years ago, as well as to furnish a test of the accuracy of the translation, by showing the rendering given to the Dean's language.[1]

The present spoken language of the Highlands of Scotland is, as is well known, a dialect[2] of that great branch of the Celtic languages termed the Gwyddelian or Gaelic, and to which belong also the Irish and Manx, or spoken language of the Isle of Man. These three dialects of the Gaelic branch of the Celtic languages, the Irish, the Scotch Gaelic, and the Manx, approach each other so nearly, as to form in fact but one language; and the peculiarities which distinguish them from one another are not of a nature sufficiently broad or vital to constitute either of them a distinct language.

The language spoken by the Highlanders of Scotland is termed by them simply Gaelic; but the name of Erse

[1] It is hardly possible to convey to the reader an adequate conception of the labour of the task undertaken by Mr. M'Lauchlan, or of the courage, perseverance, and ability with which it has been overcome. Mr. M'Lauchlan had first to read the Dean's transcript—no ordinary task, when, to a strange orthography, affording no clue to the original word, was added a careless handwriting of the beginning of the sixteenth century, faded ink, and decayed paper. He had then to convert it into the corresponding Gaelic in its modern shape and orthography, and then to translate it into English, in which he had to combine the literal rendering of an idiomatic language with an intelligible exhibition of its meaning in English.

It may be as well to take this opportunity of stating, that Mr M'Lauchlan is solely responsible for the selection made from the Dean's MS., the rendering in modern Gaelic, the English translation, and the notes at the foot of the page. The writer of this is responsible only for the Introduction and the additional notes, to which his name is attached.

[2] I use the word *dialect* throughout, in the restricted sense of the German word *mundart*, for want of a better English word to express it.

has occasionally been bestowed upon it during the last few centuries by the Lowlanders.[1] As early as the year 1690 a short vocabulary of Scotch Gaelic words was appended to an edition of Bedel's Irish Bible, to adapt it to the use of the Scotch Highlanders; and a somewhat fuller vocabulary, by the same author, was published in Nicolson's Scottish Historical Library in 1702.

In 1741, a more complete vocabulary was published by the Society for Propagating Christian Knowledge, for the use of their schools in the Highlands. It was compiled by Mr. Alexander M'Donald, schoolmaster at Ardnamurchan. Another vocabulary was published in 1795 by Robert M'Farlane; and, in 1815, a further step in advance was made by the larger vocabulary of Mr. P. M'Farlane.

In 1825, a large quarto dictionary of the Scotch Gaelic was published by R. A. Armstrong; and in three years afterwards the splendid dictionary compiled by the first Gaelic scholars, under the auspices of the Highland Society of Scotland, appeared. In this dictionary Gaelic words from all quarters are inserted; but those which belong to the vernacular dialect of the Scotch Highlands are carefully distinguished.

The small dictionary compiled by M'Alpine, a schoolmaster in Islay, affords a genuine representation of the Gaelic spoken in that island.

[1] This term is unknown to the Highlanders, who call themselves Albanaich; and was a term of reproach applied to them by the Lowlanders, from their language being the same as the Irish. It is curious that the same reproach was applied by the English to the Scotch in the twelfth century. Lambarde records that, at the battle of the Standard, when the Scots shouted *Albany, Albany!* the English soldiers retorted with *Yry, Yry!* "a term of great reproach at that time."

The only grammar of the Scotch Gaelic which it is necessary to notice, is the able and philosophic grammar by Alexander Stewart, Minister of the Gospel at Dingwall, the first edition of which was published in 1801, and the second in 1812. As a first attempt to reduce the spoken language of the Scotch Highlanders to a grammatical system, it is a work of rare excellence and fidelity, and all other grammars have been more or less taken from it.

This grammar, then, and the vocabularies and dictionaries above referred to, contain the Gaelic language as spoken, at the time of their compilation, in the Highlands of Scotland, and afford the materials for judging of the character of those peculiarities which distinguish it from the Irish and Manx Gaelic.[1]

The differences between the spoken language of the Scottish Highlands and the Irish exist partly in the pronunciation, where the accentuation of the language is different, where that peculiar change in the initial consonant, produced by the influence of the previous word, and termed by the Irish grammarians eclipsis, is unknown except in the sibilant, where the vowel sounds are different,

[1] I reject from this list the grammar and dictionary by the Rev. Wm. Shaw, published in 1778 and 1780, because, so far as they purport to be a grammar and dictionary of the Scotch Gaelic dialect, they are a deception, and not trustworthy.

Shaw was a native of Arran, where a corrupt and Irishised Gaelic is spoken; and it is well known that he failed in his attempt to compile his dictionary from the spoken language in the Highlands, where he made a tour for the purpose, and resorted to Ireland, where he manufactured his works from Irish sources and authorities, adapting the Irish grammar to a very imperfect knowledge of the language.

The subscribers complained of the deception, and refused to take the work, till compelled by a process at law. The evidence taken in this process is very instructive as to the position of Shaw's grammar and dictionary, so far as their Irish element is concerned, towards the Scotch Gaelic dialect at that period.

and there are even traces of a consonantal permutation; partly in the grammar, where the Scotch Gaelic prefers the analytic form of the verb, and has no present tense, the old present being now used for the future, and the present formed by the auxiliary verb, where the plural of one class of the nouns is formed in a peculiar manner, resembling the Anglo-Saxon, and a different negative is used; partly in the idioms of the language, where a greater preference is shown to express the idea by the use of substantives, and the verb is anxiously avoided; and in the vocabulary, which varies to a considerable extent, where words now obsolete in Irish are still living words, and others are used in a different sense.[1]

The Scotch Gaelic is spoken in its greatest purity in the central districts of the Highlands, including Mull, Morvern, Ardnamurchan, Ardgowar, Appin, Lochaber, and that district termed the Garbh chriochan, or rough bounds, consisting of Arisaig, Moydart, Moror, and Knoydart. The language here spoken is characterized by a closer adherence to grammatical rules, by a fuller and more careful pronunciation of the vowel sounds, by a selection of the best words to express the idea, and by their use in their primary sense.

In the county of Argyll, and the islands which face the coast of Ireland, the language approaches much more nearly to the Ulster dialect of the Irish, there being probably no perceptible difference between the form of the

1 A more detailed statement of the differences between Scotch and Irish Gaelic will be found in the additional Notes

language in Isla and Rachrin, or in Cantyre and the opposite coast of Antrim.

In the Gaelic of Sutherland and Caithness, again, there are marked differences of a different and opposite character, a native of Sutherland and the southern districts of Argyll having some difficulty in understanding each other; and in Perthshire, on the other hand, the influence of the English language is apparent, the pronunciation is more careless, the words selected less pure, and the secondary senses of many are only used.

The central districts afford the best type of that variety of Gaelic which forms the spoken language of the Highlands of Scotland.

Of this language two views may be taken. The peculiarities of the language may have sprung up quite recently, and the language may, at no very distant period, have been absolutely identical in form and sound with the Irish, from which it may have become corrupted by the absence of cultivation, and must be regarded merely as the rude *patois* of a people whose ignorance of the cultivated language has led to their adoption of peculiarities sanctioned by no grammatical rule; or, on the other hand, these peculiarities may partake rather of the character of dialectic differences, and enter more deeply into the organization of the language, and thus may have characterized it from that remoter period, when geographical separation and political isolation may have led to the formation, in the Highlands of Scotland, of a dialectic variety of the common language.

The first is the view taken by Irish grammarians, and if correct, these differences cannot be considered as of any philological importance. The question has not, however, been treated by them in a candid spirit, or with any grasp of the subject; and their opinion must be based upon a more accurate knowledge of the spoken dialect which is the subject of it, and upon a sounder and more impartial examination of those philologic elements which ought to enter into its consideration, before it can be accepted as conclusive. If the second view is the correct one, then it is obvious that the Scotch Gaelic is well deserving of study, as a distinct variety of the Gaelic language which was common to Scotland and Ireland; and everything that tends to throw light upon it, and upon the existence and origin of these differences, acquires a philologic value.

In the study of language, the spoken dialects are of great value. It is from the study of the living dialects, which are not merely corruptions of the spoken language, but present dialectic peculiarities, that we arrive at a full perception of the character and tendencies of the mother tongue.

It is the destiny of all languages, that they no sooner enter upon the domain of history than they begin to alter, decompose, and split into dialects. The formation of the mother tongue belongs to the prehistoric period; and it is a process which, carried on in the infancy and growth of the social state, is concealed from observation. When its possessors first emerge into view, and take their place among the history of nations, counter influences have already been at work, their language has already entered upon its downward course, and we can only watch it in its process of decomposition and alteration, and reach its primitive condition, through the medium of its dialects.

There are two opposing influences by which all languages are affected—the etymologic and the phonetic. The etymologic principle is all-powerful in the formation and original structure of the language, producing combinations of sounds demanded by the laws of its composition, but irrespective altogether of the requirements of harmony, or the tendencies of the human organs of sound. It contains in it, however, the seeds of its own destruction, and has no sooner completed its work of formation than a process of modification and decomposition commences, caused by the respective idiosyncrasies of its speakers, their craving after harmony of combination and ease of utterance, and the influence of physical situation and surrounding agents upon the organs of speech.

These phonetic causes enter at once into conflict with the strictly etymologic formations of the language, moulding its sounds, decomposing its structure, and interchanging the organs producing the sounds; and these effects are perpetuated by circumstances causing the separation or isolation of the people who have adopted them, while new words and combinations are added to their vocabulary by new wants arising in their separate state, by their advance in social condition, or by the peculiarities of their new condition. Thus innumerable dialects spring up. Whenever a difference of situation takes place among the people composing the aggregate by whom the original language was spoken, a diversity of dialect is at once created. In these dialects are preserved the bones of the mother tongue; and it is only by a comparison of these that her full character can be ascertained.

This tendency of the mother tongue, to break up into as many dialects as there are shades of difference in the position and tendencies of its speakers, is only arrested by the formation of a cultivated dialect, created when the wants of an educated or cultivated class in the community demand a common medium of interchanging their ideas. This cultivated language is usually first formed by poetry, completed by writing, and adopted by education. Its first stage is that of the language in which the songs and poems, the first literature of a rude people, are recited by its bards, its earliest literary class; and, by the introduction of the art of writing, it passes over into the written speech. It then becomes a common dialect, spoken and written by the cultivated class of the community, and to a knowledge of which a portion of the people are raised by education.

This cultivated or written language may have been originally one of the numerous dialects spoken by the people composing the community, and which circumstances have elevated into that position; or it may have been introduced from another country speaking a sister dialect, which has preceded it in cultivation; or it may, like the German, have been developed from an unspoken variety of the language created by other causes and for other purposes. In the one case, the language first cultivated by poetry passes over into the written language. In the other, it remains an indigenous, cultivated, spoken language, which is antagonistic to, and contends with, the imported written speech till the influence of the latter prevails, and it is either extinguished by it, or remains as popular poetry in the vernacular tongue, while everything prose is absorbed.

But however it originates, the spoken dialects still remain as the vernacular speech of portions of the community. They are not the children or creatures of the written speech, still less corruptions of it, but are equally ancient, and retain much of the elements of the original language which the written speech has rejected.

The formation of a cultivated or written language is always an eclectic process. It selects, it modifies, and it rejects, while the living dialects retain many of the forms and much of the structure modified and rejected by it. Hence, for the study of the character and formation of the mother tongue, the living spoken dialects are of the first importance; and a restricted attention to the written language, and the contemptuous rejection of everything in the spoken dialects which vary from it, as barbarisms and corruptions, is simply to part with much valuable material for the study, and to narrow the range of inquiry.[1]

[1] Professor Max Muller has the following excellent remarks in his recent lectures on the Science of Language, p. 49 "The real and natural life of language is

Perhaps the English language affords an illustration of these remarks. As a written and cultivated language, it took its rise in England, but was introduced from England into Scotland.

In England, the provincial dialects have remained as the spoken language of the uncultivated class in the respective provinces side by side with it; but their antiquity and their value for philological purposes is fully acknowledged. No one dreams of viewing them as merely corruptions of the written language, arising from rudeness and ignorance.

In Scotland, the English language has been introduced as the written or cultivated language, but a different form

in its dialects; and in spite of the tyranny exercised by the classical or literary idioms, the day is still very far off which is to see the dialects entirely eradicated. . . .

"It is a mistake to imagine that dialects are everywhere corruptions of the literary language. . . . Dialects have always been the feeders rather than the channels of a literary language; anyhow, they are parallel streams which existed long before one of them was raised to that temporary eminence which is the result of literary cultivation." The whole of the lecture in which this passage occurs is well worthy of perusal, in regard to the proper view and position of the spoken dialects in the study of language.

Schleicher takes the same view in his masterly work, "Die Deutsche Sprache." He says, in relation to the German language, what is equally true of the Gaelic:

"Die mundarten sind die natürlichen nach den Gesetzen der Sprachgeschichtlichen Veranderungen gewordenen Formen im Gegensatze zu der mehr oder minder gemachten and schulmeisterisch geregelten and zugestutzten Sprache der Schrift. Schon hieraus folgt der hohe Werth derselben fur die wissenschaftliche Erforschung unserer Sprache; hier ist eine reiche Fulle von Worten und Formen, die, an sich gut und echt, von der Schriftsprache verschmäht wurden; hier finden wir manches, was wir zur Erklärung der älteren Sprachdenkmale, ja zur Erkenntniss der jetzigen Schriftsprache verwerthen konnen, abgesehen von dem Sprachgeschichtlichen, dem lautphysiologischen Interesse, welches die uberaus reiche Mannigfaltigkeit unserer Mundarten bietet.

"Wer einer Mundart kundig ist, der hat beim Studium des altdeutschen einen grossen Vorsprung vor demjenigen voraus der nur in der Schriftsprache heimisch ist.

"*Nichts ist thörichter, nichts verräth mehr den Mangel wahrer Bildung als das Verrachten unserer Mundarten.*"—P. 110.

of the language, the Broad Scotch, is the vernacular speech of the people, and preceded the English language as the written language of the country in which its earliest literature was contained. Its great value, as an early form of the original Anglic tongue which formed the language of the country, is so fully acknowledged, that Jamieson's Dictionary of the Scotch language has been called the best dictionary of the English language. It has ceased to be a vehicle for prose composition; but there exists a ballad literature in the Scotch dialect which has resisted the absorbing influence of the English.

So it was also in the Scotch Highlands, where the written and cultivated language did not originate in this country, but was brought over from Ireland in the sixth century, though in this case the analogy is not so great, from the various dialects of the Gaelic having probably at all times approached each other much more nearly than the provincial dialects of England and Scotland, and been more greatly influenced by the written language.

In order to determine the philological position and value of the Scotch Gaelic, it is necessary to form a more accurate conception of the historical position of the people who spoke it, and of the influences to which they have been exposed, and by which the language was likely to be affected.

Two races seem to have entered, as original elements, into the population of Ireland and of the Highlands of Scotland. These were the race of the Scots and the people termed by the early Irish authorities the race of the Cruithne. The latter appear everywhere to have preceded the former.

Prior to the sixth century, the Cruithne alone seem to have formed the population of the Scotch Highlands. In Ireland they formed the original population of Ulster and the north part of Leinster. Connaught, the rest of Leinster, and Munster, were Scottish. The east and north of Ireland appear to have been most exposed to external influences, and to have suffered the greatest changes in their population. In the south and west it was more permanent; and from Connaught and Leinster the royal races of the Scots emerged, while their colonies proceeded from south and west to north and east.

The traditionary history of Ireland records an early settlement of the Scots among the Cruithne of Ulster, termed from its mythic founder Dalriada, and likewise the fall of the great seat of the Cruithnian kingdom, called Emania, before an expedition, led by a scion of the Scottish royal race, who established the kingdom of Orgialla on its ruins. It is certain that, while we have reason to believe that the Cruithne formed the original population of the whole of Ulster, we find them in the historic period confined to certain districts in Ulster only, although their kings retained the title of kings of Ulster.

In the beginning of the sixth century, the Scots, who are frequently recorded by the Roman writers as forming part of the predatory bands who, from time to time, assailed the Roman province, and finally overthrew their empire in Britain, passed over to the opposite coast of Argyll, and effected a permanent settlement there, which, from its mother tribe, was also called Dalriada. This settlement is recorded, by the oldest authority, to have taken place twenty years after the battle of Ocha, which was fought in the year 483, and, therefore, in the year 503. The territory occupied by this settlement of the Scots was the south part of Argyllshire, consisting of the districts of Cowall, Kintyre, Knapdale, Argyll-proper, Lorn, and probably part of Morvern, with the islands of Isla, Iona, Arran, and the small islands adjacent. The boundary which separated them from the Cruithne was on the east, the range of mountains termed Drumalban, a mountain chain which still separates the county of Argyll from that of Perth. On the north, the boundary, which probably was not very distinct, and varied from time to time, seems to have been coincident with a line extending from the Island of Colonsay through the Island of Mull to the centre of the district of Morvern, through which it passed to the shores of the Luine Loch opposite Appin.[1] The rest of the Highlands was still

[1] In the Island of Colonsay there is a cairn called Carn cul ri Erin. In Bleau's Atlas, the map of the Island of Mull marks, on the high mountain which separates the north from the south of the island, two cairns, called Carn cul ri Erin and Carn cul ri Allabyn. These seem to mark some ancient boundary, but as they are exactly in a line with Iona,—which seems to have lain so nearly on the boundary as to be claimed by both races, and also with the line which separates the ancient parishes of Killintach and Killcholumkill in Morvern, and Killintach is said, in an old document, to be in Garwmorvaren, a district which extended as far north as Loch Hourn, while Killcholumkill is said to be in Kinelbadon, which belonged to the ancient kingdom of Lorn,—there seems much reason to conclude that this may have been the line of the boundary between the Dalriad Scots from Erin and the Cruithne of Alban.

occupied by the Cruithne, who were Pagans, while the Dalriadic Scots were Christians.

In the year 563, an event took place which was destined to exercise a powerful influence both on the condition and the language of the population. This was the mission of Saint Columba, a Scot from Ireland, to convert the Cruithne to the Christian faith, and the consequent foundation of the Monastery of Iona, which became the seat of learning, and the source of all ecclesiastical authority, both for the Cruithne and the Dalriadic Scots, from whence innumerable Scottish clergy issued, who spread over the country and founded churches among the Cruithne under its influence and authority.

The platform occupied by the two populations, embracing both Ireland and the Highlands of Scotland, in the sixth century, thus showed in the south and west of Ireland pure Scots; in the north and east settlements of Scots among the Cruithne, gradually confining the latter to isolated districts; in Argyll, a Scottish settlement among the Cruithne of Alban; and in the rest of the Highlands pure Cruithne; but over both Scots and Cruithne in Alban a Scottish clergy, who brought a cultivated and literary language with them.

In Ireland the Gaelic spoken in the different provinces varies, and probably has always varied from each other. They differ in words, pronunciation, and idiom; and in grammatical construction and idiom there is a marked difference between the Gaelic of the northern and of the southern half of Ireland. The written language resembles most the language of the south and west of Ireland. It seems to have been formed from it, and to have become the common language of the literary and cultivated class, while the other dialects remained as the spoken language of their respective populations.

This written language was brought over to Scotland in the sixth century by Columba and his clergy, who introduced it, with Christianity, among the Cruithne; where, however, the native dialect must have received some cultivation, as we find that he was opposed by Magi, which implies a literary class among the Pagan Cruithne. At this time there was so little political separation between the two countries, that the Scots of British Dalriada remained subject to the Irish Dalriada, from which they emerged, till the year 573, when Aedan, son of Gabran, became king of Scotch Dalriada, and, at the great Council of Drumceat, it was declared independent of Irish Dalriada, and he was crowned as its first independent monarch. The Cruithne of Ireland, likewise, formed part of that great Cruithnian kingdom, which had its head-quarters in Scotland, till the reign of Fiacha mac Baedan, King of Ulster, who ruled over the Irish Cruithne from 589 to 626, and probably in the year 608, when they threw off the yoke of the Cruithne of Scotland.[1]

The Cruithne and the Scots of Ireland and of Scotland then first became separated from, and independent of,

[1] There were thirty kings of the Cruithne over Eri and Alba, viz., of the Cruithne of Alba and of the Cruithne of Eri, *i.e.*, of Dalaraidhe They were from

each other, and a complete political separation took place between the two countries.

The Cruithne of Scotland remained under the influence of the Scottish clergy till the beginning of the eighth century, when their king, Nectan, adopted the usages of the Romish party, and in 717 expelled the Scottish clergy out of his dominions across the boundary of Drumalban,[1] which separated them from the Scots of Dalriada, and a new clergy was introduced into that part of the country, occupied by the Cruithne, from the Anglic kingdom of Northumberland. In 731, we learn from Bede, who then closes his history, that the Scots of Dalriada were still confined within the same limits; and that no change had up to that date taken place in the relative positions of the two populations, the Cruithne and the Scots. After this date we know little of the history of the population of the Highlands till the middle of the ninth century, when we find that a great change had, in the interval, taken place in their political condition. The two populations had now become united in one kingdom, and a family of undoubted Scottish race ruled over the united people.

Of the events which brought about this great change, authentic history tells us nothing—of the fact there can be no doubt; and the question arises of how the Gaelic language originated in the undalriadic part of the Highlands.

Ollamhan to Fiachna mac Baedain, who fettered the hostages of Eri and Alba.

Book of Lecan, as quoted in Irish Nennius, lxxii.

A.D. 608. Bass Fiachiach chraich mic Baedan la Cruithnechu.—(Tigh. An.)

[1] A.D. 717. Expulsio familiæ Ie trans dorsum Britanniæ a Nectano rege.

Prior to this date, it was exclusively occupied by people of the race of the Cruithne, first Pagan under native Magi, then Christian, and for 150 years under clergy of Scottish race, who were, however, driven out in the year 717. Either then these Cruithne spoke a Gaelic dialect, or, if they spoke a different language, we must suppose that the language of Gaelic Dalriada had, subsequently to the ninth century, spread, with the rule of a Scottish king, over the whole of the Highlands not embraced in that limited territory. We have no materials for determining this question. The latter supposition has always been assumed by the Irish historians, but without proof; and they have never attempted to account for the entire disappearance of the previous language, and the expulsion of the previous population of so extensive a district, so mountainous and inaccessible in its character, and so tenacious of the language of its early inhabitants in its topography, which such a theory involves.

If the first supposition be the correct one, and the Cruithne spoke a Gaelic dialect, we can easily understand how, though originally different from the Gaelic dialect of Dalriada, it may, by the influence of the written language, and its vernacular use by their clergy for so long a period, have become modified and assimilated to it; and if, as is probable, their dialect had been so far cultivated, as the existence of popular poetry, the first literature of a rude people, was calculated to effect, the influence of the clergy would probably be antagonistic to such literature, and be employed to suppress it; and the language in which it was conveyed might remain for some time in opposition to the written language, as a vernacular and popular form of the language, the type and symbol of the anti-Christian party, till it was finally amalgamated with, or assimilated to it as the party itself was ultimately overcome.

But another event had taken place during this obscure period, extending to little more than a century, and in which the union of the two populations under a Scottish royal race had been effected, which must have interposed an obstacle to the spread of an influence from Ireland into the nondalriadic portion of the Highlands, and greatly counteracted that arising from a dominant royal family of Scottish descent. This was the destruction of Iona by the Scandinavian pirates, and their subsequent occupation of the Western Isles and western sea-board of Scotland. Towards the end of the eighth century, these hordes of Vikings or sea robbers, issuing from Norway and Denmark, had appeared in the western sea, ravaging and plundering the coasts and islands, and their course was everywhere marked by the burning and sacking of the monasteries and religious establishments. In 794, the ravaging of the islands and the destruction of Iona by these Gentiles, as they were termed, is recorded in the Irish annals. In 802, the Monastery of Iona was burnt by them, and in 806 the community or family of Iona, as it was termed, slain, to the number of sixty-eight. In consequence of the insecurity of Iona, the abbot eventually retired to Kells, another foundation of St. Columba, and the reliques of St. Columba were subsequently taken to Ireland, when Derry became the head of the Columbian houses in Ireland, while a part of the reliques were removed to Dunkeld, which represented the Columbian clergy in Scotland. The influence of Iona, as the nucleus and centre of Gaelic learning, and of its Scottish clergy upon the population of the Highlands, thus ceased for ever.

The islands were, by degrees, occupied by these pirates, till eventually the Norwegian Kingdom of Man and the Isles was formed; and after they had passed over from Paganism to Christianity, and their power became constituted, the bishopric of the Isles became included in the Norwegian diocese of Man. During this period, which lasted till the middle of the twelfth century, while the Western Isles and the western shores of the mainland were in the occupation of the Norwegians, and a royal family of Scottish race was on the throne of the united population, all that remained intact of the Gaelic population of the Highlands was mainly represented by the great province of Moray, which contained the mainland part of the modern counties of Inverness and Ross, and whose chiefs or maormors are found, during the whole of this period, maintaining a struggle for local independence against the ruling powers, whether Scottish or Saxon, till they were finally suppressed in the year 1130 by the great battle in which Angus, the Celtic Earl of Moray, was defeated and slain by David the First.

The Norwegian Kingdom of Man and the Isles was now approaching its fall, and a new power arose on the ruins of that of the Maormors of Moray, which soon became paramount in the Western Highlands, and exercised a very different influence upon its language and population. This was the dynasty of the Celtic kings or Lords of the Isles, which took its rise under Somarled, the founder of the race in the twelfth century, and maintained a powerful sway in the West Highlands till the Lord of the Isles was forfeited at the close of the fifteenth century; and, after several ineffectual attempts to maintain their ground against the Government, finally fell in the middle of the succeeding century.

Whether the race of the Lords of the Isles was of Irish descent or not, is a question which depends upon the precise degree of credibility to be given to a Celtic pedigree which reaches back to the beginning of the fourth century; but certain it is, that the spirit and tendency of the whole race was essentially Irish. The history of Somarled, the founder of the family, who may, from female connexion, have possessed a Norwegian name, is quite incompatible with the idea of his representing a Norwegian house, or deriving his position by inheritance from them. The names of his father Gillabride, and his grandfather Gillaagamnan, are purely Celtic. The interest of his family was antagonistic to that of the Norwegians; their efforts were to supplant and drive them out, and to elevate a Gaelic kingdom upon their ruins. In the foundation of this kingdom, Irish aid and Irish interest entered largely, and the connexion of the family with Ireland became always more and more closely connected,—an influence and connexion extending to the powerful Celtic families who rose under their auspices and owned their sway.

Somarled, the founder of the race, first appears in history as regulus or petty king of Oirirgaidheal, or, as it is given in the Irish form, Airergaidheal, and, in the Latin, Argathelia, a name which had sprung up subsequently to the ninth century, signifying the coast-lands of the Gael, and embracing the entire west coast from Cowall to Loch Broom.

To this district he must have had hereditary claims; and an ancient sennachy of the race thus details the steps by which he recovered possession of it:—

Gillabride, the son of Gillaagamnan, the son and grandson of the Toiseach of Argyll, and descendant of Colla, being amongst his kindred in Ireland, the clan Colla, that is, the Macguires and Macmahons, held a great meeting and assembly in Fermanagh, the country of Macguire, regarding the affairs of Gillabride, how they might restore him to his patrimony, from which he had been driven by the power of the Lochlans and Finngalls. When Gillabride saw such a large body of men assembled together, he besought them to embark in his cause, and to assist the people of Alban, who were favourable to him in an attempt to win back the possession of the country. The people declared themselves willing to go, and four or five hundred put themselves under his command. With this company Gillabride proceeded to Alban, and landing there, commenced a series of skirmishes and sudden assaults, with the assistance of friends, for his name was then very powerful. The Lochlans possessed the islands from Man to the Orkneys; but the Gael retained possession of the woods and mountains in the districts, extending from Dumbarton to Caithness, north of the two oirirs,[1] and in Mar. Somarled, the son of Gillabride, was now becoming manly and illustrious, and a band attached themselves to him, who had possession of the hills and woods of Ardgowar and Morvaren. Here he came upon a large army of Lochlans and Fingalls, and assembled round him all the soldiers he could muster and the people engaged in herding the flocks, and ranged them in order of battle. He practised a great deception on his enemies, for he made the same company pass before them three times, so that it appeared to them as if there were three companies, and then attacked them. The enemy were broken by Somarled and fled, till they reached the north bank of the river Shiell, and part escaped with their king to the Isles. Somarled did not desist from his efforts till he had cleared the whole west side of Alban from the Lochlans, except the islands of the Finnlochlans, called Innsegall.

Having married the daughter of Olave the Red, the Norwegian king of Man and the Isles, he succeeded in 1154 in obtaining one-half of the Western Isles for his eldest son Dougall, the ancestor of the M'Dougalls, Lords of Lorn, in right of his mother. The portion of the Isles thus added to the Gaelic kingdom of Oirirgaidheal were those south of the point of Ardnamurchan, including Mull, Isla, and Jura. Ten years afterwards, in 1164, he showed still further his close relation with Ireland, by placing the Monastery of Iona under the Abbacy of Derry, and in the same year he was slain in Renfrew, in an attempt which he made to subvert the Scottish throne itself, with Irish assistance. His successors remained in possession of this territory, consisting of Oirirgaidheal, or

[1] The two oirirs were the Oirir a tuath and the Oirir a deas, which make up the district known as Oirir Gaedheal, or Oirir Alban, and in Latin, Argathelia.

the western districts, from Cowall to Loch Broom, and the southern half of the Isles, till 1222, when Alexander the Second took possession of Argathelia, and annexed the north part of it to the earldom of Ross, and the central portion to the district of Moray, leaving the districts of Morvaren and Garwmorvaren, and parts of South Argyll, with the south half of the Isles, to the descendants of Somarled. On the conquest of the Norwegian kingdom of Man and the Isles by the King of Scotland in 1266, Skye and Lewis were annexed to the earldom of Ross, the rest of the Isles went to Somarled's family, their possessions were further increased by grants from Robert Bruce, and in the end of the fourteenth century they inherited the possessions of the earldom of Ross, by which they regained possession of the Oirir a tuath. A petty kingdom was thus formed, consisting of Argathelia, or the western districts, from Cowall to Loch Broom and the Western Isles, nominally subordinate to the Scottish throne, but in reality all powerful among the population of the Highlands; the clans of the centre and north Highlands, which had once looked up to the almost equally powerful Maormors of Moray, alone representing a different interest.

The marriage of the Lord of the Isles, the head of this race, with a daughter of the great Irish house of O'Cathan, princes of an extensive territory in the north of Ireland, towards the close of the thirteenth century, still further cemented the connexion with Ireland. Tradition records that twenty-four families followed this lady from

Ulster to the Scottish Highlands, and founded as many houses there, and, in the subsequent century, a scion of the House of the Isles acquired land in the north of Ireland, and founded the Antrim family. In all the Irish wars this race took generally a part, and, in their own wars at home, were rarely without assistance from Ireland.

The struggle between this great Celtic family and the Crown assumed an aspect at length which could only terminate in the ruin of the former or the humiliation of the latter, and at length resulted in the forfeiture of the Lord of the Isles in 1478, and his subsequent submission, when he resigned his hereditary Celtic title, and received in exchange the feudal dignity of Lord of the Isles; a humiliation which gave deep offence to his subjects, and was not acquiesced in by them, and produced such internal dissensions, that the Crown took advantage of them to enforce the final forfeiture of the Lordship of the Isles in the year 1493. A series of insurrections followed in favour of the descendants of the forfeited Lord, which finally terminated in the utter extinction of the kingdom of the Isles in the year 1545.

During this period, which extends to nearly four centuries, there was not only a close political connexion between the Western Highlands and Islands and Ireland, but the literary influence was equally close and strong; the Irish sennachies and bards were heads of a school which included the West Highlands, and the Highland sennachies were either of Irish descent, or, if of native origin, resorted to bardic schools in Ireland for instruction in the language and the accomplishments of their art.

The annals of the four masters record the following Irish sennachies as being recognised masters in the Highlands :—

In 1185 died Maclosa O'Daly, ollav, or chief sage or poet of Erin and Alban ; a man illustrious for his poetry, hospitality, and nobility.

In 1328 died the blind O'Carril, chief minstrel of Erin and Alban in his time.

In 1448 died Tadg og, son of Tadg, son of Giollacoluim O'Higgin, chief preceptor of the poets of Erin and Alban.

In 1554 died Tadg, son of Aodh O'Coffey, chief teacher of poetry in Erin and Alban.

The oldest of the Gaelic MSS., preserved in the Library of the Faculty of Advocates, belong to this period. They are all written in the Irish character ; the language is the written language of Ireland ; and they contain numerous specimens of the poetry of these Irish masters, especially of Tadg og and the O'Dalys.

The Betons, or, as their name was in Gaelic, Macbheatha, who were hereditary physicians in Isla and Mull, and who were also sennachies of the Macleans, were of Irish descent, being O'Neills, and are said by tradition to be one of the families who accompanied O'Cathan's daughter to Scotland ; and many of these MSS. belonged to them. The M'Vurichs, who were hereditary sennachies to Clanranald, were likewise of Irish descent, and are said "to have received their education in Irish Colleges of poetry and writing."[1] Many of these MSS. were compiled by them; and the earliest are likewise written in the Irish character and idiom. The sennachies of the other great families, comprised within the dominions of the Lords of the Isles, appear likewise to have all resorted to Ireland for instruction and training in their art.

A powerful influence must thus have been exercised upon the language and literature of the Highlands, which must have become by degrees more and more assimilated to that of Ireland; and it may well be doubted whether, towards the close of this period, there existed the means of acquiring the art of writing the language except in Ireland, or the conception of a written and cultivated literature, which was not identified with its language and learning.

We have no reason, however, to conclude, on that account, that there was not a vernacular Gaelic, which preserved many of the independent features of a native language, and existed among the people as a spoken dialect; or that a popular and unwritten literature may not at the same time have existed in that native and idiomatic Gaelic in the poetry handed down by tradition, or composed by native bards, innocent of all extraneous education in the written language of Ireland. It is, in fact, in poetry, or rather in popular ballad poetry, that the nervous and idiomatic vernacular of the

[1] Highland Society's Report, App. p. 6

people is usually preserved. Prose readily assimilates itself and succumbs to the influence of a cultivated and written language, but the tyranny of rhythm and metre preserves the language in which poetry is composed in its original form and idiom.[1]

The fall of the great House of the Isles was coincident with another event, destined to effect a great change in the position of the Highland population and of their literature. This was the Reformation of the sixteenth century and its attendant events, the establishment of a Reformed Church, the introduction of printing, and the translation of the Scriptures and religious works for the instruction of the people.

From this source sprung up a religious literature, which, commencing in the written or Irish Gaelic, gradually approached nearer and nearer to the spoken dialect of the country, and, accompanied by the preaching of the clergy in the vernacular dialect, tended to preserve and stereotype the language spoken in the Highlands in its native form and idiom.

The first printed book was a translation of the Form of Prayer issued by John Knox, which was made by John Carsewell, the Protestant Bishop of the Isles, and printed at "Dunedin darab comhainm Dunmonaidh," that is, at Dunedin or Edinburgh, otherwise called Dunmonaidh, 24th April 1567. Bishop Carsewell was a native of

[1] Prose originally written in a vernacular dialect readily adapts itself to the changes in the language, or passes into a new and cultivated form of it, but not so ballad poetry. The poems of Burns, for instance, could not be written in English without sacrificing, to a great extent, the rhyme and cadence of the verses, and almost entirely their nerve and power.

Kilmartin, in the southern part of the country of Argyll. He prefixes to his translation an address, which is written in the Irish orthography, and in the pure Irish or written dialect. In it he says, that "we, the Gael of Alban and Erin, have laboured under the want that our dialects of the Gaelic have never been printed;" and he alludes to the dialects of the language and to the manuscript literature then existing, "written in manuscript books in the compositions of poets and ollaos, and in the remains of learned men," and characterizes them not unjustly as full of "lying, worldly stories concerning the Tuatha de Dannan, the sons of Milesius, the heroes, and Finn mac Cumhal with his Feine."

The second printed book was a translation of Calvin's Catechism, which was published, along with an English edition, in 1631. This translation seems likewise to have been made in Argyllshire, and is in the Irish orthography and idiom.

In 1659, the Presbyterian Synod of Argyll took up the work of issuing translations into Gaelic of the metrical Psalms and of the Scriptures, and commenced with a portion of the Psalter, which was completed in 1694. This also is in the Irish dialect; but, in 1753, an amended version was published by the Rev. Alexander Macfarlane, minister of Kilninver and Kilmelford, who had previously, in 1750, published a translation into Gaelic of Baxter's Call to the Unconverted, adapted to the Gaelic of the central and north Highlands; and, in 1787, another version was issued by Dr. J. Smith, minister of Kilbrandon, and afterwards of Campbelltown, who had in 1781 translated Alleine's Alarm into Gaelic, and in this version the north country words and Irishisms were thrown out, and the metre suited to the west country dialect; and, finally, in 1807, an edition of the Psalter was published by Thomas Ross for the use of the northern districts, in which the Irish words, unintelligible to them, are explained at the bottom of the page by synonymous words used in that part of the Highlands.

In 1690, the first Bible was published for the use of the Highlands. It was simply an edition of the Irish version of the Bible, by the Rev. Robert Kirke, minister of Balquhidder, to which he appended a short vocabulary.

In 1767, the first translation of the New Testament was published. It was translated by the Rev. James Stewart of Killin. It was then considered as pure Scotch Gaelic, and free from Irish idiom; and, in 1796, it was revised and altered by his son, Dr. Stewart of Luss. In 1783, a translation of the Old Testament was undertaken by the Society for Propagating Christian Knowledge in Scotland, and completed in 1787, and various editions subsequently appeared. In 1816, a memorial was presented to the General Assembly of the Church, urging the necessity of a final revision of the Gaelic Scriptures, and a committee of the best Gaelic scholars appointed to superintend it, under whose auspices an amended edition was published of the Old

Testament in 1820, and of the whole Scriptures in 1826, which may now be considered as the standard of the orthography and idiom of the Scotch Gaelic.

It will be seen that the earlier printed books emanated entirely from Argyllshire, where the spoken dialect approaches more nearly to the Irish; and the work of translating and publishing the Psalter and Scriptures into Gaelic being a new and difficult task, the translators resorted to Ireland and to the written and cultivated dialect of the Irish as the medium through which to convey it; but as subsequent editions were issued, they were brought more and more near to the spoken language of the Scotch Highlands in its purest form and idiom, and the Irish orthography by degrees adapted to it, till at length the Scotch Gaelic became clothed in that orthography in which we now find it, and elevated to the position of a written and cultivated language.

Throughout the whole of this period, however, there existed, side by side with this printed religious literature, another literature in the popular poetry of the uncultivated native bards, removed from the influence of Irish training, whose compositions were expressed in the pure idiom of the spoken dialect; and in the poems of Ian Lom, the Lochaber poet of the Wars of Montrose; Duncan Ban Macintyre, whose exquisite poem of Bendoran is a beautiful specimen of pure Gaelic, and whose poems were printed in 1778; Ailen Buidhe Macdougall, W. Ross, and Allan Dall Macdougall—all natives of the central districts of the Highlands,—we find ample evidence of the existence and character of a vernacular dialect, in which the people interchanged their homely ideas, and their favourite bards composed their poems which found an immediate access to the hearts and imagination of the people; while the language in which their scriptures and formularies were conveyed was looked upon as a sort of sacred dialect, through which they received their religious teaching.

There was thus, throughout, a double influence exercised upon the language and literature of the Highlands. One from Ireland, which was associated with the written and cultivated dialect of Gaelic which had there been formed, and brought over with Christianity to Scotland. With it came the Irish orthography. It was mainly connected with learning and religious teaching, and its influence was most powerful in the western districts and islands, and the territories subject to the power of the Lord of the Isles. The other, indigenous and antagonistic to it, falling back upon a literary influence from the south and east, when not predominant, and associated more with the popular poetry of the Highlands. Its orthography seems to have resembled that of the other Celtic languages, the Welsh and the Manx; and its influence prevailed in the central and north Highlands, where the best and purest type of the Scotch Gaelic is still to be found.[1]

[1] Mr. Donald Macintosh, the Keeper of the Highland Society's MSS., in his list of MSS. then existing in Scotland in 1806, mentions that "Mr Matheson of Fernaig has a paper MS., written in the Roman character, and in an *orthography like that of the Dean of Lismore*, containing songs and hymns, some by

The literary history of the Highlands falls into periods as these influences respectively prevailed.

The first period is prior to the seventh century, when there was no political separation between Ireland and Gaelic Scotland. The great divisions of the people were regulated by race rather than by geographical distribution. The Cruithne everywhere were united by common origin and ties of race; and the Scots, wherever settled, owned the Milesian Ardrigh in Ireland. The countries were simply viewed as the east and the west, and were known as Erin and Alban, and the communication between them was free and unrestrained. The second period commences with the separation of the Scotch Dalriada from the Irish in 573, and of the Irish Cruithne from the present race, some thirty years later, when a political as well as a geographical separation between the Celtic tribes of the two countries took place; but, for upwards of a century afterwards, the church and clergy of the Highlands were Irish, and the written Irish dialect imported by them must still have remained in use, and exercised its accustomed influence on the spoken language.

After the expulsion of the Scotch clergy in 717, a period of great obscurity in the history of Scotland occurs, extending to nearly a century and a half, during which the ecclesiastical influence exercised was from the south, taking its origin from the Anglic kingdom of Northumbria; some revolution also took place, which placed a

Bishop Carsewell." This MS has not been recovered; but if we had it, we might find that, while the Bishop resorted to Ireland for his prose translation of Knox's Liturgy, his original poetry was in a different dialect and orthography.

Scottish royal family upon the throne of a kingdom consisting of the united tribes situated to the north of the Forth and Clyde. But during the same period another event took place, of great significance in the literary history of the country; the Monastery of Icholumkill or Iona, the time-honoured seat of Gaelic learning, went down amidst the troubled waters of Scandinavian piracy, and its position, as head of the learning and religion of the country, was gone for ever.

During the fourth period, which lasted for three hundred years, the Norwegian kingdom of Man and the Isles, which likewise embraced the western seaboard of the Highlands, interposed itself between the Highlands and Ireland; and the influence from the latter country must for the time have been paralysed, while the indigenous and native influence maintained itself in the extensive Highland province of Moray.

At the close of this period we have a hint of the existence of an Albanic dialect of Gaelic in the Life of St. Kentigern, first Bishop of Glasgow, by Jocelyn, the biographer also of St. Patrick, who wrote in the year 1180. He says that the name of Kentigern was justly given to one who might be called their dominus capitaneus; "nam *ken* caput Latine, *tyern Albanice*, dominus Latine interpretatur." This is nearly a phonetic orthography, and not unlike that of the Dean of Lismore's MS. In Irish orthography the words would be *cend*, signifying caput, or a head; *tigerna*, dominus, or lord; but in pronunciation the *d* in *cend* is quiescent, and the aspirated *g* in *tigerna,* so that the sound is exactly represented even as now pronounced. Jocelyn seems to recognise the existence of a native dialect designated by *Albanice;* and one of the peculiarities of Scotch Gaelic is also present in the omission of the final *a* from the word *tigerna.*[1]

The fate of the great Celtic earldom of Moray, and the decay of the Norwegian power in the Isles, was followed by the powerful sway of the Celtic Lords of the Isles, who, during the fifth period, extending from three to four centuries, were dominant in the western districts; and, as far as their sway extended, the spirit, influence, and literature were all Irish, and it was only when the fall of the almost independent kingdom of the Isles, and the Reformation again separated the country from Ireland, that a reaction towards the vernacular and spoken Scotch Gaelic took place, which has resulted in a clear development of its grammatical rules and construction, and the establishment of a fixed orthography.

It was at the close of the fifth period, during which the Lords of the Isles were all-powerful in the west, and just before the middle of the sixteenth century ushered in the Reformation, that the collection, of which selections are now published, was made by the Vicar of Fortingal, who was also Dean of Lismore. It is a col-

1 In the older life of St. Kentigern, written prior to 1164, it is said that Servanus, at Culross, when he heard of Kentigern's birth, exclaimed, "*A dia cur fir sin,* quod sonat Latine O utinam sic esset." In modern Scotch Gaelic the phrase would be, *A dhia gur fior sin.*

lection, formed upwards of three hundred years ago, from all quarters, and presents to us a specimen of the literature which was current in the Highlands during this period. There are poems by the Irish bards, whose schools extended also to the Highlands, by the O'Dalys, who lived during the fifteenth century; by Teague og O'Higgin, who died in 1448; by Dermod O'Hiffernan; and by Turn O'Meilchonair, Ollav of the Sil Murray, who died in 1468. There are poems by Allan M'Ruadrie and Gillecallum Mac an Olla, who seem to have been native bards; by John of Knoydart, who celebrates the murder of the young Lord of the Isles by his Irish harper in 1490; by Finlay M'Nab, called the Good Poet; and by the transcriber of the greater part of the manuscript, Duncan, the Dean's brother, who wrote in praise of the M'Gregors.

The great value of this collection, as regards the language, arises from the peculiar orthography used, which presents it as it must have been pronounced, and affords a means of testing one of the chief differences which characterize the different provincial dialects, the vowel and consonantal sounds, and the presence or absence of eclipsis and aspiration.

It has been found impossible to print the whole of the contents of the MS., but the selection which has been made, chiefly with reference to the literature of the Highlands, will also afford a fair specimen of the shades of difference which characterized the language in which the poems are written. Some are in pure Irish, and must have been transferred from the Irish orthography into that used in the MS. Others are in pure Scotch Gaelic, as the poems of Duncan, son of Dougall Maol, Finlay M'Nab, the bard roy, and John of Knoydart. Others are in a mixed dialect, in some of which the Irish idiom, in others the Scotch, predominates.

In general, it will be found that the language approaches more or less nearly to the Irish, as the writers appear to have had more or less cultivation in the written language, or were more or less removed from Irish influence; and the MS. may be viewed as the only known record of those vernacular dialects of Gaelic in the sixteenth century which differed in any degree from the written and cultivated language.

But while the Dean of Lismore's MS. has in this respect a philological value, it has likewise no mean literary value, from the circumstance that it contains no fewer than twenty-eight Ossianic poems, extending to upwards of 2500 lines, nine directly attributed to Ossian, two to Farris or Ferghus Filidh, and one to Caolte M'Ronan, the three bards of the Feine; two to Allan M'Ruadri, and one to Gillecallum Mac an Olla, bards hitherto unknown; and eleven poems, Ossianic in their style and subject, to which no author's name is attached.

The circumstances under which the controversy regarding the authenticity of the poems of Ossian, published by James Macpherson, arose, and the extent to which it for the time agitated the minds of the *literati* of England and Scotland, are well known.

In the summer of 1759, Mr. John Home, the author of Douglas, met Mr. James Macpherson, then a tutor in the family of Graham of Balgowan, at Moffat. Mr. Home had previously been told by Professor Adam Fergusson, a native of Atholl, and acquainted with Gaelic, that there existed in the country some remains of ancient Gaelic poetry. Mr. Home mentioned the circumstance to James Macpherson, also a Highlander, and a native of Badenoch, and was told by him that he had some pieces of ancient Gaelic poetry in his possession. After some difficulty, Mr. Home obtained translations of them from Macpherson, and took them to Edinburgh, and showed the translations to Drs. Blair, Fergusson, and Robertson, by whom they were much admired. Macpherson was importuned to translate all he had, and the translations furnished by him were published in a little volume in June 1760, under the title of "Fragments of Ancient Poetry collected in the Highlands of Scotland."

There seems little reason to doubt that these translations were made from genuine fragments in Macpherson's possession. If they existed at all, they were in his possession before any talk had arisen of translating Gaelic poetry. There was no pretext of going to the Highlands to collect them. There was no idea, at the time the translations were produced, that such poetry could have any value in the eyes of the literary world, and there seems no motive for any deception. In the fragments, or rather short poems, contained in this little work, the proper names are smoothed down from their original Gaelic form to suit English ears; and Macpherson had already hit upon that happy prose version, the conception of which has great merit, and had no little share in the popularity which immediately attached to them; but, in other respects, they have every appearance of having been translations from short Gaelic poems which really existed. The admiration which they excited in the minds of men of the great literary reputation of Home, Blair, Fergusson, and Robertson, must have first astonished, and then greatly flattered, a man of the disposition of Macpherson. He was urged to undertake a journey to the Highlands, to collect all that remained of poetry of this description, and a subscription was raised to defray the expense. This proposal must have raised a prospect sufficiently dazzling before the poor Highland tutor, who seemed likely to exchange a life of poverty, obscurity, and irksome duty, for one of comparative independence and literary fame; and he acceded to it with affected reluctance. At that time, anything like that spirit of severe and critical antiquarianism, which attaches the chief value to the relics of past ages from their being genuine fragments of a past literature, and demands a rigid and literal adherence to the form and shape in which they are found, was totally unknown. That feeling is the creation of subsequent times. At that time literary excellence was mainly looked to, their authority was usually taken on trust, and it was thought that the claims of such criticism were sufficiently satisfied when the remains of the past were woven into an elegant and flowing narrative. With Homer and other classical epics before him, such a proposal as the publication of the ancient poetry of the Highlands, assuming, as we now know to be the fact, that Ossianic poetry of some kind did exist, and looking to the high expectations formed, must have at once suggested to him the idea that he should not do justice to the task he had undertaken if he could not likewise produce a Gaelic epic. This idea seems early to have suggested itself to Macpherson's mind; it is obscurely hinted at in the preface to the Fragments; and Macpherson seems to have started on his tour with the preconceived determination to view any short poems and fragments he might find as parts of longer poems, and, if possible, by welding them together, to produce a national epic which should do honour to his country, and confirm his own reputation as its recoverer and translator. He was accompanied, in the earlier part of his journey, by a countryman of his own, Mr. Lachlan Macpherson of Strathmashie, who was a better Gaelic scholar than he was himself, and an excellent Gaelic poet. It is certain that, in this tour, a number of MSS. were collected by them, and poetry taken down from recitation; and that he was joined in it by another Gaelic scholar, Captain Alexander Morrison, who likewise assisted him. On his return, he proceeded to Badenoch, his native place and that of Lachlan Macpherson, and here he remained till January 1761, engaged, with the assistance of Lachlan Macpherson and Alexander Morrison, in preparing the materials for the next publication of Ossian; and then proceeded to Edinburgh, from whence he writes to the Rev. James M'Lagan, in a letter dated 16th January 1761,—"I have been lucky enough to lay my hands on a pretty complete poem, and truly epic, concerning Fingal. . . . . I have some thoughts of publishing the original, if it will not clog the work too much."

His task, whatever it was, had then been accomplished; and after remaining some time in Edinburgh, engaged in preparing the English version for the press, he went to London, and early in 1762 issued a quarto volume, containing the epic poem of Fingal, in six books, and sixteen other poems. In the following year another quarto appeared, containing another epic poem in eight books, called Temora, and five other poems. This volume also contained what was called "a specimen of the original of Temora," being a Gaelic version of the seventh book, and the only Gaelic bearing to be the original of any of the poems which appeared.

The English version, contained in these two quartos, possessed the same character as the English of the Fragments; the same accommodation of the Gaelic proper names to the supposed requirements of English ears, and the prose style, originated by Macpherson, sustained with equal spirit; the poems, however, were longer, and more elaborate.

The literary public, who had welcomed the Fragments with admiration, received the volume containing the epic of Fingal with startled but silent acquiescence, and exploded under the eight books of Temora. It seemed incredible that poems such as these could have been handed down by oral recitation from the supposed age of Ossian; the refined manners described, and the allusions to the Roman Emperors, awakened suspicion, and a storm of adverse criticism and questioning incredulity arose, in which Dr. Johnson—at that time in the zenith of his reputation—took the lead.

Macpherson, who found the fair breeze of flattery and laudation, before which he had been sailing so smoothly on his heavy quartos, without a suspicion that he had not attained the full success he aimed at, so suddenly changed into an adverse storm of criticism and depreciation, knew not how to meet the crisis. He had not courage to avow the truth, and state candidly to the world how much of his work was based on original authority, and to what extent he had carried the process of adapting, interpolating, and weaving into epic poems. He took refuge first in sulky silence, and eventually seemed to find a sort of compensation for his denunciation, as a detected forger, in the necessary alternative, the credit of having been a successful composer, and by half hints encouraged that view.[1]

The journey which Dr. Johnson took to the Hebrides,

[1] In 1778 and 1780 a collection of Ossianic poems, in the original Gaelic, was made by Duncan Kennedy, schoolmaster. His MS. collection was purchased by the Highland Society, and is now in the collection of MSS. in the Advocates' Library. There is appended to it a list of the persons from whose recitations the poems were taken down

In 1780, Dr. Smith, of Campbellton, published a quarto volume, entitled Gaelic Antiquities, containing versions

in order to examine the question, and of his Journal of which, one passage seems to have adhered to men's recollections almost as pertinaciously as that of Ossian's Address to the Sun did to the Highland reciters of his poems—the celebrated description of Iona—was not likely to do much in the way of solving the question.

A man of the obstinate prejudices and overbearing temper of Dr. Johnson, with a firm belief that no Ossianic poems really existed, and that Gaelic was not a written language, with an entire ignorance of that language, and a colossal reputation as a critic, bursting suddenly among the frightened Highland ministers, who believed in him, and trembled before him, could hardly return with any other result than that he had found no poems of Ossian, and no one bold enough to avow, in his presence, that he believed in their existence; and most men now subsided into the conviction that the whole

in English of poems attributed to Ossian, Ullin, etc.: and in 1787 the originals were published under the title of Sean Dana.

Unhappily, Dr. Smith, instead of publishing the poems as he got them, with a literal English version, was ambitious of shining, like Macpherson, as an editor of Ossian, and of sharing in his notoriety, but the poems of the latter had already lost their lustre, and Smith did not possess the wonderful tact and originality Macpherson really showed in producing his English version, and which alone made them bearable; his version was diffuse, heavy, and turgid, and his book fell dead from the press.

The Sean Dana showed that he had largely made use of Kennedy's collection.

Kennedy, with the strange desire that all of these collectors of Ossianic poems showed to be supposed capable of composing them, and thus to acquire literary credit at the expense of their honesty, laid claim to the authorship of part of them, and furnished the Highland Society with a statement of those parts of the poems he had really taken down from recitation, and those he claimed to have composed.

It is strange that the passages he claimed as his own composition are just those which have been most clearly established to be genuine.

Thus, lines which Kennedy marked as his own composition, are found *verbatim* in the Dean's MS.

I believe that there was little or no truth in Kennedy's assertion, which was dictated by vanity, and that his collection is, *on the whole*, genuine.

thing was an imposture, an opinion embodied and elaborately worked out by Malcolm Laing.

This led to the Highland Society of Scotland undertaking an inquiry into the authenticity of the poems of Ossian published by Macpherson, which involved the subsidiary inquiry of whether such poems existed in the Highlands in the original Gaelic. The result of this inquiry is contained in the elaborate report prepared by Henry Mackenzie, the author of the Man of Feeling, and published in 1806.

The inquiry was conducted with much candour. The committee were aided by receiving from Mr. John Mackenzie, Secretary of the Highland Society of London, and executor of Mr. James Macpherson, all the Gaelic MSS. in his possession, including those which Macpherson had left behind him; and they resorted to every means within their reach to obtain information.

The whole of the materials for forming a judgment which they had collected were placed impartially before the public; and the subject, so far as such materials then existed or were at their command, is really exhausted by this report.

The committee were cautious in giving an opinion, but the result they arrived at seems to have been—

1*st*, That the characters introduced into Macpherson's poems were not invented, but were really the subjects of tradition in the Highlands; and that poems certainly existed which might be called Ossianic, as relating to the persons and events of that mythic age.

2*d*, That such poems, though usually either entire poems of no very great length, or fragments, had been handed down from an unknown period by oral recitation, and that there existed many persons in the Highlands who could repeat them.

3*d*, That such poems had likewise been committed to writing, and were to be found to some extent in MSS.

4*th*, That Macpherson had used many such poems in his work ; but by joining separated pieces together, and by adding a connecting narrative of his own, had woven them into longer poems, and into the so-called epics.

No materials existed, however, to show the extent to which this process had been carried, and the amount of genuine matter the poems, as published by Macpherson, contained.[1]

[1] A comparison of the poems in the Fragments, with those in the first quarto, containing the epic of Fingal, shows indications of the mode in which Macpherson dealt with his materials.

There are sixteen poems in the Fragments, all short ; and some bearing the usual mark of a complete poem, by the first line being repeated at the end.

Thus, the second fragment begins with the sentence, "I sit by the mossy fountain ; on the top of the hill of winds." And the same expression is introduced at the end—"By the mossy fountain I will sit; on the top of the hill of winds ;" marking a complete poem.

The first and fourth fragments we find in the quarto volume, containing Fingal, forming part of a longer poem termed Carrickthura, and here they are joined together by intermediate passages of some length, evidently interpolated by Macpherson.

The sixth and twelfth fragments contain dialogues between the poet and the son of Alpine. This was no doubt, in the original, the usual dialogue between Ossian and Patrick, always called in Scotch Gaelic poems Macalpine. The sixth fragment appears also in the quarto, in the so-called Epic of Fingal ; but the dialogue is omitted, and the translation greatly altered.

To the fourteenth fragment there is appended the following note :—"This is the opening of the epic poem mentioned in the preface. The two following fragments are parts of some episodes of the same work," and they accordingly appear in the quarto, in the epic poem of Fingal.

The fourteenth fragment, however, relates to Cuchullin alone ; and in those tales and poems which we know to be genuine, Cuchullin and Fingal are never brought together.

Macpherson seems, at this stage of

Such was the result to which the committee appeared to come, and which may fairly be deduced from this inquiry; all intelligent inquirers seemed now to adopt this result, and the unbiassed public generally acquiesced in it,—the only difference of opinion being as to the greater or less extent to which Macpherson carried his process of adaptation and amalgamation.

The publication in 1806 of what was called the original Gaelic of Ossian, did not affect this conclusion, or tend to alter the general acquiescence of the public in it. Instead of consisting of genuine extracts from old MSS., or copies of pieces taken down from oral recitation, it proved to be a complete version in Gaelic poetry of the English version transcribed under James Macpherson's eye, and left by him in a state for publication. It was a smooth and polished version in Gaelic verse of the entire poems, in the same shape as they were presented in English, and written in the modern Gaelic of that time.

It is very difficult, however, to believe that this Gaelic version had been composed subsequently to the publication of the English Ossian, and translated from it. To any one capable, from a knowledge of Gaelic, of judging, such a theory seems almost impossible; and it is difficult to acquiesce in it. A review of all the circumstances which have been allowed to transpire regarding the proceedings of James Macpherson, seems rather to

his collection, to have conceived the idea of weaving the short poems into one epic, but his unskilful junction of Cuchullin and Fingal in the same transactions, betrays its artificial construction.

lead to the conclusion that the Gaelic version, in the shape in which it was afterwards published, had been prepared in Badenoch, during the months Macpherson passed there, after his return from his Highland tour, with the assistance of Lachlan Macpherson of Strathmashie, and Captain Morrison, and that the English translation was made from it by Macpherson in the same manner in which he had translated the fragments,—a conclusion which is the more probable, as, while James Macpherson's acquaintance with the language seems not to have been sufficiently complete to qualify him for such a task, there appears to be no doubt of the Laird of Strathmashie's perfect ability to accomplish it.[1]

But while from this date the controversy in England may be said to have terminated, with the exception of

[1] Some years ago I happened to pass a couple of months in the immediate neighbourhood of Strathmashie, and I recollect having been informed at that time, but by whom I cannot now tell, that, after Lachlan Macpherson's death, a paper was found in his repositories containing the Gaelic of the seventh book of Temora, in his handwriting, with numerous corrections and alterations, with this title,—"First rude draft of the seventh book of Temora."

Mr Gallie sent to the Highland Society a part of the Gaelic of Fingal, which afterwards appeared in the Gaelic version subsequently published He said he had taken it from a MS. he had recovered, written by a friend "who was at that time with Mr. Macpherson and me, a gentleman well known for an uncommon acquaintance with the Gaelic, and a happy facility for writing it in Roman characters."

On being pressed to say who this friend was, he says, "his name was Lachlane Macpherson of Strathmashy. He died in 1767."

This Gaelic version seems, therefore, to have been put together before 1767; and if before 1762, it will account for the original of the seventh book of Temora having been published in that year, and also for an advertisement which appeared soon after the publication of the second quarto, that the originals were lying at the publisher's, and would be published if a sufficient number of subscribers came forward, but as few subscribers appeared, and fewer came to look at them, they were withdrawn.

The so-called originals were, no doubt, this Gaelic version, which there is every reason to believe had preceded the English version in its preparation

an occasional reproduction of old arguments and of criticism long superseded, by enthusiastic young Highlanders, and occasional discussions at young debating societies, it broke out from a new quarter, and in a different shape.

The Irish, who had been long murmuring under the neglect of their claims to literary notice, and the absorbing attention obtained by the Highlands, suddenly burst forth with a succession of violent and spasmodic attacks, of which the partial detection of the Ossian of Macpherson afforded a favourable opportunity.

In 1784 Dr. Young, afterwards Bishop of Clonfert, a good Irish scholar, had made a tour in the Highlands, with the view of collecting Gaelic poems, and ascertaining from what materials Macpherson had constructed his Ossian. He published an account of his journey in the first volume of the Transactions of the Royal Irish Academy, in which he maintained that any poems that existed were Irish, and that Macpherson had founded his Ossian on some of these, "retrenching, adding, and altering as he judged proper."

In 1789 a collection of Irish Ossianic poems was published by Miss Brooke, termed Reliques of Irish Poetry. They consisted of short poems, either attributed to Ossian or on Ossianic subjects, and were accompanied by the original Irish version from which they were translated. Where that was obtained is not stated.

In 1807 the Dublin Gaelic Society was formed, for the purpose of publishing the contents of Irish MSS.;

and in the only volume of transactions published, the subject of Ossian was taken up. The prose tale of Deirdre, the original of Macpherson's Darthula, interspersed with fragments of poetry, is there given; and the volume likewise contains strictures upon Macpherson, in which his work is boldly denounced as an entire fabrication and imposture from beginning to end, and the assertion made, that no poems of Ossian ever existed in Gaelic except those in Ireland.

In 1827 the Royal Irish Academy offered a prize for the best essay on the poems of Ossian. The subject proposed was "to investigate the authenticity of the poems of Ossian, both as given in Macpherson's translation and as published in Gaelic (London, 1807), under the sanction of the Highland Society of London." The prize was awarded in 1829 to Dr. Drummond, their librarian, whose essay is published in the sixteenth volume of their Transactions. In this essay the arguments of Dr. Johnson and Malcolm Laing are adopted; and the assertion of the former is re-echoed, that "there does not exist in the whole Highlands a person who can repeat one poem of Macpherson's Ossian." Another essay, given in by Edward O'Reilly, the author of an Irish dictionary of no great repute, is printed in continuation of Dr. Drummond's, also asserting the modern fabrication of the whole of the poems published by Macpherson, and that the Gaelic poems of Macpherson contain in them the substance stolen from Irish poems.

In 1853 a society was formed in Dublin, "whose

object should be the publication of Fenian poems, tales, and romances illustrative of the Fenian period of Irish history, in the Irish language and character, with literal translations and notes explanatory of the text." This society was termed the Ossianic Society, and they have already issued six volumes of Transactions.

In the fifth volume there is an essay on the poems of Ossian by Macpherson, which may be considered as a summary of the case of Ireland against Scotland as to these poems.

This essay is, like the others, violent in language and uncandid in spirit. It deals with the controversy as it existed in the last century, and its strength consists in simply ignoring altogether the inquiry made by the Highland Society of Scotland, the whole of the great mass of facts collected by them being passed over in silence, and in imputing to the Scots of the present day the views and feelings of those of a century back, before the rise of a true spirit of historic inquiry and genuine criticism had led them to a just appreciation of their national history, and of the claims of Macpherson's Ossian to be viewed as an authentic work.

The publications of the Dublin Gaelic Society and of the Ossianic Society have, however, not merely assailed the Ossian of Macpherson as a fabrication, and denied to Scotland the possession of any Ossianic poems whatever; they have at length given to the world those genuine Ossianic poems alleged to exist solely in Ireland.

The former contains the prose tale of Deirdre, interspersed with short poems. The latter have presented to the public a number of poems in the original Irish, with literal translations. The first volume contains a poem extending to no fewer than 180 quatrains, termed the Battle of Gabhra, to which is added a short poem termed the Rosg Catha of Oscar son of Ossian; but, strangely enough, though there is an elaborate introduction, no hint is given of where the originals of these poems were obtained. The second volume, besides a short poem given in a long and elaborate introduction, contains a prose tale called the Festivities of the House of Conan of Ceann-sleibhe; and in this volume, for the first time, the source from which this tale and the poem in the previous volume was taken is stated. They are from a MS. collection made by a celebrated scribe named Foran, who resided at Portland, in the county of Waterford, in the year 1780, that is, twenty years after Macpherson had published his Ossian.

The third volume contains a long prose tale, interspersed with poetry, termed the Pursuit of Diarmaid and Grainne; another prose tale, termed How Cormac mac Art got his Branch; and a poem, termed the Lamentation of Oisin after the Feinne. And the sources of these tales are stated to be—1*st*, The collection made by Laurence Foran in 1780, termed Bolg an tsalathar; and 2*dly*, A closely written quarto of 881 pages, from the pen of Martan O'Griobhta or Martin Griffin, an intelligent blacksmith of Kilrush, in the county of Clare, 1842-43, called an Sgeulaidhe, and containing thirty-eight Fenian and other legends, some of which are said to have been transcribed from MSS. of 1749.[1]

The fourth volume contains ten poems, which, with the exception of two, were taken from the collection of 1780, from another collection made in 1812 by the Rev. Thomas Hill of Cooreclure, and from the volume of the intelligent blacksmith in 1844.

The fifth volume contains a long prose tale termed the Proceedings of the Great Bardic Institution, an essay on the poems of Ossian, published by Macpherson, and several short poems which are ancient, but not Ossianic.

And the sixth and last contains nine Ossianic poems, which are stated to be taken from Foran's collection in 1780, from that of Mr. Hill in 1812, and from the intelligent blacksmith of 1844.

No information whatever is given as to the sources from whence these respectable collectors obtained their poems; they are all posterior to the publication of Ossian's poems by Macpherson; and, so far as we are yet informed by the Irish editors, the Ossianic poems published by them stand in no better position in regard to their antiquity or authenticity than those of Macpherson.[2]

Professor O'Curry, in his valuable lectures on Irish literature, with that scrupulous accuracy which always distinguishes him, admits that there exists in Ireland

[1] In vol. iv. p. 230 of these Transactions, it is admitted that some of the poems transcribed in 1749 were the composition of the writer, Michael Comyn.

[2] Those poems published by the Ossianic Society which are of any length, and especially the poem termed the Battle of Gabhra, show evident indications of the same process of patching and dovetailing together of shorter poems which characterize Macpherson's Ossian.

only eleven Ossianic poems prior to the fifteenth century —seven ascribed to Fionn himself, two to his son Oisin, one to Fergus Filidh, and one to Caoilte. Most of these are extremely short, and are found principally in the book of Leinster, supposed to be compiled in the twelfth century, and in the book of Lecan in the fifteenth.

The theory, that Macpherson stole his poems directly from Ireland, is obviously untenable and inconsistent with all that we know of his proceedings, for he never was there, and had apparently no communication with Irishmen, or access to their MSS. What he obtained, he got in the Highlands of Scotland, and the collection of poems made by the Dean of Lismore and his brother tends to confirm the result which had been attained by the inquiry made by the Highland Society of Scotland, for it contains poems attributed directly to Ossian and others which may be called Ossianic, collected in the Highlands of Scotland upwards of three hundred years ago. The persons named, and the subjects, are of the same character with those in Macpherson, and such poems must have been handed down by oral recitation, as many of the poems obtained from recitation during the Highland Society's inquiry are the same as those in this MS.

Assuming, then, that Ossianic poems existed in the Highlands of Scotland, and were both preserved by oral tradition, and transcribed in MS. collections, the question arises, What is their real position in the literature of the Highlands? and this question leads to a preliminary question which will materially aid its solution.

Who were the Feinne of tradition, and to what country and period are they to be assigned?

To this question the Irish historians give a ready response.

They were a body of Irish militia, forming a kind of standing army, employed for the purpose of defending the coasts of Ireland from the invasion of foreign foes. They were billeted upon the inhabitants during winter, and obliged to maintain themselves by hunting and fishing during summer. Each of the four provinces had its band of these warriors, termed Curaidhe or champions. Those of Ulster were termed the Curaidhe na Craoibh Ruaidhe, or champions of the red branch, and were stationed at Eamhain or Eamania, near Ulster. To this body belonged the celebrated Cuchullin and the sons of Uisneach. The militia of Connaught were the Curaidhe or champions of Jorras Domnan, otherwise called the Clanna Morna, to which belonged Goll Mac Morn, stationed at Dun Domnan, in Mayo. The militia of Munster were the Curaidhe Clann Deaghadh, to which belonged Curigh Mac Daire, stationed at Cathair Conrigh, in Kerry. The militia of Leinster were the Curaighe Clanna Baoisgne, to which belonged the renowned Finn Mac Cumhal, his sons, Ossin and Fergus Filidh, his grandson Oscar, and his relation, Caoilte Mac Ronan. Cuchullin lived in the first century, in the reign of Conaire Mac Eidersgeoil, Kingof Ireland, and Conchobar Mac Nessa, a king of Ulster; and at the same period lived Curigh Mac Daire, who was slain by him. Finn

Mac Cumhal lived in the reign of Cormac Mac Art, who ruled from A.D. 227 to 266, and whose daughter Graine he married, and Goll Mac Moirna was his cotemporary. Finn was slain in the year 285, his grandson Oscar having fallen in the battle of Gahbra, fought in the following year. Oissin and Caoilte survived to the time of St. Patrick, whose mission to Ireland fell in the year 432, and related to him the exploits of the Feinne; one conversation between these aged Feinne and the apostle of Ireland having been preserved, and is termed Agallamh na seanorach or the Dialogue of the Sages.

Such is the account of the Feinne given by the Irish.

If this is history, *cadit questio.* The ancient Irish militia, like their more modern representatives, could not, it is presumed, be called upon to leave their country, except in case of invasion; and poems narrating their adventures and exploits must have been as Irish as the heroes which were the subject of them.

But we cannot accept it as history in any sense of the term. It is as illusory and uncertain as are the dates of St. Patrick, and the narrative of which the one forms a part, is as little to be regarded as a veracious chronicle, as the life of the other can be accepted as a genuine biography. The chronology of the one is as questionable as the era of the other.

Prior to the year 483, the Irish have, strictly speaking, no chronological history. The battle of Ocha, fought in that year, which established the dynasty of the Hy'Neills on the Irish throne, and the order of things which existed subsequent to that date, is the great chronological era which separates the true from the empirical, the genuine annals of the country from an artificially constructed history.

Prior to that date, we find the reigns of a long succession of monarchs recorded, with a strange mixture of minute detail, chronological exactness, and the wildest fable, a wonderful structure of history palpably artificial, and ranging over a period of upwards of 3000 years. Passing over the arrival of Casar, Noah's niece, who landed in Ireland forty days before the deluge, on the fifteenth day of the moon, the so-called Irish history records the arrival of four colonies before that of the Milesians. First, that of Partolan and his followers, who landed at Inversceine, in the west of Munster, on the 14th day of May, in the year of the world 2320 or 2680 years B.C., and who all perished by a pestilence in one week to the number of 9000 on the Hill of Howth, thirty years after their arrival. Secondly, the Nemedians, under their leader Nemedius, thirty years after, who, after remaining 217 years in the island, left it, in consequence of the tyranny and oppression of the pirates, termed the Fomorians, in three bands,—one going to Thrace, from whom descended the Firbolg; the second to the North of Europe or Lochlan, from whom descended the Tuatha De Danann; and the third to Alban or Scotland, from whom descended the Britons. The third colony were the Firbolg, who returned to Ireland 217 years after the arrival of the Nemedians, and consisted of three tribes, the Firbolg, the Firdomnan, and the Firgailian under five leaders, by whom Ireland was divided into five provinces. With Slainge, the eldest of the five brothers, the Irish historians commence the monarchy of Ireland and the list of her kings. The fourth colony were the Tuatha De Danann, who went from Lochlan to Alban or Scotland, and from thence to Ireland, where they landed on Monday the 1st of May, and drove out the Firbolgs, after they had been thirty-six years in Ireland, to be in their turn driven out by the Scots, under the three sons of Milesius, Eremon, Eber, and Ir, who, with their uncle's son Lughadh, the son of Ith, led the fifth and last colony from Spain to Ireland. The island was divided between the two brothers Eremon and Eber, the former having the north, and the latter the south half of Ireland; Ir obtaining Ulster under Eremon, and Lughadh a settlement in Munster under Eber.

From the sons of Milesius to the reign of Lughadh, who was placed on the throne by the battle of Ocha, there proceeded a line of monarchs amounting to 116 in number, and extending over a period of upwards of twenty-one centuries, the descendants of the different sons of Milesius alternating with each other from time to time, and the reign of each given with an exactness of date and minuteness of event which betrays its artificial character. As part of this narrative is introduced the existence of these bands of Fenian militia, with the dates at which their leaders are said to have lived.

Is it possible, however, to accept this extraordinary bead-roll of shadowy monarchs during Pagan times, with their exact chronology, and the strange and almost ludicrous peculiarities by which each are distinguished, as serious history, or even to attempt to discriminate between what may be true and what is false? Are there any materials, or any data upon which we can even fix upon a date, within a reasonable compass of time, and say all before that is fable, all after may be history, till we arrive on firm ground, after the introduction of Christianity? Professor O'Curry is right when he says, in his admirable lectures on the MS. materials of ancient Irish history, that he cannot discover any ground on which the annalist Tighernac was able to say, "omnia monumenta Scotorum usque Cimbaoth (a king of Ulster, who flourished in the seventh century, B.C.) incerta erant."

From Slainge, the first king of the Firbolgs, who began to reign 1934 years B.C., and ruled only one year, or even from Eremon, the first monarch of all Ireland of the Milesian race, who began to reign 1700 years B.C., down to Dathy, who was killed by a flash of lightning at the foot of the Alps in the year 428, and Laogarc, his successor, who was slain by the elements for refusing obedience to St Patrick's mission which is said to have taken place during his reign, every reign is stamped with the same character; and what to accept and what to reject is a problem, for the solution of which the history itself affords no materials.

If this narrative is to be submitted to historic criticism,

is the later portion less an object of such criticism than the earlier? There seems no reason why we should accept the history of Neill of the nine hostages, who reigned from 379 to 405, and had subjected all Britain and part of France to his sway, and reject that of Ugony More, who reigned 1000 years earlier, and whose conquests were equally extensive and equally unknown to European history, or why Ugony's twenty-five sons are less worthy of credit than the thirty sons of Cathoirmor, who reigned 750 years later. Why the division of Ireland into the two great portions of north and south, between Conn of the hundred battles and Modha Nuadhat, in the second century, is to be accepted in preference to the original division into the same districts between Eremon and Eber, the sons of Milesius; or which of the divisions of Ireland into five provinces, that by Tuathal the acceptable, or Eochaddh, called Feidhlioch, from the deep sighs which he constantly heaved from his heart, or that by Slainge, the first king of the Firbolgs, is to be held to represent the event which produced it.

Are the conquests in Scotland by Crimthan mor, and Dathy in the fourth and fifth centuries, to be accepted, and these equally detailed battles of Aongus olmucadha and Rechtgidh righ-derg, some centuries earlier, to be rejected because they occupy a different place in this succession of unreal monarchs? Are we to accept the reign of Conchobar Mac Nessa in the first century—to whom the death of Christ upon the cross was revealed by a Druid at the time it happened, and who became

Christian in consequence, and died from over-exertion in attacking a forest of trees with his sword which he mistook for the Jews; and the reign of Cormac Mac Art, called Ulfada, either from the length of his beard and hair, or because he drove the Uladh or Ultonians far from their country, where, however, they are ever after found notwithstanding; who was also miraculously converted to Christianity two centuries before the supposed arrival of St. Patrick, the apostle of Ireland, and died by choking upon the bone of an enchanted fish, or, according to other accounts, was strangled by a number of infernal fiends,—as history, in preference to the reigns of scores of older monarchs, the events of whose reigns cannot be said to be less probable.

Must we hold that the chronology of Cuchullin and Corroi, of Finn Mac Cumhal and Goll Mac Morn, is fixed, because the two former are placed in the reign of Conchobar Mac Nessa, and the two latter in that of Cormac Ulfada, or that their Irish character is demonstrated because they are woven into this Milesian fable?[1]

[1] The following passage is quoted by Petrie (*Round Towers*, p. 96) from an ancient tract termed the Senchas na Relec, preserved in the leabhar na h'uidhre, a MS. of the year 1100:—

"Cormac Mac Art was the third person who had believed in Erin before the arrival of St. Patrick; Conchobar Mac Nessa, to whom Œtno had told concerning the crucifixion of Christ, was the first; Moran, the son of Cairpre Cinncait, was the second; and Cormac was the third."

Cairpre Cinncait was the leader of the Attachtuatha in the insurrection above referred to; and it is remarkable that the reign of Conchobar, in which Cuchullin and Curoi are said to have flourished, the era of the occupation of the country by the Attachtuatha, the descendants of the ante-Milesian population, and the reign of Cormac Mac Art, in which Finn Mac Cumhal and Goll Mac Morn are said to have lived and fought, should be connected by the link of a conversion to Christianity. It seems to synchronize these three periods in tradition with each other, and

In fact, the whole of this history presents a structure so artificial, so compact, and so alike in all its features, that it is impossible for any one, like Samson, to withdraw any two pillars without bringing the whole edifice about his ears, and crushing the entire bead-roll of unbaptized monarchs beneath its ruins.

The truth is, that notwithstanding the claims of the Irish to an early cultivation and to a knowledge of letters in Pagan times, the art of writing was unknown in Ireland till after the introduction of Christianity, and written history there was none. The only materials that existed for it were poems, legends, historic tales, and pedigrees, handed down by tradition ; and from these, at a subsequent period, when, as in all countries, the leisure hours of monks and ecclesiastics were employed in constructing a history of ante-Christian times, in imitation of more classical histories, a highly artificial system was by degrees constructed, embodying the substance of traditions and myths, real facts and imaginative poems, with bardic and monkish creations, and the whole based upon the classical model, by which the different ethnological elements which entered into the population of the country were cloaked under an artificial and symbolical genealogy.

But it is not chronological history. The dates are quite artificial, and the whole creation melts and resolves itself into its original elements upon investigation. The pre-Milesian colonies are found existing

with the first introduction of Christianity into Ireland.

The same tract states, that the mythic King Cormac Mac Art "was slain by Siabhras, *id est*, the Tuatha De Danaun, for they were called Siabhras."

and occupying large tracts of the country down to a late period of the ante-Christian history. The provincial kings, when closely examined, lose their Milesian name, and are found ruling over Firbolgs, Firdomnan and Cruithne; and notwithstanding that the Milesians had been for 1600 years in possession of the country, and a flourishing monarchy is supposed to have existed for so long a period, we find, as late as the second century after Christ, the Attachtuatha, as the descendants of the Firbolg, Firdomnan, and Tuatha De Danann were termed during the Milesian monarchy, in full possession of the country for nearly a century, and in close alliance with the Cruithne of Ulster; during which time the Milesian kings were in exile, and the process of subjugating these tribes, supposed to be completed 1600 years before by Eremon and Eber, is again repeated by Tuathal teachtmhar, who arrives with an army from Alban.

The descendants of the different sons of Milesius likewise assume foreign characteristics. The race of Ir, son of Milesius, who possessed the whole of Ulster till the Heremonian settlements almost within the domain of history, are found calling themselves on all occasions Cruithne. The descendants of Ith called themselves Clanna Breogan, and occupy the territory where Ptolemy, in the second century, places an offshoot of British Brigantes. Eremon and Eber seem to represent the northern and southern Scots distinguished by Bede, a distinction reproduced in Conn of the hundred battles, and Modha Nuadhat

The legend of St. Patrick, too, in its present shape, is not older than the ninth century; and, under the influence of an investigation into older authorities, he dissolves into three personages; Sen-Patricius, whose day in the calendar is the 24th August; Palladius *qui est Patricius*, to whom the mission in 432 properly belongs, and who is said to have retired to Alban or Scotland, where he died among the Cruithne; and Patricius, whose day is the 17th of March, and to whom alone a certain date can be assigned,—for he died, in the chronological period, in the year 493,—and from the acts of these three saints the subsequent legend of the great apostle of Ireland was compiled, and an arbitrary chronology applied to it.

The Feine also, when looked at a little more closely, emerge from under the guise of a Milesian militia, and assume the features of a distinct race. Cuchullin, Conall cearnach, and the children of Uisneach belong to the race of Ir, and are Cruithne. Goll Mac Morn and his Clanna Moirne are Firbolg; Curigh Mac Daire and his Clanna Deaghadh are Ernai; and though they are called Heremonians in Irish history, yet they are also said to be a Firbolg tribe of the same race with the Clanna Morna; and in the poem of Maolmura, who died in 884, they are said to be of the race of Ith, and, therefore, probably Britons,—a conjecture singularly corroborated by the fact that there exists, in Welsh, a poem on the death of Curigh Mac Daire; and, finally, Finn Mac Cumhal and his Clanna Baiosgne, although a Heremonian pedigree is given to them, it is not the only one known to the old Irish MSS. There is a second, deducing him from the Clanna Deaghaidh, the same race with that of Curigh Mac Daire; and a third, and probably the oldest, states that he was of the Ui Tairsigh, and that they were of the Attachtuatha, as the descendants of the non-Milesian tribes were called, a fact corroborated by Maolmura, who says—

> Six tribes not of Breoghan's people
> Who hold lands,
> The Gabhraighe Succa, *Ui Tairsigh*,
> Galeons of Leinster.

The fact is, when the fictitious catalogue of Milesian kings was extended over so many centuries, and the Milesian monarchy drawn back to so remote a period, it became necessary to account for the appearance of non-Milesian races in the old traditional stories, and they were either clothed with a Milesian name and pedigree, or some device hit upon to account for their separate existence; and thus the Feinne, a pre-Milesian warrior race they could not account for, appear under the somewhat clumsy guise of a standing body of Milesian militia, having peculiar privileges and strange customs.

The Irish Ossianic poems, as well as those in the Dean's MS., indicate that the Feinne were not a body of troops confined to Ireland, but belonged, whoever they were, to a much wider extent of territory.

Thus, the poem on the battle of Gabhra, published in the first volume of the Transactions of the Ossianic Society—a battle in which Oscar the son of Ossian was slain, and the Feinne from all quarters took part—we find the following verses :

The bands of the Fians of Alban,
And the supreme King of Breatan,
Belonging to the order of the Feinne of Alban,
Joined us in that battle.

The Fians of Lochlin were powerful.
From the chief to the leader of nine men,
They mustered along with us
To share in the struggle.

Again—

Boinne, the son of Breacal, exclaimed,
With quickness, fierceness, and valour,—
I and the Fians of Breatan,
Will be with Oscar of Eamhain.

There were thus in this battle, besides Feinne of Erin, Feinne of Alban, Breatan, and Lochlan.

Alba or Alban was Scotland, north of the Firths of Forth and Clyde.

Breatan was not Wales, but the southern districts of Scotland, of which Dunbreatan, now Dumbarton, was the chief seat.

Lochlan was the north of Germany, extending from the Rhine to the Elbe ;[1] and the name of Lochlanach was originally applied to the ancient traditionary pirates termed the Fomorians. When the Norwegian and Danish pirates appeared in the ninth century, they were like-

[1] A passage in one of the oldest of the MSS., deposited in the Library of the Faculty of Advocates, shows that the term Lochlan was anciently applied to the districts east of the Rhine "Cœsar came with some entire legions of the ruthless youth of Italy into the rough land of Gallia, and the wide and long country of Lochlain. For these are one and the same country ; *but for the interposition of the clear current of the Rhine, which divides and sunders the two lands.*"

wise called Lochlanach ; and the name of Lochlan was transferred to Norway and Denmark, from whence they came. There is every reason to believe that the Low German race were preceded, in the more ancient Lochlan, by a Celtic people.

The Feinne then belonged to the pre-Milesian races, and were connected, not only with Erin, but likewise with Alban, Breatan, and Lochlan. Now, there are just two people mentioned in the Irish records who had settlements in Ireland, and who yet were connected with Alban, Breatan, and Lochlan. These were the people termed the Tuatha De Danann, and the Cruithne.

The traditionary migration of the Tuatha De Danann brings them from Lochlan, where they possessed four cities, to Alban, where they inhabited a district termed Dobhar and Jr Dobhar; and from thence they went to Erin, where they drove out the Firbolg, to be subdued in their turn by the Milesian Scots.

The Cruithne are likewise brought from Lochlan to Erin and from Erin to Alban, where they founded a kingdom, which included, till the seventh century, the Cruithne of Ulster, and which was subverted in the ninth century by the Milesian Scots.

These two tribes were thus the prior race in each country. Both must have been prior to the Low German population of Lochlan. The Cruithne were the race prior to the Scots in Alban, and the Tuatha de Dannan the prior colony to the Milesian Scots in Erin. The Feinne are brought by all the old historic tales into close contact with the Tuatha De Danann; a portion of them were avowedly Cruithne; and if they were, as we have seen, in Erin, not of the Milesian race, but of the prior population, and likewise connected with Alban, Breatan, and Lochlan, the inference is obvious, that, whether a denomination for an entire people or for a body of warriors, they belonged to the previous population which preceded the Germans in Lochlan and the Scots in Erin and Alban.

This view is corroborated by the fact, that in the old poems and tales the Feinne appear, as we have said, in close connexion with the Tuatha De Danann. They are likewise connected with the Cruithne, as in the Lamentation of Cuchullin over the body of his son Conlaoch, in Miss Brooke's collection, where he says—

Alas! that it was not in the land of the Cruithne
Of the Feinne bloody and fierce,
That thou didst fall, active youth,
Or in the gloomy land of Sorcha.

While the traditions of the Cruithne, in narrating their migration and the names of their leaders, mention, as the mythic poet of their race, a name singularly like that of Ossian—

Cathmolodar the hardknobbed,
And Cathmachan the bright,
Were glorious youths;
The two valiant sons of Cathluan,

His hardy puissant champions;
Heavy, stern was their trampling,
Cing victorious in his victory.
Im, son of Pernn, were their names;

Huasein was the name of his poet,
Who sought out the path of pleasantry.

In answering, then, the preliminary questions of who were the Feinne? and to what period do they belong? we may fairly infer that they were of the population who immediately preceded the Scots in Erin and in Alban, and that they belong to that period in the history of both countries, before a political separation had taken place between them, when they were viewed as parts of one territory, though physically separated, and when a free and unrestrained intercourse took place between them; when race and not territory was the great bond of association, and the movements of their respective populations from one country to the other were not restrained by any feeling of national separation.

It was natural that the deeds and events connected with this warrior race, associated as they must have been with the physical features of the country in which they dwelt, should have formed the subject of the early poems and legendary tales of their successors, and that a body of popular poetry should have sprung up in each country, which occupied itself with adventures, expeditions, and feats of bravery of this previous race, which were common to both countries, and which, attributed to their mythic poets, and full of the names of heroes, and of the scenes of their exploits, would be appropriated by the bards of each country to their own districts. The names of the places connected in tradition with these events would, as they were localized in the respective countries, be identified with its scenery and physical features, and thus a species of Fenian topography would spring up in each country, which, having a common origin, would bear the same character, and possess a mutual resemblance. Each country would thus claim the Feinne as their exclusive property, and could point to a body of popular Ossianic poetry in support of their claim, and to the Fenian names of their localities, in proof of the events which form the subject of the poems having there occurred.

The allusions to Fingal in the older Scottish historians who wrote long before Macpherson's Ossian appeared, or the controversy arose, show that stories of the Feinne were current in Scotland, and that they were regarded as belonging to this country as much as to Ireland, while the Fenian names of localities in charters and other documents evince that a Fenian topography likewise existed in Scotland before that period.[1]

[1] It is unnecessary here to repeat these references. They will be found in the Report of the Highland Society, page 21.

The quotation from Barbour shows that the name of Fingal was known long before the time of Macpherson; and as most Gaelic proper names had a corresponding name in English which resembled it in sound, and was held to represent it, as Hector for Eachin, or Hugh for Aodh, it is not unlikely that Fingal may have been known as the recognised representative in English of Finn.

In fact, Finn and Fingal are both real names, and closely related to each other.

Gal is a syllable of unknown origin and meaning, which enters largely into the composition of Gaelic proper names Thus we have Aedgal, Aelgal, Angal, Ardgal, Artgal, Bodgal, Comgal, Congal, Donngal, Dubhgal, Dungal, Feargal, Fingal, Gormgal, Leargal, Maengal, Riagal, Saergal, Smiorgal. Some also take the form of *galach*, as Congalach, Dungalach, Fiangalach, Irgalach

Those in which the first syllable expresses a colour appear both alone and with the affix *gal*, as Dubh and Dubhgal, Finn and Finngal, and are really the same name. The annals of the Four Masters mention several persons of the name of Finn, and, in 741, Finghal of Lismore.

Kirke, in his Psalter, published in 1684, adds the following address :—

> Imthigh a Dhuilleachan gu dan,
> Le dan glan diagha duisgiad thall ;
> Cuir failte arfonn fial nab fionn,
> Ar-gharbh chriocha is Inseadh Gall.

That is,—

> Little volume go boldly forth,
> Rouse whom you reach to pure and godly strains ;
> Hail the generous land of the Feinne,
> The Roughbounds and the Western Isles.

The Roughbounds were the districts from Morvaren to Glenelg, which, with the Isles, are thus called the land of the Feinne.

The districts in which the Fenian names enter most largely into the topography of the Highlands are Atholl, Lochaber, Lorn, and Morvaren, Glenelg, and the districts about Loch Ness; and the antiquity of this topography in the Highlands of Scotland is proved by an old gloss to a charter by Alexander the Second to the monks of Kinloss of the lands of Burgyn, within the ancient Celtic province of Moray, which is preserved in the Chartulary of the Bishopric. The boundary of the lands passes by a place called Tuber na Fein, meaning literally the well of the Feinne, and the gloss is " or *feyne*, of the grett or kempis men callit *ffenis*, is ane well."

Cuchullin was of the race of the Cruithne, and belongs both to Ulster and to Scotland. In Ulster his seat was Dundealgan, and the scene of his exploits the district of

Cuailgne and the mountains of Sleave Cuillin; but even Irish tradition admits that he was reared by Sgathaig, in the Isle of Skye, and here we have Dunsgathaig and the Cuillin Hills.

The children of Uisneach were likewise Cruithne, and must have preceded the Scots, for the great scene of their Scotch adventures are the districts of Lorn, Loch Aw, and Cowall, afterwards the possessions of the Dalriadic Scots; thus, in the vicinity of Oban, we have Dun mhic Uisneachan, now corruptly called in guide-books Dun mac Sniachan, a fort with vitrified remains; and here we have on Loch Etive, Glen Uisneach, and Suidhe Deardhuil. The names of the three sons of Uisneach were Ainle, Ardan, and Naoise; and it is remarkable that Adomnan, in his life of St. Columba, written in the seventh century, appears to mention only three localities in connexion with St. Columba's journey to the palace of the king of the Picts, near Loch Ness, and these are Cainle, Arcardan, and the flumen Nesae. Two vitrified forts in the neighbourhood of Lochness are called Dundeardhuil.[1]

The hunt of Diarmed O'Duine after the boar on Bengulbain, and his death by measuring his length against the bristles, enters into Scotch topography in three different localities; in Glenshee, where there is a hill called Bengulbain, also in Glenroy, where we have also a Bengul-

[1] It is remarkable that the ancient legends of Cuchullin and the sons of Uisneach connect them with those remarkable structures termed vitrified forts. Dun Scathaig, Dun mhic Uisneachan, and Dundheardhuil, are all vitrified forts, and the latter is a common name for them. There is probably a mythic meaning under this.

bain and an Eassroy, and also on the south bank of Loch Ness. Daire donn, who appears in the Cath Finntragha identified by the Irish with Ventry, has also deposited his name on a mountain in Ardgour, close to the west sea, called Meall Dayre donn.

The mountain streams and lakes in these districts of the Highlands are everywhere redolent of names connected with the heroes and actions of the Feinne, and show that a body of popular legends connected with them, whether in poetry or in prose, preserved by oral recitation or committed to writing, must have existed in the country when this topography sprung up, though it does not follow that the events, though now associated with the scenery of the country, originally happened there any more than does the Fenian topography of Ireland.

These legendary poems and tales seem to have passed through three different stages.

In the first and oldest form they were pure poems, of more or less excellence, narrating the adventures and deeds of these warrior bands, whose memory still lingered in the country; each poem being complete in itself, and constructed upon a metrical system which brought the aid of alliteration and of rhyme, or correspondence of sounds, to assist the memory in retaining what had been received by oral recitation, and to render it less easy to forget or lose a part. These poems seem generally to have been attributed to one mythic poet of the race they celebrate.

Then, as the language in which these poems were composed became altered or modified, or as the reciters were less able to retain the whole, they would narrate, in ordinary prose, the events of the part of the poem they had forgotten, and merely recite the poetry of what they recollected; and thus they would pass into the second stage of prose tales, interspersed with fragments of poetry.

Bards who were themselves composers as well as reciters, besides composing poems on the subjects of the day in which they lived, would likewise select the Fenian legends as their themes, and become imitators of the older Ossianic poetry. The prose narrative would form the basis of their poem; and thus would arise the third stage of their poems, in which they were reconstructed from the prose tales, and again appear as long poems, the names and incidents being the same as in the older poems, and the fragments of them preserved in the prose tale, imbedded in the new poem.

The poems of the first stage were probably common to Ireland and to Scotland, and traces of them are to be found wherever the Feinne were supposed to have once existed; though, in countries where their successors were of a different race, and spoke a different language, the continuity of the tradition would be at once broken.

Among the ancient poems in the Welsh language which have been preserved, there exists an Ossianic poem called Marwnad Coire map Daire, or the death-song of Curoi, son of Daire, the traditionary head, according to Irish history, of the Fenian militia of Munster, but who, as we have seen, appears to belong to the body called the Feinne of Breatan; and the poem, no doubt, belongs to the northern Cumbrian kingdom, which had Dunbreatan for its chief seat. Curoi is called Chief of the Southern Sea, and the contest between him and Cuchullin is mentioned.[1]

Poems of the same character seem also to have been known in the Isle of Man, as O'Connor, in his catalogue of the Stow MS., mentions a MS. containing "Finn and Ossian,—a Manx coronach, with Manx on one side of the page, and Irish on the other."

The oldest which has been found in any MSS. preserved in the Highlands is a poem of five quatrains, at the end of a glossary contained in a MS. written prior to the year 1500. It is in old Gaelic, and there is an interlineal gloss, explaining the meaning of the expressions in more familiar language. At the end there is a line stating that Ossian was the author of the poem.

It may be not uninteresting to insert here the text of the poem, with its glosses :—

.i. do chodladar mo shuile
Tuilsither mo dherca suain
.i. mo sleagh .i. mo sgiath
mo ruibhne mum luibhne ar lo
.i. mo cladhiomh um dhorn
mo ghenam um dhuais ro bhaoi
.i. mo dhorn fam chluais
agus mo dhuais fam o

.i. aislinge .i. tarla
Adhbhul fisi ar mo ta
.i. dar leiges .i. mo chu
dar cinnius go dian mo chuib

[1] This poem, with a translation, is given in the Additional Notes, pp 143, 144.

.i. ar mhuic
ar criobhais a leirg ar art
.i. saill go fiacuil a carbui
fo cheird bracht go feic a cuil

.i. throigh .i. gun broigh
Triocha treathan damh gun naibh
.i go moing a srona
iona taoibh go a tul moing tuinn
.i orladh .i. na fiacuil
Triocha nena Finn na feic
.i. a sa cionn amach
asseicsi tuas re fa thuinn

.i. coimed re coire gach sul di
Meidis re habhron a dherc
meidis re mes afert fo
.i. tesgus mo cladhiomh a muineal
Sealus mo ghenam a muin
.i. mo chu as a cluais
agus mo chuibh as a ho

.i. muic
Criobais mhara Tallann tair
.i ria cloic ris ambenann tonn
benus ria hail tairges tnu
.i. mo bhoill as comairce diob nert
mo leo uam fhaosamh domniadh
.i. ni lag mar tu
mar tusa ni triath mar tu

Oisin ro chan ann sin attraigh mara tallann.
ar nia na muice.

TRANSLATION.

My eyes slumbered in sleep,
My spear was with my shield,
My sword was in my hand,
And my hand under my ear.

A strange dream happened to me,
I set swiftly my dogs
On a sow in the plain upon flesh.
She was fat to the tusk in her jaw,
Thirty feet for me with my shoes
In her side to the beard of her snout.
Thirty inches for Finn in her tusk
Fat above on her under her hide.
Large as a caldron was each eye,
Large as a vessel the hollow beneath.
My sword hewed in her neck,
And my dogs fixed on her ear.
Sow of the sea of eastern Tallann,
Which strikes the rock where the wave touches.
My limbs were to me a protection to me strong,
As thyself not weak like thee.

Ossian sung this at the shore of the sea of Tallann, for the champion of the sow.[1]

The tales of Cuchullin and Conlaoch, and the tale of the Sons of Uisneach, are good specimens of the second class. The latter is one of three tales, called the Three Woes, the two others relating to families of the Tuatha De Danann; but though these tales may be Irish, and of this

[1] The scene of this poem is in Scotland, the sea of Tallann being said to be in the east, and it must have been written in Scotland, as the accent is placed on the first syllable of the name Oisin

The Highlanders call a whale *muic mhara*, and, from the description, this creature appears to have been a whale.

On communicating this curious poem to Professor O'Curry, he informs me that there is a copy of it in the Book of Leinster, an MS. of the thirteenth century. The text is the same, but the glosses a little different

I may take this opportunity of calling attention to Professor O'Curry's admirable Lectures on the MS. literature of Ireland, just published. They are most interesting and instructive, and for the masterly and complete survey taken of the subject, as well as for accurate and minute detail, they are almost unexampled in the annals of literature. They will well repay perusal.

period, they contains fragments of poems probably much older, and which may have been derived from another source. One of the poems in the tale of the Children of Uisneach contains such a tender recollection of and touching allusion to Highland scenery, that it is hardly possible to suppose that it was not originally composed by a genuine son of Alban.

It is the lament of Deirdre or Darthula over Alban, and the following is a translation :—

Beloved land that Eastern land,
Alba, with its wonders.
O that I might not depart from it,
But that I go with Naise.

Beloved is Dunfidhgha and Dun Finn;
Beloved the Dun above them;
Beloved is Innisdraighende,
And beloved Dun Suibhne.

Coillchuan! O Coillchuan!
Where Ainnle would, alas! resort;
Too short, I deem, was then my stay
With Ainnle in Oirir Alban.

Glenlaidhe! O Glenlaidhe!
I used to sleep by its soothing murmur;
Fish, and flesh of wild boar and badger
Was my repast in Glenlaidhe.

Glenmasan! O Glenmasan;
High its herbs, fair its boughs.
Solitary was the place of our repose
On grassy Invermasan.

Gleneitche ! O Gleneitche !
There was raised my earliest home.
Beautiful its woods on rising,
When the sun struck on Gleneitche.

Glen Urchain ! O Glen Urchain !
It was the straight glen of smooth ridges
Not more joyful was a man of his age
Than Naoise in Glen Urchain.

Glendaruadh ! O Glendaruadh !
My love each man of its inheritance.
Sweet the voice of the cuckoo on bending bough,
On the hill above Glendaruadh.

Beloved is Draighen and its sounding shore ;
Beloved the water o'er pure sand.
O that I might not depart from the east,
But that I go with my beloved ![1]

The third class of Ossianic poems belongs principally to that period when, during the sway of the Lords of the Isles, Irish influence was so much felt on the language and literature of the Highlands, and when the Highland bards and sennachies were trained in bardic schools, presided over by Irish bards of eminence. It was at this period mainly that the Irish poems assumed so much the shape of a dialogue between the Ossianic poets and St.

[1] The oldest copy of this tale, which was the foundation of Macpherson's Darthula, is in the Glenmasan MS., in the collection in the Advocates' Library, which bears the date of 1238, and this translation is made from it.

The scenery is all in Argyllshire. Inis Draighen is Inistrynich in Loch-awe ; Dun Suibhne, Castle Sween ; Glenlaidhe is now called Glenlochy, where is Benlaoidhe ; Glenmasan still bears the name , Gleneitche, in another copy called Loch Eitche, is Glenetive and Loch Etive , Glenurchain is Glenurchay ; and Glendaruadh is now called Glendaruail.

Patrick, the apostle of Ireland; and the Highland bards imitated this form, often adding or prefixing a few sentences of such dialogue to older poems, or composing poems in imitation of Ossian in this form; but the imitation, in this respect, of Irish poems by native bards is apparent from this, that Patrick is in the Irish poems correctly called Mac Calphurn or M'Alphurn, his father, according to his own "Confessio," having been Calphurnius, but the Highland bards, to whom Patrick's history was strange, and this epithet unintelligible, have substituted the peculiarly Scotch form of Alpine, and styled him Patrick Mac Alpine.

One of the poems in Macpherson's fragments has been one of these—the sixth fragment,—which begins and ends with a dialogue between Ossian and the son of Alpin.

It was at the same period that the collection of Gaelic poems was made by the Dean of Lismore, and it includes many poems in which this dialogue occurs, but in most the saint is termed Macalpine, showing its non-Irish source.

The Ossianic poems in this collection attributed to Ossian, Fergus Filidh, and Caoilte, the three Fenian bards, and those which are either anonymous or composed by imitators, as Gillecalum Mac an Olla and Allan Mac Ruadhri, with the other poems which are not Ossianic, afford a fair specimen of the poetic literature current in the Highlands of Scotland at the close of this period, and before the fall of the Lords of the Isles, and the Reformation again severed that country from Ireland,

and ushered in a period of reaction and return towards the native dialect and literature.

On the whole, then, we fully admit the claims of Ireland to Fenian legends and tales, and their attendant poems, but not to an exclusive possession of them.

We admit that its Fenian topography is authentic, but it is not the only one.

We admit its claim to an early written and cultivated speech, but not to the only dialect of Gaelic in which such poems once existed.

We hold that Scotland possesses likewise Fenian legends and Ossianic poetry derived from an independent source, and a Fenian topography equally genuine; and we consider her dialect of the common Gaelic tongue not undeserving of the attention of philologers.

W. F. S.

CONTENTS OF THE DEAN OF LISMORE'S MS.

NOTE.—The figures on the left hand refer to the pages in the original MS.; and those added on the right—to the poems selected for publication—refer to the pages in this volume where the translation and the original text will be found.

P. of MS.		Eng.	Gaelic.
	The first four pages illegible.		
5.	Earl Gerald. 6 lines. Indistinct.		
6.	Author's name defaced. 38 lines on John, son of Sir Robert Stewart. Illegible.		
7.	Duncan M'Dougall Maoil. Quatrain on John, son of Colin Campbell.		
8.	Anonymous. Obscure—apparently on O'Ruark. 34 lines		
10.	Duncan Campbell. 12 lines. Satire on Women.		
11.	Earl Gerald. 6 lines. Indistinct.		
11.	Duncan O'Daly. 6 lines. Religious.		
12.	—— fynn O'Daly. 88 lines. Religious.		
15.	Anonymous. 20 lines. Indistinct.		
16.	Cochondach Mac Thearlaich bhuidh. 65 lines. On Irish Chiefs.		
19.	Muireach Albanach. 14 lines, ...	157	120 121
19.	Do. 8 lines, ...	158	120 121
20.	Muireach Lessin Dall O'Daly. 60 lines. Counsels to Chiefs.		
23.	Duncan Mor from Lennox. 10 lines, ...	93	68 69
23.	Gilchrist Taylor. 32 lines, ...	93	68 69
25.	Anonymous. Ossianic. 14 lines, ...	71	50 51
26.	Do. 15 lines. Illegible.		
27.	Six lines in Latin on the Scotch Kings.		
27.	Scotch. A legal deed.		
27.	Dean's Autograph. *Vide* Fac-simile, inserted at p. xcvi.		
27.	Anonymous. A Quatrain.		
28.	Duncan M'Dougall Maoil. 9 lines.		
28.	Gilliecallum Mac an Ollaimh. On the Macdonalds, .	95	70 71
30.	Anonymous. 31 lines. An Ursgeul, or Tale.		

P of MS.		Eng.	Gaelic.	
31.	Ossian. 8 lines. The household of Finn,	1	2	3
32.	Anonymous. 36 lines. On M'Glass M'Gluaire.			
33.	Do. 23 lines. Satire on Women.			
35.	Dougall. Dialogue with his Wedder.			
36.	Anonymous. 33 lines. Eulogy on a Lady.			
37.	Duncan M'Cailein. 16 lines.			
38.	Scotch. The three perilous days in each season.			
39	M'Eachag. On John M'Leod,	140	106	109
41.	John Mor O'Daly. 84 lines. On Tuathal Teachdmhar.			
44.	Anonymous. Note on the hanging of Cochrane in 1480.			
45.	Do. 14 lines. On Conall M'Scanlan,	98	72	73
48.	Notes of purchases in Perth, etc., in Scotch.			
48.	Lines on Marriage, in Scotch.			
49.	Anonymous. 18 lines. Indistinct.			
50.	Ossian. A Lament,	3	2	3
51.	Maoldonaich M'Aonghuis Mhuilich. 50 lines To the Virgin Mary.			
53.	Gorrie Finn O'Daly. 30 lines. In praise of Gormlay.			
54.	Gilliepatrick M'Lachlan A Quatrain.			
55.	John of Knoydart. On O'Cairbar,	99	72	73
55.	Gormlay Ni Fhlainn. Lament for Nial Glundubh,	100	74	75
56	Nial M'Eoghain bhig. A Quatrain.			
57.	Gormlay Ni Fhlainn. Lament for Nial Glundubh,	101	74	75
57.	Anonymous. 30 lines. On Tabblisk (Tables).			
58.	Do. A Quatrain,	104	78	79
59.	Do. 8 lines,	102	76	77
59.	Phelim M'Dougall Aphorisms,	102	76	77
60.	Anonymous. A Quatrain,	108	82	83
61.	John M'Murrich,	108	82	83
62.	William M'Lachlan. A Quatrain.			
62.	Gormlay Ni Fhlainn,	118	90	91
63.	Ossian "Sliabh nam ban fionn,"	4	4	5
64.	Duncan M'Dougall Maoil. A Quatrain.			
64.	Duncan M'Pherson,	110	82	83
64	Anonymous.			
65.	Gille Thuirse O'Sluabhainn. 57 lines. Indistinct.			
68.	Anonymous. Aphorisms,	104	78	79
68.	Earl Gerald. A Satire,	105	78	79
69.	Andrew M'Intosh,	106	80	81
70.	The Bard M'Intyre,	107	80	81

P of MS		Eng.	Gaelic.	
71.	Allan M'Dougall bain. 32 lines. A Satire on Women.			
73.	Astronomical Notes.			
73.	Colin Earl of Argyle. 12 lines. Satire on Women.			
74.	Notes of purchases in Dunkeld, etc.			
75.	Anonymous. 49 lines. On Muircheartach, an Ulster Prince.			
77	Scotch. Satirical. 13 lines.			
77.	Two anonymous Quatrains.			
78.	List of Scottish Kings, from Boece.			
84.	Eoin M'Dhunchaidh Ruaidh. 12 lines. Indistinct.			
85.	Anonymous. On Alexander the Great, ...	110	84	85
87.	Song of the Three Brothers. 32 lines. Moral.			
88.	Gerald 6 lines. A Satire on Women.			
88.	Fearchar M'Phadruig Grannd (Grant). 6 lines. Do.			
88.	John M'Murrich. A Quatrain, ...	112	84	85
89	Duncan M'Pherson. 4 lines. On Eoin Riabhaich.			
91.	List of Names. Genealogical. Robert "clarsair Leoid," "harper of Lude," among them.			
No number.	Fragments on Astrology, etc			
93.	Ossian. "Cath Fionntraigh,"	7	6	7
97.	Anonymous. 81 lines. On M'Ricard of Connaught.			
101.	Duncan Mor O'Daly. 26 lines. On Cathal's Belt.			
103.	Finlay, the red-haired bard. M'Gregor's Horse, . .	112	84	85
104.	Do. do. On M'Gregor, . .	114	86	87
106.	Teague òg O'Huggin. 49 lines. Religious.			
106.	Sir Duncan M'Kermont. 20 lines. Satire on Women.			
109.	Duncan M'Cailein. On a Miser, ...	116	88	89
111.	Do. Satire on Donald donn. 14 lines.			
112.	Dermod O'Heffernan. 36 lines. An Eulogy.			
113.	Muireach Albanach. A Quatrain.			
114.	Ossianic. "Am brat,"	72	50	51
115.	Eoin Liath M'Aonghuis. 6 lines.			
117.	Author's name defaced. 80 lines. Indistinct. On John Lord of the Isles.			
120.	Gilchrist Taylor. 48 lines. An Ecclesiastical Legend.			
122.	Duncan Mor O'Daly. 36 lines. Do.			
124.	Gorry finn O'Daly. 44 lines. On O'Brien.			
126.	Ossian. "Feeble this Night,"	13	10	11
128.	Earl Gerald. On Death. 27 lines.			
129.	Duncan M'Cabe. On the Macdougalls, . .	119	90	91
130.	John M'Ewen M'Eacharn. Do.	121	92	93

P. of MS		Eng.	Gaelic	
133.	Caoilte M'Ronan,	62	42	43
141.	Continuation from page 215,		122	123
143.	Finlay M'Nab. On the Book of Poems,	125	94	95
144.	Earl Gerald. 6 lines.			
144.	Genealogy of Writer, and date 1512,	161	124	125
145.	Fergus the Bard. "Rosg Ghuill,"	43	28	29
147.	Allan M'Rory. "Bàs Dhiarmaid,"	30	20	21
148.	Eafric M'Corquodale. Elegy on M'Niel,	126	96	97
149	Duncan M'Cailein. 16 lines.			
150.	Muireach Albanach. 81 lines. Hymn to the Virgin.			
153.	Gilchrist Bruilingeach, bard an Lymin. 43 lines.			
155.	Dougall M'Ghille ghlais. 48 lines. On M'Gregor,	128	98	99
157.	Duncan Campbell, the good knight. 12 lines.			
158.	Gillepatrick M'Lachlan. 78 lines. On James, son of John. Indistinct.			
161.	Anonymous. 14 lines. A Lament.			
161.	Do. The Clans.	131	100	101
163.	Notes on Adam's Family.			
164.	Ossianic. The Expedition of Eight,	74	52	53
165.	Gorry finn. 21 lines. Moral.			
166.	Teague Og. 72 lines. Religious.			
170.	Robert M'Lamont "a Gassgaitr." 16 lines. Moral.			
171.	Ossianic. "Binn guth,"	80	58	59
171.	Date 12th February 1526. Indiction 15. 4th year of Pope Clement VII.			
171.	Anonymous. 6 lines.			
172.	Ossianic. The Banners of the Feinn,	76	54	55
174.	Do. "Which is the sweetest Music?"	80	58	59
174	Do. Finn's Feast,	82	60	61
176.	Anonymous. A Quatrain on "Ruaraidh Rodasach."			
177.	Do. 20 lines. On a Harp.			
179.	Baron Ewin M'Comie. On Sickness,	133	102	103
179.	Ossian. "Here I saw the Feinn,"	15	10	11
181.	Fili fuge ebrietatem.			
181.	Three Quatrains. The authors of two, Andrew M'Intosh and Gillespick M'Niel.			
182.	Latin Genealogy of our Lord.			
183.	Scotch. The divisions of Ireland.			
184.	Verses in Scotch.			
185.	Physiological Notes in Latin.			

P of MS		Eng	Gaelic
185.	Et ego Jacobus Gregorii.		
186.	Chronicle in Latin, beginning with the death of Malcom Kenmore.		
199.	Measurements of Noah's Ark		
199.	Domhnull liath M'Dhughaill Mhic Grigoir. 62 lines. Satire.		
202.	Duncan Campbell, the good knight. 26 lines. On Old Age.		
204.	Author's name wanting. To Archibald Earl of Argyle,	134	102 103
208.	Dunchadh M'Dhughaill Mhaoil. The M'Gregors,	137	104 105
209.	Mac Gille Fhiontaig, the poet. The M'Gregors,	141	108 109
212.	Ossianic. Dialogue with St. Patrick,	84	62 63
215.	Ossian. "Urnuidh Oisiain,"	17	12 13
216.	Finlay, the red-haired bard. On Allan M'Ruarie,	143	110 111
217.	Two Quatrains by Finlay M'Nab.		
217.	Anonymous. On the M'Leods of Lewis,	146	112 113
219.	Latin Notes.		
220.	Ossian. "Fainesoluis,"	20	14 15
223.	Dunchadh M'Dhughaill Mhaoil. 29 lines. Satire.		
225	Duncan Campbell. 12 lines. Satire on Women.		
225.	Anonymous. 6 lines		
226	Gillebride beag M'Conmidhe. 85 lines. On M'Eachain.		
230.	Fergus the bard. "Cath Ghabhra,"	48	32 33
232.	Allan M'Rory. "Cath Ghabhra,"	35	24 25
236.	Gilliecallum Mac an Ollaimh. "Bàs Chonlaoich,"	50	34 35
239.	Duncan Og. The Seven Mortal Sins,	155	128 129
240.	Gilliecallum Mac an Ollaimh. On John Lord of the Isles,	148	112 113
242.	Genealogy of Malcom Kenmore.		
244.	Gilchrist Bruilingeach, bard an Lymin 48 lines. On Irish Chiefs.		
246	Turn O'Meilchonor. 84 lines. On Irish Chiefs.		
249.	Quatrain by Finlay the red.		
250.	Fragments. Two lines on St. Patrick.		
251.	Contissa Ergadien, Isabella. 8 lines.		
251.	Duncan Campbell, the good knight. On Priests		
252.	Teague òg O'Huggin 63 lines. On the Cross.		
255	Muireach Albanach. 111 lines. Do.		
260.	Teague òg O'Huggin. 92 lines. Religious.		
263	Arthur dall M'Gurkich. Attack on Castle Sween,	151	116 117
266.	The Bard M'Intyre. A Ship on Loch Rannoch.		
267.	M'Pherson. 28 lines.		
269.	O'Meilchonor. 51 lines. On Nial frasach.		

P. of MS.		Eng.	Gaelic.
271.	Gilchrist Taylor. 36 lines. Moral.		
271.	M'Cailein mòr, *id est*, Cailean maith. An Epigram.		
273.	Duncan òg Albanach. 37 lines. A Dream.		
275.	Gilchrist Taylor. 62 lines. On the Host.		
278.	Gille glas Mac an Tàileir. 48 lines. On M'Gregor.		
279.	Earl Gerald. 10 lines.		
280.	Ossianic. The Greatness of the Feinn, . .	87	64 65
281.	Finlay the red. 26 lines. On M'Gregor.		
282.	The Bard M'Intyre. 26 lines.		
284.	Muircach Albanach. A Prayer, ...	159	122 123
285.	Isabella Ni vic Cailein. 6 lines.		
286.	Anonymous. 36 lines. Indistinct.		
287.	Ossianic, ...	88	64 65
291.	Latin. The Ages of the World.		
292.	Isabella Ni vic Cailein, ...	155	118 119
293.	Teague òg O'Huggin. 26 lines.		
294.	Ossian. Eulogy on Finn, ...	26	18 19
296.	Duncan mor O'Daly. 54 lines. To the Virgin.		
301.	An caoch O'Cluain. "Fraoch,"	54	36 37
303.	Earl Gerald. 20 lines.		
304.	Finlay, the red-haired bard. 39 lines. On M'Diarmad. Illegible.		
306.	Duncan M'Cailein. 8 lines.		
307.	Anonymous. 15 lines. Indistinct.		
307.	Muireach Albanach. A Lament. 98 lines. Indistinct.		

P 27

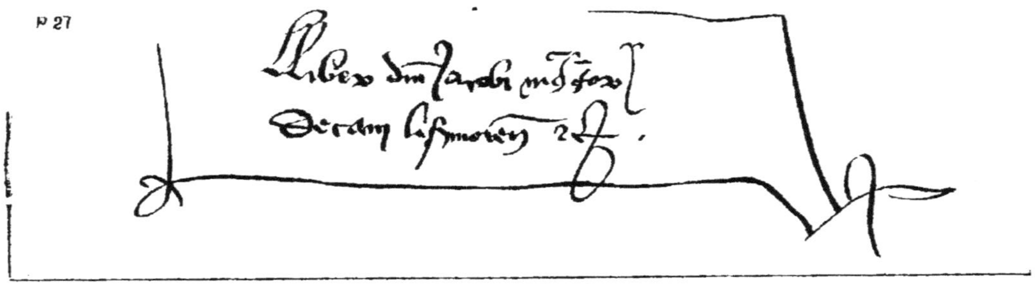

I AUTOGRAPH OF DEAN M'GREGOR

P 294

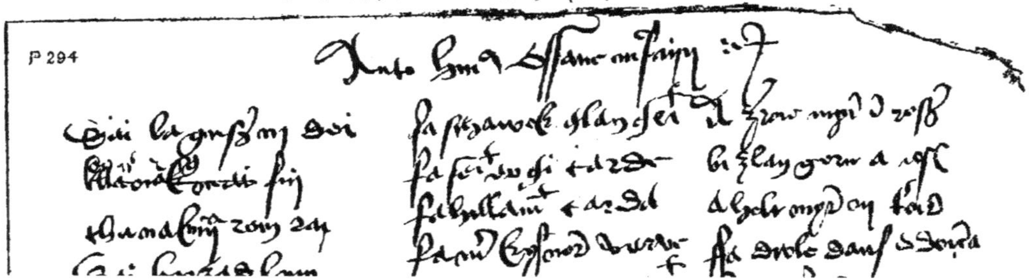

II

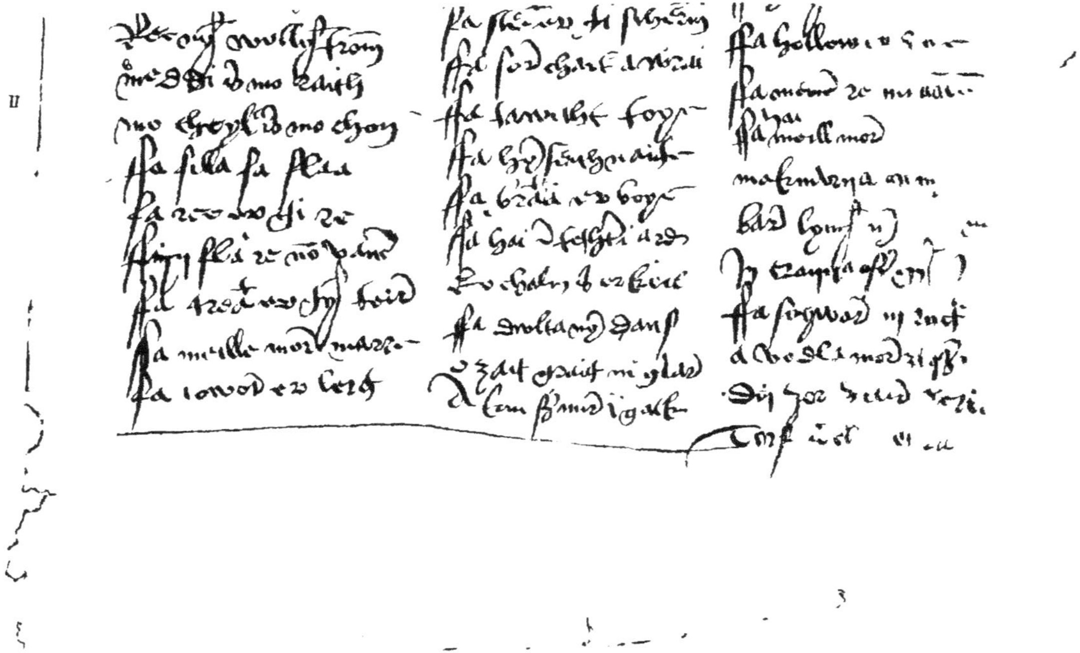

THE BOOK OF THE DEAN OF LISMORE.

THE author of this is Ossian,[1] the son of Finn:[2]

I've seen the household of Finn,
No men were they of coward race.
I saw by my side a vision
Of the hero's household yesterday.

[1] The name of this poet has given rise to some controversy between the Scotch and Irish Gael. By the latter it is pronounced *Oisìn*, the accent falling on the last syllable; by the former it is pronounced *Ossian*, the accent falling on the first. Dean M'Gregor spells the word sometimes *Ossan*, but usually *Ossin*. It is manifest from the use of the *ss* that he intends the accent to fall upon the first syllable, according to the Scottish mode. The Scottish pronunciation would appear to have been the same in his days as now. This form of the word we have retained in our translation. We do not mean to institute any comparison between the Irish and Scottish mode. The difference clearly arises from the peculiarity of each dialect, the Irish almost uniformly, in words of two syllables, laying the accent on the last, and the Scottish upon the first syllable.

[2] The Dean's Finn is the Fingal of some writers. "Fionn," pronounced "Fiūghn," genitive, "Fhinn," pronounced "Ighn," is the present Scottish and Irish form of the word, and we have preserved this in M'Gregor's own orthography. Scottish writers have, however, been unjustly accused of manufacturing the term "Fingal." It is not, as some Irish scholars have maintained, a modern corruption of Fin mac Cùl, but a word known and in use for centuries. John Barbour, who wrote his metrical life of King Robert Bruce in 1375, uses it as a familiar term:—

"He said, Methinks Martheoke's son
Right as Gow-mac-Morn was won,
To have from Fingal his menzie."

It would appear, from the analogies of the Gaelic language, to be the complete form of the word. "Fionn" means *fair*,

I've seen the household[1] of Art,[2]
He with the brown-haired son of gentle speech;
No better man I ever saw.
I've seen the household of Finn.
Who ever saw what I have seen?
I've seen Finn armed with Luno's son.[3]
How sad the mournful memory.
I've seen the household of Finn
Never can I recount the ills
Which now do crown my head.
Do thou free us for ever from pain.
I've seen the household of Finn.
I've seen, etc

being in reality an adjective noun, "Gal" is a common termination of Celtic proper names. Hence, "Fionn Ghal," or "Fingal," means the "fair-haired one." In like manner, we have "Dubh," *black*, "Ghal," "Dubhghal," or "Dugald;" "Donn," brown, "Ghal," "Donnghal," *Dungal, Donald*, the brown-haired one. Hence, Fionn is a contraction of the name It is remarkable as an instance of the changes which take place in the use of words, that in modern times "Fionnghal" is the name of a woman, and is usually translated "Flora."

1 In the original the word translated here, "household," is "tylych," or "teaghlach," *a family*. The literal translation would be, "the family of Art." But this would not convey the idea in the original, the Celtic *family* in such a case as this implying the military followers of the head or chief It seems probable that these ancient Celtic chiefs, like chiefs in more recent times, had their armed followers in constant attendance on them.

2 Art was King of Ireland, according to Irish authorities, in the beginning of the third century Tradition says that he was the father of Grainne, the wife of Finn, whose defection and escape with Diarmad led to the event so famous in ancient Celtic poetry, the death of Diarmad A poem relating the event will be found in this collection

3 "Mac an Loinn," or "Luno's son," was the famous sword of Fingal, manufactured by Loinn mac Liobhaidh, the celebrated smith, or "Vulcan," of the Celts. The sword was so effective that in no case was it ever required to give a second stroke. The Gaelic words are, "Cha d' fhàg e fuigheall beuma,"—It left no remnant for its stroke. We have heard of a remarkable instance of the effective use of this phrase in the pulpit by a distinguished Highland minister, Mr. Lachlan M'Kenzie of Lochcarron In illustrating the completeness of the one sacrifice of our Lord, he said, and to a Highland audience it was electrifying, "Chuala sibh mu 'n chlaidheamh bh' aig Fionn, nach d' fhàg riamh fuigheall beuma,"—*You have heard of Fingal's sword, which never needed to give a second blow* "Loinn mac Liobhaidh," the "Vulcan" of the Celts, is in reality *Brightness, the son of polishing*, a fact which would go far to prove the mythical character of this famous artisan.

The author of this is Ossian :[1]

Long are the clouds this night above me ;
The last was a long night to me.
This day, although I find it long,
Yesterday was longer still.
Each day that comes is long to me,
Such indeed was not my wont.
Now is no fight, or battle-field,
No learning noble feats of arms
Without maiden, song, or harp ;
No crushing bones or warlike deeds,
No studious learning any more,
No hospitable heart or board,
No soft wooing, and no chase,
In both of which I took delight
Without the battle-march or fight,
Alas ! how sorrowful life's close ;
No hunting of the hind or stag,
How different from my heart's desire !
No trappings for our hounds, no hounds
Long are the clouds this night above me.
No rising up to noble feats,
No mirthful sport as we would wish,
No swimming heroes in our lakes.

[1] This piece is extracted and printed in the report on the Poems of Ossian, published by the Highland Society. Dr Smith, however, who made the extract, appears not to have read it with much care or accuracy, and the concluding portion, from the twentieth line downwards, is suppressed altogether. This seems to have arisen from a desire to suppress all the references in those poems to St. Patrick, and thus to establish by all possible means their Scottish origin. If any of the Poems are the genuine compositions of Ossian, there is sufficient evidence that the references to the Saint are of more recent introduction, in the fact, that if Ossian saw Art, who lived in the opening of the third century, as he tells us in the preceding fragment, he could hardly hold a dialogue with St. Patrick, who flourished in the fifth. In the present publication the poems of every kind are given just as they stand, without any reference to the effect on existing systems and theories, Scotch or Irish.

Long are the clouds this night above me ;
In this great world none is like me,
So sad, how sad my case !
A poor old man now dragging stones.
Long are the clouds this night above me,
The last man of the Feine am I,
The great Ossian, the son of Finn,
Listening to the sound of bells.[1]
Long are the clouds this night above me

Find, O Patrick, from thy God
What our eternal state shall be.
Freed may we ever be from ill.
Long are the clouds this night above me.
Long are the clouds, etc.

The Author of this is Ossian :

Once on a time when Finn my loved
Went to hunt on the "Fair maids' hill," [2]
With three thousand nobles of the Feine,
Their shields aloft o'er their heads.

[1] The bells used in Christian worship. "Patrick of the bells," is a common appellation of St. Patrick in these compositions.

[2] "Sliabh nam ban fionn," or the "hill of the fair-haired women," is said to be one of the mountains of Tipperary, in the neighbourhood of Clonmel. It is now called "Sliabh nam ban," and has several traditions of the Feine associated with it. The writer is not aware of any mountain of the name in Scotland ; besides, although the word "Sliabh" is well known and in common use among the Scottish Highlanders, it is seldom found in the topography of the country, in which the almost uniform term for a mountain is "Beinn," the English "Ben." This is one of the marked differences between Irish and Scottish topography. The term under consideration has sometimes been called in Scotland "Sliabh nam beann fionn," "the hill of the fair hills," a manifest mistake, which the meaningless tautology should be enough to prove. Topographical phrases in the Gaelic language are usually not only grammatically accurate, but of remarkable elegance in their structure The interpretations often put upon them are a monstrous outrage upon this sound and invariable principle.

Ossian! thy words are sweet to me,
My blessing on the soul of Finn[1]
Tell us the number of the deer
That fell on the "Fair maids' hill."

How vigorously we shook our spears,
For never hast thou sung the deer
Slain on the "Fair maids' hill,"
By the hand of Finn of the feasts
Tell them the tale in full,
My blessing on thy guileless lips.
Had you your dress and your armour
When you went forth to the chase?

We had our dress and our armour
When we went forth to the chase;
There was no Fian amongst us all
Without his fine soft flaxen shirt,
Without his under coat of substance soft,
Without a coat of mail of brightest steel,
The covering for his head adorned with gems,
And in his hand he bore two spears,
Besides a fierce and conquering shield,
And sword that never failed to cleave the skull.
Wert thou to search the universe
Thou would'st not find a braver man than Finn;
Of noblest race and fairest form,
No arm from him could carry victory.
As he went forth to try his snow-white hound
Who 'mongst us all was like to Finn?
Westward we went, an ordered band,

[1] It is obvious that parts of these compositions are dialogues, for the most part between Ossian and St. Patrick. The dialogue portion in these editions of Dean M'Gregor's is generally either prefixed or added to the body of the poem. This is quite consistent with the genuineness of the work, and can be explained upon the supposition, that these portions were either prefixed or adjoined at an after period by some other hand to serve a purpose. This cannot be said of those poems which are in the form of dialogues throughout.

To hunt on the "Fair maids' hill."
O Patrick, pupil of the church's head,
Bright was the sun above us,
As in the midst of us sat Finn.
Eastward and westward sweetly rung,
From hill to hill the voice of hounds,
Arousing boars and harts.
Then Finn and Bran[1] did sit alone
A little while upon the mountain side,
Each of them panting for the chase,
Their fierceness and their wrath aroused.
Then did we unloose three thousand hounds
Of matchless vigour and unequalled strength
Each of the hounds brought down two deer,
Long ere 'twas time to bind them in their thongs.
That day there fell six thousand deer,
Down in the vale that lies beneath the hill;
There never fell so many deer and roe
In any hunt that e'er till this took place.
But sad was the chase down to the east,
Thou cleric of the church and bells,
Ten hundred of our hounds, with golden chains,
Fell wounded by ten hundred boars:
Then by our hands there fell the boars,
Which wrought the ill upon the plain.
And were it not for blades and vigorous arms,
That chase had been a slaughter.

O Patrick of the holy crosier,
Eastward or westward, hast thou ever seen,
Another chase, in all thy days,
Greater than that of Finn and of the Feine?

[1] Bran was the famous hound of Finn. The word means "a raven," but used as an adjective it signifies "black," which is apparently the origin of the name. Another of his dogs was called "Luath," or "Swift," also an adjective. These are common names for staghounds in the Highlands at this day. Reference is made a few lines before this to a white dog, "a choin ghil," translated "snow-white," "geal," implying the most intense whiteness.

This then was the hunt of Finn,
Thou son of Alpin[1] of the holy relics,
More than thy howling in the church
Do I love to tell the day.
Once on a time, etc.

The author of this is Ossian :[2]

Once on a time as Patrick of the holy crook
Betook him to his cell,
He sought as his companion
Ossian of gentle mien.

Now let me hear, he said,
Ossian, whose courage has made foes retreat,
Who of all those whom thou ne'er sang'st,
Most vexed the Feine of Finn?

Priest of the spotted crook,[3]
Thy lifetime it would take

[1] The Irish call this word "Ar-pluinn," in Latin, "Calphurnius" In the Highlands the name is uniformly "Alpin,"—"Padruig mac Alpain."

[2] This composition the Irish call the battle of "Ventry Harbour," a place in the county of Kerry in Ireland There are, however, Fintrays in Scotland, which are apparently the same name, and Mr. Skene has called the attention of the writer to the fact, that there is a Sgùir Dhaire dhuinn, "the hill of Daire donn," in Duror in Argyleshire. Irish Antiquaries say the battle was fought in the third century between the Féine of Ireland and Daire donn, or Daire the brown, King of the world It will be seen in this copy that Daire is introduced as King of Lochlin or Scandinavia, although afterwards called King of the world. It is very probable that both to the Scotch and Irish Celt Scandinavia was at this period synonymous with the world This poem is here attributed to Ossian, although it is very doubtful whether it is so in the MS The writing is so indistinct, that it is impossible to read the title correctly. It is hardly necessary to remind the reader that the poem is in the form of a dialogue between the bard, whoever he may be, and St. Patrick. The name of the saint seems to have been a favourite one with the bards, and was used no doubt to give consequence and currency to their compositions

[3] The crozier of St. Patrick. Several ancient Celtic croziers are still in exist-

To tell in human speech
The glory of the Feine of Finn.

Since without guile thou art,
And now that they are dead, dost live,
Watch thou for ever on,
And tell the deeds done by the Feine.

Should I be spared for fifty years,
Hearing thy music in thy cell
Till my death's day, I could not tell
The noble deeds of the Feine of Finn
The kingdoms of the earth in all its breadth
Belonged to us on every side
Tribute we raised from all of them for Finn,[1]
Else filled them with the shout of war.
In this wide earth there was not one
That dared refuse us,
Not ev'n in Alve[2] of the spotted spears,
With all its power and its untold renown

ence Two are well known in Scotland One of them is the Quigrich, or crozier of St. Fillan, now in possession of a family of the name of Dewar in Canada, to whose progenitor it was intrusted by Robert Bruce at the battle of Bannockburn. An interesting notice of this relic has recently been published by Dr D Wilson of Toronto. Another is the crozier of St. Munn, now in the Museum of the Society of Antiquaries in Scotland, and long in possession of a family called the Barons of Bachul (a *crozier*, from the Latin *Baculus*), in the island of Lismore. A notice of this relic will be found in the transactions of the Scottish Antiquaries, from the able pen of Mr Cosmo Innes The word "breac," or *spotted*, applied to the crozier, must refer to its ornamentation The term will be found elsewhere applied to spears or swords

[1] This is a curious piece of Bardic exaggeration. But there may be some history hidden within its folds. There is sufficient evidence to prove that the Feine, whoever they were, were not confined to Ireland We have numerous ancient Celtic compositions in which reference is made to the Féine of Scotland, and the Féine of Britain, meaning either Wales, or England and Wales together. The truth with regard to Finn and his Féine seems even yet to be a long way off.

[2] This is said to be "Almhuin," or Allen, the residence of Finn, according to Irish accounts, in the county of Kildare. The word has a strong resemblance to "Alba," the Gaelic name for Scotland; and in reading ancient Gaelic MSS., care must be taken to distinguish the two We give the name in the Dean's orthography, whatever the place may be.

Would'st thou but tell them now,
Ossian, of the fierce assaults,
Which was the stoutest arm
Among the men that followed Finn.

Thou sett'st me to a painful task,
O Priest, thou pupil of the heavenly king,
I could not till the judgment day,
Tell of the Feine, the men and deeds

Yet since it so fell out that thou outliv'st them
Ossian of sweet and pleasing songs,
Which would'st thou chuse of all the Feinn,
To stand in battle by thy shield ?

Oscar and Caoilte and Gaul,
And Luthy's son, of sharpest swords;
Round Cumhal's son,[1] they well might stand,
No nobler band in battle fought;
Bloody Fargon, son to the king,
And Carroll with the murderous spear;
Dermin, brave and fair, who nothing feared,
And bore his pointed shield aloft,
Coll Caoilte's son, so gentle at the feast;
Corc, a warrior of no tender blows;
Ryno, son to the king;—
A band than which no braver fought
The fair-haired Fillan, who was son to Finn,
And Garry, than whom no bloodier foe;
The guileless Dyrin, Doveran's son,
Hugh, son of Garry of the powerful arm,
I, myself, and Gaul the son of Smail,

[1] Finn was Cumhal's son. The word is pronounced "Finn mac Cúil,"—very much as M'Dougal is pronounced in the speaking of Gaelic. The writer has been led to think that traces of "Cual" (Cumhal) might be found in the King Coil of Ayrshire The whole region about the scene of Coil's territory and sepulchre has been purely Celtic, and the grave itself bears marks of being constructed in the early Celtic method.

And Daire of oaken frame, brave Ronan's son;
The armourer's three sons, men without guile,
Whose ruddy armour gleamed, adorned with gold.
Now that I tell my tale to thee,
Cleric that dwell'st at Port-na-minna,
No man of all the Feine was known to me
But one, to whom all other men must yield.
But, now, do thou be seated in thy chair,
Take up thy pen, we'll number all the host,
The host of brave and noble men
Who came, well-ordered bands, unto the Feine.
Across the sea the King of Lochlin came,
The brown-haired[1] Daire of famous shield,
From Conn to wrest the tribute paid by Erin,
A mournful tale for us and all our host.
Our Feinn had friends who came to give them aid,
Men from the sides of every hill,
Led on by Cairbar of the sinewy arm.
Of these four bands came safe to land
Of the Feinn themselves came seven bands,
Three from the east, the half of Erin called from Conn.[2]
The greater number in the battle fell,
But few escaped the bands of Daire donn.
Down with his fleet lay Daire donn
Himself and all his host
Of these were thirty score[3]
Who ne'er again did see their native land
There watched them near the shore
Conn Crithear of the well-aimed strokes.
He seized the men of India there,
And raised the king's head on the mountain side.

1 As already observed, Daire donn, or "Daire the brown," is called here the King of Lochlin

2 Ireland was divided into two great sections: the northern, called Leth Chuinn, or Conn's half, from Conn of the hundred battles, King of Ulster; the southern, called Leth Mhogha, or Mogh's half, called from Mogha Nuadhat, King of Munster, both in the second century.

3 The Celts always count by twenties up to 400 When a Highlander speaks of 340 or 360 of anything, he uniformly says seventeen score or eighteen score The numbers given here are an instance of the poetic license

This famous Conn, the son of Ulster's king,
And Dollir, no less famed for warlike deeds,
We left upon the strand,
Drowned in mutual clasp beneath the waves.
Dathach's three sons, no braver men,
Ascending from the place where lay the ships,
Feartan and Kerkal, he with the large round head,
We left their bodies naked on the strand.
Owar,[1] the armed daughter of the King of Greece,
And Forna of the heavy sturdy blows
We left, a vacant grin upon their faces.
We knew no sorrow as we left them there.
Four of the King of Lochlin's sons we left,
Slain by our fierce, resistless arms.
The three Balas from Borrin in the east,
Hardly escaped our murderous blows.
Great as was the king of the world,
Daire donn, with shield of purest white,
We left his body, too, upon the strand,
Slain by the blows of the victorious Feine.
Of all the world's hosts, brave though they were,
None did escape the slaughter
Except the King of France alone,
Who, like a swallow as it grasps the air,
Fled from fear of noble Oscar,
And even once his sole ne'er touched the earth
Until he got to Glenabaltan, as men relate;
Then and there only did he find him rest.
It was on Fintray's strand, down at the sea,

[1] This daughter of the King of Greece is well known in Celtic tradition. In Mr. J. F. Campbell's *Tales of the West Highlands*, vol. ii. p. 470, it will be seen that traces of her existence are found still in the island of Barra Greece was not unknown to the ancients. Cæsar tells us that the Gauls, although not committing their religious mysteries to paper, in common writing which was familiar to them, used the Greek letters. This is a remarkable statement, and one of which too little use has been made in discussing the social condition of the early Gael. At the same time, we learn from the history of the Gallic war that the literature of Gaul was drawn from Britain, at least her priests studied there, which can have no other meaning.

Our people made this slaughter,
Of these, the kings of all the world,
And drank our full of vengeance.
Our fierce and conquering arms
Laid many a noble warrior low;
Many a sword and shield
Lay shattered on the strand,
The strand of Fintray of the port;
Many dead bodies lay upon the earth,
Many a hero with a vacant grin.
Much was the spoil we gathered in the fight
Patrick, son of noble Alpin,
Even of the Feine themselves, none did escape
The fierce and murderous fight
Except two ordered bands,
Nor were their bodies whole.
The sons of Boisgne[1] made one band of those,
A race, with hands that knew no tender grasp,
Then came the sons of Morn,[2] who with the sons of Smail
Made up the second band.
By thy hand, O noble Priest
In that sore fight, there perished of our Feine
Five well-trained bands
Who left us for the strand.
Thirty luckless bands,
A thousand score in each,
We numbered of the men of Daire donn,
That never reached the waves.
Were I to answer thee, O Priest,
As thou desir'st to hear my every tale,
Down to the time we[3] Gawra's battle fought,

[1] The race of the Féine to which Finn belonged. The Irish say they occupied Leinster and the eastern part of Ulster.

[2] The race to which the famous Gaul belonged. They are said to have occupied Connaught and the west of Ireland. These are the Irish accounts, and must be taken as contributions to a correct elucidation of the history of these events, if they have a real history.

[3] A poem on this famous battle will be found in a subsequent part of this collection.

We never lost our power
Then did we seize the ships;
We took the heavy silver of the king,
The gold, the garments, and the other spoil;
Each half of Erin had its share.
Holy Patrick of the relics,
Shall I meet death within thy house of prayer?
Cover thou my form with earth,
Since thou knowest well my tale.

Ossian, since thou art wearied now,
Make thy peace, that thou may'st die,
Take up thy prayer and ask for mercy,
Early each day call on thy God,
And when, on the judgment day, thou reachest Sion,
Where all men shall be gathered,
May Michael, Mary, and the Son of God
Take thee kindly by the hand.

May the Twelve Apostles, with their song of praise,
Each holy cleric, and each prophet,
Me save from hell,
For I've been very sinful in my day.
Once on a time.[1]

The author of this is Ossian:

Feeble this night is the power of my arm,
My strength is no more as it was;
No wonder though I should mourn,
Poor old relic that I am;
Sad that such should be my lot,

[1] It will be seen in this and the previous pieces, that the first few lines are repeated at the close of every poem. This practice is uniformly followed in all ancient Celtic Poetry, and is a sure indication that we have reached the end of the piece.

Beyond all men who tread the earth,
Wearily dragging stones along
To the church on the hill of the priest.
I have a tale which I would tell
Regarding our people, O Patrick :
Listen to Finn's prediction.
Shortly ere thou cam'st, O Priest,
The hero was to build a fort,
On Cuailgne's[1] bare and rounded hill.
He laid it on the Feine of Fail[2]
Materials for the work to get.
Two-thirds of all his famous fort
He laid upon the sons of Morn ;
The other third he laid on me,
And on the other sons of Boisgne.
I answered, but not aright,
The son of Cumhal, son of Trenmor.
I said I would cast off his rule,
And would submit to him no more.
Then for long Finn held his peace,
The hero hard to vanquish,
He who knew no guile nor fear,
When my answer he had heard,
His words to me were these,
The words of Finn, prince of the Feine :

Thou shalt be dragging stones awhile
Ere to thy mournful home thou goest

[1] A hill said to be in the county of Armagh, celebrated in the ancient poem of "Tain bo Chuailgne," or "The cattle spoil of Cuilinn." It is said to have been here that Cuchullin resided, whence probably his name, Cu Chuailgne, or Cuchullin, the Hound of Cuillinn. In Irish History Cuchullin is said to have lived a couple of centuries previous to the era of Fingal.

The reader may be reminded that there is a mountain in Skye called Cuilinn, one of the grandest of the Scottish mountains. The person from whom both this and the Irish hills of the name were called, is said to have been Cuilionn, a Druidical priest of great fame. The word means also the Holly tree, from whence the derivation is sufficiently probable.

[2] "Fail" is an ancient name for Ireland. The word signifies *fate;* hence "Innisfail," or the "Island of fate," or, more probably, "the sacred island."

Then did I rise up in wrath,
From Cumhal's son of bloody sword
There followed me of all the Feine,
The fourth battalion, hardy and brave.
Then was I long with the Feine,
On all things I my judgment gave.
Many were there with me then,
But now, alas, I'm feeble, feeble;
I was counsellor to the Feine,
In all emergencies, how feeble
How many men that do not know
That on this earth I'm feeble, feeble
This night my body's frame is feeble,
Patrick, I believe thy words
My hands, my feet, and head,
All of them are feeble, feeble.
Feeble, etc.

The author of this is Ossian:

Here have I seen the Feine,
I have seen Conan and Gaul,
Finn, and Oscar my son,
Ryno, Art, and brown-haired Diarmad,[1]
Brave M'Luy,[2] he of noble mien,
The red-haired Garry,[3] also Hugh the less,

1 Diarmad was the Adonis of the Feine. He is celebrated for his beauty, which led finally to his death, as will be seen in a future poem. He is said to have been the Ancestor of the clan Campbell, who are hence called "Clann Diarmaid," or the "children of Diarmad" The M'Diarmads, as well as some other subordinate clans, are also said to be of the same stock.

2 A grandson of Finn by his son Daire dearg His mother's name was Luigheach, whence he was called the son of Luigheach, pronounced Luy. He was a famous man among the Feine, according to Irish authorities.

3 There were several among the Feine of this name. The name is widely known in the topography of Scotland. There are two Rivers Garry, two lochs, and two large rivers These are found in Inverness-shire and Perthshire.

Hugh Garry's son, who never quailed,
The three Finns, and with them Fead,
Glass and Gow and Garry,
The long-haired Galve, and the impetuous Conan;[1]
Gaul and Crooin, Gaul's son,
Socach, the son of Finn, and Bran;[2]
Caoilte, the son of warlike Ronan,[3]
Who swiftest ran, and leaped o'er valleys,
The readiest to scatter gold,
One of them of sweetest voice;
Bayne, son of Brassil of the swords,
The son of Cromchin, son of Smail,
And Oscar, son of powerful Garry,[4]
The three Balas, and the three Skails,
Three battalions from Glenstroil,
Three bands from Monaree;
Caoilte's seven sons best trained to fight;
The three named Glass from Glassrananseir;
The three Beths from Cnokandurd,
Three of unfailing excellence;
Deach Fichid's son from Borruinn mor,
Of them who always conquered.
Here have I seen the Feine
Whose liberal hand did music buy,[5]

[1] Conan is usually called "Conan maol," or "Conan the bald," and was known among the Feine for his thoughtless impetuosity. He was, in consequence of this peculiar temperament, ever getting into difficulties, and exposing himself to the ridicule and reprehension of his companions. There are both a river and valley in Scotland called after him, the River Conan and Strathconan in Rosshire.

[2] "Bran," the name of Finn's celebrated hound, is here obviously the name of a man There is a "strath" or valley in Rosshire which still retains his name, Strathbran. The extent to which Fenian names are found in Scottish topography, goes far to show the close connexion of the Feine themselves with that country.

[3] Caoilte was one of the most famous of the Feine. He was distinguished for his swiftness, and not without reason, as is shown in his chase of Loinn mac Liobhaidh, the Fenian blacksmith, whom he overtook, although he could cross a valley at a stride.

[4] This Oscar must be distinguished from the famous Oscar, the Poet's son. Of the latter he never speaks without applying to him some term of endearment, as "my son," "my own son," etc.

[5] This line refers to the liberal rewards

Ranged around Ossian and Finn,
Traversing valleys to dispense their gold.
Fearton and brave Carroll were there,
Who never fought but where they won.
I sing them, and generous Felan,
All of whom here have I seen.
Here have I seen.

The author of this is Ossian, the son of Finn.[1]

Tell us, O Patrick, what honour is ours,
Do the Feine of Ireland in heaven now dwell?

In truth I can tell thee, thou Ossian of fame,
That no heaven has thy father, Oscar, or Gaul.

Sad is the tale thou tellest me, Priest,
I worshipping God while the Feine have no heaven.

Shalt thou not fare well thyself in that city,
Though ne'er should thy father, Caoilte, and Oscar be there?

Little joy would it bring to me to sit in that city,
Without Caoilte, and Oscar, as well as my father.

Better see the face of heaven's son each day,
Than all the gold on earth, were it thine to possess.

which the Bards usually received among the Celts. A eulogy was sometimes rewarded by the Chief with a silver cup. Even poetry had need to be purchased; and probably were it not for the hope of reward of some kind, many of the noblest Poems which have adorned human history would never have seen the light. At a meeting of Skye gentlemen on some public occasion some years ago, the question was put, "Where are the bards?" One of the company replied, "They are gone." "No," said Nicolson of Scorrybreck, "they are still with us; but the men who fostered them are gone."

[1] This piece is what is usually called "Urnuidh Oisiain," or "Ossian's prayer." There are many such colloquies in the Gaelic, many of them bearing no marks of great antiquity. It will be found that in the Gaelic the poem is divided. This arose from a misplacing of different parts of it in the MS., which was not observed till the first part was printed off. In the English the whole is given consecutively.

Tell us, thou Priest of the Holy city, the tale ;
In return I'll recount thee the battle of Gaura.

If the tale of that city thou desir'st, old man,
No thirst, no hunger, want, reproach are there.

Who are heaven's sons ? more noble are the Feinn :
Are they hard of heart ? have thou mercy, Cleric ;

Unlike them are the Feine, unlike them altogether,
Never on the green plain did they seek the chase.

For thy love's sake, Patrick, forsake not the heroes,
Unknown to heaven's King, bring thou in the Feinn.

Though little room you'd take, not one of your race,
Unknown to heaven's King, shall get beneath his roof.

How different Mac Cumhail, the Feinn's noble king,
All men, uninvited, might enter his great house.

Sad is that, old man, and thy life's close so near,
That thou should'st so unjustly judge of my great king.

Better the fierce conflict of Finn and his Feinn,
Than thy holy master, and thyself together.

Mournful, poor old man, that thou should'st folly speak,
Better God for a day than all of Erin's Feinn.

Though few be my days, and my life's close near,
Patrick defame not the nobles of clan Boisgne.

Thou can'st never tell, Ossian, son to the Queen,
How different your nobles from those of my Lord.

Were even Conan living, the least of the Feinn,
He would not suffer thy insolence, Cleric.

Speak not thus, Ossian, savage are thy words,
Take thee now thy rest, and guide thee by my rule.

Did'st thou see the fight, and the noble banners,
Never would'st thou think but of the glory of the Feinn.

Ossian, Prince's son, 'twill be thy soul's great loss
That thou now think'st only of the battles of the Feinn.

Did'st thou hear the hounds, and the sounds of the hunt,
Thou would'st rather be there than in the holy city

That is sad, old man, if the glory of the chase
Be greater than all which Heaven above can yield.

Say not so, Patrick, empty are thy words,
Indeed and in truth, better Finn and the Feinn.

By thy hand, Boisgne's son, not empty are my words,
Better is one angel than Finn and the Feinn.

Were I only now as I was at Gaura's fight,
I would punish thy reproach of Erin's noble Feinn.

Thy pride is all gone, for all thy future days,
None are now left of thy band but thyself

Were my men in life I'd not hear thy howling,
And I'd make thee to suffer in return for thy talk.

Though all of these yet lived, and were now joined together,
I'd still not speak only of the Feinn's seven bands

Seven times the number that thou hast of priests,
Fell all in battle by Oscar alone.

Thou'rt now in thy last days, old and senseless man,
Cease now thy speaking, and come away with me;
Did'st thou see the men of cowls, Finn's son, in Alve,
Thou would'st not as thou dost reproach the men of heaven

No less was our great band, when we were met in Taura,
Reproachful are the words thou speak'st of the great king,
I will forgive thee, Cleric, although thou dost not tell
Tell.

The author of this is Ossian.[1]

I know a little tale of Finn,
A tale that we should not despise,
Of Cumhal's son, the valorous,
Which our memory still preserves.
Once we were a little band,
At Essaroy,[2] of gentle streams,
Near the coast was under sail,
A currach, in which sat a maid;
Fifty men stood by the King,
Brave in any fight or field,
Sad for them who faced their right arm,
For we ruled in every land.
All of us rose up in haste,
Save Finn of the Feine and Gaul,
To welcome the boat as it sped,
Cleaving the waves in its course.
It never ceased its onward way
Until it reached the wonted port.
Then when it had touched the land,
The maid did from her seat arise,
Fairer than a sunbeam's sheen,
Of finest mould and gentlest mien.

[1] This composition is known usually by the name of "Fainesoluis," or the sunbeam, derived manifestly from the comparison of the sunbeam in the twenty-first line. In Ireland it is called "Laoidh an Mhoighre Bhoirb," or "The song of Mayre Borb." The "Mayre" of Ireland will be found to be "Daire" in Scotland.

[2] The topography of these poems is a subject of very deep interest to the student of our national antiquities. In the valley of the Roy in Lochaber, so famous for its parallel roads, is a waterfall called "Eas ruaidh," or "Essaroy," the "fall of Roy." Was this the scene of the story of Fainesoluis? It may be objected that from there the sea lies at a distance of fifteen miles. On the Earn, near Ballyshannon, in the county of Donegal, is "Assaroe," or "Eas Aoidh Ruaidh," "The waterfall of Hugh the red," who was drowned there. This is nearer the sea; but at the period ascribed to Ossian, the name could not have been given to the spot, as the death of Aedh ruadh mac Badhairn, from whom the cascade was named, occurred, according to the Four Masters, in A.M. 4518.

Then before this stranger maid,
We stood and showed courtesy;
"Come to the tent of Finn with us."
With grace she all of us salutes;
'Twas Cumhal's son himself replied,
And salutes her in return
Then did the King of noblest mien
Ask of the maid of fairest face,
"Whence is it thou hast come, fair maid?
Give us now in brief thy tale."
"The King of the land beneath the waves,[1]
My father is, such is my fate,
Through all lands where the sun revolves,
Thee and thy men I long have sought."
"Princess, who hast searched each land,
Youthful maid of beauteous form,
The reason why thou cam'st so far,
Tell us now, and tell us all."
"If thou be Finn, I ask defence,"[2]
So now did speak the youthful maid,

1 Kings among the Celts were, at an early period, persons of much less consequence than the name would now seem to imply. In Ireland, there were four provincial sovereignties besides the national one. But even this does not give an accurate representation of the Celtic polity The fact is, every ruler of a district and leader of an army was called a King Of this we have ample evidence in Cæsar's account of the state of Britain at the period of the Roman invasion. In Scotland, tradition points to several kingdoms. In the Western Highlands the Island of Mull is said to have formed a kingdom by itself, called "Rioghachd na Drealluin," "the Kingdom of Drealinn," from "dreall," a "bar" or "sneck," applied to the Sound of Mull, which shuts out all strangers from the Island. Islay was called "Rioghachd Modheadh," or the "South-west Kingdom," from its position Morvern was called "Iorruaidh," to which frequent reference is made both in Scottish and Irish Celtic tradition. Ardnamurchan was called "Sorcha," the kingdom of Daire Borb's father, from its mountainous character, "Sorcha" meaning "high," whence "sorchan," "a tripod" "Tir bàr fo thuinn," or the land beneath the waves, was Tyree, from the lowness of the land appearing from a distance as if its surface were on a level with the sea If there be any historical accuracy in these traditions, which have been gathered up from an intelligent old Highlander, skilled in the lore of his country, this story of Fainesoluis is one in which a daughter of the ruler of the Island of Tyree is pursued by a son of the ruler of Ardnamurchan. Poetry gives a consequence and magnitude to the event, which in all probability the naked reality did not possess.

2 "Mo chomraich ort," "my protec-

"Thou of soft speech, and purest race,
Grant me protection, grant it now."
Then spoke the wise and knowing King,
"Tell us now from whom thou flee'st;
Protection I thee grant, fair maid,
'Gainst every man that dares thee hurt."
"There comes in wrath across the sea,
Swift in pursuit, a warrior brave,
The well-armed son of Sorcha's King,
He whose name is Daire the fierce.[1]
I laid me under heavy bonds[2]
That Finn should from the sea me have,
But that his wife I ne'er should be,
Though famed his beauty and his deeds."
Then Oscar spoke, of hasty speech,
The warlike conqueror of Kings,
"Though Finn should not thy pledge sustain,
Never shalt thou with him wed."
Then do we see borne by his steed[3]
A hero of unequalled size,
Travelling with speed across the sea,
Following the maiden in her course;
His helmet close about the head
Of this brave and dauntless man;
His right arm bore a round black shield,

tection be on thee," was an appeal which the Celtic warrior could never reject when made by the weak and helpless. In Christian times, the word "Comraich" came to be applied to the "girths" or "sanctuaries" around places of worship and other sacred spots, where accused persons might flee for security. Hence the Gaelic name of the parish of Applecross in Rosshire, "A Chomraich," or "the Sanctuary," formed round the church dedicated to St. Malrube, an early Christian missionary.

[1] As already observed, this name is in Irish editions of the poem "Mayre." See Miss Brooks' "*Reliques of Irish Poetry*."

[2] "Geasan," "bonds." The word here appears to mean a simple pledge, although in most cases it implies the exercise of some magical power. In those cases of metamorphosis so common in Celtic tales, the persons who have been made to undergo the change are said to be "fo gheasaibh," "under spells." The mythology of the Celts has much in common with that of Eastern nations.

[3] The magical steed of Daire borb was capable of carrying its master over sea and land. In many ancient Celtic Tales we read of ships which could also traverse sea and land.

The surface of its back engraved ;
A heavy, large, broad-bladed sword,
Tightly bound, hung by his side ;
He comes in attitudes of fence,
As where we stood he swift approached ;
Two javelins, with victory rich,
Rest on the shoulder of his shield ;
For strength, for skill, for bravery,
Nowhere could his match be found.
A hero's look,—the eye of a king
Shone in that head of noblest mould,
Ruddy his face, his teeth pearl-white,
No stream ran swifter than his steed.
Then did his steed bound on the shore,
And he in whom we saw no fear.
Of us did fifty warriors then
Approach him as he came to us ;
Fear of the hero as he neared us
Filled the bravest of them all.
Now as he landed from the waves,
Our famous King the question put,
" Can'st thou tell me now, fair maid,
Is that the man of whom thou spak'st ?"
" I know him well, Finn Cumhal's son,
Nor does his coming bode you good ;
Me he will rudely strive to seize,
Despite thy strength, O noble Finn."
Then Oscar and Gaul arose,
The fiercest of all in the fight,
Near to the men they firmly stood,
Between the giant and our chief.
The well-formed warrior then approached,
In rage sustained by his great strength,
The maid he rudely bears away,
Though by Finn's shoulder she had stood.
The Son of Morne then hurled his spear,
With wonted force, as he bore off ;

No gentle cast was that, in truth,
The hero's shield was split in twain.
The wrathful Oscar then did shake
The red-dyed belt from his left arm,[1]
And killed the hero's prancing steed,
A deed most worthy of great fame.
Then, when the steed fell on the plain,
He on us turned in fiercest wrath,
And battle does, the onset mad,
With all our fifty warriors brave.
On the same side with me and Finn,
The fifty stood in front of him :
Yet though they oft stood firm in fight,
His arm did now them force to yield
Two blows, and only two he gave,
With vigour to each sep'rate man,
When we were stretched upon the earth,
Each man of us with whom he fought.
Three vanquished nines he tightly bound,
Ere from the furious fight he ceased.
Firmly the three smalls'[2] usual tie
On each of these he firmly placed.
Then did the manly Gaul advance,
The conquering hero to assail.
Whoe'er he was could see them then,
The struggle and the fight were fierce.
Then did Mac Morne slay with his arm
The King of Sorcha's son, most strange!
Sad was the coming of the maid,
Now that the brave in fight had fallen.

1 The word in the original here is "criss zerk," the "red belt." This is, however, in all probability, a mistake of the Dean's for "craoiseach," a "javelin." It is not easy to see what could be meant by the "red belt" on Oscar's left arm. It could hardly signify the straps of the shield. If it be "craoiseach," the bard would seem to indicate that Oscar was left-handed, like the sons of Benjamin.

2 "Na tri caoil," or the "three smalls," were the neck, the ankles, and the wrists. Prisoners of war had this triple binding applied to them.

And now that he had fallen thus,
Beside the sea, a sad event,
She of the land beneath the waves,
With Finn and his Feine remained a year.
Flann, son of Morne, in battle brave,
Was killed, it is a piteous tale ;
None of all our men escaped,
Whose body was not full of wounds,
Except my noble Father, Finn,
The generous friend of all distressed.
And now at last the deed is done.
Of Finn this little tale I know.
I know a little tale of Finn.

As our fifty warriors brave [1]
Were now subject to his arms,
Helpless were we in his hands,
Our precious rights were all now lost.
His sword without a single check,
Did hack our bodies and our shields
Any fighting like to his,
In my day never have I seen.
We buried then close to the fall
This noble, brave, and powerful man.
And on each finger's ruddy point
A ring was placed in honour of the King.
For ten long years his conquering arms,
To the victor did the King forbid ;
For all that time the son of Morne
Was healing with Finn of the Feine.

[1] These supplementary lines would appear to be either additional lines or various readings. There are two given in the Gaelic, which are not translated, as being of little consequence, and which seem intended to come in between the ninety-eighth and ninety-ninth lines. The first eight lines of this additional fragment are probably intended to fall in between the hundred and twenty-eighth and the hundred and twenty-ninth lines, the last eight to close the poem. Dr. Smith, in the Report on Ossian's Poems given in to the Highland Society, states, that the Edition given in this supplement is inconsistent with that in the body of the Poem, and must be held to contain various readings.

The author of this is Ossian, the son of Finn.[1]

'Twas yesterday week
I last saw Finn;
Ne'er did I see
A braver man;
Teige's[2] daughter's son,
A powerful king;
My fortune, my light,
My mind's whole might,
Both poet and chief.
Braver than kings,
Firm chief of the Feinn.
Lord of all lands,
Leviathan at sea,
As great on land,
Hawk of the air,
Foremost always.
Generous, just,
Despised a lie.
Of vigorous deeds,
First in song.
A righteous judge,
Firm his rule.
Polished his mien,
Who knew but victory.

[1] The following seems to have been Ossian's eulogy on his father Finn. The editor has not met with any similar composition either among Scottish or Irish collections, except a few lines extracted by Miss Brooks from a composition which she calls "Buille Oisein," and it is therefore rescued from oblivion by having been seized by the Dean while floating on the stream of oral tradition, and treasured in his miscellany. In the original, the poetry is worthy of the name of Ossian, more so, indeed, than any of the pieces in this collection. It is quite impossible to produce in English the effect of the rhythm and alliteration of the Gaelic; but the editor has endeavoured, while giving an exact rendering, to retain, in as far as possible, the peculiar measure of the original. The piece is a fine tribute of filial love and admiration, nor is there much room to doubt its genuineness.

[2] Muirne Finn's mother is said to have been a daughter of Teige, a famous Druid, or, as others say, of a princely family of Bregia, in Meath.

Who is like him
In fight or song?
Resists the foe,
In house or field.
Marble his skin,
The rose his cheek,
Blue was his eye,
His hair like gold.
All men's trust,
Of noble mind.
Of ready deeds,
To women mild,
A giant he,
The field's delight.
Best polished spears,
No wood like their shafts.
Rich was the King.
His great green bottle,
Full of sharp wine,
Of substance rich.
Excellent he.[1]
Of noble form,
His people's head,
His step so firm,
Who often warred.
In beauteous Banva,
Three hundred battles
He bravely fought.
With miser's mind
From none withheld
Anything false
His lips ne'er spoke.
He never grudged,

[1] Some of the lines in this part of the original MS are very much defaced from age and bad usage. The editor has been obliged in consequence to guess one line and a few additional words. The line is the forty-fifth, where he has introduced a phrase sufficiently general to prevent the charge of in any measure tampering with his author. The other words will be seen by referring to the Gaelic.

No, never Finn ;
The sun ne'er saw King
Who him excelled.
The monsters in lakes,
The serpent by land,
In Erin of saints,[1]
The hero slew.
Ne'er could I tell,
Though always I lived,
Ne'er could I tell
The third of his praise.
But sad am I now,
After Finn of the Feinn !
Away with the chief,
My joy is all fled.
No friends 'mong the great,
No courtesy.
No gold, no queen,
No princes and chiefs.
Sad am I now,
Our head ta'en away !
I'm a shaking tree,
My leaves all gone.
An empty nut,
A reinless horse,
Sad, sad am I,
A feeble kern.
Ossian I, the son of Finn,
Strengthless in deed.

[1] The word "naoimh," here translated "saints," is not necessarily associated with Christianity. The word "naomh," *holy*, is one belonging originally to the Gaelic language, and not introduced, like many ecclesiastical terms, from the Latin and Greek. The phrase may be rendered "sacred Erin," a character belonging to the island, in popular belief, even previous to the Christian period It is a curious fact, that the feat of destroying all the vermin in Ireland was, in a later age, attributed to St. Patrick. It would appear that this was but a transference of a portion of the glory of Finn to the Christian Saint,—a remarkable instance among many of early Christianity borrowing, not very wisely, the laurels of heathenism.

When Finn did live
All things were mine.
Seven sides had the house
Of Cumhal's son.
Seven score shields
On every side.
Fifty robes of wool
Around the King.
Fifty warriors
Filled the robes.
Ten bright cups
For drink in his hall.
Ten blue flagons,
Ten horns of gold.
A noble house
Was that of Finn.
No grudge nor lust,
Babbling nor sham;
No man despised
Among the Feinn.
The first himself,
All else like him.
Finn was our chief,
Easy his praise,
Noblest of Kings.
Finn ne'er refused
To any man,
Howe'er unknown;
Ne'er from his house
Sent those who came.[1]

[1] Hospitality was one of the highest qualifications of a Celtic chief. Ossian never fails to sing the generous, open-handed hospitality of his father Finn. Till a late period the same feature of character distinguished the Scottish Highlander, although modern civilisation is fast uprooting it, and overlaying the character of the simple Highlander with the selfishness peculiar to itself. Even now, in most part of the Highlands, the door of a hut is never closed by day,—a practice said to originate in the universal sense of the ready reception due to the wayfarer and the stranger. Is the *seven* sides of Fingal's house an orientalism?

Good man was Finn,
Good man was he.
No gifts e'er given
Like his so free.
'Twas yesterday week

The author of this is Allan M'Rorie.[1]

Glenshee,[2] the vale that close beside me lies,
Where sweetest sounds are heard of deer and elk,
And where the Feinn did oft pursue the chase,
Following their hounds along the lengthening vale.
Below the great Ben Gulbin's[3] grassy height

[1] This Poet is obviously a Scotchman; but judging from another of his compositions in this volume, he was, like the Scottish bards of his time, well acquainted with the bardic literature of Ireland. This arose from the frequent intercourse between the two countries during their early history, and the number of Scotchmen educated both in the Medical and Bardic Schools of Ireland. This is one of the circumstances which renders it so difficult now, in the absence of authentic historical documents, to extricate much of the social history of the two countries. Hence the rival Scottish and Irish claims to many of our Celtic literary remains. There is no doubt that the poets of both countries interwove with their compositions the traditions of the race, without much regard to whether these were Scotch or Irish. The Irish trace this common literature to the fact of the Irish colonization of Scotland, which they maintain was the origin of the Celtic population of the latter country; but it is by no means necessary to go so far back in order to find sufficient cause for the fact. Christianity seems to have formed the first solid basis of union between the two countries, and a common Christianity was without doubt the means of long maintaining it. This composition is usually called "Bàs Dhiarmaid," *The death of Diarmad.*

[2] A valley in the eastern part of Perthshire, where the grave of Diarmad is pointed out to this day. M'Rorie appears to have been an inhabitant of the neighbourhood, for he speaks of Glenshee as being close beside him. The name of Glenshee is derived from the word "Gleann," *a valley*, and "sìth," *a hill* of a peculiar form. This word is found in the names of several Scottish hills, as "Sìth challain," *Schihallion;* "Beinn shìth," *Ben Hi*; "An t-Sìth mhòr," *the great pointed hill.* "Sìthan," a hillock. The word has been often mistaken for "Sìth," *peace*, whence the name "Sìtheach, sìthichean," *a fairy, fairies*, has been absurdly rendered *the peace folk*, instead of *the folk of the hills*, referring to their reputed residence in earthen mounds.

[3] "Ben Gulbin," *the mountain of the beak*, lies at the head of Glenshee. There is a hill with a similar name in Ireland, whence Conall Gulbain, one of the kings of Ulster, took his designation. There is a "water of Gulbin," and a "Torgul-

Of fairest knolls that lie beneath the sun,
The valley winds. Its streams did oft run red,
After a hunt by Finn and by the Feinn.
Listen now while I detail the loss
Of one, a hero in this gentle band:
'Tis of Ben Gulbin, and of generous Finn,
And Mac O'Duine,[1] in truth a piteous tale.
A mournful hunt indeed it was for Finn,
When Mac O'Duine, he of the ruddiest hue,
Up to Ben Gulbin went, resolved to hunt
The boar,[2] whom arms had never yet subdued.
Though Mac O'Duine, of brightest burnished arms,
Did bravely slay the fierce and furious boar,
Yet Finn's deceit did him induce to yield;

bin," in the braes of Lochaber; but the reference to Glenshee fixes the scene of the death of Diarmad in Perthshire. There is, as is common in Highland topography, a stream called Gulbin, whence a valley of the same name, and then a mountain. The names in similar cases seem to have been primarily attached to the streams, whence they ascended through the valleys to the hills. We have an instance of this in the River Nevis, Glen Nevis, Ben Nevis, the "neamhais," referring to its impetuosity, having been in all likelihood originally applied to the stream.

[1] Mac O'Duine is the patronymic of Diarmad. Hence the Campbell clan, besides being called "Clann Diarmaid," *The race of Diarmad*, are called also "Clann O'Dùine," or *The children of O'Duine*.

[2] The chase of the boar was a favourite employment among the ancient Celts. It is celebrated in many of their tales. Besides this, the sow enters largely into their ancient mythology. Even in this case the boar was possessed of magical properties, as will be seen in the subsequent portion of this poem. It is not unlikely that at an early period the Celts worshipped the sow like the Egyptians, whose worship of it might have been one reason why it was pronounced unclean. Whether the Celts worshipped it or not, it is manifest that it was held in high esteem, for its figure is engraved on most of the ancient sculptured stones of Scotland. Among the Welsh it is a national emblem, and hence one argument for the ancient Picts being British, as these stones are found confined to the ancient Pictish territory. The word "muc," *a sow*, enters largely into Scottish topography. We have "Eilean nam muc," the *Isle of muck*, or *Sow island*. The ancient name of St. Andrews was "Muc ros," *the Sow's headland*, and we know that the sow is associated with the memory of St. Regulus. There is a "Bridge of Turk," or *the Boar's bridge*, near the Trosachs. There is a "Slochd muice," or the *Sow's hollow*, near Inverness, on the Highland road, a name derived from a hillock shaped like a sow's back, in the bottom of the chasm a little to the west of where the coach road crosses, and there is "Sròn muice," *The Sow's snout*, on the north side of Loch Ness, derived from the resemblance of a hill-face to that part of the animal. These two latter names are manifestly derived from natural resemblances, and have nothing to do with mythology.

And this it was that did his grievous hurt.
Who among men was so beloved as he?
Brave Mac O'Duine, beloved of the schools;[1]
Women all mourn this sad and piteous tale
Of him who firmly grasped the murderous spear.
Then bravely did the hero of the Feinn
Rouse from his cover in the mountain side,
The great old Boar, him so well known in Shee,
The greatest in the wild boar's haunt e'er seen.
Glad now was Finn, the man of ruddiest hue,
Beneath Ben Gulbin's soft and grassy side;
For swift the boar now coursed along the heath;
Great was the ill came of that dreadful hunt.
'Twas when he heard the Feinn's loud ringing shout,
And saw approach the glittering of their arms,
The monster waken'd from his heavy sleep,
And stately moved before them down the vale.
First, to distance them he makes attempt,
The great old boar, his bristles stiff on end,
These bristles sharper than a pointed spear,
Their point more piercing than the quiver's shaft.
Then Mac O'Duine with arms well pointed too,
Answers the horrid beast with ready hand:
Away from his side there rushed the heavy spear,
Hard following on the course the boar pursued.
The javelin's shaft fell shivered into three,
The shaft recoiling from the boar's tough hide.
The spear hurled by his warm red-fingered hand
Ne'er penetrated the body of the boar.
Then from its sheath he drew his thin-leaved[2] sword,
Of all the arms most crown'd with victory;

[1] The "schools," referred to frequently in Ossianic tales, were probably military, although there can be no doubt that there was a learned class among the ancient Celts. Cæsar tells us, as already observed, that the Gauls used the Greek letters, and that their priests were educated in Britain. The "oghum" character, whose antiquity is pretty thoroughly established, is another evidence of ancient literary cultivation.

[2] The Gaelic is "tan-lann," the *thin sword*. Was this steel or merely bronze? The thinness would seem to indicate steel.

Mac O'Duine did there the monster kill,
While he himself escaped without a wound.
Then on Finn of the Feinn did sadness fall,
And on the mountain side he sat him down;
It grieved his soul that generous Mac O'Duine
Should have escaped unwounded by the boar.
For long he sat, and never spake a word,
Then thus he spake, although 't be sad to tell,
"Measure, Diarmad, the boar down from the snout,
And tell how many feet 's the brute in length."
What Finn did ask he never yet refused;
Alas! that he should never see his home.
Along the back he measures now the boar,
Light-footed Mac O'Duine of active step.
"Measure it the other way against the hair,
And measure, Diarmad, carefully the boar."
It was indeed for thee a mournful deed,
Youth of the sharply-pointed piercing arms
He went, the errand grievous was and sad,
And measured for them once again the boar.
Th' envenomed pointed bristle sharply pierced
The sole of him,[1] the bravest in the field.
Then fell and lay upon the grassy plain
The noble Mac O'Duine, whose look spoke truth;
He fell and lay along beside the boar,
And there you have my mournful, saddening tale.
There does he lie now wounded to the death,
Brave Mac O'Duine, so skilful in the fight;
The most enduring ev'n among the Feinn,
He lies upon the knoll I see on high,
The blue-eyed hawk that dwelt at Essaroy,[2]
The conqueror in every sore-fought field,

[1] It is hardly necessary to point out the resemblance here between the sole of Diarmad and the heel of Achilles Achilles could only be wounded in the heel, Diarmad only in the sole of the foot. The Adonis of the ancient Greeks was slain by a boar. There are remarkable analogies between classical and Celtic tradition.

[2] Essaroy, *vide supra*, p. 18, n. This is manifestly the Essaroy of Scotland, which is in the heart of one of the finest

Slain by the poisoned bristle of the boar.
Now does he lie full stretched upon the hill,
Brave, noble Diarmad Mac O'Duine!
Slain, it is shame! victim of jealousy.[1]
Whiter his body than the sun's bright light,
Redder his lips than blossoms tinged with red,
Long yellow locks did rest upon his head,
His eye was clear beneath the covering brow,
Its colour mingled was of blue and grey;
Waving and graceful were his locks behind,[2]
His speech was elegant and sweetly soft;
His hands the whitest, fingers tipped with red;
Elegance and power were in his form,
His fair soft skin covering a faultless shape,
No woman saw him but he won her love.
Mac O'Duine crowned with his countless victories,
Ne'er shall he raise his eye in courtship more,
Or warriors' wrath give colour to his cheek;
The following of the chase, the prancing steed,
Will never move him, nor the search for spoil.
He who could bear him well in every fight,
Has now us sadly left in that wild vale.

Glenshee.

hunting regions in the world. Nor is it at any great distance from either of the Gulbins.

[1] Grainne, the wife of Finn, had formed an unlawful attachment to Diarmad. The latter had what is called a "Ball seirce," or *beauty spot*, which no woman could resist. Hence Finn's jealousy and desire to destroy Diarmad. The word rendered here "naire," *shame*, is in the MS. "noor," *gold*. If this be the accurate reading, Grainne's dowery must have formed an element in the conflict.

[2] Yellow was the favourite colour of the ancient Celt. "Falt buidh," *yellow hair*, is an object of the highest admiration, and the longer and more waving the locks, the greater the admiration. The account the Celt gives of himself is somewhat different from that given by his neighbours, who would paint him a wiry, thin, black-haired, black-eyed man. Tacitus gave a different description, and any man who travels the Highlands of Perthshire, where, perhaps, we have the purest Celtic blood in Scotland, will have ample evidence of the accuracy of the Roman historian. With reference to the admiration of the yellow colour among the Celts, it is interesting to trace how it intermingles itself with the vocabulary of the language, thus, a *fine* day is a *yellow* day. The name given to Beltin day, the opening of summer, is, "la buidhe Bealltenne," *yellow Beltin day*; and anything propitious is called

The author of this is Allan M'Rory.[1]

To-night my mourning is great,
Thou tonsured priest whom I love,
While I reflect on the fight,
With red-tree[2] Cairbar we fought,
Son to great Cormaig O'Cuinn,
Woe to the Feinn whom he seized;
A king who ne'er shunned the fight,
And feared not the face of man.
The Feinn to a man did serve,
Finn and the good race of Conn,
Till the day of Cairbar Roy;
Nor evil nor weakness fear'd.
Brave Cairbar his people addressed,
Deceitful indeed was the speech

yellow, as, "is buidhe dhuit e," *it is yellow or propitious for you;* and a man satisfied after a meal is called "buidheach," *yellow or satisfied.*

[1] This is the second composition of M'Rory's given in the Dean's MS. The present is as purely Irish in its incidents as the former was Scotch, the author having been in all likelihood, as already shown, a Scotchman, but perfectly familiar with the events of Irish history, and equally so with what is called the Irish dialect, although in the day of the Dean it was common to the literature of both countries, with a few variations It will be seen, for instance, that in several of these pieces the Irish negative *ni* and the Scottish *cha*, are used indifferently This composition has been published at much greater length than here, under the name of Ossian, but from MSS apparently of no antiquity. This poem is usually called "Cath Ghabhra," "the battle of Gaura," or "Bàs Osgair," "the death of Oscar."

[2] The "red-tree" knights were the knights of Emania, or Ulster. Cæsar mentions the order of *equites*, or knights, as one of the three great leading classes into which the Gauls were divided; so that the existence of such an order in Ireland, at an early period, is in no way inconsistent with what history relates of ancient Celtic policy. Cairbar was the son of Cormac, son of Art, son of Conn of the hundred battles, Irish kings of the Emanian race. Finn, according to O'Flaherty, was married to a daughter of Cormac, so that this battle with Cairbar was in reality with his brother-in-law. It seems to have originated in the Feinn, who are said to have been a species of militia, or rather a standing army in Ireland, becoming disposed to stretch their prerogative farther than was agreeable to the monarch, and that the object of Cairbar in this battle was to put them down It is said that the Feinn were supported by the provincial king of Munster. This is Irish history, and it is remarkable to find these events sung by a Scottish Poet.

In battle would he choose to fall,
The Feinn and he together,
Ere even as a King he'd live
With Erin beneath the Feinn.
Barrin then spoke boldly out,

Remember Muckrey[1] and Art;
How your great ancestors fell,
Resisting the Feinn's deceit;
Remember their cruel bonds,
Remember their pride and guile;
And that we ne'er knew of war,
But such as was stirr'd by Mac Cùil.

Then did the race of Conn resolve,
In counsel with Cairbar Roy,
That they'd at once assail us,
And the whole of us destroy.
They'd have days of joy and feasting,
Great Alvin cleared of the Feinn.
Then would all grief be dead,
Nor could they a tax demand.
Fiercely and bravely we fought,
That fight the fight of Gaura;
There did fall our noble Feinn,
Sole to sole with Ireland's kings.
From India far in the east,
To Fodla[2] here in the west,

[1] Muckrey, or "The island of Swine," is an ancient name for Ireland, derived obviously, not as it might be in modern times, from the abundance of the animal in the country, where it is the sum total of the family possessions in many instances, but from the place which the sow held, as referred to already, in the national mythology. It is obvious from the reference in this line to a difference with the Feinn, that that was no new event in the history of the Irish monarchs

[2] Another name for Ireland O'Flaherty says there were five names for the island, and quotes a scholiast of the name of Fiach, who lived a thousand years before The names are Ere, Fodla, Banba, Fail, and Elga Might we not add to these the much-disputed name of Scotia, which our Irish neighbours claim, yet don't possess. Surely it is time now

The kings did all own our sway,
Till the battle of Gaura was fought
But since that horrid slaughter,
No tribute nor tax we've raised.
Nor to us was tribute due,
Save by part of Erin's soil.
Many were there on the earth
Of the folk who felt no grief.
To both sides how great the loss,
When we each other did destroy,
Should strangers fierce come over,
And seize on beauteous Erin.

Ossian, what would Finn have done
Were burdens laid on Erin?

By thy hand, most holy Priest,
There were none in all fair Banva,[1]
Save a few aged heroes,
And some younger untried men;
What king might there plant his foot,
Could Fodla have for taking.
No fight, no conflict he'd need,
No stratagem nor struggle

Eastward we sent ambassadors,
To Fatha of Con's great son;

to perceive that the only true and satisfactory solution of the question regarding it, is that the name was applied to both countries, latterly under the distinctive appellation of Scotia Major and Scotia Minor, as the countries of the Scots. Surely Scotland was as much a Scotia as Ireland, and Ireland as much as Scotland, in so far as they were both occupied by Scottish inhabitants. This identity of race, language, and at an early period religion, is not sufficiently allowed for in discussing questions involving the several claims of Scotland and Ireland to much of what was common to both. Scotland has suffered more than Ireland from the destruction of her early archives; but is not the life of Columba, so recently given to the world under the able editorship of Dr. Reeves, in reality a Scottish work?

1 "Banva" is another name for Ireland. This is the Gaelic name for a *sucking-pig*, so that it also is probably mythological. It is in all likelihood the same name with our Scottish Banff

That he might lead us on,
To seize on Erin's kingdom.

Great grief had now come on you,
From Tara's loud-spoken King:
New reason had ye given
Why all of you should perish.

Ossian, tell us now the tale,
When ye fought that sturdy fight.
Did thy son in battle die,
Or had he speech when you him found?

I bent me over valiant Oscar,
Soon as was the slaughter o'er;
Caoilte too did bend him o'er
His seven valiant sons;
Each living man among the Feinn
Bent him o'er his own dear friends.
Some of them had still their speech,
From others life had parted.
Priest of the crosier white,
Whoever saw that slaughter,
'Tis an everlasting grief,
Erin's nobles thus to die.
Many were the hard round shields,
Many precious coats of mail,
And lifeless warriors on the field.
Nor would our people grieve for this
Were they not a vanquished race.
Little from that field was left us,
Save a king's or chieftain's spoil.
There found I my own dear son
Laid, on his left arm resting,
His shattered shield beside him,
While his hand still grasped his sword;
His precious blood on every side,

Flowed swiftly through his harness.
My spear I rested on the earth,
And o'er him stood as he lay;
Then thought I, O tonsured Priest,
What, now lonely, I could do.
Oscar towards me now turns,
'Twas for me a grievous scene;
Forth to me he stretched his hand,
Wishing I should him approach.
Then my dear son's hand I seized,
And cried out with a bitter cry.
Forward from that time till now,
In this world I've useless been.
Thus to me my own son said,
As life was fast departing,

Thanks to the powers above,
That thou'st escaped, dear father.

Nothing do I tell but truth,
A word I could not answer.
Then approached the noble Caoilte,
Who to visit Oscar came.
Gently did Mac Ronain[1] say,

How find'st thou thyself, dear friend?

Just as thou would'st have me be,
Going to a better world.

Cairbar Roy's spear had pierced,
'Neath the navel, red-armed Oscar;
The arm of Caoilte up to its bend,
Followed in its course the spear.
Caoilte did deeply search the wound,
And well saw how all stood there.
The wound was through to the back,

[1] Another name for Caoilte.

Torn by the murderous spear.
Mac Ronain gave a loud shriek,
And, fainting, fell to the earth.
Then spake Caoilte, the warrior brave,
Recovering from his faint,

Dear Oscar, no more art thou ours;
Thou and the Feinn must part,
So part must the Feinn with war,
Conn's race the tribute shall raise.

We had been thus a brief space,
Thou priest, the son of Alpin,
When leaving the slaughter we saw,
All of Fail's Feinn now living,
There were but two thousand men,
The old and the young together,
And none unwounded returned,
Even of these hundred score.
Nine wounds them grievously pierced,
There were few of them with less.
Then raised we the noble Oscar,
Aloft on the shafts of our spears;
To a fair green knoll we bore him,
That we his dress might remove.
Of his body one hand's breadth
Was not whole, down from his hair,
Till you reached the sole of his foot,
Save his face, and that alone.
The entrails, the liver, the spleen,
Each draining the body till day.
The sons of the Feinn did then
To a fair knoll them betake;
His own son did no man mourn,
Nor did he mourn his brother:
As they saw how lay my son,
All, all did mourn for Oscar.

Thus was it with us a while,
Watching the fair-skinned hero,
When we saw approach at noon
Finn Mac Cumhail, mac Treinvor.
From the fierce slaughter escaped,
A third of the Feinn still lived,
When they laid the sons of Boisgne
Upon their biers, the fight being o'er.
With gashed limbs the men were halt,
The chiefs a dreadful sight.
We saw the standard of Finn
Raised on the shaft of a spear,
Which from the slaughter they bore;
Gladly to meet it we went.
All of us saluted Finn,
But no salute was returned,
As he climbed the warrior's hill,
Where deadly-armed Oscar lay.
When by Oscar Finn was seen,
As o'er him sadly he bent,
He turned to him his face,
His grandfather saluting.
Then did my Oscar thus speak
To him who was first of us all:

In death I have my desire,
Noble Finn of pointed arms.

Sad it is, my brave Oscar,
Thou good son of my own son;
After thee I'm but feeble,
And after Erin's brave Feinn.
The heavy curse of Art aenir
Is on us to our great grief,
From the east it me pursued,
Following me along the field.
Farewell to battle and fame,

Farewell to the victor's spoils,
Farewell to the many joys,
Which in this body I've had.

When Oscar had heard Finn's wail,
Convulsive pangs did him seize.
Both of his hands he stretched forth,
And his soft fair eyelid fell.
From us then Finn turned away,
And shed many bitter tears.
But for Oscar and for Bran,
Never did he shed a tear.
There was none but Finn and I,
Greater than him of the Feinn.
Then did the men give three shrieks,
Which rung through fair Erin all
Five score hundred, ten hundred and ten,
There were who belonged to us,
Of the Feinn dead on the field,
The number was nothing less.
No lie it is that double,
With Erin's king, great tale,
Perished on the other side,
Of Erin's well-armed men.
Finn cheerful or peaceful never
Was from that down to his death,
Since that fight it touched him sore
That our kings should want their land.
Ever since Gaura's battle
My speech has lost all its power.
No night or day has e'er passed
Without a sigh for each hour[1]

To-night

1 It may be interesting to many readers to have here a specimen of this poem, as taken down from the oral recitation of a Christina Sutherland, an old woman in the county of Caithness, in the year 1856. It commences thus:

Is trom an nochd mo chumha fein,
Guilgeantach mo rian,

The author of this here is Fergus the Bard.[1]

High-minded Gaul,[2]
Who combats Finn,
A hero brave,
Bold in assault,

Smuaineachadh a chath chruaidh,
Chuir mise 'us Cairbar claon ruadh,
Am macsa Chormaic O Chuinn,
Is mairg sinn a thàradh fo 'laimh,
Laoch gun ghràin cha do chuu,
Annsa dh' a laimh iuthaidh, etc

Translation:—

My mourning is grievous this night,
Weeping is my condition,
As I think of the fierce fight,
Fought with red, squint-eyed Cairbre,
That son of Cormac O Chuinn;
Woe to them fell into his hands,
Hero who knew no coward fear,
Whose hand took delight in the arrow, etc.

The composition is very much the same with that of the Dean, but in many portions contains lines which the latter wants, and in others is comparatively defective. Although frequently superior in force, it is not, upon the whole, so smooth and regular as the Dean's edition. It will be given at greater length in the Appendix to this volume.

1 Fergus the Bard was one of the sons of Finn, and consequently brother to Ossian. He was, from all we can learn, the chief Poet of the Feinn. Ossian was both warrior and poet; Fergus was chiefly poet. Fergus was probably somewhat like a modern Gaelic Bard, John Macdonell, commonly called Ian Lom, who, on being urged to fight at the battle between Montrose and Argyle at Inverlochy, replied with well-assumed indignation, "Cha-n e sin mo ghnothuch, cathaichibh sibhse 'us innsidh mise," *that is not my business,—fight you and I'll relate.* In one of the odes preserved in the Dean's MS., Fergus is called "Filidh Feinn Eirinn," *Bard of the Feinn of Erin.*

2 This composition is usually called, "Rosg Ghuill," or the *Ode to Gaul.* Gaul was chief of one branch of the Feinn, the branch denominated "Clann Moirn," or *the children of Morn*, as Finn was chief of the other branch, called "Clann Baoisgne," or *the children of Boisgne.* The word "Gall" means *a foreigner;* "muirn" means *a body of men*, or *beauty, elegance*, in either sense giving a marked significance to the name. This poem represents a difference between Gaul and Finn, the cause of which will appear as the poem proceeds. Fergus, as was customary with the Bards, interposes as peacemaker, and represents to his father, whom he manifestly holds to be in the wrong, the danger of a difference with Gaul. The ode is a very remarkable one, having a striking resemblance to Ossian's eulogy on Finn, as given already in this volume. Both bear decided marks of genuineness and antiquity. The language is peculiar, many of the words being obsolete. Indeed, the phonetic orthography of the Dean, the peculiar handwriting, and the discoloration and bad condition of the MS., with the obsoleteness of many of the words, made it a matter of no little labour to decipher the composition at all. There is an edition of it in Miss Brooks' "Reliques of Irish Poetry," from which, however, the present differs considerably in many of the lines, besides having several additional lines, and several deficient in some parts. The peculiar rhythm of the origi-

His bounty free,
Fierce to destroy.
Beloved of all,
Gaul, gentle, brave,
Son of great Morn ;
Hardy in war,
His praise of old,
A comely man,
King, soldierly, free,
Of no soft speech,
No lack of sense,
Cheerful as great:
In battle's day
He moved a prince;
Though soft his skin,
Not soft his deed,
Of portly mould,
A fruitful branch,
His heart so pure,
He trains the young.
'Bove mountains high
Rises in victory,
We ever fear
When he assails.
I tell you Finn,
Avoid the man,
Terror of Gaul
Should make you quail;
Soothe him rather,

nal, with the alliterations and vocalic concords, give it remarkable smoothness and force. The rhythm has, as far as possible, been retained in the translation. But besides the language, the sentiment of the piece is strong evidence of its antiquity. Those features of character are commended which have always been in favour in a rude age. Bodily strength, courage, manliness, and size, are dwelt on with all the warmth of an ardent admiration; while as much of literary cultivation is pointed out and commended, as would show the acquaintance of the hero with the traditions of his race. Gaul is said to have been "eagnaidh a stair," *learned in history.* This and the ode to Finn have internal evidence of being compositions belonging to a very remote age.

Better than fight
Skilful and just,
He rules his men,
His bounty wide,
A bloody man,
First in the schools,
Of gentle blood,
And noble race,
Liberal, kind,
Untired in fight,
No prince so wise,
Brown are his locks,
Marble his skin,
Perfect his form,
All full of grace,
Fierce to exact,
When aught is due,
In vigour great,
Of fairest face,
No king like Gaul.
I tell thee Finn,
His strength as waves
In battle's crash,
Princely his gait,
Comely his form,
Gaul's skill'd fence
No play when roused.
Ready to give,
Dreadful his strength,
Manly his mould,
Soldierly, great,
Ne'er could I tell
His grace and power;
A fearful foe,
Ready his hands,
Conceal'd his wrath,
A cheerful face.

Like murmuring seas,
Rushed to the fight,
A lion bold,
As great in deed,
Powerful his arm,
Choice amidst kings.
Joyful his way,
His teeth so white.
'Tis he that wounds,
The greatest foe.
His purpose firm,
A victor sure,
Desires the fight,
In history learn'd,
Warrior bold,
Sharp is his sword,
Contemptuous Gaul,
Plunders at will.
A fearless man,
Wrathful he is,
Dreadful in look,
Leopard in fight,
Fierce as a hound,
Of women loved.
A circle true
E'er by him stood.
He hurls his dart,
No gentle cast.
Soft are his cheeks,
In blossom rich,
Of beauteous form,
Unchanged success;
No stream so swift
As his assault,
Mac Morn more brave,
Than any told,
Of powerful speech,

It far resounds,
He 's truly great,
Liberal, just,
Does not despise,
Yet firm resolves,
Gentle, yet brisk,
Forsakes no friend,
In fight of kings,
No powerless arm.
There, fierce his mien,
And strong his blow.
When roused his wrath,
He 's third of the chase.
Noble Mac Cumhail,
Soothe and promise,
Give peace to Gaul,
Check wrath and guile.

During my day,
Whate'er it be,
I'd give without guile,
A third of the chase.[1]

Let's hear no more,
Soft dost thou speak,
Finn's love to Gaul,
And third of the hounds.

[1] It would appear from this latter part of the poem, that the difference between Finn and Gaul concerned the right to hunt. It would appear that such a cause of controversy is no modern affair, but that game and game-laws had their place among human interests and human contentions from the earliest period of our country's history. Finn seems to have claimed the right of chase over the whole territory of the Feinn. Gaul resisted and claimed a share for the race of Morn. Hence the contest giving Gaul the appellation of "Fear cogaidh Fhinn," or *resister of Finn.* Fergus's intervention resulted in Gaul's obtaining from Finn, with good will, one-third of the territory called here "fiodh," or *wooded territory,* and one-third of the hounds. There is a curious reference to these hunting rights in one of the poems in praise of the M'Gregors, given in an after-part of this volume, in which it is said that Finn himself dare not hunt without leave.

Gaul, leave thy wrath,
With us have peace,
Now without grudge,
Thou'st of Finn's forest third.

That will I take,
Fergus, dear friend,
My wrath is gone,
No more I ask.

Friend without guile,
Lips thin and red,
Bounty and strength,
Shall win thee praise.
High-minded Gaul.

The author of this is Fergus the Bard.[1]

Tell us now, Fergus,
Bard of Erin's Feinn,
How did fare the day
In Gawra's furious fight

Not good, son of Cumhail,
The tidings from Gawra's fight.
Dear Oscar lives no more,
He who bravely fought;
Caoilte's seven sons are gone,
With the commons of Alvin's Feinn
The youth of the Feinn have fallen,
All in their warlike robes.

[1] This is another of the compositions of Fergus, the son of Finn, and brother of Ossian. It will be found to be an account of the death of Oscar at the battle of Gaura. One composition on this subject by Allan M'Rory has been given already. M'Rory's appears to be the more modern of the two, besides being inferior in many respects to this. The account of Oscar's death given here, is in the way of reply to an inquiry of Finn.

Mac Luy too is dead,
With six of thy father's sons.
Fallen are the youth of Alvin,
Dead are the Feinn of Britain.[1]
Lochlin's king's son is dead,
Who came to give us aid,
He of the manly heart,
And arm at all times strong.
Tell them now, O Bard,
My son's son, my delight,
How it was that Oscar
Hewed the helmets through.
It would be hard to tell,
'Twould be a heavy task,
To number all that fell,
Slain by the arms of Oscar.
No swifter is a cataract,
Or hawk in sweeping stoop,
Or rapids rushing fast,
Than in that fight was Oscar.
You saw him, last of all,
Like leaves in windy weather,
Or like a noble aspen,
When hewers strike its stem.
When Erin's King he saw,
Still living 'midst the fight,
Oscar swift approached him,
As waves break on the strand.
When Cairbar this observed,
He shook his hungry spear,
And through him drove its point.
Chiefest of all our griefs!
Yet Oscar did not quail,

[1] Here we have in this very ancient composition reference to the Feinn of Britain, Britain including then as now England, Scotland, and Wales. If the Feinn belonged to Britain as well as Ireland, they could not have been a mere Irish militia.

But made for Erin's King;
With force he aimed a blow,
And smote him with his sword.
Then Art mac Cairbar fell,
Struck with the second blow.
So 'twas that Oscar perished,
With glory, as a King.
Fergus the bard am I,
I've travelled every land,
I grieve after the Feinn,
To have my tale to tell.
Tell.

This tale is by Gilliecallum M' an Olave.[1]

I have heard a tale of old,
A tale that should make us weep;
'Tis time to relate it sadly,
Although it should fill us with grief.
Rury's[2] race of no soft grasp,
Children of Connor and Connal;
Bravely their youth did take the field,
In Ulster's noble province.
None with joy returned home
Of Banva's proudest heroes.

1 This is the composition of a Poet of whom we know nothing save what we find in this volume. From a poem of his in praise of the M'Gregors, he would appear to have been a Scotchman. The name signifies Malcom, the son of the chief bard or the physician. It is found still in the form of M'Inally. This poem is the Celtic edition of the Persian tale of Zohrab and Rustum. The incidents are so similar, that the two tales must have had a common origin. Whether the Persians received the tale from the Celts, or the Celts from the Persians, or both from some other and older source, it is hard to say. The composition is in Gaelic, usually called, "Bàs Chonlaoich," or *The death of Conlach.*

2 Clann Rughraidh, a powerful race, who occupied the province of Ulster at an early period, after having expelled the Clann Deaghaidh, or the Dalcassians, afterwards of Munster.

For as they once more tried the fight,
Rury's race did win the day.
There came to us, fierce his mien,
The dauntless warrior, Conlach,
To learn of our beauteous land,
From Dunscaich[1] to Erin.
Connor spoke thus to his men,
"Who's prepared to meet the youth,
And of him to take account;
Who will take no refusal?"
Then the strong-armed Connal went,
Of the youth to take account;
The end of their fight was this,
Conlach had bound Connal.
Yet the hero did not halt,
Conlach, brave and vigorous,
He bound a hundred of our men,
It is a strange and mournful tale.
To the hounds' great chief[2] a message
Was sent by Ulster's wise king,
To sunny, fair Dundalgin,[3]
The old, wise fort of the Gael,
That stronghold of which we read,
And the prudent daughter of Forgan.[4]
From thence came he of great deeds
To see our generous king;
To know of Ulster's great race,
There came to us the red branch[5] Cu,

1 Dunscaich, a stronghold in the Isle of Skye, on the coast of Sleat, of which the ruins still exist.

2 Cuchullin, or the hound of Cullin, was a famous Celtic warrior, whose fame is celebrated both in Scotland and Ireland. The name is a curious one, and is thought by some critics to indicate the existence of Anubis worship, or the worship of the dog, among the ancient Celts. There is a Cullin in Skye, and another in Ireland. From which of these the name was taken it is difficult to say. Certainly the Skye mountain is by far the more magnificent natural object, and Dunscaich is unquestionably in Skye.

3 Dundalgin is said to be the modern Dundalk.

4 Cuchullin's wife is said to have been unwilling that he should engage Conlach.

5 Cù is a dog or hound. The "red

His teeth like pearl, cheeks like berries
"Long," said Connor to the Cu,
"Has been thine aid in coming,
While Connal, who loves bold steeds,
Is bound and a hundred more."
"Sad for me to be thus bound,
Friend, who could'st soon unloose me."
"I couldn't encounter his sword,
And that he has bound brave Connal."
"Refuse not to attack him,
Prince of the sharp, blue sword,
Whose arm ne'er quailed in conflict,
Think of thy patron now in bonds."
When Cuchullin of the thin-leaved sword
Heard the lament of Connal,
He moved in his arm's great might
To take of the youth account.
"Tell us now that I have come,
Youth who fearest not the fight,
Tell us now, and tell at once,
Thy name, and where's thy country?"
"Ere I left home I had to pledge
That I should never that relate;
Were I to tell to living man,
For thy love's sake I'd tell it thee."
"Then must thou with me battle do,
Or tell thy tale as a friend.
Choose for thyself, dear youth,
But mind, to fight me is a risk.
Let us not fight, I pray thee,
Brave leopard, pride of Erin,
Boldest in the battle field,
My name I would tell unbought."
Then did they commence the fight,
Nor was it the fight of women.

branch" heroes were the knights of Ulster, the most famous of the Irish military orders. Cuchullin is often called "Cù nan con," or *The hound of hounds*.

The youth received a deadly wound,
He of the vigorous arm.
Yet did Cuchullin of battles,
The victory on that day lose.
His only son had fallen, slain,
That fair, soft branch, so gentle, brave.
" Tell us now," said skilful Cu,
" Since thou art at our mercy,
Thy name and race, tell us in full,
Think not to refuse thy tale."
" Conlach I, Cuchullin's son,
Lawful heir of great Dundalgin,
It was I thou left'st unborn,
When in Skiath[1] thou wast learning.
Seven years in the east I spent,
Gaining knowledge from my mother;
The pass by which I have been slain
Was all I needed still to learn."
Then does the great Cuchullin see[2]
His dear son's colour change;
As of his generous heart he thinks,
His memory and mind forsake him;
His body's excellency departs,
His grief it was destroyed it;
Seeing as he lay on the earth
The rightful heir of Dundalgin;
Where shall we find his like,
Or how detail our grief?
I have.

[1] The Isle of Skye.

[2] The touching incident in this story is the death of the son by the hand of his own father. It is said that Conlach's mother, in revenge for Cuchullin's forsaking her, had laid her plans for securing this object, and had sent her son into Ireland under vow never to disclose his name until overcome in battle.

The author of this is the Blind O'Cloan.[1]

'Tis the sigh of a friend from Fraoch's green mound,
'Tis the warrior's sigh from his lonely bier,[2]
'Tis a sigh might grieve the manly heart,
And might make a maid to weep.
Here to the east the cairn, where lies
Fraoch Fitheach's son of softest locks,
Who nobly strove to favour Mai,
And from whom Cairn[3] Fraoch is named.
In Cruachan east a woman weeps,
A mournful tale 'tis she laments;
Heavy, heavy sighs she gives
For Fraoch mac Fithich of ancient fame.
She 'tis, in truth, who sorely weeps,
As Fraoch's green mound she visits oft;
Maid of the locks that wave so fair,
Mai's daughter so beloved of men.
This night Orla's soft-haired daughter,
Lies side by side with Fraoch mac Fithich.

[1] The author of this composition is altogether unknown, nor is it easy to decipher even the name accurately. In the original it is distinctly "in keich o cloan." According to the Dean's usual orthography, this should be "An caoch O'Cluain," which means the *blind O' Cloan*, or the *blind man from the green mound*. Some of the readers of the MS. have made it out to be the name of a woman. We have given the form of the name most likely to be accurate. The composition itself is usually called "Bàs Fhraoich," or *the death of Fraoch*.

[2] "Caiseal chrò," usually translated *bier*, is a curious term. "Caiseal" means a *castle* or *stronghold*, "crò," a *fold* or *pen*; so that the word really means the *stone pen*, or *fortified pen*. Is not this in all likelihood the stone coffin, with which we are so familiar in ancient Celtic sepulture?

[3] It is not easy identifying the topography of this poem. It is generally believed in Perthshire that the scene of Fraoch's death was in Glen Cuaich, a valley lying between those of the Tay and the Almond. We have a Loch Fraoch there, but I have not been able to identify Carn Fraoich, or Carn Laimh. Cruachan is spoken of as lying to the east, which goes rather in favour of the opinion, that the scene of the poem was in Argyleshire, Ben Cruachan being to the east of the locality so designated in that part of the country. I cannot find any lake in Scotland now called Loch Mai, although Loch Fraoch may have been so called.

Many were the men who loved her,
She, of them all, loved Fraoch alone.
Mai is filled with bitter hate,
As the love of Fraoch she learns.
His body got its grievous wounds,
Because with her he'd do no wrong;
She doomed him to a bitter death:
Judge not of women by her deed,
Grief 'twas that he should fall by Mai,
Yet I'll relate it without guile. A sigh.[1]

A rowan tree stood in Loch Mai,
We see its shore there to the south;
Every quarter every month,
It bore its fair, well-ripened fruit;
There stood the tree alone, erect,
Its fruit than honey sweeter far;
That precious fruit so richly red,
Did suffice for a man's nine meals;
A year it added to man's life,—
The tale I tell is very truth.
Health to the wounded it could bring,
Such virtue had its red-skinned fruit.
One thing alone was to be feared
By him who sought men's ills to soothe:
A monster[2] fierce lay at its root,
Which they who sought its fruit must fight.
A heavy, heavy sickness fell
On Athach's daughter, of liberal horn;
Her messenger she sent for Fraoch,
Who asked her what 'twas ailed her now.
Mai said her health would ne'er return,
Unless her fair soft palm was filled

[1] The introduction of the "sigh," would seem to indicate that a sigh was expected at certain parts of the poem from the reciter.

[2] It is needless to point out the analogy between this tale and that of Hercules and the garden of the Hesperides. It will strike any one acquainted with the classical story.

With berries from the deep cold lake,
Gleaned by the hand of none but Fraoch.
" Ne'er have I yet request refused,"
Said Fithich's son of ruddy hue;
" Whate'er the lot of Fraoch may be,
The berries I will pull for Mai."
The fair-formed Fraoch then moved away
Down to the lake, prepared to swim.
He found the monster in deep sleep,
With head up-pointed to the tree. A sigh.

Fraoch Fithich's son of pointed arms,
Unheard by the monster, then approached.
He plucked a bunch of red-skinned fruit,
And brought it to where Mai did lie.
" Though what thou did'st thou hast done well,"
Said Mai, she of form so fair,
" My purpose nought, brave man, wilt serve,
But that from the root thou'dst tear the tree."
No bolder heart there was than Fraoch's,
Again the slimy lake he swam;
Yet great as was his strength, he couldn't
Escape the death for him ordained.
Firm by its top he seized the tree,
And from the root did tear it up:
With speed again he makes for land,
But not before the beast awakes.
Fast he pursues, and, as he swam,
Seized in his horrid maw his arm.
Fraoch by the jaw then grasped the brute,
'Twas sad for him to want his knife:
The maid of softest waving hair,
In haste brought him a knife of gold.
The monster tore his soft white skin,
And hacked most grievously his arm.
Then fell they, sole to sole opposed,
Down on the southern stony strand,

Fraoch mac Fithich, he and the beast,
'Twere well that they had never fought.[1]
Fierce was the conflict, yet 'twas long,—
The monster's head at length he took.
When the maid what happened saw,
Upon the strand she fainting fell.
Then from her trance when she awoke,
In her soft hand she seized his hand:
"Although for wild birds thou art food,
Thy last exploit was nobly done."
'Tis from that death which he met then,
The name is given to Loch Mai;
That name it will for ever bear,
Men have called it so till now. A sigh.

They bear along to Fraoch's green mound
The hero's body to its grave.
By his name they call the glen,
Sad for those he left behind.
Cairn Laive is the hill beside me,
Close by it many a happy day
The hero lived, of matchless strength,
The bravest heart in battle's day.
Lovely those lips with welcomes rich,
Which woman liked so well to kiss;
Lovely the chief whom men obeyed,
Lovely those cheeks like roses red,
Than raven's hue more dark his hair,
Redder than hero's blood his cheeks;
Softer than froth of streams his skin,
Whiter it was than whitest snow;
His hair in curling locks fell down,
His eye more blue than bluest ice;
Than rowans red more red his lips,

[1] The story is simple and intelligible. Mai loved Fraoch, and became jealous of her own daughter, usually called Gealcheann, or Fairhead. She accordingly planned and accomplished Fraoch's destruction as related.

Whiter than blossoms were his teeth ;
Tall was his spear like any mast,
Sweeter his voice than sounding chord ;
None could better swim than Fraoch,
Who ever breasted running stream.
Broader than any gate his shield,
Joyous he swung it o'er his back ;
His arm and sword of equal length,
In size he like a ship did look.
Would it had been in warrior's fight
That Fraoch, who spared not gold, had died ;
'Twas sad to perish by a Beast,
'Tis just as sad he lives not now

'Tis the sigh

The author of this is Connal Cearnach M'Edirskeol.[1]

These heads, O Connal, are worthless ;
Though thou must have blooded thine arms.
These heads thou bear'st upon that withe,
Can'st tell their owners, now thy spoil ?

Daughter of Orgill of the steeds,
Youthful Evir, so sweet of speech,
'Twas to avenge Cuchullin's death,
That I took these numerous heads.

Whose is that hairy, black, great head,
With cheeks than any rose more red,

[1] This is the most ancient of all the Ossianic Poets. He was contemporary of Cuchullin, who flourished, according to Irish historians, in the first century. Cuchullin was his foster-son, and upon his being slain, Conall took vengeance upon his enemies by putting them all to death. In this poem he tells Evir, who was either the wife or the betrothed of Cuchullin, the names of those thus put to death, and whose heads he carried on a withe. The name M'Edarscoil is represented now by that of O'Driscol ; "Cearnach" means *victorious*, so that the poet's name is really, The Victorious Conall O'Driscoll.

That which hangs nighest thy left arm,
The head whose colour has not changed?

That head the king of swift steeds own'd,
Said Cairbar's son of vigorous lance;
In vengeance for my foster son,
I took that head and bore it far.

What head is that I see beyond,
Covered with smooth, soft, flowing hair,
His eye like grass, his teeth like bloom,
His beauty such as none is like?

Manadh, the man that own'd the steeds,
Aoife's son, who plunder'd every sea;
I left his trunk 'reft of its head,
I slew his people, every man.

What head is that I see thee grasp,
Great Connal of the gentle streams;
Since that Cuchullin[1] now is dead,
Whom to avenge him did'st thou take?

'Tis the head of Mac Fergus of steeds,
He in extremity so bold,
My sister's son from the tall tower,
His head I from his body wrenched.

What fair-haired head is that to the east,
Whose hand might well have seized the heads;
Well did I know his voice of old,
For he and I were friends awhile?

[1] Cuchullin, or *The Hound of Cullin*, is often spoken of simply as "An Cu," or *The Hound*. In the Gaelic this is either "Cu" or "Con," according as the word is in the nominative or genitive case. In the English version it is uniformly translated Cu, as it would be impossible to follow intelligibly the variations of the Gaelic grammar in the cases of a proper noun.

Down there it was the Cu did fall,
His body cast in fairest mould ;
Cu, son of Con, of poets' king,
Among the last I took his head.

What two heads are those farthest out,
Great Connal of the sweetest voice ;
Of thy great love hide not from me
The names of them so dark in arms ?

'Tis Laoghar's head and that of Cuilt,
The two who fell pierced by my arms ;
One of them had Cuchullin struck,
Hence his red blood my weapons dyes.

What two heads are those to the east,
Great Connal of the famous deeds ;
Alike the colour of their hair,
Than hero's blood more red their cheeks ?

Cullin the handsome, and Cunlad brave,
Two who e'er triumphed in their wrath ;
Evir, their heads are to the east,
I left their bodies streaming red.

What are those six hideous heads
I see in front facing the north ;
Blue in the face, their hair so black,
From which thou turn'st thy look, brave Connal ?

These are six of Cuchullin's foes,
Calliden's sons, who triumphed oft ;
These are now the senseless six
Who all, full armed, fell by my hand.

Great Connal, father to a king,
What is that head, noblest of all ;

How bushy the golden yellow locks,
Covering it with so much grace?

The head of M'Finn, M'Ross the red,
The son of Cruith, slain by my stroke;
Evir, he was king, chief of them all,
In Leinster of the spotted swords.

Great Connal, now please change thy tale,
Tell us the number slain by thine arm,
Of all the noble famous men,
In vengeance for the head of Con?

Ten and seven score hundred men,
I tell the truth, the number is,
That fell by me, all back o'er back,
Fruit of my bravery and power.

Connal, tell how the women feel
In Innisfail, the Cu being dead;
Do they sadly, sorely mourn,
Now that like me themselves have grief?

O Evir, what am I to do,
Now that my Cu is ta'en away;
My foster-son of fairest form,
Now that he's left me desolate?

O Connal, lay me in my grave,
And raise my stone o'er that of Cu;
In grief I'll soon from this depart,
Let my lips touch Cu's lips in death.

Evir am I, of fairest form,
No vengeance can me satisfy;

In tears no pleasure I can find,
'Tis sad that I am left behind.[1]
Connal.

The author of this is Caoilte Mac Ronan.[2]

I set me off to rescue Finn,
To Taura of the joyful streams;
With arms sure of victory,
To Cormac, son of Art Aonir.[3]
I will not put forth my strength,
Though bloody and light of foot,
Until that with the Feinn of Fail,
We have reached the shore of Loch Foyle.
Then did we slay the mighty hero,
When we had slain Cuireach.[4]
We killed a mighty warrior
When we had killed their leader.

1 This poem is usually called "Laoidh nan ceann," or *The Lay of the Heads* It bears many marks of genuineness and antiquity It is well known in the Highlands, but the Editor has never seen or heard any reference to its authorship, except in the MS. of the Dean.

2 This is a remarkable composition, descriptive of an attempt of Caoilt to deliver his friend and patron Finn from the hands of Cormac M'Art, King of Ireland, against whom the Feinn had been stirring up rebellion. Caoilt, after various strange doings, is told that he can only have Finn's liberty on condition of bringing to Tara a pair of all the wild animals in Ireland. A portion of the poem has been translated in Ireland, and published in the *Dublin University Magazine* for March 1854, in connexion with an interesting paper upon the food of the ancient Irish, and the early zoology of their country, by Dr. Wilde. The translation is by that eminent Irish scholar, Mr. E O'Curry. In that paper the poem is said to be at least a composition of the ninth century. It must be of extreme antiquity, as a reference to the language of it presents an amount of difficulty owing to obsolete words and phrases rarely met with The Editor had the advantage of submitting his work to the review of Mr. O'Curry. For the topography of the poem, which is altogether Irish, the Editor has to refer the reader to the notes to the paper in the number of the *Dublin University Magazine*, referred to above, which are very full and very instructive.

3 Art, King of Ireland, was called "Aonfhir," or *The Solitary*, from his love of solitude.

4 Cuireach was a famous Leinster prince.

We bore his head up to the hill,
Which lies above Buadhamair.[1]
Then indeed I had my triumph,
For I made a total havoc.
For the hero's sake I slew
A man in every town[2] in Erin.
Then indeed I had my triumph,
For I made a total havoc.
For the hero's sake I brought
Grief into every house in Erin.
Then indeed I had my triumph,
For I made a total havoc.
The calves I slew with the cows,
Whom I found in all fair Erin.
Then indeed I had my triumph,
For I made a total havoc.
The doors on which the red wind[3] blew,
I threw them each one widely open.
Then indeed I had my triumph,
For I made a total havoc.
The fields all ripe throughout the land,
I set them then a blazing brightly.
Then indeed I had my triumph,
For I made a total havoc.
In my day there won't be seen
Either mill or kiln in Erin.
Then it was they loosed against me
The horse of Albin and of Erin.
My fleetness gave me victory,
Until I reached Ros illirglass.
Then I westward took my way
To Taura, although great the distance;
Not one horse of all the troop

1 Buadhamair, the ancient name of Cahir, in Tipperary.

2 In Gaelic, a farm is called "baile," *a town*.

3 The red wind, a magical wind said to blow in Ireland, and to be very destructive.

Had Taura reached so soon as I did.
In Taura then I gave that day
The wife of him who cared not for her.
I gave the wife of him who cared not,
To him who cared for his as little;
In noble Taura then I gave
The wife of Cairbar to Cormac.
The wife of Cormac also gave,
Just as I had done, to Cairbar.
The king's sword then I firmly seized,
A sword of matchless power and virtue;
My own sword, fit for little now,
I left it in the sheath of Cormac.
Then I passed me quickly over,
And from the door-keeper got his garment.
From whence it happened, it is true,
I became candlestick to Cormac.
Then did I many strange things do,
In presence of the King of Erin.
"Though ye may wonder at my speech,
Caoilte's two eyes are in my candlestick."
"Say thou not so," said noble Finn,
The fair-haired prince of all the Feinn;
"Though I may now thy prisoner be,
Cast not reproach upon my people,
Such is not Caoilte's noble nature,
Nought he does but what is generous.
He would not hold a servile candle
For any gold that earth may yield."
Then did I draw forth his drink
For the excellent, manly king.
Four steps, one after the other,
I went along with him to serve him.
Then I betook myself to his right,
'Twas one source of my sharp sorrow;
I gave him of my own free will
A dirge so grating, loud, and mournful.

"Strange that he should give me this,"
Said the clever, well-formed king.
"The music smells of Caoilte's own skin,
This mournful, unharmonious dirge."
"Do not thou say so, O King,"
Said I, in his servant's garb;
"These are boastful words thou speak'st.
'Tis worthy of one loving music."
"By my hand, most noble Caoilte,
As Finn has been the Feinn's great chief,
Though, as I am, no pledge I'll give
To the men of Alb' or Erin."
As I plainly saw he knew me,
I now did boldly ask of Cormac,
"Thou wilt tell me how I may
Freedom purchase for my patron."
"Thou shalt not have Finn made free,
I say, on any one condition,
Save this condition, noble Caoilte,
One thou never can'st fulfil;
That thou should'st obtain for me
Of all wild animals a pair,
Then to thee I'd give thy patron,
So soon as thou such pledge redeem'st."
I seized upon the pleasing words
Of Cormac Mac Airt Inir,
That he would freedom give the king
So soon as I fulfilled such promise.
When I had thus by promise bound
Erin's noble fair-haired king,
Though I had a trying task,
I set off to keep th' agreement.
From Taura I a journey took,
A journey over all the land.
I gathered in the flocks of birds,
Though they were so very scattered.
Two fierce *geilts* I brought along,

And two fine tall and long-clawed ospreys,
And ravens from Fee ya von ;
Two wild ducks from Loch a Sellin,
Two crows down from Slieve Cullin,
Two wild oxen brought from Borrin,
Two swans I brought from Dobhran gorm,
Two owls from the wood of Faradrum,
Two polecats from Coiltie creive,
On the side of Druma Dabhran.
Two otters also I took with them,
From the rock of Donavan doivin,
Two gulls from the strand of Loch Lee,
Two *rualls* from Port Lairge,
Four woodpeckers from Brosna ban,
Two plovers from Carrig dunan,
Two *eachts* from Eachta ard,
Two thrushes from Letter Lomard,
Two wrens from Dun Aoife,
Two *geingeachs* from Corrie dhu,
Two herons from Corrin Cleith,
Two gledes from Magh a Foyle,
Two eagles from Carrig nan clach,
Two hawks from Ceindeach forest,
Two sows from Loch Meilghe,
Two water-hens from Loch Earn,
Two moor-fowls from Monadh maith,
Two sparrow-hawks from Dulocha,
Two stone-chats from Magh Cullin,
Two tomtits from Magh Fualainn,
Two *caschans* from Glen Gaibhle,
Two swallows from the Old Abhla,
Two cormorants from Dublin,
Two wolves from Crotta cliath,
Two blackbirds from Traigh dha bhan,
Two roe from Luachair Ir,
Two pigeons from Ceis Charran,
Two nightingales from Letter Fin chul,

Two plovers from Letter roy,
Two starlings from Taura the green,
Two rabbits from Sith dubh donn,
Two wild boars from Cluaidh chur,
Two cuckoos from Drum a daive,
Two grey birds from Laigheande,
Two lapwings from Lanan Furrich,
Two woodcocks from Craobh maidh,
Two hawks besides from Sliabh glé,
Two grey mice from Limerick,
Two otters from the Boyne,
Two larks from Monadh mòr,
Two bats from the cave of Cno,
Two badgers from the lands of Ullanach,
Two cornrails from Shannon valley,
Two water-wagtails from Bruach Bire,
Two curlews from the sea of Galway,
Two hares from Muirtheimhne,
Two eagles from the wood of Luaraidh,
Two hinds from Sith Buy,
Two *geiseadachs* (peacocks) from Magh Mall,
Two *cith cenceachs* from Cnamh choille,
Two yellow-hammers from Bruach Bru,
Two eels from the Black Water,
Two goldfinches from Sliabh da eun,
Two *cathails* from Bray an Turla,
Two birds of prey from Magh builg,
Two coloured swallows from Granard,
Two fierce ospreys from Gruing,
Two redbreasts from the Great wood,
Two *bliorachs* from Dun nam barc,
Two rock cod from Cala cairge,
Two whales from the great sea,
Two eels from Loch M'Lennan,
Two *gearrgarts* from Magh nan Eilean,
Two little birds (wrens) from Mias a chuil,
Two fish (salmon) from Eas M'Moirn,

Two fine roe from Glen Smoil,
Two cows from Achadh Maigh Moir,
Two swift otters from Loch Con,
Two wild cats from the cave of Cruachain,
Two sheep from Sith Doolan gil,
Two sows of the sows of Mac Lir;
A ram and a red nimble sheep
I brought with me from Ennis.
I brought with me a horse and mare
Of the fine stud of Mananan;
A bull and cow in calf from Drumcan,
These I had from Muirn Munchain.
Ten hounds of the hounds of the Feinn
Did Cormaig insolently require.
Whatever thing he asked of me,
I brought it with me as I came.
When I had them all collected,
And brought them to one plain,
And sought to have them in control,
They all of them did scatter widely
The raven flew away to the south,
A cause to me of much vexation;
I caught it in Glen da bhan,
By the side of deep Loch Lurgan.
The duck did also me forsake,
Nor was it easier to take it;
Over swift and swollen streams,
I chased it to Achin dughlas.
Then I seized it by the neck,
Although it was not very willing.
I took this duck along with me
That I might liberate Finn from Cormaig.
Of all the ills that I have met,
During all my life on earth,
Never shall my heart forget
This, till my body is in the grave:
With small birds, and with other birds,

How I strove along to drive them,
Travelling over hills and ditches,
That with them I soon might reach him;
While he still held Finn in bonds,
And thought that I could never find them;
And if I could but find him these,
Then was he bound to give him freedom.
This race that I had swiftly run,
Was such as no man ran before me.
Then I brought them all to Taura,
To the chief who ruled the palace;
Then had I further much to suffer,
That night was to me very grievous.
Within the town there was a stronghold,
To which by nine doors there was entrance.
Cormaig 'twas gave me the house,
As I now was very wearied.
Where I saw that they were placed
In the narrow, horrid dungeon;
Then came a loud and vigorous scream
From the throats of all the gathering.
There was a little ray of light
Reached them in through fifty openings.
Every door was closely shut,
Nor was the case an easy one;
They mournfully shut closely up,
While I as sadly was excluded.
My heart did now pour out its grief,
Watching by the doors till morning.
Though great the evil I had suffered,
As before they flew so swiftly,
Not one I suffered to escape
Till the day rose in the morning.
The name men gave to this great rabble
Was "Caoilte's rabble," and no wonder.
To see them standing side by side,
Was all the profit got by Cormag.

For when Finn did get his freedom,
All of them did scatter widely ;
No two nor three of all did go
From Taura in the same direction.
My own swiftness and Finn's escape
Was a miracle from heaven;
The three great things to me which happened
Were these and gathering that host.
It is security for my fame,
I believe in Christ, and in this,
Though great my gathering for Finn,
I have nought of which to boast.
Though long my leap to the east,
In Taura of the Fenian heroes,
Long was my leap to the west,
In Taura, twenty hundred feet,
Agile then was my leap,
Which amongst strangers I did take,
While the point of my foot alone yielded,
Slow is now any expedition I make.
I set me off.

No author's name given.[1]

There lies beneath that mound to the north
Mac Cumhal's son, in battle firm.
Of Dearg's daughter the white-tooth'd son,
In wrath who never harshly spoke.
There lies beneath that mound to the south
Mac Conn's son, his skin like bloom,
The man who never met his match,

[1] The Fenian poetry to which the Dean has attached the names of the authors, is now all given. We proceed with those whose authors' names are not attached to them. Many of these are manifestly of the same period with the others, and they may with equal accuracy be attributed to Ossian or others of the Fenian bards.

Whose arm in fight dealt no soft blows.
There lies beneath that mound to the east
Oscar, so brave, famous in deeds.
Though the Clan Morn were famous men,
He counted them of little weight.
There lies beneath that mound to the west
The man by women thought so fair,
M'Ronan for his beauty famed,
Beneath the mound to the west he lies.
Beneath the mound that is below me
Lies he so famed for ugly pate;
Conan, in every virtue rich,
Beneath the mound below me lies.
There lies.

GORRY, let us go to Finn,
A service which we do not like,
To ask of him the head of Gaul,
That we may lay it down to rest.
I am unwilling to go,
Since I hear not aught of the head,
And that we cannot have revenge,
For the head of the great Mac Morn.
Whether thou willest or not, I will,
Said the great but foolish Conan ;
I will slay all the men I can
In vengeance for the yellow-haired Gaul.
Let us kill the three princes of the Feinn,
As we can't slay Finn himself.
Speak, Gorry, speak quickly out,
Let us be found at once on their hands
Thou shalt kill great Ossian M'Finn,
I will kill the valorous Oscar,

Dyre shall kill the dauntless Caoilte,
Let them have us all assault.
I shall show no foolish softness,
Gentleness doesn't suit with Finn;
Though in our arms we all should fall,
We will have no help from Gaul;
If Finn is there his strength will be there,
Let us send Finn down to his grave.
True and guileless are the words
Which to thee I speak, Gorry.
Gorry.

The author of this is ——.[1]

'Twas on a day Finn went to drink
In Alve, with his people few;
Six women and six men were there,
The women fair, with whitest skin.
Finn was there and guileless Diarmad,
Caoilte and Ossian too, and Oscar,
Conan the bald, slow in the field,
With the wives of these six men;
Maighinis the wife of dauntless Finn,
The fair-bosomed maid, my own dear wife,
Fair skin Gormlay, of blackest eye,
Naoif, and the daughter of Angus.
When drunkenness had the women seized,
They had a talk among themselves:
They said that throughout all the earth
No six women were so chaste.
Then said the maiden without guile,
"The world is a many-sided heap;

[1] This is a curious episode in Fenian history. Maighineas was the wife of Finn according to Irish writers on Fenian history. The daughter of Deirg was the mother of Ossian, and consequently another of Finn's wives.

Though pure are ye, they are not few
Women quite as chaste as you."
They had been a short time thus,
When they saw a maid approach,
Her covering a single seamless robe,
Of spotless white from end to end;
The maiden of the pure white robe
Drew near to where M'Cumhal sat.
She blessed the king of guileless heart,
And close beside him there sat down.
Finn asks her to give them her tale,
The handsome maid of whitest hand:
"Maid of the seamless robe, I ask,
What virtue 's in thy spotless veil?"
"My seamless robe has this strange power
That women, such as are not chaste,
Can in its folds no shelter find,—
None but the spotless wife it shields."
"Give my wife the robe at once,"
Said the bulky, senseless Conan,
"That we may learn what is the truth
Of what the women just have said."
Then Conan's wife does take the robe,
And in vexation pulls it on;
'Twas truly pity it was done,
Her fair-skinned breast was all exposed.
Then when the bald-pate Conan saw
How that the robe shrunk into folds,
He seized in passion his sharp spear,
And with it did the woman slay.
Then the loved Diarmad's wife
The robe from Conan's wife did take;
No better did she fare than she,
About her locks it clung in folds.
Then Oscar's wife seized on the robe,
Which looked so long and softly smooth;
But wide and large as were its wings,

The robe her middle did not reach.
Then fair Maighinis took the robe,
And put it also o'er her head;
The robe there creased and folded up,
And gathered fast about her ears.
" Give my wife the robe," said Mac Rea,
" For the result I have no fear,
That we may see, without deceit,
Of her merit further proof."
" I would pass my word for it,
Though I claim not to be learned,
That never have I once transgressed,
I've been faithful aye to thee."
Mac Rea's wife now showed her side,
The robe was then put o'er her head;
Her body was covered, feet and hands,
None of it all was left exposed.
Her bosom then one kiss received
From Mac O'Duine, from Diarmad;
The robe from her he then unfolds,
From her who thus did stand alone.
" Women, give me now my robe,
I am the daughter of Deirg the fierce,
I have done nought to cause me shame,
I only erred with sharp-armed Finn."
" Bear thou my curse, and quick away,"
These were then the words of Mac Cumhail.
On women he denounced a curse,
Because of her who came that day.
'Twas on a day.

THE expedition of eight I remember,
Which oft returns to my mind;
Some of their exploits I'll relate,

Though now my strength is all gone.
Oscar and manly Caoilte were there,
And Mac Luy of ceaseless praise;
Finn and white-toothed Diarmad,
Of the eight heroes these were five.
There were myself and Ryno and Caroll,
A gentle, matchless band;
Bred were we all in Banva's soil,
These were the names of the eight.
When we set forth, true the tale,
'Twas with a proud and manly step.
From Mac Cumhal's fort we set out,
The expedition of eight I remember.
First of all we made for Albain,
'Twas with a struggle we reached it,
There a king fell by Mac Cumhal,
The expedition of eight I remember.
We then strove to get to Sasunn,[1]
Exploits and slayings were there;
Every stronghold was seized by Finn,
The expedition of eight I remember.
To Italy we then carried the battle,
And fiercely fought in its harbours;
Triumphs and treaties we had then,
The expedition of eight I remember.
In France did we then make war,
Where we had many great hardships;
Submission and treaties were made,
The expedition of eight I remember.
After that we fought in Spain,
There we had prey and great spoil;
I have traversed the earth in my day,
The expedition of eight I remember.
We next carried war to Britain,
'Twas fearful and full of danger;
Yet did we earn a triumph,

[1] Sasunn, "England," after the Saxon invasion.

The expedition of eight I remember.
We bore along "Crom nan carn,"[1]
O'er the fierce, stormy sea;
Every land made to us submission,
The expedition of eight I remember.
After it we led the chiefs,
Most gentle and holy Patrick,
Who made their submission to Finn,
The expedition of eight I remember.
Sanctify, O Patrick, my soul,
Thou blessed and privileged man,
For I have sinned in thy sight,
The expedition of eight I remember.
The expedition

NINE[2] of us once did bind ourselves
To find material for a pup's head,
To find material for a dog-pup's head;
Though no attempt was more laborious.
We searched the plain of Leny Leirg,
And Glen Frenich of bloody swords;
True, we found not there one hound
From which we could obtain a pup.
Then did we search a dark, black glen,
A glen of deep corries, full of stones;
True, we found not there one hound
From which we could obtain a pup

[1] It is difficult to say what this is. "Crom" was a Celtic deity. Here the word seems to indicate a banner. The word "Crom nan cairge" will be found in the second volume of the publications of the Ossianic Society of Ireland, pp 53, 58.

[2] This is a curious piece. The dog without doubt entered largely into the mythology of the ancient Celts. Some have supposed that it was an object of worship with them. Mr O'Curry informs the editor that the "Concheannaich or Dogheads were an ancient race who inhabited Magh O'Coin-chinn, now Moygonihy, in Kerry. They were said to be great enemies of Finn. This poem may really describe an attack upon them." One of the Irish kings was called "Cairbar Cinn Chait," or *Cairbar of the Cat's-head.* The latter portion of the poem, referring to the banners of the Feine, has been preserved in tradition, although the editions of it are various.

We searched the Sian of Drum Cliff,
Fair after it seemed the plain of Liff;
True, we found not there one hound
From which we could obtain a pup.
We searched in Thurles of liberal hosts,
In Bregian Tara and Dun Dobhran;
True, we found not there one hound
From which we could obtain a pup.
We searched, too, through Glen a Cuaich,
Looking out for something noble;
True, we found not there one hound
From which we could obtain a pup.
We searched Moylena of slopes,
Through Bregian Tara and Kinsale;
True, we found not there one hound
From which we could obtain a pup.
We searched the whole of Eire,
Men and dogs ranging together;
True, we found not there one hound
From which we could obtain a pup.
Shortly were we thus engaged,
Ourselves, our followers, and friends,
When three battalions were seen,
Sons to the King of Rualay.[1]
Cat-headed one battalion was,
Dog-headed was the one beside it;
The other behind them was white-backed,
Brown the rest, though white the back.
Aloft the mighty javelin shone
Of Finn, hero of bloody strength;
Above his noble, murderous shield,
He bore that spear of hundred fights
Bright was the glitter of the spear
In the white hand of Finn himself.

[1] This seems to have been an imaginary monarch, like many of those in the "Ursgeuls," or prose tales of the Highlands. At least the Editor has not met with the name elsewhere

Beneath the shield of cheerful Caoilte
Was the javelin, bloody in fight;
The javelin glittering below,
Held by Caoilte of joyful heart.
Beneath his round and handsome shield
Cruinchan's son his javelin bore.
Caoilte gave a loud, far-sounding shout,
In distant Alvin it was heard,
And in Magh Lena of sharp spears,
In Tavar and in Dun Reillin.
'Twas answered loud by Gaul Mac Morn,
The noble chief of Cronwoyn,
Where Faolan, son of Finn, is found,
The Balwas, too, from Borrin.
'Twas answered by Manwoe Breck's two sons,
And by Mac Elle from Uabreck,
Fair Sciath, the son of Daithein Dian,
And Ceall the brave, of sharp-edged arms.
Keangach the bold gave answer too,
And Iolunn of the bloody edge,
And Ceall the brave, of handsome form,
Who ne'er to scandal's tale gave ear.
Pleasing the sound of clashing spears,
Pleasing, too, the hum of warriors,
Of waving banners sweet the sound,
As in morn's frosty wind they rose.
The "Image of the Sun"[1] we raised,
The banner of great Fenian Finn,
Studded all around with gold,
Great was its price as red it gleamed
We raised "Fulang Duari"[2] aloft,

[1] Finn's banner had inscribed upon it, according to this bard, "Dealbh Ghréine," or *The image of the Sun*. This word has been corrupted by tradition to "Deo ghréine," said to be *the sun-beam*, though upon no authority, "deo" in no case signifying "*a beam*.",

[2] The Editor has not attempted to translate these and several others of the emblems of the Fenian leaders. He has given the words as he found them, except when the meaning was obvious and unquestionable.

The banner of great Gaul Mac Morn.
Oft when the javelins were in motion,
'Twas both the first and last to move.
Aloft we raised the "Mincheann Oir,"
Banner of Ryno and his men;
Under its folds were bones and heads
Cloven, and ankles steeped in blood.
The "Cineal chath" we also raised,
The banner of the oaken Faolan;
Finn's son, chief of the Feinn,
Who cast with powerful arm his spear
Then we raised aloft "Dun nimh,"
The banner of Ossian of the brave;
The banner of Mac Ronan, "the Red-hand,"[1]
Whose other side was all adorned.
"Sguab Ghabhaidh," too, we raised aloft,
Banner of the well-armed Oscar,
When the stormy conflict raged,
Oft was "Sguab Ghabhaidh" waving seen.
The "Lia Luinneach" aloft we raised,
The banner of nimble, powerful Diarmaid;
Oft when the men began their march,
'Twas seen to flutter vigorously.
Then was the "Bearn Reubainn" raised,
Banner of Oscar, no saintly sign;
The echo of the glens replied
To its fierce sounds, waving on high.
The "Bloody hand" aloft we raised,
Banner of Mac Luy, and his men;
When the Feinn went forth to fight,
Its place was always in the van.
Then did we fight a bloody fight,
As round the noble Finn we stood,
Round the steel of manly Finn,

[1] This heraldic emblem of Caoilte M'Ronan has descended through a long course of ancestors to the modern M'Donalds. It is probably the oldest of the kind in the kingdom.

First of all the valorous Feinn.
The whole of the Catheads were killed,
The Dogheads we seized to a man;
The whole of the Whitebacks fell
Round dauntless Finn of Alvin.
We found a little hill to the south,
On which was built a double fort;
There indeed we found a hound
From which we could obtain a pup.
The whole of Eire we had searched,
All of us, both men and dogs.
In all its length we could not find
A hundred who could match our nine.
Nine.

SWEET is man's voice in the land of gold,
Sweet the sounds the birds produce,
Sweet is the murmur of the crane,
Sweet sound the waves at Bun Datreor,
Sweet the soft murmuring of the wind,
Sweet sounds the cuckoo at Cas a choin
How soft and pleasing shines the sun,
Sweet the blackbird sings his song;
Sweet the eagle's voice of Easaroy,
Above the sea of great Mac Morn;
Sweet the cuckoo 'mongst the branches,
Sweet the silence of the crane.
Finn Mac Cumhail is my father,
Who nobly leads the Feinn's seven bands;
When he his hounds lets loose to hunt,
To follow him is truly sweet.
Sweet.

A NOBLE tale of sweetest music,
To Carn Vallar now I'll bring;

That whether others hear or not,
It may be heard by Mac Cumhail.
Mac Cumhail once had a feast
On Almhuin's slope, of finest gold;
O'er the music he presided,
Finn who ever graced the feast.
Brave Oscar and Diarmad were there,
And good Mac Luy, warriors bold;
With other two who ne'er shunned fight,
Conan himself, and with him Oscar.
"Tell me now, my warriors brave,
As at the feast of Finn ye sit,
Which do ye count the sweetest music?"
"The clang of gaming," Conan said,
"The sweetest sounds I ever heard."
Vigorous his arm before the foe,
Yet ne'er a man who more lacked sense.
"The sound of swords drawing on the foe,"
Said he who never spared in fight,
"Cleaving of men's heads and legs,"
The sweetest music Oscar heard.
"The sounds which ever pleased me most,"
Said Diarmad of slow rolling eye,
"That I loved most all my life,
Was woman's voice, as soft she talked."
"My music, thou son of Morn,"
Said Mac Luy of the glittering arms,
"Is leaping 'midst the tumult of my dogs,
As swift upon the deer they gain."
"'Tis this that music is for me,"
Said Finn, the chief of all the host,
"To have my banner in the wind,
Heroes ranged by its golden side."
"When of the bards I had no fear,
Ossian," he said, as still he spoke;
"And when my Feinn were still around me,
Sweet its music in my ears."

A GREAT feast was made by Finn,[1]
I tell thee now, O tonsured Priest,
Many were the men were there,
Of the Feine of Alba and Erin.
The great Mac Morn did ask
Of the queen of whitest hand,
"Did'st thou see so rich a feast
Since thou cam'st 'mongst the Feine of Erin?"
Finn of the Feine himself replied,
Chiefest of all both east and west;
He said she saw a richer feast
Than any Fenian feast in Erin.
We then saw coming from the waves
A warrior tall, manly, fair-haired,
No man was with him but himself,
And a noble man he was.
When he had come near the Feine,
Thus did he mildly, wisely say,
"Come, Finn, come along with me,
And take with thee a hundred men;
Thirty sons of the great Morn,
Let them be the first around thee;
One man and eight of thy own sons,
Take them and Oscar of the Feine's Fians;
Let ten of the sons of Smoil be there,
And twenty of the sons of Ronan;
Let some of Muin's sons be there,
Other ten, not counting Diarmad;
Take with thee Diarmad O'Duine,
He who could either court or hunt,
Both him and Caroll in thy ship;

1 Hospitality was the most esteemed feature in the character of the Celtic chief. That of Finn is sung with untiring admiration by the poets. This virtue, with bravery, generosity, and liberal giving, no doubt to the poets themselves especially, seemed to make up what they looked upon as a perfect character for their leader. These feasts were apparently affairs of great moment, as the like are in our own day.

Let there be ten of men and crew,
Of thy men take with thee nine,
Of those whom thou'dst most like to have;
Besides them all thyself, O Finn,
Thou dauntless and well-armed man.
Take o'er the waves a hundred men
Of those that follow Finn Mac Cumhail,
A hundred shields with golden studs,
For Finn Mac Cumhail, Mac Tranevor.
Take now with thee also, Finn,
The two best hounds that are in Erin;
Bran and Scoilean[1] take them with thee,
The swiftest-footed of the pack.
Have no fear about thee, Finn,"
The tall and cheerful warrior said;
"Let them all be brought in peace,
And trouble not our men or ships."
"Foolish the speech thou now hast made,
Thou man who cam'st amongst us;
Wert thou to approach nearer Finn,
Thy body soon would want its head."
"Little care I for what thou say'st,
Bald-headed Conan of the gibes;
Pity for thy friends that thou art there,
Ugly and feeble as thou art."
"Rise ye up, ye sons of Boisgne,"
Then spoke Conan, so well known;
Each man did seize a hero's arms,
From every side the Fians came fast.
Then fell there slain a son of Finn,
One of the stalwart, white-hand Fians,
A man of Mac Morn's followers too,
A vigorous hand 'midst battle's blows.
"Fergus, now go rouse thee up,
And mingle boldly in the fight;
Ask whether Gaul has aught to give

[1] Scoilean was the second favourite hound of Finn.

To Conan, whom he knows so well."
"Let Finn himself then be the judge,"
Said the great Gaul of mighty blows;
"Conan or I shall take his head,
Or else his brains we will dash out."
Fergus, Caol, and thirty are in the glen,
Who never more shall see this earth,
Unknown to all the Feine of Finn.
Sad is my tale, O tonsured Priest.
Much do I weary, valiant Priest,
For now I never see the Feine,
Hunting, as wont, from glen to glen,
With herds of deer on every side.
Much loved I Ossian, son of Finn,
He only never yet forsook me;
But above all the men I saw,
Finn of the feasts I loved most.
A great feast.

'Tis sad that the hill of the Feine,
Should now by the clerics be held,
And that the songs of men of books
Should fill the halls of clan Baoisgne
I myself was once in Rath Cruachan,[1]
Happily beneath thy banks,
I little thought I e'er should find
A priest upon thy summit dwelling.
There would be found my shield and spear,

[1] Rath Cruachan, as Irish tradition says, was the chief seat of the Feinn of Connaught, usually called the Sons of Morn. The word "Rath" means a *Fort*, and Cruachan an elevation more than usually steep. It sometimes stands upon another hill, as in Argyleshire, where we have "Cruachan Beinne," *The hillock upon the mountain*, usually called Ben Cruachan. The word "Rath" enters largely into Scottish topography, and assumes different forms in English, as *Rath*, *Roth*, *Rothie*, *Rait*, *Raits*, etc.

My dogs and hounds along thy ridge,
Although to-night the Fenian hill
Is under clerics and their crosiers.
Were the sons of Morn alive,
The priestly order soon must quit;
You would find yourselves cut up,
Ye men of the spotted crooks.
Were Mac Luy alive,
With his six heroes bold,
Ere you had quitted the hill
You'd find your garments curtailed.
Were the sons of Ceard alive,
Who never hypocrisy knew,
Neither your bells nor crooks
Would in place of their banners be found.
Were the sons of Muin alive,
Who knew no weakness in fight,
Men would not see thy people
So powerful amidst our hills.
Were the sons of black Garry alive,
Or Caoilte, who was ever so brave,
Neither the sounds of bells or priests
Would now be heard in Rath Cruachan.
Were red-haired Ryno alive,
And brave Caol, son of Revan,
Thy books would not be so whole,
Oh man, who readest the Bible.
And for all thy hooked crosiers,
Which have travelled over the earth,
Thy staves would be in splinters,
Were only brave Oscar alive.
Thou of the yellow[1] garment,
Who sittest so much at thine ease,
'Tis well for thee that Conan is dead,

[1] "Yellow" was the favourite colour of the Celts. It seems that St. Patrick adopted it as the clerical colour, very probably as a means of commending himself and his cause to the good-will of the people.

Else thou'dst feel the weight of his fist.
Were the blue-eyed hero alive,
Bald Conan, the son of the Feine,
Cleric, though thy office be sacred,
With his fist he'd strike thee down.
Were the son of O'Duine alive,
Thou man of the crooked staff,
Thy staff should be all in shivers,
Smashed at the pillar of stone.
Thou man of the bell, I do think,
If Daoruinn were now in life,
Thy bell would be now in pieces,
Scattered before the pillar.
Were the red point seen, old man,
Of the swift-flying spear of Mac Ronan,
Thy bell would not be faintly sounding,
Thou who sing'st the howling song.
I cannot be joyful now,
I see not Mac Cumhail in life,
I see not Diarmad O'Duine,
I see not Caoilte Mac Ronan.
No wonder though I should be sad,
As I sit on this mound, Patrick.
I see not the son of Luy,
I see not the hero so loved,
I see not Fearluth by my side,
I see not the Fenian Oscar;
I see not warlike exercises,
I see not the noble hounds;
I see not the sons of Smoil,
I see not Gaul of great feats,
I see not the generous Faolan,
I see not with him the Feine.
I see not Fergus, my brother,
So gentle and worthy of praise;
I see not Daire of the songs,
Whose music we always enjoyed.

I see not Fatha[1] Canan,
Whose presence filled us with joy;
I see not one of our band,
Whose noise was like thunder in war.
I see neither music nor joy,
I hear not if music there be,
Ere I was laid in my cave
Freely I scattered my gold.
Patrick, I tell thee it now,
If I chose my knowledge to give,
That 'tis not in my power to relate
How much of their joy I have seen.
I and the mass-book clerics,
Are two that can never agree.
Though this night so mournful I am,
I'm sad for the hill of Feine.
'Tis sad.

I now will tell thee, O Grainne,[2]
What I have seen with Mac Cumhail.
The misery I suffer now
I cannot much longer endure.
I have seen sport and rejoicing
'Mongst those who now are despised.
I have seen maidens and men,
I now will tell thee, O Grainne.
Courtesy and cheerfulness too,

[1] Fatha Canan appears in several of these pieces. He appears as Fatha son of Mac Con, and Faycanan. He was son of Lughaidh Mac Con, a King of Ireland, of the race of Ith, who flourished in the middle of the third century. Hence his name Fatha Mac Mhic Con, *Fatha son of Mac Con's son.* The Irish say he settled in Scotland, and was progenitor of the Campbells.

[2] Grainne was the wife of Finn, and the poet, whether it be Ossian or some other of the Fenian bards, addresses this description of the glory of Finn and his followers to her.

I've seen with feasts, steeds, and shouting.
I've seen the violin played,
I now will tell thee, O Grainne.
Great Caoilte and Mac Luy,
A couple who can't be despised,
We oft gained nought by their wrath
I now will tell thee, O Grainne.
Gaul and Oscar and Ossian,
A brood who did nought by halves;
These all loved us well,
I now will tell thee, O Grainne.
Finn himself of fearless heart,
Whose welcome was always sure,
We've seen him cheerful too,
I now will tell thee, O Grainne.
I have in nine battles been,
To me no joy is now left.
Looking on nought but their graves,
I now will tell thee, O Grainne.
In wrath we crossed over hills,
And over Banva's fierce tops;
Then in singing their praise,
Employment was found for my lips.
We feared for nought in the valleys,
I now will tell thee, O Grainne.
I was both long time and short
Traversing Erin the fair;
We were famous and powerful then,
I now will tell thee, O Grainne.
I now will tell.

ONCE on a day there was in Dundalgin,[1]
Cuchullin of the handsome form;

[1] The following piece seems to be made up of fragments Mr. O'Curry, who has obligingly taken the trouble to examine it, suggests that it contains fragments

Joy and merriment were his,
All his people were with him.
When from the drinking hall we rose,
We saw the whole of the Feine.
We strove from their hiding-place to raise
The flocks of birds in the two hills.
The most loved thing of all we had
Was the women of Clan Rury province.
The valley we were in was rough,
We drove the birds to its mouth,
In hopes that we might find a hero.
The father of Conlach chased
The birds with handsome Daoruing,
The sweet-spoken noble of Coll in Galway.
The well-formed sling was then used
With skill by great Cuchullin,
He with the arm of well-known strength;
The birds with speed he kills.
The game was then divided,
None was forgotten but Evir.[1]
Evir took wrath for her share,
'Tis true that prudence was lacking
'Twas promised her in reparation
That she should have the first birds slain,
Killed on the mountain side,
With the skill of the shot for her fired.
As they travelled they came to a place
Where poets were wont to resort;

of four different pieces: The Irish bardic account of the name of "Srubh Brain," or the "Raven's snout," at Loch Swilly; the legend of "Cuchullin's sick-bed;" the death of Conlaoch; and a short but imperfect account of the battle of Cnucha, in which Cumhal was killed. The piece is given as in the MS., and if thus made up, is just as it was written in the beginning of the sixteenth century. The Editor has to state, however, that the leaves which contain it are so discoloured, and the writing so defaced, that he has had the greatest difficulty in deciphering it at all, and for many of the words he cannot be answerable except as guesses. Mr. M'Lachlan of Aberdeen, who transcribed the greater portion of the MS., did not transcribe this piece; and it is given now merely from the desire to withhold nothing in it that may be of value or interest.

[1] Evir was the wife of Cuchullin.

Each of them wore round his neck
A chain of the purest gold.
The wife of Cuchullin fell in love
With one of our Ulster Fians,
With the willing and handsome friend
Who came from the Ulster bounds.
Evir of the weighty locks asks
Her agreement with Cuchullin,
That she should now have her birds,
Without excuse about them.
Twice or thrice did he shoot at
The wild birds, but missed his aim;
'Twas a victor's leap as he shot
Three shots amongst the birds.
The last blow he had struck ere then
Had pierced his own dear son.
Without joy, or women at feasts,
Had he been, as he sadly mourned.
For a whole year he did nought
But grieve for the hero now dead.
'Twas not tales of the Feine he sought,
But to have that tale rehearsed.
If the story men tell be true,
The Cu never ceased to grieve;
The blossomed branch whom women loved,
Sad and grievous was his state.
It happened at length of a time,
A few of the Feine met together.
Finn himself had joined the hunt,
And sent us in pairs to search.
I myself sat with Garry,
Side by side with the King.
Finn put the question to Garry,
As by the King's side he sat:
" Since that thou wert there,
How was't ye slew Cumhal?"

"I will now pass my word,[1]
Since to me the question thou putt'st,
That mine was the powerful arm
Which gave the first wound to Cumhal."
"That is a cold welcome for me,
Ye sons of Morn, as a follower;
'Tis hard indeed for me to bear,
To know that ye slew my father."
"If that be a cold welcome for you,
Finn, son of Cumhal from Alvin,
Put aside pretended love,
And show your usual hatred."
"Should I now raise my arm,
Ye hated children of Morn,
I could do all I chose alone,
Without the help of any man."
"Ere ever thou had'st so moved,
Walking in the steps of thy father,
Lightly could we leap o'er streams,
Were it not for the wiles of Cumhal
'Twas Cumhal got influence o'er us,
'Twas Cumhal oppressed us sore,
'Twas Cumhal that banished us far,
To the land of the stranger away.
Some he sent to Albin fair,
And some to Lochlin the dark,
The third band to Greece the white,
We all from each other were torn.
Sixteen years were we all
Severed from Erin; 'tis truth,
No small calamity was this,
Never each other to see.

1 It is here that Garry's account of the battle of Cnucha commences. The account, as Mr. O'Curry says, may be imperfect, but the gathering together of such fragments, and comparing them with one another, cannot but be interesting to the student of early Celtic history. There is interest in the variety, irrespective of the question of comparative merit as between the different compositions. This may be a Scotch version of an Irish story.

The first day we set foot on shore
In Erin's isle, so much loved,
We slew, and it is no lie,
At least sixteen hundred men.
These all were slain by Clan Morn,
Their heroes and their chiefs;
There was not a man of them all
But such as their women would mourn.
With that their castles we seized,
We, the noble Clan of Morn,
Our race did bravely then
Before the men of Erin
By thy hand, hero of the Feine,
There ne'er was seen, east or west,
One thing to cloud my eye,
But seeing the slaughter there;
My heart became tender and soft
As I saw the terrible scene.
We all surrounded one house,
In Munster of the red towers;
But such was the strength of the man,
'Twas easier to find than to kill.
They slew on the opposite hill
All that lived of Cumhal's race.
We made a joint and rapid rush
To the house where Cumhal still was;
Each man of us gave a wound
With his spear to the body of Cumhal.
Though it was my lot to be there
At the time that Cumhal was slain,
For the deed which then was done,
Take vengeance now if you will."

Once on a day.

The author of this is Duncan Mor from Lennox.[1]

Pity the man who lost his voice,
When he is called on to recite,
Who cannot speak so fast as needs be,
And yet 's unwilling to give up.
Who cannot sing an air or tune,
And cannot well recite a lay.
Who cannot put aside his harp,
Yet cannot sing as he would wish.
Pity him ever with his "dring, drang,"
Trying his verses to recite,
When men can neither hear his harp,
Nor understand the songs he sings.
Pity the man neglects his health,
And strives not his vigour to retain.
Pity the man who ever strives
To have the fruit he cannot reach.
Were I to wish to have such fruit,
Fruit which I could not reach on high,
I'd cut the tree down at the root,
Let men be angry if they will.
Pity.

The author of this is Gilchrist Taylor.[2]

Bless, O Trinity, thy household,
King of heaven, place of jewels ;

1 The fragments of Ossianic or Fenian poetry in the miscellany of Dean Macgregor are now exhausted. They afford some idea of the amount of such poetry in the Highlands at the time he lived. We now proceed with those pieces which profess to be of a more recent date. These will be found to consist chiefly of compositions of the fourteenth and fifteenth centuries. The first short composition here given is one by a poet hitherto unknown to modern fame. Duncan the big, from Lennox or Dumbartonshire, might be a man of some note in his day, but time has obliterated all knowledge of him. His composition is of a class well known in his day, and highly popular, being aphoristic. Several compositions, consisting of a series of aphorisms, will be found in the sequel.

2 There are several pieces by this poet in the Dean's MS., but we know nothing of his history. He was probably an ecclesiastic.

Black thy family was not formed,
All by thyself in wisdom made.
By thee 'twas Adam's race was shaped
The cheek like berries richly red;
Thou who blessest place and people
Curse them that 'gainst thee fierce contend.
There is a pack of cruel hounds,
Who the king's children sorely grieve;
I hear the baying of these dogs,
Every glen is full of it.
Such as war on Adam's race,
Since that they cannot silence keep,
Joined together in their evil,
Powers of the king of light them smite;
Such as war on Adam's race,
Of crafty Lucifer the slaves,
Give them no rest, to them give none,
King of lights do thou them burn.
Mounted on two ugly steeds,
When vicious packs abound the most,
They furiously commence the hunt,
Belching out death on every side.
Curse thou their hunt and devastation,
Their two steeds so black in hue;
Lay them, their backs stretched on the turf,
Scatter the heads of this black band
There is a band of cruel hounds
Harbouring at Inch Ald Art,
They're horrid brutes, Thou God forsake them,
Let bags out of their skins be made.
Though many be the skins of wolves,
Covering our harps, both small and great,
The cold and empty skulls are many,
Given us by these fierce hounds.
Father of Christ, with speed them strike
From Lochaber to Raon Fraoich,
Soon let the plague their bodies waste;

'Tis sad that thus I have to speak.
Though no reparation for a true hound,
For Robert's son[1] of clustering locks.
From Loch Venachar of rich glens,
Many's the ugly head laid low.
Though from Ben Gulbin's sunny side,
Many the dogs to Tummel's stream,
Who know to hunt along its side,
The eye of Christ is on them all.
'Twas told me when at Inverness,
That greyhounds were scattering the pack
Pity the man who's seized with fear,
'Tis like the falling sickness, sore.
Pleasing to witness hounds pursue,
Them who would slay the fine grey steeds.
May God's Son with His holy power,
Destroy all surly cruel hounds.
Smoke every den in Schiehallion,
John Stewart of the bounding steeds,
Ere I must call a sweet-voiced pack
This litter of ugly, snarling curs.
By Garry of John Stewart of the white steed,
No antlers are seen without the head,
While 'mongst the rocky rugged woods,
Are seen the grey-skinned pack of hounds.
Bless.

The author of this is Gilliecallum Mac an Olla.[2]

There is no joy without the clan Donald,
No battle when they are awanting;

[1] The piece is extremely obscure, but the reference to Mac Robert and the Athole Stewarts would seem to indicate that the subjects of the poem were the murderers of King James the First. The infamous persons whom the poet denounces are said to have done evil to the race of kings.

[2] This bard has been met with already as an imitator of Ossian. He was in all

First of the clans in all the earth,
Each man of them is a hundred.
The noblest clan which you can find,
A race as brave as they are peaceful;
The clan whose praise does fill the lands,
Famed for their faith and godliness.
The clan so faithful, bold, and brave,
The clan so swift amidst the fight,
The clan so gentle among men,
And yet in battle none so fierce;
The clan most numerous of all
Whose number has been ever known.
The clan which never vexed the Church,
And ever dreaded its reproach.
Of all that dwell in Albin green,
This is the bravest e'er baptized.
The third of every land is theirs,
Their bravery is like the falcon's.
The clan most numerous and famous,
Of finest form and fairest mould;
The clan that has the largest hearts,
Most patient and most liberal.
They, sons of kings, deserved no gibe
When asked in trouble to give help.
Noble were they since the time
When there was giving and poor ones.
The clan for wine and shelter best,
The first in prowess and in strength.
'Tis sad how short the length extends
Given by him who spins your thread.
They were not wicked and rough,
Nor were they gentle and weak.

likelihood an ecclesiastic. Several of the early Lords of the Isles were liberal benefactors to the Church, and it is not unlikely that this liberality called forth the praises of our bard. The word "bochd," *poor*, associated in one of the lines of this composition with "brontachd," *bestowing*, is often by early Gaelic writers applied to monks and hermits, who lived upon the beneficence of the wealthy, and became finally enriched by their gifts.

In midst of trial and hardships,
Not harder than them was the rock.
The clan without pride or misdeeds,
When the spoil of battle is theirs.
'Mongst them you'd find gentlemen,
And common people with them.
Pity him who has lost their defence,
Pity him who forsakes their protection.
There is no clan like the clan Donald,
The noble clan of firmest mind.
Who is there can number their gifts?
Who is there can count their nobles?
Without limit, commencement or close,
Of excellencies among their gentry.
First of all with the clan Donald,
There is knowledge which they learn;
Last of all, there is among them
Polish, generosity, and modesty.
'Tis in sorrow and in grief
Understanding and learning are got,
By him who them would have.
No joy without the clan Donald.
Loud was the sound of their thunder,
This race so wise and faithful,
Though now they be reproached,
There is no joy without the clan Donald.
This people so great in fame,
In courtesy, mind, and firmness,
There is no right without them,
There is no joy without the clan Donald.
The son of his virgin mother,
Who hath earned for us freedom from pain,
Though he be faithful and true,
There is no joy without the clan Donald.
There is no joy.

ALAS! alas! this is the head[1]
Which belonged to the blue-armed Conull;
The head where understanding was found,
Noble it was and most lovely.
Alas! alas! this is the eye
That dwelt in generous Conull's head;
Round which the eyelid wound,
Benevolent it was and manful.
Alas! alas! this is the mouth
In which no bard did folly find;
Its lips so thin, like apples red,
Sweet as honey the mouth of Conull.
Alas! alas! this is the hand
That Conull Mac Scanlan owned;
The hand of him so brave in battle,
The hand of Conull my first beloved.
Alas! alas! this is the side
By which our noble side we laid;
It was a hound from Mull that came,
John did lie upon his side.
Alas! alas! this is the foot
Which ne'er before a warrior fled;
The foot of him in fight most brave,
The foot of the shielded son of Scanlan
Alas! success e'er followed Conull,
Where'er it was he battle fought;
But now that my tale is done,
This place is the dwelling of tears.
Alas!

[1] Mr. O'Curry says regarding this Conull Mac Scanlan, "I don't know any person in our history whose name would agree with his but Congal Claen, son of Scanlan, Prince of Ulster, who fought the battle of Magh Rath in A.D. 634, in which the Four Masters say he was killed. The old account says he was disabled, and disappeared no one knows where. It would be curious if your elegy could be traced up to this hero."

The author of this is John of Knoydart.[1]

Thou head of Diarmad O'Cairbre,[2]
Though great be thy trouble and pain,
I grudge thee not all thou hast suffered,
Although it be painful to tell.
I grudge not though thy ragged locks
Be searched by the winds from the glens.
I grudge thee not that thou art bound,
Thou head of Diarmad O'Cairbre;
Pity the thought e'er filled men's breasts,
That thy friendship was not hatred;
Pity, alas! thou turn'dst not back,
Thou head of Diarmad O'Cairbre;
Thou hast the King of Isla slain,
Who freely gave his wine and money,
Him of the soft and flowing locks,
Thou head of Diarmad O'Cairbre;
Isla, king of well filled horns,
Who with his friends so kindly dealt;
Alas! who gashed his soft white skin,
Thou head of Diarmad O'Cairbre!
Beloved was that liberal hand,
Which never grudged his gold or silver,
And which in feast or hunt was first,
Thou head of Diarmad O'Cairbre.

1 Of the author of this fragment we have no tradition. All we learn here is that he was a Knoydart man, that mountainous region lying between Loch Hourn and Morar, on the west coast of Inverness-shire, till lately possessed by the Macdonells of Glengarry.

2 In a transcript of a MS. history of the Macdonalds, published in the Transactions of the Iona Club, it is said that Angus Og of Isla, or of the Isles, who fought against his father in the battle of the Bloody Bay, was assassinated by Art O'Carby, an Irish harper, instigated by M'Kenzie, whose daughter had captivated the impressible musician. In the Irish annals this harper is called Diarmad. This lay seems to commemorate the event by commemorating the punishment of the assassin, which was inflicted by drawing him between horses. The lines being composed shortly after the event, which took place about the year 1490, and being taken down by the Dean, are sufficient evidence of the historical accuracy of the statement.

It is my prayer to th' Apostles' King,
He who preserves by His great power,
That He from pain may him e'er keep,
Thou head of Diarmad O'Cairbre.
Thou head.

The author of this is Gormlay, daughter of Flann.[1]

Melancholy earth upon the breast of Nial,
Melancholy its depth upon his grave;
Neither nobility nor fame can save,
Since that the King of the North is dead.
Whose back is turned upon this joyful world,
Now that his death-wound he received.
He from the noble race of Nial is traced,
The men who proudly governed all this land.
I, the gentle, kind, Mac Cuilenan,[2] did leave,
With Muireagan mòr I also joyful lived.
With Nial I spent a truly happy life;
Bright was my honour as with him I drunk,
Of feasts and wine I could abundance have;
My gold I freely gave the church.
If any there be who heaven reach,
How could Nial be without heaven?
Never have I seen one like Nial.
Fair was he all except the knee,
Great were his beauty and his fame,
Soft were his locks, and grey his eye.
Wrath grew upon the mighty deep,
The wind in strength blew from the east,[3]
Nial then bent him on his knee,

[1] Gormlay was the wife of Nial Glundubh, *Nial of the Black Knee*, who succeeded to the throne of Ireland in 916. He was of the northern O'Neills, hence called "Righ Tuaisgearta," or *King of the North.*

[2] The famous Cormac M'Cuilenan, the King-bishop of Munster and Cashel, to whom M'Geoghagan says Gormlay was first married.

[3] Nial Glundubh was killed in battle by the Danes in 919, having reigned only three years.

Stronger it blew and without fail;
It suffered no happiness nor peace.
The wind never ceased its sound,
Neither fort nor tree was spared,
Since that the courteous king is dead.
Since Nial[1] Aidh's son died yesterday,
Numbers on numbers sorely mourn;
And though cups and horns are filled,
Sore is the blow to Conn's great race.
Without him prosperity is joyless,
His form my heart with sorrow fills,
That I'm till judgment left behind,
Is that which fills my heart with grief.
Melancholy.

Gormlay, daughter of Flann.[2]

Monk, remove thy foot,
Lift it off the grave of Nial.
Too long dost thou heap the earth
On him with whom I fain would lie;
Too long dost thou, Monk, there
Heap the earth on noble Nial.
Thou brown-haired friend, though gentle,
Press not with thy sole the earth
Do not firmly close the grave,
O Priest, whose office is so sad.
Raise off the fair, black-kneed Nial,
Monk, remove thy foot.
Mac O'Nial of finest gold,
'Tis not of my will thou 'rt bound.[3]

[1] Nial was son of Aidh Finliath, King of Ireland. O'Flaherty mentions an elegy of Gormlay on her husband, as preserved in the Annals of Donegal.

[2] This is another elegy of Gormlay, Queen of Ireland, on her husband, Nial Glundubh. There is something extremely mournful in these compositions of the youthful queen. Mr. O'Curry has kindly furnished the Editor with Irish copies of these two elegiac pieces, which he is about to publish in a second volume of his admirable Lectures.

[3] Referring, undoubtedly, to the mode of laying out the dead.

Leave his stone and his grave,
Monk, remove thy foot.
I am Gormlay, who order keeps,
Daughter I of Flann the bold;
Stand not thou upon his grave,
Monk, remove thy foot.
Monk.

WOUNDED thou hast been, great man,[1]
Whate'er the men were thou hast met;
Though thou art truly sad and sick,
'Tis joy to us that thou'st got fame.
Ten hundred ships from Greece of the Gael,
While of them only three were noble,
Thou didst attack with sharp-edged arms,
Sore was the strife while life did last,
That people with their many spears;
They live not now who were so pure,
Thy six nobles at last they slew,
Many their bold deeds at thy side.
That of thy wounds thou may'st be healed,
I pray for thee, pray thou thyself,
To Mary, the mother of the poor,
My Pater and my Creed's for thee.
Wounded.

The author of this is Phelim M'Dougall.[2]

'Tis not good to travel on Sunday,
Whoever the Sabbath would keep;

[1] The allusion in this fragment is not very clear Celtic poetry is full of reference to Greece, whence a portion of the race are said to have come; but what this battle with Greeks was, the Editor cannot say. These allusions belong, without doubt, to the period when both Scotland and Ireland were brought into contact with Greek literature.

[2] We have here a curious specimen of

Not good to be of ill-famed race;
Not good is a dirty woman;
Not good to write without learning;
Not good are grapes when sour;
Not good is an Earl without English;
Not good is a sailor, if old;
Not good is a bishop without warrant;
Not good is a blemish on an elder;
Not good a priest with but one eye;
Not good a parson, if a beggar;
Not good is a palace without play;
Not good is a handmaid if she's slow;
Not good is a lord without a dwelling;
Not good is a temple without a burying ground;
Not good is a woman without shame;
Not good is a harper without a string;
Not good is fighting without courage;
Not good is entering a port without a pilot;
Not good is a maiden who backbites;
Not good is the poverty of a debtor;
Not good is a castle without an heir;
Not good is neglecting the household dogs;
Not good is disrespect to a father;
Not good is the talk of the drunken;
Not good is a knife without an edge;
Not good is injustice in judging;
Not good is the friendship of devils
For thy son, oh Virgin most honoured;
Though he has saved the seed of Adam,
Not good for himself was the cross.
Not good is a reader without understanding;
Not good for a man to want a friend;
Not good is a poet without a subject;
Not good is a tower without a hall;

aphoristic poetry, the idea borrowed probably from the Proverbs of Solomon. These aphorisms throw some light upon the habits and modes of thought of the age in which they were produced.

Not good is a web without fulling;
Not good is sport without laughter;
Not good are misdeeds when prosperous;
Not good is marriage without consent;
Not good is a crown without supremacy;
Not good is ploughing by night;
Not good is learning without courtesy;
Not good is religion without knowledge.
Not good.

I MYSELF, Robert, went[1]
Yesterday to a monastery,
And I was not allowed in,
Because my wife was not with me.

I DISLIKE to journey for a year;[2]
I dislike the table where a woman sits;
I dislike sorrow and sadness;
I dislike a great house without joy;
I dislike seeing a good man with a bad wife;
I dislike a frown upon a prince's face;
I dislike weak drink at a high price;
I dislike a noble without courtesy;
I dislike war when it is peace,
When nothing is allowed to pass;
I dislike a rough and cruel chief;
I dislike the men who cannot fight;

[1] These lines are given as indicative of the state of public feeling at the time with respect to a great social question. The writer of these lines was manifestly no friend to monasteries, and no believer in their purity.

[2] We have here another specimen of aphoristic poetry. In the original the lines are in rhyme. The author's name is not given, though it is probably Phelim M'Dougall.

I dislike being long at a tune;
I dislike the men who grudge me food;
I dislike a jealous woman if unchaste;
I dislike the dog who cannot kill a stag;
I'm loath to go to Erin in the west,
Now that Brian of the tunes is dead;
I dislike a widow who is not cheerful;
I dislike the man of melancholy mind;
I dislike an ill-favoured old woman,
Whose tongue is sharp and rapid too;
I cannot tell to any man
All the things that I dislike.
I dislike.

Earl Gerald.[1]

Pity the man who overleaps his horse;
Let him that likes, my meaning understand,
That from myself my means have taken flight;
'Tis best to have nought to do with women.
May my curse 'mongst women rest,
Although for a time I mixed with them;
As for men who still are single,
'Tis best to have nought to do with women.
That man who early is on foot,
Cannot but many evils find;
Were I to tell what I have seen,
'Tis best to have nought to do with women.
The man who has got a useless wife,
Cannot do much before the foe,

[1] The following is the composition of Gerald Fitzgerald, the fourth Earl of Desmond. He is known in Ireland as Earl Gerald, the poet. There are several of his compositions scattered over the MS.; but as they are mostly of the same character—satires on the female sex—it has been thought that one specimen is sufficient. The Editor thought it desirable to give one of those, with a view to a fair representation of the contents of the MS., although there is not much in the composition itself to render it worthy of being rescued from oblivion.

The first milch cows that bellow loud;
'Tis best to have nought to do with women.
The wife who listens to my speech,
Who listens to my voice and cry,
Just as if wax were in her ears;
'Tis best to have nought to do with women.
Her husband she to wrath provokes,
Different her manner with all else,
For them she lightly steps about;
'Tis best to have nought to do with women.
Were she to see a weeping eye,
With any youth of handsome form,
To him she would not run but leap,
'Tis best to have nought to do with women.
Where is the young and sprightly maid,
Who would not quietly give her kiss,
To any lips that she might meet?
'Tis best to have nought to do with women
Though married from th' altar and the church,
From the good priest's worthy hand,
Still are her way and temper bad;
'Tis best to have nought to do with women.
'Tis best to have nought to do with women,
Wrath and annoyance they provoke;
He who does not this proclaim
Is sure to find a woe himself.

Pity.

The author of this is Andrew M'Intosh.

The coquetry of Duncan from Taid's daughter,
The most impudent coquetry men have seen,
The coquetry of the wife of David,
Coquetting like the wind in her red-tailed skirts,
Men had thought that I was dumb,
Whilst I'd three reasons not to speak.

The author of this is the Bard M'Intyre.[1]

What is this ship on Loch Inch,[2]
Of which we now may speak ?
What brought this ship on the loch,
Which songs cannot o'erlook ?
I would like much to ask,
Who was it brought that ship,
Afloat upon that angry loch,
Where changes often come ?
The fierce wind from the hills,
And bitter storms from the glens,
Oft has the vessel from the shore,
Stolen upon the dangerous sea.
Stranger, who sawest the ship,
On the rough and angry stream,
What should hinder thee to tell
About her and about her crew ?
An old ship without iron or stern,
Never have we seen her like,
The vessel all with leather patched,
Not even beneath the waves is't tight.
Her boards are trifling bits of deals,
Black patches down along her sides,
Useless nails to fix them on
Upon her scanty, stinted ribs.
What woman cargo is in the black ship

1 Nothing is known of this poet. The modern M'Intyre, the bard of Glenurchy, has a place second to none among the composers of Gaelic poetry; but it would appear that there was an older poet of the name, and one not unknown to fame. Four hundred years may produce no little change in the place which not a few men of note in our day hold in the temple of fame, and greater stars than the bard M'Intyre may have their lustre dimmed by time. He is another writer of satires on women, a kind of composition wonderfully popular, judging from our MS. at the period. We only give a few specimens of these, but there are several in the miscellany, and some of a character which, in modern days, one wonders the Dean could have admitted to his collection.

2 The only loch of this name with which the Editor is acquainted is Loch Inch, on the Spey, in Badenoch.

Pulling her on betwixt the waves,
The cargo heartless and senseless too ?
Widows of a foolish mind,
A boasting, talkative crew,
A load vexatious and bad,
Quarrelsome and covetous,
Of evil minds and evil deeds.
Their ways and conversation bad,
A band of well-known fame,
No substance in what they say,
Drunken, singing, with levity,
A band ill-shapen, mischievous,
Who live by both sides of Loch Inch.
In spite of thee and of their ship
On the stormy sea's dun face,
No good woman could take that ship,
However pressing the constraint.
The worst of women go to sea,
Others cannot give them help
Let this ship be driven from the loch,
Down to the fierce and roaring deep,
Let the wind pursue the ship,
To the old point of Seananach.
There will I leave upon the stream,
The ill-favoured, ill-doing ship,
Of wicked widows full on the sea,
Without a psalm or creed e'er said,
What.

THE fame of the house of Dunolly, little favour where they drive a herd.[1]
This brute is much like a dog, greedy aye for stolen flesh

[1] These satirical lines on the family of Dunolly are given as a specimen of the strain indulged in at times by the bards, to gratify their animosity against hostile clans. It need hardly be added, that the Macdougalls of Lorn were a race as distinguished for the antiquity of their descent, as for the high character of many of the name.

The author of this is John M'Murrich.[1]

Sad to me's my fate,
Though men don't understand,
Suffer not, Son of God,
Me to have pain to-day.
Little thought the school
That such should be my fate,
The fate which me o'ertook,
'Tis it has me destroyed.
The pain in it I have,
Is threefold what I've felt,
The trouble I have found
Is weighted with a stone.
For her who caused my grief,
My wrath and rage are great.
Her skin like froth of waves,
Ruddy and soft her hand,
Her lips like berries red,
My soul she gently seized.
Since I slept last night,
Sad indeed my state.
I thought she was beside me,
That I saw her smile.
She's not been since the day,
When began my grief.
She of curling locks,
And colour richly red,
Five jewels in a knot,
In the maiden's name.

[1] This John M'Muirich, or M'Vurrich, was in all likelihood a member of the family who were so long bards to Clanranald, and who derived their name from their great ancestor in the thirteenth century, Muireach Albanach. A list of the names of these bards is given for eight generations by Lachlan, who lived in 1800, in his declaration, as given in the Report of the Highland Society on Ossian, but it does not embrace this John. The piece is chiefly interesting from the historical references at the close.

Pity she 's not with me,
And others have her not.
That I myself might get
For evermore that friend.
Were I to suffer from,
What other men have felt,
The spear of great Cuchullin,
The horse of white-steed Teague,
The purple shield unbroken,
Famous all in war;
The speed of Mac Erc's coursers,
Though much it is to say,
Alas, more sad for me
The trouble I endure.

Duncan M'Pherson.[1]

Alexander, hast thou left thy sadness,
Or is it so that thou canst not?
Hast thou without God passed another year,
Or dost thou mean to live thus ever?
Hast thou not found thy God,
Now that thou'rt aged and grey?
If sadness be prosperity,
Rich are the gifts thou'st got from God.

FOUR men met at the grave,[2]
The grave of Alexander the great;
They spoke the words of truth,

[1] This writer was probably an ecclesiastic, but nothing is known of him.

[2] This composition is one of the few of the more recent fragments in this MS. which appear elsewhere. We have a copy of it in the collection of Gaelic poems made by Ronald M'Donald, schoolmaster of Eigg, son of Alexander M'Donald, the famous Skye bard. M'Donald's edition was most likely taken down from oral recitation, and it is remarkable how little it differs from this of the Dean's, 250 years before.

Over the hero of Greece the fair.
The first man of them said,
"There were yesterday with the king,
The world's great hosts, sad the tale,
Though to-day he lonely lies."
"Yesterday the world's great king
Proudly rode upon the earth;
But to-day it is the earth
That rides upon the top of him."
Then did the third wise speaker say,
"Yesterday Philip's son owned the world;
But to-day he only owns
Of it all not seven feet."
"Alexander, brave and great,
Who won and treasured gold and silver,
To-day," the fourth man wisely said,
"The gold it is that treasures him."
The palm among trees was Philip's son,
The moon among the lesser stars,
As gold above the finest gems,
As among fish leviathan.
The lion amidst carrion,
The eagle among other birds,
As Sion hill amidst the hills,
As Jordan amidst other streams.
The polished gem 'mongst common stones,
The sea amidst all lesser streams,
Noble was the fearless man,
The man above all other men.
The man above all other men,
Save heaven's great and holy King.
King he was of herds and boars,
Ruler of hosts and heroes too.
True was the talk these speakers had,
As at the great king's grave they met.
Unlike to women's empty talk,
Were the sayings of the four.
Four.

John M'Murrich said this.

The men of Albin, and not they alone,
Unless that M'Gregor survived,
How much wrath would them destroy!
All excellence in Alexander.[1]

Finlay, the red-haired bard, said this.[2]

Gael-like is every leap of the dun horse,
A Gael she is in truth.
It is she who conquers and wins,
In all that I'll now sing.
The praise of speed to her limbs,
In every fierce assault.
Marked, and famous her strength,
While quiet at the house of prayer.
The birds are they who could,
Strive with her in the race.
Not false is the fame of that horse,
The steed both sturdy and swift,
Liker she was to Duseivlin,[3]
Than to the beast of Lamacha.[4]
They who would view her size and triumphs,
Can nowhere find her match.

[1] Alexander was a family name of the Macgregors of Glenstrae. In the obituary contained in this MS. is the following entry:—1526 Obitus Gregorii filii Johannis M'Gregor, alias M'Evine M'Allester de Glenschray. This would indicate the period of Alexander as about the middle of the fifteenth century.

[2] This Finlay is the author of several pieces in this miscellany. He is apparently the Finlay M'Nab to whom another composition is attributed, and is called in one place "Am bard maith," *The good poet*. He seems to have been the family bard of M'Gregor, the praise of whose horse he here proclaims in most poetic strains.

[3] Duseivlin was one of the famous steeds of the Feinn.

[4] The beast of Lamacha, "Aidhre an Lamacha," is entirely unknown to the Editor. The animal is called "Beisd," *a beast*, in a subsequent part of the poem. It must have been some animal famous in the country for its ugliness.

Just like the wheeling of the mountain winds,
Is the action of the prancing steed.
Hundreds admire her paces,
Like one in frenzy passing.
Like the point of an arrow this horse,
Famous are all her doings.
Bands of the great witness her course,
As with speed she rushes.
Though far before her stands the groom,
No blunderer is her rider.
Few are the words would tell her praise,
Like birds on wing her movements.
Her triumphs and paces the same,
Whether 'mong rocks or bogs she moves.
Before that horse all men do fear,
When she comes in the trappings of war.
In the troop, the hunt, or the conflict,
That horse a noble horse is.
That horse is all full of spirit,
As fameworthy she follows the banner.
That wave-like steed, hardy and keen,
Will win for her rider the praise of men.
Forth from her stall she takes the lead,
That gentle, great, and active horse.
She will triumph in speed and slaughter,
Till that the day in evening sinks.
Ready to treasure the girdle of gold,[1]
The field with violence shakes.
Startling, rounded, bright, well shod,
Gentle, broad-backed, coloured well.
A horse of such great fame as this,
I long had heard that they possessed.
Where was ever found her match,
Not he, the beast of Lamacha.
Mac Gregor 's the master of that horse,

[1] The girdle of gold would seem to have been the prize conferred upon the victor in a race.

Prince of the house to poets free.
From Banva men do come to praise,
To Albion they do come to seek,
The man who robs from the Saxon,
And e'er puts his trust in the Gael.

Finlay the red-haired bard.

I am a stranger long to success,
'Tis time that I should have it.
'Tis time now to desist,
From satire justly due.
The way that I shall take,
To seek a noble branch,
Is to the Prince of the Gael,
Where are no worthless guests.
To Mac Gregor the brave,
Head of all the schools; [1]
He's neither cruel nor sparing,
To praise him is our duty.
To whom courage is a right;
When summer time comes round,
Peace he never knows,
He's in the throat of all his fellows.
When men of him do speak,
As Gregor of the blows,
'Tis his delight to drive,
Flocks and herds before him.
Of that flock John's [2] the head,

1 The schools of the bards. Many Highland bards at this period were trained in Ireland, of which these poems bear evident marks.

2 In his obituary the Dean enters at 1519, May 24-26, death of John dubh Mac Gregor of Glenstrae, at Stronmelochane. He was buried in Dysart (Glenurchy), north of the great altar, in a stone coffin, upon the 26th of May 1519, on which day there was a great mourning in Glenurchy. The Elizabeth afterwards mentioned was probably the wife of this chief.

The king at lifting cattle,
I myself will sing,
Mouth with mouth at daybreak.
When his sharp-armed men see,
Mac Gregor at the Bealach,[1]
His way so gently soft,
No weight to them their burdens.
Then when war arises,
Proclaimed in enemies' hearts,
It is to him they'd gather,
Clothed in martial dress.
'T is of Mac Gregor's fame,
When fighting 's left behind.
To men not to be cruel,
His castle full of mirth;
When victory I had left
Upon the field of war,
When of the fight I spoke,
Nought loved my patron more.
Though sad, on the stormy lake,
To tell men of my grief,
To have a crew of mariners,
Is best in battle's day.
Remember I'll be with thee,
Mac Gregor without stain,
In face of any foe,
Long, long 's the time.
Gentle Elizabeth,
Change thou my state;
Woman of softest locks,
And of the loftiest brow.

I am.

[1] "Bealach," the modern "Taymouth," was, with the territory around, in possession of the M'Gregors down to about 1490, when it passed by Royal charter into the possession of the Knights of Glenurchy.

The author of this is Duncan Mac Cailein, the good knight.[1]

Who is now chief of the beggars,
Since the famous man is dead?
Tears flow fast for the man,
For beggary has lost its strength.
The orphan is in a piteous case,
Beggary's gone since Lachlan's death.
In every homestead this is sad,
That beggary should want for knowledge.
If he be dead, I've never heard,
Of one that could compare with Lachlan,
Since God created man at first;
It is a source of bitter grief,
That without mother or a father,
Poor beggary should be so weak.
Since that Bretin's son is dead,
Why should I not mourn his loss?
There is no man now on earth
Who can beg as he could do.
Since Lachlan the importunate's dead,
Great's the grief that is in Erin.
Who will now beg a little purse?
Who will even beg a needle?
Who will beg a worthless coin?
Since that rough-palmed Lachlan's dead.
Who will beg a pair of brogues,
And then will beg a pair of buckles?
Who will beg a shoulder plaid?
Whose begging now will give us sport?

[1] This poet is generally supposed, by those who have seen the Dean's MS., to have been Sir Duncan Campbell of Glenurchy, one of the most distinguished of the ancestors of the present noble family of Breadalbane. There are several pieces in the MS. attributed to him. These are remarkable for caustic humour, indulged in in several cases at the expense of the female sex. He almost uniformly receives the title of "An Ridir maith," *The good Knight*. The present piece is a strange satirical elegy on a miser.

Who will beg soles for his shoes?
Who will ask a peacock's feather?
Who will beg an eye for his belt?
Who will mix in any mischief?
Who will beg an old felt hat?
Who will beg a book to read?
Who will beg an early meal?
Who is it wears arms with his dress?
Who will beg for boots and spurs?
Who is it will beg for bristles?
Who will beg for sids and meal?
Who will beg a sheaf of rye?
Who will ask a sporran spoon?
Who will gather without shame?
Since Lachlan the hero is dead.
Who will now afford us sport?
Who will beg for maidens' shifts,
Since old shoe'd Lachlan is dead?
Sad the fate that he should die,
Who will ask men for a rullion?
Who will steal the servant's feather,
And who is it can't tell the truth?
Who likes to travel in a boat,
And likes his old friends to visit?
Who will beg the hen with her eggs?
Who will beg a brood of chickens?
Who will ask the hen's overplus,
After a handful of money?
Who will beg a headless pin?
Who can read as he can do?
That Lachlan should leave no heir,
Is that which mournful makes his death.
Who will beg for a hook and line?
Who will seek for open doors?
Who will beg for unboiled rennet?
Who will beg for anything?
Who won't give a penny to the poor,

And yet e'en from the naked begs?
Who would oppress the very child,
And is cruel to the infant?
Who would beg for wool and butter,
That they may have it, after Lachlan?
Who would beg a woman's collar?
Who is it likes a dirty heap?
Who would beg from young women,
From little dogs and weasels?
Who would take the fire from an infant?
Who would steal e'en the dead?
Who is sick when he is well?
Who on his gruel begs for butter?
More sad for me than this man's death,
Is that he has left no heir.
For fear that beggary should die,
And none be found to keep it up
Do not ye forget the man,
Men of the earth, do ye,
Each of you for himself make rhymes,
My malison on him that won't.
If Lachlan died on Monday last,
Every man will joyful be.
Sad it is that for his death,
None there is who will lament.

Who is now

Gormlay, daughter of Flann, the good wife.

Alas! alas! my own great pain,
Alas! that I've my beauty lost,
To-night sore is my wound,
Since that Mac O'Neill is dead.
Alas! to want the son of Dervail,
Alas! my fate now left behind,

Guaire's hospitality is nought,
Erin's a desert without him.
Alas! for the good king of Banva,
How fair thy form down to this night,
Since he, my life, in battle died,
Nought will I say but alas! alas!
Alas!

The author of this is Duncan M'Cabe.[1]

M'Dougall of bright armour,
A noble chief's thy famous son,
All that I think is true
Of thy fair-formed, prudent child.
'T were better that thy fair head
Were now exposed than mine, kind friend.
Duncan Carrach[2] is his name,
A name that triumphed ever.
Duncan of bravest deeds,
Remember thy first honoured name;
Son of Allan,[3] do not merit,
Reproach thy race did ne'er deserve
Since now that thou art so well known,
With every reason to esteem thee,
To thee is given the foremost place,
Since thou the favourite art of all.

[1] We know nothing of this poet. The name is a rare one, although still existing in the Highlands. He would appear to have been a family bard of the Macdougalls of Dunolly.

[2] In the Dean's chronicle of deaths, contained in this MS., is the following entry in Latin —1512, Jul 13. The death of Duncan M'Dougall, who was slain A.D. 1512, who was the son and heir of Alexander M'Dougall of Dunolly, and Duncan was buried in Ardchattan 13th July. "Carrach" means a *scald head*, from which he seems to have got his name in childhood. The poet refers to his head as now more smooth than his own.

[3] In Innes' Orig. Par vol ii. part 1, p. 115, it is said, on the authority of the Acts of Council, that, in 1478, Colin Earl of Ergile was sued by Alane Sorlesone M'Cowle for warrandice of the lands of Lereage and Wouchtrouch, etc. This is probably the Alan referred to by the bard

True it is thou art indeed
The man to take the richest spoil.
Like a bull that's fierce for fight,
'Tis thus thou goest to make war.
'Tis thou who traversest Cruachan,[1]
Casting thy spear beneath its knolls
Thy fame is as that of the leopard,
Thou art Duncan of Durinis.
Thou quellest quick thy foe,
Thou stainest both hands with blood
Thou cheerest us when we are weary,
Thou art the source of all our joy.
He is the man whom 'tis easiest
In song like mine to praise,
Which among heroes I compose,—
The generous dragon of Connal.[2]
Other fame belongs to him,
The art that is in his gun.
The bravery and skill of Erin
Bound firmly up in all his blows.
Whatever skill a king's son has,
That he has, with no defect
The purest speech has come to him,
This will in thy son be found.
Now I see thee raise the tax,
Truly out of every homestead,
Noble king of bravest deeds,
Descendant of that martial race
Macdougall.

[1] "Ben Cruachan," the highest mountain in Lorn, the ancient territory of the clan Dougall.

[2] Connal Ferry, the remarkable narrow at the mouth of Loch Etive, where the stream at times becomes a salt-water cascade. The name "Connal," "Conthuil," means a *roaring stream*.

The author of this is John M'Ewen M'Eacharn.[1]

A mournful cry amongst Conn's[2] race,
Heavy indeed is now their loss;
As every one now follows John,
Silent they can't be at his grave.
What grief did ever them o'ertake,
The race of Conn ne'er honour lost.
For John each man does weep,
Necessity leads us to his grave;
Sad is the land because of thy death,
Son of the noble race from Allan.
Great is our grief as thee we mourn,
Few are the men that shed not tears.
Sorely has it touched us all,
Grievous the tale that John is dead.
Tidings from the Dun went through the land,
The stranger now does o'er us rule.
Changeful the world down till John's death,
Now they rise not to the fray;
Since then indeed thy race is sad,
This grief now has them sorely wounded.
'Tis grief to them that thou art thus,
Clan Dougall mourn for their great chief;
The conflict of their grief is long,
The tale which now is told is grievous;
Thou messenger who brought the news,
God made thee messenger of evil;

[1] We have no written or traditional account of this poet. He was manifestly one of the bards of the clan Dougall. The difficulty of deciphering the Dean's writing is in this case increased by the peculiar measure of the composition, which is one of those well known to Irish scholars, and where the accentuation is in accordance with the Irish mode. The Editor does not pretend to have deciphered every line with perfect accuracy, but he is pretty well assured of having caught the meaning of the poet throughout.

[2] The clan Dougall, as well as the cognate clan Donald, were held by the bards to have descended from "Conn Ceud chatha," *Conn of the hundred battles*, King of Ireland.

Ere men thy tidings did recite,
Pity they had not lost their ears.
The abundance of my racking grief
Has almost my eyesight ta'en away;
No feeble mourning is 't for John,
Tears for him I cannot shed;
Mourning for our buried prince,
The death of Macdougall of Dunolly.
His was the form of Conn's great race,
Like a nut kernel, fair and rounded;
His death has been a grievous breach,
The very waves sing his lament.
Above the beach,[1] since John has died,
No ceasing is there of men's sorrow;
Men speak not even now of joy,
Since that this grief has on them seized;
Bitter sorrow has them filled,
No word of sport, of music none;
That way is called the sacred way,
That from the beach leads to the grave.
So do men thus mourn their loss,
And women too, who loved thee well.
Shall I from thy soft locks have honour?
In place of it I have but ruin.
I mourn as on thy grave I stand,
All I see makes me lament;
Women will not leave thy grave,
So truly heavy is their sorrow.
Raise up a tomb for our fair prince,
Let it be wide as Cruachan's cell,
That men may see by what they do,
How heavily on them weighs their grief
The clan with weeping do thee mourn,
Their soul is sad, they cannot sleep.
Dougall's race before thy death,

[1] The Macdougalls of Dunolly buried at the old Priory of Ardchattan, on the banks of Loch Etive.

Never did fear the face of foe.
Chieftain, thy death has come on them,
'T would be no boast to rule them now.
Not few the women at John's grave,
Pouring their tears from day to day;
Of women bands even by night,
With bare heads gathering on the plain;
No wonder is 't that they should mourn,
Because of John of brightest fame.
No day can pass but hearts are full
Of this sad tale, that wakes our mourning.
I care not though 't be thus with them,
Though they should feel what I don't like;
Thy death for us is ill to bear,
Sore the state to which it brings us;
I stand amidst the gloom of death,
No word is there of wonted song;
My heart is truly rent in twain,
As we speak of his departure;
Never were we thus before,
That it is grief to ask, how fares he;
'Tis cause of sorrow that he is absent,
I mourn that he is no more with us;
Now that he sleeps in his cold grave,
'Tis melancholy what men feel to tell;
They cannot cease from shedding tears,
Castle and cottage both in sorrow;
The rising tide has swept o'er hills,
So for John do mourn his comrades;
Yet there's no heaving of the sea,
Not of the boisterous sea at Connal;[1]
For thou art mourned, great chief of Conn,
In all the borders of clan Dougall;
The land for thee does seem to weep,
Loud is the cry, with much distress,
From the musicians of Dougall's race,

[1] Connal Ferry, on Loch Etive.

The learned men, and leading bards.
On John's grave lies a heavy stone,
'Tis grief to me to tell the story;
Far otherwise than Neil[1] would wish,
Does every scandal now appear;
Have they no care to see his grave,
Since that John has overcome them?
The race of Conn are now but few,
Since death has ta'en away Macdougall;
No pleasure in the violin's sounds,
Nor writing poetry without him;
Poetry brings no honour now,
Since death has seized the son of Mary;
Few are the mouths that now can tell,
How commanding is her privilege,
Now that on their backs are laid,
Both the heads of the clan Dougall;
That John's great power I do not find
Soon after losing John his father;
May God preserve thy noble nature,
Who wisdom learned from thy Isla[2] teacher;
Horses can't insure a triumph,
Men must leave them, and depart;
After the three, our loss is great,
My heart, in truth, can find no comfort;
Mournful in youth to see such loss,
Death has seized two Johns and Alexander;[3]

[1] There is considerable obscurity about these lines. It would serve to elucidate the meaning if we knew of any feud between this chief and the clan Neil, or any person of the name of Neil belonging to any other Highland clan. The Editor has not been able to find any information on this subject.

[2] The original here is indistinct. The word "noid illeich," made "an oide Ilich," may be "nord Illeich," or "an uird Ilich, *The Isla order*, meaning some ecclesiastical order in Isla, by whom he was educated, or it may refer to the weapons of war for which Isla was famous.

[3] Alexander was Laird of Dunolly in 1493; Greg High. p. 83. His son Duncan Carrach was slain young; Dean's Obit. Greg. Ed. In Innes' Orig. Par. vol. ii. pt. i. p. 114, we find that, in 1451, Stewart Lord of Lorn granted to John M'Alan of Lorn, called M'Cowle, and to John Keir ("ciar," *dark*), his eldest son and heir, etc., twenty-nine marklands of the island of Caruvray, etc. These are pro-

Alexander, whom no restraint could bind,
That I of him should also tell;
Thy breast was stout to the rushing wave,
Thy body now! alas my sorrow;
Never do ye seek again
That John's young heir should go to battle;
That he should stand 'midst battle's storm,
Lest soon he come to his long grave.

The author of this is Finlay M'Nab.

The sluggard's Book of Poems,[1]
If 't were your wish to write in it,
Among what they have left you'll find
Enough wherewith to fill it.
Though many the men there be,
Who cruelly the people oppress,
Never will these be found,
Honoured in famous songs.
Of all the fruits of sluggards,
Though there be of them a thousand,
The house in which these do meet,
They ne'er can by any means reach.
They are both gentle and simple,
Dressed in their Sunday coats;
And yet of all their productions,
It happens we never can hear.
I won't their genealogy tell,
Of their history nothing I know,

bably the two Johns and Alexander of our bard. This holding of the Stewarts may explain the bard's reference to the rule of the stranger.

[1] The word "duanaire," here used in the original, means "a miscellany of poetical compositions." The Dean's MS. is a "duanaire," but not a "duanaire nan strangair," for the Dean seems to have been a most industrious compiler. This piece of M'Nab's is a satire on lazy composers or compilers. It is valuable as showing that the ancient bards wrote their compositions. The number of such books must have been large, although during the course of centuries they seem to have perished with few exceptions.

But that they are out at evening,
Followed close by their hounds.
Dugall, thou art their fellow,
John's son of the polished blade,
In whom flows the sluggard's blood,
Write thou in the Book of Poems.
Write knowingly, intelligently,
Write their history and their life;
Don't bring a poem on the earth,
To have it read by Mac Cailein
Remember this my claim on thee,
Gregor, as thou hast heard
That I have as an obligation,
All thine to put in the Book of Poems.
Let there be nothing in this poem
Of priests or of tenantry;
But nothing of this band there is,
Which is not in the Book of Poems.
The sluggard's

The author of this is Eafric M'Corqudale.[1]

Jewel,[2] who has roused my grief,
Beloved hast thou been of me,
Beloved that joyous, generous heart,
Which thou hadst until this night.
Thy death has filled me with grief,
The hand round which I lived so long,
That I hear not of its strength,
And that I saw it not depart;
That joyful mouth of softest sounds,
Well was it known in every land.

[1] This poetess seems to have been the wife of the last M'Neil of Castle Sween The name M'Corqudale is common in Kintyre.

[2] The word "paidrein," derived from "Paidir," *The Lord's Prayer*, really means *a rosary*.

Lion of Mull, with its white towers,
Hawk of Isla, with its smooth plains,
Shrewdest of all the men we knew,
Whom guest ne'er left without a gift.
Prince of good men, gentle, kind,
Whose mien was that of a king's son,
Guests came to thee from Dunanoir,[1]
Guests from the Boyne[2] for lordly gifts.
Truth it is they often came,
Not oftener than gave thee joy.
Shapely falcon of Sliabh Gael,[3]
Protection to the bards thou gav'st,
Dragon of Lewis of sandy slopes,
Glad as the whisper of a stream;
The loss of but a single man
Has left me lonely, now he 's gone.
No sport, no pleasing song,
No joy, nor pleasure in the feast;
No man whom I can now love,
Of Nial's race down from Nial òg;[4]
Among our women there 's no joy,
Our men no pleasure have in sport,
Just like the winds when it is calm,
So without music is Dun Sween.[5]
See the palace of a generous race,
Vengeance is taken on clan Neil,
The cause of many a boastful song,
And will till they lay us in the grave;

[1] Dunanoir was a castle on the island of Cape Clear, on the south-west coast of Ireland. See *Miscell. of Celt. Soc.* p. 143.

[2] The river Boyne. From Dunanoir to the Boyne included all Ireland.

[3] Sliabh Ghaidheael, a range of hills in Kintyre.

[4] In Innes' Orig. Par. vol. ii. pt. i p. 41, we find that Hector M'Torquil Mac Neil was constable of Castle Sween in 1472. In 1481 the office and lands were conferred on Colin Earl of Argyle. Between these two periods M'Neil would appear to have died, leaving no heir in the direct line.

[5] Castle Sween is an ancient stronghold at the mouth of Loch Sween in Knapdale, said to take its name from Sween of Argyle, who flourished in the thirteenth century; but the Irish annalists make mention of it at a much earlier period. It was probably a stronghold of the Dalriadic monarchs.

And now 'tis hard to bear, alas!
That we should lose on every side.
Didst thou, son of Adam, crush
Any cluster of three nuts,
It is to him thou lovest most
The largest third of them thou 'dst give.
Thus of their husk the topmost nut,
Does to clan Neil, ungrudged, belong.
The bountiful have often poured
Their gifts on the dwelling of clan Neil
The prince, who was the last of all,
Is he who me with gloom has filled.
In half my purpose I have failed,
Jewel, who has roused my grief.
Broken my heart is in my breast,
And so 't will be until I die;
Left by that black and noble eyelid,
Jewel, who hast roused my grief.
Mary, mother, foster-mother of the king,
Protect thou me from every shaft;
And thou, her Son, who all things mad'st.
Jewel, who hast roused my grief.
Jewel.

The author of this is Dougall Mac Gille glas.[1]

Bold as a prince is John[2] in each gathering,
'T were long to sing his race's glory;
Of this there is no doubt 'mong men,
That he is the first of the race of kings.
Mac Gregor of the bravest deeds,

[1] This poet was probably a M'Gregor.

[2] In the Dean's Obits, as already quoted, we find that, in 1519, died John Dow M'Patrick M'Gregor of Glenstray, at Stronmelochan. He was apparently the subject of this laudatory ode. He is called grandson of Malcolm. Accordingly, we find among the Dean's Obits, that Malcolm M'Gregor, son and heir to John M'Gregor of Glenstray, died in 1498.

Is the boldest chief in any land;
Between his gold and Saxons' spoil,
Well may he live in ease and peace.
Choice for courage of the Grecian Gael,
Whose meed of praise shall ne'er decay,
Abounding in charity and love,
Known in the lands of the race of kings.[1]
White-toothed falcon of the three glens,[2]
With whom we read the bravest deeds,
The boldest arm 'midst fight of clans,
Best of the chiefs from the race of kings.
When on Mac Phadrick of ruddy cheeks,
Wrath in battle's hour awaked,
The men who with him share the fight
Are never safe amidst its blows.
Grandson to Malcom of bright eyes,
Whom none could leave but felt their loss,
The generous, gentle, shapely youth,
The readiest hand when aught's to do.
The race of Gregor stand round John,
Not as a weak one is their blow;
The famous race without a fault,
Round him like a fence they stand
Clan Gregor who show no fear,
Even when with the king they strive,
Though brave Gael may be the foe,
That they count of little weight.
Gael or Saxon are the same,
To these brave men of kingly race,
Sons of Gregor bold in fight,
Bend not before the fiercest foe.
Prince[3] of the host of generous men,

[1] The original is "sliochd an row," or "an rudha." It is translated as if the word were "righe," *kings;* but the Editor is in doubt if this be the word meant.

[2] The M'Gregor's glens were Glenurchay, Glendochart, and Glenlyon

[3] "Braineau," the word here translated *prince,* is the ancient Gaelic form of the Welsh "Brenhin," *a king* The word is now obsolete in the Highlands.

To Gregor of golden bridles, heir,
Pity the men whom you may spoil,
Worse for them who you pursue.
Chief of Glen Lyon of the blades,
Shield and benefactor of the Church,
His arm like Oscar's in the fight,
To whom in all things he is like.
Kindness mantles on his red cheek,
Thy praise he justly wins, ungrudged;
Benevolence when to men he shows,
Horses and gold he freely gives.
Mac Gregor of the noble race,
No wonder though bards should fill thy court;
To his white breast there is no match,
But he so famous 'mong the Feinn.
Three fair watches him surround,
Never as captives were his men;
His arm in battle's struggle strong,
Well did he love to hunt the deer.
In mien and manners he was like
The king who ruled amongst the Feinn.
Mac Gregor of the spoils, his fortune such
That choicest men do covet it.
Good and gentle is his blue eye,
He's like Mac Cumhail of liberal horn,
Like when giving us his gold,
Like when bestowing gifts on bards,
Like in wooing or in hunt,
To the Cu Caird[1] among the Feinn.
Fortune attends the race of kings,
Their fame and wisdom both are great,
Their bounty, prudence, charity,
Are knit to them, the race of kings,

[1] "Cu caird," *The artificer's dog*, is an old name for Cuchullin. It is said in Ireland to have originated in Cuchullin having killed the watch-dog of Cullin, artificer to King Cormac; whereupon he undertook to watch himself, and hence obtained the name of Cullin's dog, or Cuchullin, also "Cu caird."

Wine and wax and honey,
These, with the stag-hunt, their delight.
Famous the actions of John's clan,
Like to the sons of the Fenian king;
John himself was like to Finn,
First and chief 'mongst all his men.
Though many sought to have Finn's power,
'Mongst those who fought against the Feinn,
On Patrick's son fortune attends,
His enemies he has overcome
Mac Gregor who destroys is he,
Bountiful friend of Church and bards.
Of handsome form, of women loved,
He of Glenstray of generous men.
Easy 't is to speak of John,
His praise to raise loud in the song,
Giving his horses and his gold,
Just as a king should freely give.
King of Heaven, Mary virgin,
Keep me as I should be kept;
To the great city fearless me bring
Where dwells the Father of the king.
Bold.

FOND[1] are men of being high-born,
Whatever their wealth may be;
Great scorn of the illegitimate,
Who seek to approach the king.
Hear me, though ye may mock,
Ye race of commons and gentles,
The number of famous chiefs,

[1] This is a curious fragment, and is of interest from the references in it to the Highland clans. The writer, who towards the close gives his name as Maol-domhnaich, *Servus Domini*, was apparently the illegitimate son of some man of note, and was in all likelihood a Mac-lean.

Who go to make up my fame.
I'm of the blood of clan Dougal,
A race of unquestioned right;
But brave and bold though they be,
'T is not of them I've my all.
My kinsman is Mac Chailein,
Who freely gives gold to the bards;
Why should I be sorrowful,
My native place is in Earla.[1]
My native place is in Earla,
Clan Donald lie off to the west;
My dwelling is with clan Gillean,
The men who in battle can fight.
Mac Phee of Colonsay,
No stranger is he to my race,
And Mac Niel of Barray,
Of pure and gentle descent.
Mac Nee I also remember,
And also the powerful Mac Sween,
Clan Leod and clan Ranald,
Chiefs from whom I descend.
Cattanachs and Mac Intoshes,
They too are among my friends;
The Camerons and clan Gregor,
The men from Breadalbane who come
Stewarts, though widely they be
Scattered throughout the whole earth,
Old, certain, swift-footed the tale,
That of them was my father's grandmother.
In Balquhidder and Breadalbane,
My friends are numerous found;
Kindly men in bringing aid,
These are my kindred true.
Clan Lauchlan and clan Lamond,
Clan Neil, who learn feats of war;

[1] There is, between Tobermory and Aros in Mull, a place marked in the maps Arile. This was probably the residence of our bard

Friends of mine are clan Tavish,
'Midst their green hills and their braes.
These little vigorous men,
Who dwell in the straths of the land,
I visit M'Dougal of Craignish,
I've a friend besides in Mac Ivor.
Gillean who has come from Mull,
Woman from the race of mariners,
Never did compass the earth,
The man whom she did not attract.
Faithful and steadfast friend,
Chief who was kind to Maol Donich,
In the liking which this man has,
No man more favour could get.
Fond.

The author of this is the Baron Ewen M'Omie.[1]

Long do I feel my lying here,
My health to me is a stranger;
Fain would I pay my health's full price,
Were mine the numerous spoils.
A spoil of white-haired, heavy cows,
A spoil of cows for drink or feasting,
I'd give besides the heavy bull,
If for my cure I had the price.
The herds and flocks of Mannanan,[2]
The sword and horn of Mac Cumhail,
The trumpet of Manallan[3] I'd give,

[1] The Editor has not been able to identify the author of this poetical complaint. During the existence of baronies, with their bailies or local judges, the number of barons or baron bailies in the Highlands must have been large. Of this class was most likely our poet.

[2] An ancient Celtic hero, from whom the Isle of Man takes its name, as well as the district in Scotland called Slamannan.

[3] The Editor has not been able to obtain any account of this person. There is a contraction over the second *a* in the MS., which makes the reading doubtful.

And the quiver of Cuchullin,
Ir, Evir, and Eireamon,[1]
And were I to possess them,
The harp of Curcheoil,[2] which hid men's grief,
The shield of the King of Golnor.[2]
Lomond's[3] ship of greatest fame,
Had I it upon the strand,
All I've seen I'd freely give,
Ere as now I'd long remain.
Long to me appears the coming
Of Alexander Mac Intosh,
That my disease he might drive away,
And thus I might no longer lie.
Long.

No Author.[4]

For the race of Gael, from the land of Greece
There is no place where they can rest;
Doubtless thou would'st much prefer
To raise the Gaelic race on high.
Now that thou risest 'gainst the Saxon,
Let not thy rising be a soft one;
Have your swords with sharpened blades,

[1] The three sons of Milidh of Spain, from whom the Milesian races are descended, according to Celtic story.

[2] The Editor can give no account of these names. The traditions respecting them seem to have perished.

[3] A famous Celtic hero, from whom Ben Lomond and Loch Lomond are said to derive their names.

[4] There is a portion of the beginning of this ode wanting, and we have no means of knowing who the poet was. A reference to the history of the time, and the names introduced into the poem, however, suggest very emphatically the occasion of it. It is addressed to Archibald, Earl of Argyle, Chancellor of Scotland, who was killed at the battle of Flodden in 1513. The Saxons assailed so virulently by the poet are, in all likelihood, not the Lowland Scotch but the English, and the poem is probably a "Brosnachadh catha," or incitement to the rising of the Scotch, and particularly the Argyle men, previous to the disastrous battle of Flodden. This invests the fragment with peculiar historical interest. There seems not to be much of the poem wanting, probably only a few lines.

Let your spears stand by your sides,
Let us not forsake our country,
Let us fiercely, bravely fight.
It is said by the Gael of Banva,[1]
Our fathers did the tale repeat,
And I have heard there was a time,
Long ago, that Innis Aingin[2]
Was ruled by the Fomorian[3] race,
Who raised from it a heavy tax.
Thus for a while the Saxons have
Our country burdened heavily;
And now each clan is full of fear,
And we are plunged in grievous doubt.
But now that a gathering 's begun,
There 's need that chiefs should rouse them up;
For with them, 'tis my opinion,
We will share a common fate.
Who is the man, whom we can tell,
Will from the Saxon save the Gael?
Who in our day has won much fame,
And whose house is truly noble?
Know a man, were he but willing,
Of whom we readily might tell,
His power in Banva widely known,
Men all bound with him to gather.
Archibald of the pointed head,
Of thee it is that men now speak.
Earl of Argyle,[4] I thee beseech,
Be as a hero in the conflict;

[1] Ireland

[2] There was an Innis Aingin, an island in the Shannon, famous as being the place to which St. Ciaran retired to spend the latter part of his life. It is here apparently taken to represent a portion of Ireland. See Mr. O'Curry's Lect. p. 58.

[3] An early race of pirates, said to have infested the Irish coasts. The word is said to be derived from "fo mhuir," *under the sea*, and is supposed to indicate their coming from the low sea coasts of Holland or Denmark.

[4] Archibald, Earl of Argyle, Chancellor of Scotland, who was killed at Flodden in 1513. He is called Iarla "Oirthir Ghaidheal," *The sea-coast of the Gael*, which would seem to be the true etymology of "Argyle."

A hero who shall reign supreme
O'er Gael from the famous land;
Noble, high-born prince of the Gael,
Thou 'lt in apportioned Albin reign
Hero, who 'll desert no fight,
With sword, so long as right remains,
Who for the Gael from Greece, subjection
Ne'er suffer would at Saxon's hand.
The very roots from whence they grow,
Pluck them that thou may'st us deliver,
Suffer not a Saxon hence to live,
After that thou overcom'st them
Burn all their women, ugly in form;
Burn their children, every one;
Burn their black huts, burn them all;
And crush their enmity to us.
Drown their warriors in their streams,
When their accoutrements are burnt.
Cease not, while a Saxon lives,
To drown them weakened in their streams
Remember thou, of ruddy cheeks,
The claims we on the Saxon have;
Oppression and beggary all thy days,
When that their oppression throve
Remember thy own father Colin;[1]
Remember Archibald,[2] father to him,
Remember Duncan,[3] the prosperous,
He who was liberal and friendly;
Remember thou that other Colin;[4]
Remember Archibald[5] as well;

[1] Colin, second Earl of Argyle, and Chancellor of Scotland, who married Isabella, second daughter of Stewart, Lord of Lorn.

[2] Sir Archibald, first Earl of Argyle, called "Gillespuig Ruadh," *Archibald the red.*

[3] Sir Duncan of Argyle, commonly called "Dunchadh an aigh," or *Duncan of good fortune*

[4] Sir Colin of Argyle, called "Cailean iongantach," *wonderful Colin,* and also "Cailean maith," *good Colin.*

[5] Sir Archibald of Argyle, called "Gilleaspuig mòr," *Archibald the great.*

Remember Colin[1] first of all,
He who was brave amongst the Gael.
Remember that they never gave
Their tax from terror of the Saxon;
Much more it now belongs to thee
To see that thou bear'st not this tax.
Now that there is but thy sire's blood,
Of Gael from the famous land,
Let the men together come,
Let them fill with fear their foes.
Let them attack the Saxon now,
Wake thee up then, son of Colin,
Golden-haired one, war is begun,
'T is not good to sleep too much.
Great.

The author of this is Duncan Mac Dougall Maoil.[2]

The history of the secret origin of John Mac Patrick,[3]
Why should I conceal it?
What belongs to his race is not feeble,
The bearing of that race we love.
Seldom of a feeble race it is,
Among the Gael of purest fame,
That inquiry of their origin is made,
By the men who read in books.
Firm the belief to them and me,
During the evening time so dark,

1 Sir Colin of Argyle, called "Cailean òg," *young Colin*, son of Neil, son of Colin, called "Cailean mòr," from whom the family take the patronymic of "Mac Chailein mhòir," *The son of great Colin.* Cailean mòr was also called "Cailean na Sreang," from a mountain between Loch Awe and Lorn, where he was killed in a feud with the Macdougalls. (MS. Gen. not. of fam. of Argyle, pen. Ed.)

2 This author is one of the writers of the MS., and a Macgregor. By referring to the genealogy at p. 143 of the MS., we find him designating himself as Dunchadh daoroglach, Mac Dhughaill, Mhic Eoin riabbaich — Duncan the apprentice, son of Dougall, son of John the grizzled.

3 John dow M'Patrick M'Gregor of Glenstrae, who died in 1526.

That in the blood of noble kings
Were the rights of true clan Gregor.
Now that I'm by thy green dwelling,
Listen, John, to thy family story:
A root of the very root we are,
Of famous kings of noble story.
Know that Patrick was thy father,
Malcom father was to Patrick.
Son of black John, not black his breast,
Him who feasts and chariots owned.
Another John was black John's father,
Son of Gregor, son of John the lucky.
Three they were of liberal heart,
Three beneficent to the Church.
The father to that learned John,
Was Malcom, who his wealth ne'er hid,
Son of Duncan, surly and small,
Whose standard never took reproach.
His father was another Duncan,
Son of Gillelan of the ambush,
Noble he was, giving to friends,
Son of the famous Hugh from Urquhay.
Kennan[1] of the pointed spear,
Of Hugh from Urquhay was the father.
From Alpin,[2] of stately mien and fierce,
Mighty king of weighty blows
This is the fourth account that's given
Of thee, who art the heir of Patrick.
Remember well thy back-bone line,
Down from Alpin, heir of Dougal.
Twenty and one, besides thyself,

1 This is manifestly a mistake for Kenneth. The person meant is Kenneth M'Alpin, King of Scotland. In the genealogy given in p. 144 of the MS, this Kennan is said to have been high King of Scotland, to distinguish him from lesser chiefs, whom the Celts called kings.

2 Alpin, King of the Scots, who flourished in the beginning of the ninth century. Several of the links in the Macgregor genealogy must be wanting in this poem. Even the name of Gregor, from whom the clan is called, does not appear at all.

John the black, not black in heart.
Thy genealogy leads us truly
To the prosperous Fergus M'Erc.
Of thy race, which wastes not like froth,
Six generations wore the crown.
Forty kings there were and three,
Their blood and origin are known.
Three there were north and three to the south,[1]
After the time of Malcom Kenmore.
Ten of the race did wear the crown,
From the time of Malcom up to Alpin.
From Alpin upwards we do find
Fourteen kings till we reach Fergus.
Such is thy genealogy
To Fergus,[2] son of Erc the prosperous.
How many are there of thy race,
Must have been from thee to Fergus!
Noble the races mix with thy blood,
Such as now we cannot number.
The schools[3] would weary with our tale,
Numbering the kings from whom thou 'rt sprung.
The blood of Arthur[4] is in thy bosom,
Precious is that which fills thy veins;
The blood of Cuan, the blood of Conn,[5]
Two wise men, glory of the race.
The blood of Grant in thy apple-red cheek,
The blood of Neil, the fierce and mighty.
Fierce and gentle, at all times,
Is the story of the royal race.

The history.

[1] Both sides of Loch Tay, the ancient Macgregor territory, are still called "Tuaruth" and "Deasruith," *north and south sides.*

[2] First king of the Dalriadic Scots.

[3] The schools of the bards which abounded in Scotland and Ireland at this period, chiefly in Ireland, as may be discovered from this collection, for most of the composers were undoubtedly trained there. Poetry and genealogy were the chief branches studied.

[4] Arthur, King of the Strathclyde Britons, from whom the Campbells also are said to be descended.

[5] "Conn ceud catha," *Conn of the hundred battles,* King of Ireland.

The author of this is Mac Eachag.[1]

Displeased am I with the south wind,
Which hinders the coming of John,[2]
And that he is kept away out,
On his way from the north to M'Leod.
Janet's son, of whitest sails,
Well would he like to cross the sea;
But the south wind will not listen
To John, William's son of swift steeds.
By night or by day as I sleep,
From the beach I see to the north,
The rushing bark of whitest sails,
The bark of him who stays defeat
This is the fame which every man
Awards to M'William from Clar Sgith,[3]
An ardent, white-toothed, ready youth,
One who for aught he did ne'er mourned.
This is the eighth day without John,
Heir to M'Leod of bluest eye;
Like he is in mien and strength
To the great house of liberal heart.
Cheerful he is, does nought conceal,
Such is the fame of sharp-armed John.
In battle's day he takes the lead,
Ever ready fame to win.
William's son, my foster child,
Son to Janet, royal her race,
Did I but hear thou cam'st from the north,
All my gloom would disappear.

[1] This name is very indistinct in the MS, and cannot be given with certainty.

[2] In 1480, William Macleod of Dunvegan was killed at the battle of the Bloody Bay, and was succeeded by his son Alexander, usually called "Alastair Crotach," or *hump-backed* (Greg. High. p. 74). The charters give no information as to John, if a son of this William Macleod. But William's father was John, whose father was also in all likelihood a William, and this John, whose *floreat* was early in the fifteenth century, might be the person here meant.

[3] The old name for Skye, and throws some doubt on the derivation of the name "Sgiathanach," usually accepted.

The author of this is Mac Gillindak,[1] the man of songs.

Lords have precedence of chiefs,
It has been so from the beginning;
It is commendable in young men,
That each should have knowledge of this.
The first who was lord of this land
Was Duncan beg (little) of the great soul,
He who as a legacy has left
Their bravery to clan Gregor.
Duncan, great by many spoils,
Was the blessed father of Malcom;
Grandfather he was to princely John,
Him who never broke his pledge.
Gregor, excellent son of Duncan,
Was son to John, and was his heir;
Famous man he was of the country,
From the bright shore of Loch Tullich,[2]
Swarthy John, so pure in speech,
Princely son of John M'Gregor,
Hunter of the well-formed deer,
He like a king aye led the fight.
Malcom of unbending truth,
Know thou John, succeeds his father,
Southwards in fair Glenurchay,
Handsome he was amongst its valleys.
The first place 'mong their ancestors
Is given by the Saxon to clan Gregor,
Of whom were three chiefs loved the hunt,
And were most active in the fight.
In the days of Conn of hundred battles,
I heard of something like this,

[1] We have no tradition respecting this poet. But he must have been a bard of the M'Gregors'. The allusion to the Feinn will be understood by referring to the war-song of Gaul.

[2] Elsewhere translated Loch Tummell. "Tolve" is the word in the original. Loch Tullich lies at the head of Glenurchay.

Of Finn of spears and sharp sword,
Cumhal's son of famous deeds.
That of Erin the hunting and lordship
Belonged to Mac Cumhal of long locks,
Patrimony and lordship he had n't
Over the lands of the race of Gaul.
Forest right they had all his life,
From Kerry north to Carn Valair.
But he possessed the old rights
Which previously were his.
From Hallowmas on to Beltin,
His Feinn had all the rights.
The hunting without molestation,
Was theirs in all the forests.
Many the tributes I cannot tell,
Belonged to Finn and his men.
Tribute in Erin possessed
By Mac Cumhail from the forests.
A noble's forest right to the Feinn,
On the banks of every stream.
But Malcom's large tributes
Did not belong to Mac Muirn;[1]
Finn himself would never hunt
Without first asking leave.
The hunting of Scotland, without leave,
Belongs, with its spoil, to Malcom.
Constant in the hunt together
Are M'Gregor and his fierce men,
No oftener did the blood-red hounds
Enter the fort of clan Boisgne
A fighting band of chieftains
Arose with him in battle's day,
Men whose dress sparkled with gold,
Men who conquered in the fight.
The head of clans and of huntsmen

[1] This is usually the name of Gaul, but here it is Finn, whose mother's name was Muirn.

Is the common fame of his race.
No trial of bravery or skill
Will show weakness in M'Gregor.
Many in his halls are found together,
Men who carried well-sharped swords,
Red gold glittered on their hilts,
The arms of the lion of Loch Awe.
Harmonious music among harps,
Men with dice-boxes in their hands,
Those who leave the game of tables,
Go and lead forth the hounds.
Mac Gregor of red-pointed palms,
Son of Dervail, the Saxon's terror,
No hand like his amidst the fight,
He 't is that ever victory won.
Liberal he ever was to bards,
Gifts which Mac Lamond[1] knows to earn
Famous for managing his hounds,
A hand so ready with its gifts.
Mary, who stands by his side,
Of noble mind and handsome form,
Poets unite to give her praise,
Her with cheeks as berries red.

Lords

The author of this is Finlay, the red-haired bard.[2]

The one demon of the Gael is dead,
A tale 't is well to remember,
Fierce ravager of Church and cross,
The bald-head, heavy, worthless boar.
First of all from hell he came,

[1] Probably the chief bard of the MacGregors.

[2] It has been suggested to the Editor that this poet might have been the chief of the Macnabs, the chief of this period being Finlay Macnab of Boquhan; and we know that the Macnabs counted themselves of the same lineage with the MacGregors. There is much in the composition given here, however, to indicate his being an ecclesiastic.

The tale 's an easy one to tell,
Armed with the devil's venomous spear.
But he was surely, firmly bound,
Ere quitting the black house of hell,
To the same stronghold to return,
And leave the Star of Paradise.
Then, when came the black-skinned boar,
Many the devils in his train,
Each of them with horrid sound,
Their voices all in one loud strain.
Lest that he should nothing have,
It was apportioned by Mac Ruarie,[1]
As a covenant firmly fixed,
That in hell he 'd live a dog.
Righteous and just is now the claim
Which Allan has against the devils.
Whatever share may be their own,
He, I think, should have much glory.
'T is time to cease now from that band,
Of horrid sounds, and cruel heart.
Mac Ruarie from the ocean far,
Wealth thou 'st got without an effort.
'T is a report we can't neglect,
For with Columba I must meet,
'T is a report that fills the land,
Bald-head Allan, thou so faithless,
That thou hast, not thine only crime,
Ravaged I[2] and Relig[3] Oran.
Fiercely didst thou then destroy
Priests' vestments and vessels for the mass.

[1] We learn from Greg. High. pp. 65, 66, that Allan MacRuari, great-grandson of Ranald, and chief of clan Ranald, was one of the principal supporters of Angus, the young Lord of the Isles, at the battle of the Bloody Bay; and that he also followed Alexander of Lochalsh in his invasion of Ross and Cromarty in 1491, receiving a large share of the booty taken on the occasion. The poet describes him as a sacrilegious marauder.

[2] The ecclesiastical establishment at Iona. The Reformers had probably less to do with the destruction of the buildings in Iona than is generally thought.

[3] The church of St. Oran in Iona.

Thou art Inche Gall's[1] great curse,
Her revenue and stronghold spoil'st;
Thou art the man whose heart is worst
Of all who followed have thy chief,
Save one who stands at his left hand,
And he, Mac Ruarie, is thy brother.
Now thy fight we never hear,
But from the cross we hear thee cursed;
The two are good who are about thee,
Black indeed they are in form.
At the time thou first mad'st war,
There was the Abbot's horrid corpse,
Besides that other lawless raid
Against Finan[2] in Glengarry.
Thine own cruel, hateful deeds,
Have cursed thy bald-head body, Allan,
Just as crime will always do,
Revenge itself on who commits it.
The country side, with its protest,
Has stamped mad rage on Allan's face.
Thine own country and thy friends,
Thou hast cruelly oppressed.
The last of thy goodness was lost
Between the Sheil and the Hourn.
'T is no wonder thou didst keep
Far away, Allan, from the gallows.
The fame which men had given thee,
Extends to thy mother and thy sister.
Time it is to cease from satire,
Worthless, cruel son of Ruarie.
Though learning which helps not manners,
The sound of thy wailing is pleasant.
The one demon.

[1] The Hebrides were known as "Innse-gall," or *the islands of the strangers*, probably since the rise of the kingdom of the Norsemen there.

[2] The church of Kilfinan, at the eas end of Loch Lochy, where is still the burying-place of the M'Donells of Glengarry.

THE son has been found like his father,[1]
Above all chiefs whom we have known,
His bearing, countenance, and mind,
And with me he dwells in Lewis.
The knowledge and mind of a chief,
With which he'll make prosperous times.
I say of this young son we've got,
That he is just another Roderick;[2]
How like each other are their locks,
His father's honour to his ringlets.
In battle, too, how like the praise
Of Torquil[3] and his famous father.
Of all that in Torquil's time may come,
None of his friends shall suffer loss,
Great deeds and victories will be,
Such as Mac Calman[4] may relate.
Many his gifts which we might praise,
Torquil of the famous race;
His are a hero's strength and vigour,
Which he brings into the fight.
I say of him, and say in truth,
Since I have come so well to know him,
That never was there of his age
Better king who ruled in Lewis
To him belonged the "Cairge mhordha,"[5]
The richest jewel sailed the sea,
Given it was to Mac Vic Torquil,
With which to reach his people's land.

[1] There is no author's name given for this spirited eulogy. The author was probably a family bard of the Siol Torcuil, or M'Leods of Lewis.

[2] Roderick M'Leod of Lewis was head of the Siol Torcuil, or sons of Torquil, in 1493. (Greg. High. p. 73.)

[3] Torquil was second son of Roderick M'Leod of Lewis, the eldest having been killed in the battle of the Bloody Bay. Torquil was forfeited for harbouring Donald dubh, son of Angus Og of Islay. (Greg. High. p. 73.)

[4] Probably the chief bard of the Siol Torcuil.

[5] "Cairbhe" is *a ship*. This was probably the name of Torquil's galley, although spelled "cairge" by the Dean.

Mac Ruarie of cheerful music,
Had also the old cleaving sword,
Another jewel of sure effect,
'T was given him by the King of Aineach.[1]
Since he so many presents had,
'T was needless for him to go and seek
A shield he had cleft in the head,
Another jewel, sounding loud.
Without he had a noble herd
Of horses, with their trappings red;
'T would n't suit a man like him
Not to have many swift-paced steeds.
His was the Du Seivlin,
M'Leod's, whom the bards would sing.
'T was hard for those to take that horse,
Whoe'er they were that might him seek.
Torquil had many youths
Who never trembled in battle,
Who for his race seized on all lands,
A race that aye the conflict loved.
Not braver of his age was Cuchullin,
Not hardier was he than Torquil,
Him of the ready, vigorous arm,
Who boldly breaks through any breach.
Beloved though Mac Vic Torquil is,
I can't enough his beauty praise;
He who is fair as he is the brave,
The key to every woman's heart.
There is no son of king or chief
Of whose fame we've ever heard,
Though we've had much to do with such,
That better are to us than Torquil.
Catherine,[2] daughter of Mac Cailen,
Whose soft hand's worthy of thy race,

[1] "Aineach," a castle of the O'Kanes, within a few miles of Derry. The King of Aineach was chief of the O'Kanes.

[2] Catharine, daughter of Colin, 2d Earl of Argyle, who married Torquil Macleod of the Lewis.

Daughter of the Earl of Argyle,
Best of the women we have found.
To our isle we've got a woman,
Branch of a great and famous tree.
Daughter of Mac Cailen, young and gentle,
Whose locks in flowing ringlets fall.
The son.

The author of this is Gilliecalum Mac an ollave.[1]

The cause of my sorrow is come,
This year has not prospered with me;
Foolish who cannot understand
How my grief has on me come;
He who cannot understand
How my grief has come at once;
Since these wounds my body got,
Such wounds I've got I mourn.
Pleasant now, though bitter too,
To mourn my sad distress;
Sorrow fills my inmost heart,
Great was my love for him who's gone;
My heart is broken in twain,
No wonder it should be so;
My body has neither flesh nor blood,
Like a strengthless sufferer.
'T is no wonder if I so grieve
For Margaret's[2] son who now is gone,
Remembering all his virtues,
And that chiefless we are left.

[1] It has been said in a previous note that nothing is known of this poet. But the present composition would indicate his being one of the celebrated Beatons, physicians and sennachies to the Lords of the Isles. There is a charter of lands in Islay, written in Gaelic by Fergus Beaton in 1411. There were several of the family whose name was Gilliecallum. "Mac an Olaimh" means *son of the physician*.

[2] Margaret Livingstone, daughter of Sir Alexander Livingstone, married to Alexander Lord of the Isles.

Sore is the loss that he is gone,
Now that in the world we're weak,
My grief now that thy days are ended,
Is the injury done by Angus[1]
Though it be hard for me to part
With John's[2] son of sweetest speech,
What is worst of all is this,
That ne'er to his place he'll return.
Though I were from happiness far,
Pursued by my foes' reproach,
Whatever good might me o'ertake,
From them never would I buy.
No wonder though heavy my heart,
As another lord's seen in thy place,
That my whole man should be feeble,
Now that my king is dead.
Bitter is my pain since he left,
'T is easy the tale to relate,
'T is hard my great sorrow to bear,
For the hero so famous who's gone
Great is my grief, and no wonder,
My mourning is true, sincere;
That which sorely has me pained,
Is that in Albin we've no race.[3]
Now since that I must leave,
As others with reproach me load,
Since he is dead, I fain would go,
Away from the rough isles of Albin.
Yet 't is sore for me to leave,
Although I feel that go I must,
Now that my beloved is dead,
My country I must leave behind.

1 Angus Og, son of John last Lord of the Isles, who fought the battle of the Bloody Bay against his father.

2 John, son of Alexander Lord of the Isles.

3 Both John and Angus, sons of the last Lord of the Isles, died before their father. He was forfeited, and died in a monastery in Paisley.

Last of all, what grieves me is,
And truly the cause is enough,
That my beloved will not return,
To Islay on this side of Innis.[1]
And then, besides, it is so sad,
That this during his time should come,
Wringing hearts, and bodies rending,
Without revenge being in our power.
No men on earth could think
How ready he was foes to crush,
'T was nothing both for us and thee
That champions should come against us.
But thy foes now have pierced thee,
Pity we had not with thee died,
Fair-handed, sweet-voiced son of Mary,
That we should have none to help.
He of the fairest countenance,
Our loss is not to follow him.
All the fame thou didst enjoy,
Was such as to thy race belonged,
They who had the long curled locks,
Whose company men loved much.
Now their hearts are sore depressed,
Every comfort poor without thee.
'T would be hard to find one like me,
And that from my lord I had,
The fellowship of priests and poets;
These are plenty, but his hand absent.
When others to the banquet go,
Of the honour my share is this,
Ever to mourn in grief unchanged,
And of sorrow drink my fill.
'T is sad for me I do not follow,
Much his absence do we grieve;

[1] This word is spelled "Eithnis," and "Einis," and "Eins." It is translated *Angus* and *Innis*. But it is difficult to decide which it means; probably "Inis" in Ulster, where the Lords of the Isles had extensive possessions.

And then o'er that which makes me mourn,
Many the other men who weep.
Many the men before our time,
Who by sorrow were brought low;
And what I've said does find its proof,
In a tale I've told before.
"I've heard a tale of old," etc.[1]
As follows in another place.
The fellow of this noble man,
Foster-son of Caoimh and Conull.

Blind Arthur Mac Gurkich.[2]

The assembled fleet at Castle Sween,
Pleasant tidings in Innisfail,
Of all the riders of the waves,
A finer ship no man e'er owned.
Tall men did manage the ship,
Men, I think, to urge their way;
No hand without a champion,
A slashing, vigorous, noble band.
With coats of black all were supplied,
In this bark, noble their race,
Bands with their brown, broad belts,
Danes and nobles were they all.
Chieftains with ivory and gold,
The crew on board this brown-sailed ship,

[1] See above, p. 50.

[2] Who this blind poet was the Editor cannot say. He can find no notice of him anywhere, nor of the attack on Castle Sween, which he describes. He was an Irish bard, and composes in the Irish dialect, making use, like the later Irish poets, of language much more difficult to understand than the older composers. The Editor encountered more difficulty in reading this piece, than in reading any other in the Dean's MS. "Broin" is an ancient word for a *troop* or *band*, and "cleath," "comhlan," "nòs," are words for a *warrior*, but these words are entirely obsolete; so "glantair," as the comparison of "glan," is unknown in the modern language. There is a manifest attempt in the composition to use obsolete words; but the Editor trusts the meaning has been correctly rendered.

Each with a sheaf of warriors' spears,
Shields on their hooks hung round the sides.
Wide-spread wings, speckled sails,
Bearing purple, all of gems;
A long, handsome, gentle band,
Stood along the stout-made spars.
The blue sea at the swift ship's prow,
The ship laden when the tide is full;
Wattled baskets full of swords,
With shields all brought on board the bark.
Fair women, too, were in the ship,
Modest, their beds were placed on high,
Spotted cushions were provided,
Couches for the nobles' wives.
Spotted coverings of fine linen,
This was the covering of the ship;
Handsome, easy, as she rocked,
Purple linen round each mast.
No hardened hands, no tightened belt,
Nor roughened by their usual toil;
Heroes were there, nor did they labour,
Bands of men of sweetest lips.
We heard not of so many nobles,
Of our isle from labour free;
From Erin princely champions,
A troop with soft and ruddy hair.
Not ship of all did she count swifter,
None has there been nor will be,
No sigh, no sorrow, and no grief,
Nor is there any end of all.
No ship of ships she counted swift,
Full of princely men she is,
Scattering gold among the bards,
While round the ship resounds the sea.
Many the men of sword and spear,
Many men quick in fight to mix;
Down by the sea the fighting men,

Above, the gentle women were.
Who is he provides this fleet,
At Castle Sween[1] of many hills?
A vigorous man who fears no blast,
His masts upraised, seeking his right
John M'Sween,[2] sail thou the ship,
On the ocean's fierce-topped back;
Raise aloft the vessel's masts,
Let thy bark now test the sea.
A leading wind then for them rose,
At Kyle Aca[3] as rose the tide;
The speckled sails were roundly bellied,
As John ran swiftly for the land.
We entered the cheerful anchorage
In the bay of fruitful Knapdale;[4]
The noble hero, lordly, shapely,
Comely, masted, swift, victorious,
He was then near Albin's walls,
Helpful, welcoming his men.
Fair was then the youthful hero,
Abundant dew distilling round,
Favourable at Slieve Mun's[5] streams,
To Mac Sween, him of Slieve Mis.
Speakers then come near to ask,
They deal as with him of sharpest eye
Branches are laid beneath their knees,
To welcome those of valour great.
Their safety in each harbour nook
Suffers from the welcome they give John
The men of Albin's isles then come

[1] We can find no trace in our history of this attack by the Irish Mac Sweenys on Castle Sween. The event cannot be of a very ancient date, as the Mac Sweenys are not a very ancient tribe in Ulster

[2] One of the Mac Sweens or Mac Sweenys of Slieve Mis in Antrim.

[3] This cannot be Kyle Akin in Skye, but is probably the ancient name of the entrance to Loch Sween

[4] Knapdale, on the west coast of Argyle, south of Crinan.

[5] Not known to the Editor, but is probably on the Knapdale side of Loch Sween.

With welcome from the narrow sea
The men who sweetest are that sing,
Tenfold welcomes to him bring.
For a while there was a conflict,
Between them and our men of song;
They come at last to know full well,
How fair the hill from whence came John.
Then did we fight at Castle Sween,
Just as a slender, furious hawk,
We set us down around that rock,
Every limb endowed with strength.
We pierced the bodies of our foes,
Just as a serpent fiercely wounds;
Our thin-bladed, well-edged swords,
The foreigners' bodies fiercely hacked.
We raised the cry of great Mac Sween,
Amidst the rolling of the sea;
True it is that roll won't help,
Broad-backed, long although it be,
Their javelins have no power to pierce
The shields which our brown coats protect.
Rathlin of the sharp rocks, hears
The music of our ringing swords.
The thin-bladed sword, in Europe best,
A spear that swift obeys the wish,
What shield on earth can it resist?
Fierce and fearless Erin's sons.
John Mac Sween of stratagems,
With his thin, powerful, cutting sword,
He whose shield is spotted brown,
A blind man found him brave and wise.
The assembled fleet.

Isabella Ni vic Cailein.[1]

Pity whose complaint is love,
Whate'er my reason thus to speak,
'T is hard to separate from its object,
Sad 's the condition I am in.
The love which I in secret gave,
Of which I 'd better never speak,
Unless I quickly get relief,
Withered and thin I 'll soon become.
The man whom I have so loved,
A love I never must confess;
Has me put in lasting bonds,
For me a hundred times 't is pity.
Pity.

The author of this is Duncan Og.[2]

Seven arrows me assail,
Each of the arrows does me wound,
Between me and my God they come,
Such of my body is the desire.
The first one of these is Pride,
Which wounds me under my belt,

[1] This lady is elsewhere called "Contissa Ergadien," *the Countess of Argyle* From the name given her here, she would appear to be a daughter of the Earl of Argyle, but she might as countess be styled Ni vic Cailein, or the daughter of Colin. We know that Sir Colin Campbell of Glenurchy, was uncle and tutor to Archibald, first Earl of Argyle, and that having himself married Margaret, eldest daughter of Stuart last Lord of Lorn, he arranged a marriage between his nephew and Isabella, the second daughter, who became Countess of Argyle. She was most likely the authoress of these lines, but we have no key to the piece of domestic history to which they refer.

[2] There is a Duncan Og Albanach among the writers of religious poetry in the MS., who was most likely one of the Mac Vurrichs, and the author of these lines. It is hardly necessary to say that the poet refers in this composition to the seven mortal sins of the Roman Catholic Church

Often of a triumph it has me spoiled,
Which otherwise I might obtain.
The second arrow is Lust,
To whose power I'm such a slave;
Since this shaft trait'rously has me pierced,
I cannot live beyond its reach.
The third of these arrows is one
Which pierces 'midst my very joints;
Laziness, which suffers not
That I the right way e'er should chuse.
The fourth arrow is Covetousness,
O God, 't is mournful where it wounds;
Deliverance I can never have
From this load of earth upon my back
The fifth of these shafts is Gluttony,
Which has brought me much reproach;
Besides that it pains my self-respect,
From it my body is not free.
The sixth sore arrow of them all
Is Anger, which me from men divides;
May Mary stay them when they're shot,
Otherwise I have no help.
The seventh shaft does pierce the eye,
Envy, which grudges others' good;
A shaft which, however we may feel,
Is one which never does us good.
When these in his hand the enemy takes,
Many they are by 's arms destroyed;
He never shoots but what he strikes,
And never strikes but what he kills.
Son of God, I'll place a pater,
And the apostles' creed as well,
Between me and these wounding arms,
With five psalms, or six or seven.

Seven

The author is Murdoch Albanach.[1]

'T is time for me to go to the house of Paradise,
While this wound 's not easily borne,
Let me win this house, famous, faultless,
While others can tell of us nought else.
Confess thyself now to the priest,
Remember clearly all thy sins;
Carry not to the house of the spotless King,
Aught that may thee expose to charge.
Conceal not any of thy sins,
However hateful its evil to tell;
Confess what has been done in secret,
Lest thou expose thyself to wrath.
Make thy peace now with the clergy,
That thou may'st be safe as to thy state;
Give up thy sin, deeply repent,
Lest its guilt be found in thee.
Woe to him forsook the Great King's house,
For love of sin, sad is the deed;
The sin a man commits in secret,
Much is the debt his sin incurs.
This is a sermon for Adam's race,
I think I 've nothing said that 's false,
Though men may death for a time avoid,
'T is true they can't at length escape.

[1] Murdoch of Scotland was the first of the great race of Macvurrichs, bards to Macdonald of Clanranald. From all that can be gathered regarding him, he was an ecclesiastic, and, according to the measure of light he possessed, a man of earnest and sincere religion. It was not known, until this volume of Dean M'Gregor's was searched, that any remains of his compositions existed; but here we find several, all very much of the same character. There is one long poem to the cross, which appears to have been modelled on the early Latin hymns. Murdoch of Scotland, or Muireadhach Albanach, would appear to have lived between A.D. 1180 and 1220. Mr. Standish H. O'Grady, late President of the Ossianic Society of Dublin, kindly sent to the writer some years ago a poem, still preserved in Ireland, containing a dialogue between Muireadhach and "Cathal Cròdhearg," the red-handed Cathal O'Connor, King of Connaught, on the

Thou who hast purchased Adam's race,
Their blood, their body, and their heart,
The things we cherish may'st thou assail,
However we may them pursue.
'T is time

The above Murdoch.

That there should be in God's Son's heart
A sinner like me, how great the tale,

occasion of their embracing a religious life. Cathal's "floruit" is known to have been between A.D. 1184 and 1225. As the lines are curious, they are inserted here.

Cathal croibhdhearg agus Muireadhach Albanach maraon iar n-dul anns na braithribh dhoibh, cecinerunt :—

A Mhuireadhaigh, meil do sgian, go 'm bearram inn do 'n Aird-righ,
Tabhram go milis ar mòid, 'us ar dhà trillis do 'n Trianaid,
Bearraidh mise do Mhuire, an bhreath so is breath òr-chridhe,
Do Mhuire bearr am bàrr so, a dhuine seang, sùlmhal so
Anamh leat, a mhaca ghlan, sgian tar do bharr do'd bhearradh,
Fa mhionca rioghain bhinn bhog, a cireadh a cinn thugad
Gach ré n'uair do foilcthi dhuinn, us do Bhrian ard bhairr chladh-ùir,
'Us do fhoilcinn uair eile ri stuaidh fhoilt-fhinn Bhoroimhe
Do ghrinn comh-shnamh 'us Ua Chàis, air linntibh fuara Forghais,
Air teacht air tìr leis o'n linn, do ghrinn 'us Ua Chais coimhshling,
An dha sgian so leath air leath, do rad dhuinn Dunchadh Cairbreach,
Níor b'fhearr dhà sgian de sginibh; bearr gu mìn a Mhuireadhaich.
Meil do chlaidheamh, a Chathail, chosnas am Banbha braonsgathaidh,
Ni chuala gun fhachuin d'fhearg, a Chathail chuanna, chròdheirg,
Dion air fhuachd 's air ainteas inn, a inghin uasail Ioachaim,
Dean ar coimhead 's an tìr theith, a ro gheag mhìn, a Mhuire.

A Mhuireadhaich

TRANSLATION.

Cathal Crodhearg and Murdoch of Scotland, on entering among the brethren, sung :—

Murdoch, whet thy knife, that we may shave our crowns to the Great King,
Let us sweetly give our vow, and the hair of both our heads to the Trinity.
I will shave mine to Mary, this is the doing of a true heart,
To Mary shave thou these locks, well-formed, soft-eyed man
Seldom hast thou had, handsome man, a knife on thy hair to shave it,
Oftener has a sweet, soft queen, comb'd her hair beside thee.
Whenever it was that we did bathe, with Brian of the well-curled locks,
And once on a time that I did bathe, at the wall of the fair-haired Boroimhe,
I strove in swimming with Ua Chais, on the cold waters of the Fergus.
When he came ashore from the stream, Ua Chais and I strove in a race.
These two knives, one to each, were given us by Duncan Cairbreach,
No knives of knives were better, shave gently then, Murdoch
Whet your sword, Cathal, which wins the fertile Banva,
Ne'er was thy wrath heard without fighting, brave, red-handed Cathal,
Preserve our shaved heads from cold and from heat, gentle daughter of Joachim,
Preserve us in the land of heat, softest branch, Mary

Murdoch.

And that there should to me be given,
On my lips to have the cross of Jesus Christ.
Jesus Christ, sanctify as thou art wont,
My two feet, and my two hands,
Sanctify me of thy good will,
Even my blood, and flesh, and bones.
I never cease committing sin,
Because that my body loves it well;
May consecration come from afar,
Upon my head and on my heart.
Glorious great One, save thou me
From every grief which me has seized,
Ere I 'm laid beneath the turf,
May my way be plain and smooth.
That.

The author of this is Murdoch Albanach.

Thou Trinity, do thou me teach,
Thou Lord, whose praise all men must sing,
Thou Trinity, come on my tongue,
Bless it in thy judgment great.
Holy Trinity in the heavens,
Strengthen thou my spiritual arms;
Come to, and dwell in my heart,
Thou head of all thy holy race.
Guide thou my hand, and teach my heart,
Teach my eye, thou King of truth;
Come to my voice, move on my tongue,
Quicken my ear, and bless my lips.
This is the mouth which ye have torn,
Which checks men's conflicts, nought forgets;
This is the tongue that ne'er spared speech,
Bless it, Beloved of my soul.
From thee, O Trinity, alas! O Trinity,

Let healing come, speak thou to me;
There is, as in the white-wood oak,
In me a sinful, corrupt heart.
Though sinful, I never man destroyed,
Ne'er did I steal, O Son of God;
Never did my hand slay man,
For Mary's love, answer thou me.
'T is true, I've made lying refuges,
Deceived by lies of men of fame,
Building on others' lie my lie,
O King, shall I in this succeed?
Thou who in me prayer begett'st,
'T is no sin to follow thee;
'T was neither righteous men nor great,
But God a refuge found for me.
No man in this world can me teach,
But only thou, O Lord, alone,
None keepeth truth but heaven's King,
To His wisdom none is like,
If I am in the way of truth,
My tonsure vow requires it all;
If, O Trinity, on a lie I rest,
Lead me to the way of truth.
Earth or clay shall not me cover,
But waves of judgment, little the wrath,
Nothing else shall be to hide me,
But, O King, burning red-flamed fire.
Trinity, thou mad'st this world,
Both of fire and of earth;
Of earth and fire all men are made,
So at the end it will be found.

GENEALOGY OF THE MACGREGORS.

John son of Patrick, son of Malcom, son of John the black, son of John, son of Gregor, son of John, son of Malcom, son of Duncan the little, son of Duncan from Srulee, son of Gilelan, son of Hugh of Urchy, son of Kenneth, son of Alpin; and this Kenneth was head king of Scotland, in truth, at that time; and this John is the eleventh man from Kenneth, of whom I spoke. —And Duncan the servitor, son of Dougal, son of John the grizzled, wrote this from the books of the genealogists of the kings; and it was done in the year of our Lord One thousand five hundred and twelve.

THE ORIGINAL GAELIC

OF

THE BOOK OF THE DEAN OF LISMORE

WITH A

MODERN VERSION.

THE ORIGINAL GAELIC.

A houdir Ossan M'Finna.

Di chonna mee tylych finn, is ner vai tylych teme trea,
Aggum di chonna mee scheve, di vontir in ir in nea
Di chonna mee tylych art, far lar vac donna binni
Far is farre ne agga mi. Di chonna mee tylych finn
Dane vaga mir a chonna mee, chonna m'ynlain fa ynna
Owcht is mark na vagga ea Di chonnek mai tylych finn
Goym ree ni iyg noch gi olk, za vil er mo chinni.
Sin serra marroine o faynna, dyth chonna ma tylych finn
Di chonna mee tylych.

A houdir so Ossin

Is fadda noch ni nelli fiym, is fadda liym in nycheith ryr
In lay dew gay fadda zoyth, di bi lor fadda in lay de
Fadda lwmmi gych lay za dik, ne mir sen di cleachta dom
Gin deowe gin danyth cath, gin wea feylim class dlweth
Gin nenith gin choill gin chrut, gin fronith crewi gin zneiwe gray
Gin deillych ollom zor, wea gin neilli, gin oill fley
Gin chin er swrri na er selgi, in da cherd rey in royth me
Gin dwlli in glaow no in gath, oichane ach is derrich dow
Gin wraith er ellit no er feyg, ne hawle sin bi wane lom
Gin loeg er chonvert no er chon, is fadda noch na nelli fiym
Gin errith gaske gnaath, gin nimert mir abaill linni
Gin snaw zar leithire er loch, is fadda, etc.
Din teill mir a ta mee, is trowig er bea mir a ta sinn

MODERN VERSION.

An t-ùghdair Ossian mac Fhinn

Do chunnaic mi teaghlach Fhinn, 'us nior bu teaghlach tioma tréabh,
Agam do chunnaic mi sabh, de mhuinntir an fhir an dé.
Do chunnaic mi teaghlach Airt, fear le'r mhac donna binn,
Fear is fearr ni faca mi. Do chunnaic mi teaghlach Fhinn.
Do ni fhac mar a chunnaic mi, chunnaic mi mac an Luinn fa Fhinn.
Och ! is mairg na faca e. Do chunnaic mi teaghlach Fhinn.
Do'm ré ni ioghnadh gach olc, dha bheil air mo cheann.
Sinn saora marruinn o phèin. Do chunnaic mi teaghlach Fhinn
Do chunnaic mi teaghlach.

Is e ùghdair so Ossian.

Is fad an nochd na neula faim, is fada leam an oidhche an raoir,
An la an diugh ge fada dhomh, do bu leor fada 'n la an dé,
Fada leam gach la a thig, ni mar sin bu chleachdadh leam
Gun deabhtha gun deanamh catha, gun bhi foghlum cleas dlù
Gun nigheanaibh, gun cheòl, gun chruit, gun phronnadh cnaimh gun ghniomh gré,
Gun tuilleadh fhoghluim gheire, bhi gun fheill, gun òl fleidh,
Gun chion air suiridh, no air sealg, an da cheard ri an robh mi,
Gun dol an gleò no an cath, ochan ! ach is deurach domh,
Gun bhreith air eilid no air fiadh, ni h'amhuil sin bu mhiann leam,
Gun luaidh air chonbheart no air chon, is fad an nochd na neula faim,
Gun eiridh gaisge ghnàthaich, gun imirt mar a b'àill leinn,
Gun snàmh d 'ar laochruidh air loch, is fad an nochd na neula faim,
Do 'n t-saoghal mar a ta mi, is truagh ar bith mar a tha sinn,

Menir a tarruing clach, is fadda, etc.
Derri ni feyni far noiss, is mee Ossin mor m'finni,
Gesticht re gowow clokki, is fadda, etc.
Faye a phatrik zocin o zea, fiss in nini in bea sinni
Gith serrir marrien roith locht, is fadda, etc.
Is fadda.

Auctor hujus Ossin.

La zay deacha finn mo rayth, di helg er sleyve ny bau finn
Tri meillith wathyon ny wayn, ne zeaath skaow vass in ginn
Ossin is vinni lwmmi di zloyr, bannicht foiss er anmyn finn
Agus innis gay wayd feyg, hwtti er sleyve ny ban finn.
Ga mor lewe crathamar slee, or ni deatha voylte in loy
Di hutti er sleyve ny ban finn, di zeyith lay fin nyth wlygh
Innis doyf royth gith skayle, bannith er a waill gin zoyth
A bayig eaddith no ermmi, a doll leive a helg gi lay
Di weith eaddith agus ermmi, a doll leine a helg mir senni
Ni weith feanee zeiwe ym zoe, gin leynith roylle is men
Gin chottone schee schave, gin lurych sparri zeyr zlynn
Gin chenvart clooth di choirrith, s zay ley in norn gi fer
Gin skay neynith warryth boye, gin lanni chroye eskoltith kenn
A nearryth in doythin fayn scheath, ne royth nath bi zer no finn
Is schea a barri enicht is awge, ne zeath lav vassa chinn
Doll in dastill a choyn zill, gi aggin er farri mir finn
Cath eggr a choymir schear, a helg er sleyve ni bau finn
A phatrik ayd chinni ni glar, di balin grann vass ir ginni
Noyr a hwyth finni r gonni da binni seirri agus schear
Gow gyir o chnok gow cnok, a meskeith hork is feaygh
Di weith finn agus brann, nane swe selli er in tleywe
Gyth fer rewe in nayd helg, no ger eirryth kolg in feark
Di leggymir tre in cowe, a barri lowe syth way gi garga
Warwe gith cowe zewe da eyg selli fa neyd yn eyll na hard
Di hwtti vi meill feyg bar er a zlann di weith fane tleyve
A haggus eyg agus arbe ne zarne selgi mir sen reywe
Gir bee deirrith ir selgi hear, a clarre oyd ni glar is ni glok
Deich kayd kow fa lawre oyr hutti fa leon x c tork
Di huttidir lyne ni twrk, a roynith ni helg er in lerga
Mir a weyg r lanith is r lawe di verdis air er in telga
A phatrik ni baichill fear, a wakka tow hear no horri
Selga in lay raid lin a waynew fin bi woyth no sen

'Nam sheanair a tarruing chlach, is fad an nochd na neula faim.
Deireadh na Feinn far nis, is mi Ossian mòr mac Fhinn,
Ag eisdeachd ri guthaibh chlog, Is fad an nochd na neula faim.
Faigh a Phadruig dhuinn o Dhia, fios an inbhe am bi sinn,
Gu saorar marrainn roimh lochd, is fad an nochd na neula faim.
Is fad.

Is e ùghdair so Ossian.

La dhe 'n deachaidh Fionn mo ghràidh, do shealg air Sliabh nam ban fionn,
Tri mile de mhaithibh na Feinn, na deagh sgiathan os an cionn.
Ossian is binn leam do ghlòir, beannachd fòs air anam Fhinn,
Agus innis cia meud fiadh, thuit air Sliabh nam ban fionn.
Cia mòr luath chratham ar sleidh, oir ni deachaidh uait a luaidh
Do thuit air Sliabh nam ban fionn, do theidh le Fionn nam fleadh.
Innis doibh romhad gach sgeul, beannachd air a bheul gun ghò'
Am bitheadh éideadh no airm, a dol leibh a shealg gach lò ?
Do bhitheadh éideadh agus airm, 'dol leinn a shealg mar sin,
Ni bhitheadh Fian dhiubh a 'm ghuth, gun léine sroil is min,
Gun chotan 'us i seimh, gun luireach 'us barr geur glan,
Gun cheannbheart cloch de chorr, 's a dha shleagh 'an dorn gach fir,
Gun sgiath nimhneach bheireadh buaidh, gun lann chruaidh a sgoltadh
cheann,
An iarraidh an domhain fa seach, ni robh neach bu gheir no Fionn,
Is e a b'fhearr fhineadh 'us agh, ni dheachaidh lamh os a chionn,
Dol an tasdail a choin ghil, cia againn fear bhàrr mar Fionn ?
Gu h- eagar chaidhmir siar, a shealg air Sliabh nam ban fionn.
A Phadruig oide chinn na cleir, do b'aluinn grian os ar cionn,
'An uair a shuidh Fionn m'ar coinnimh, do binn sear agus siar,
Guth gadhar o chnoc gu cnoc, a mosgladh thorc agus fhiadh.
Do bhi Fionn agus Bran, 'nan suidh seal air an t-sliabh,
Gach fear dhiubh 'an eud seilg, no gur eireadh colg am feirg,
Do leigeamar tri mile cù, a b'fhearr lùth 's a bha garg.
Mharbh gach cu dhiubh sin da fhiadh, seal fa'n deachaidh iall 'an aird
Do thuit se mile feidh barr, air a ghleann do bhi fo 'n t-sliabh
Na th' agaibhse fhiadh agus earb, ni dheanadh sealg mar sin riamh.
Gur b 'e deireadh ar sealg shear, a chleirich oide nan cleir 's nan clog,
Deich ceud cu fo shlabhraidh òir, thuit fo leòn deich ceud torc,
Do thuit leinn na tuirc, a rinn na h-uile air an leirg.
Mar bhitheadh ar lann 'us ar lamh, do bheirdeas àr air an t-seilg
A Phadruig nam bachull fior, am faca tu shear no shoir,
Sealg an la ri d' linn, o Fhianaibh Fhinn bu mho na sin ?

Ach sen selga a roinith finn v'alpin ni minni blayth
Gar ni goyllane ansi cheille, gi bi winni laym ane lay
Lay za deach.

Actor hujus Ossin.

Lay za deach say zai keill, Patr[k] zrynn ni bachal . . .
Rug e in tossin less er wurn, gow was aa gi . . sl . . .
Is di bail awzail uoid, Ossan nan roak nach teym
Coo in tein neaach gin a loyith, smow chur groym er feanow fynn
A cleryth ni bachill brek, bi wor ym beacht zut reid lin
A churri a wrayr a znaath, ne wai zaw er fanaw fynn
Onyth harly zut gin noine, a Ossin gin doll nane dey
Bee say er chathris gi braa, how gathris di znaa nyn fane
Kegit blyin di bein boa, a geyskych reid choel syth heill
Ne hynossit zut gow maik, a luit eacht a rin feanow fynn
Fa ranew in doyn traane, wa agginn fene er gyth . . .
Keiss ga hokwail gow fane fin, na noe in tegwail . . .
Ne reive ansyth si doythin vor, nach da bi chor bea na . .
Ne reive in nalwe nin lann brek, a darveith . . .
Da nynnosit zeive in ness, a Ossin nin gress noch mein.
Coo yn tein neach bi zar lave, wa sreyith . . .
Mor in feine, a churris orm, a cleyrrith oyd nyth f . . .
Ni hynossit gow lay looin, ne way loye . . .
Onyth harlyth how nane dey, a Ossin da dane . . .
Coo nyth leich bar lat mait skay, ri dol din ane ansyth gath
Oskir is keilt is gowle, is m'lowith nyn lanni maath
Fa hymchill v'kowle ayl boyin di bi raa si chath
Farzone fullych m'ynreith is kerrill ri sneive zaath
Dermin daath alin gyn nawle, re hor skaath chin bi waath
Collyth m'cheilt er wley mynni, kyrkeith curri nyn genk maath
Agus rynnith m'ynreith, myrychin nar wenyth in gaath
Felane foltinn bi wakith ind, agus garryth in deim narv
Derring m'doyrin gyn none aygh m'garryth bi waath law
Me fene is g. m'smail is dyryth darrith m'ronane
Tre mek nyth kerd gyn chalk, re oyr hentyth di barm yark
Mir a zana ma zut goo, a cleryth wor furt nyth mynni
Cha noch banit dossyth din nane ach gith fer fane a braath a zille
Soo id chaithir is gawe di fenni is wayassi in narm gi ler
Gi ein neach ga bi zar laiwe, hanyth o chaaith guss in nane
Hanyth reith lochlin er ler, daor done skaa by wor gnaa

Ach sin sealg a rinn Fionn, mhic Alpainn nam mionn blath,
Thar na gòlan anns a chill, gum bu bhinne leams' an la.
La dh' an deachaidh.

Is e ùghdair so Ossian.

La de 'n deachaidh se do 'n chill, Padruig grinn a bhachuill . . .
Rug e an t-Ossian leis air mhuirn, gu bhitheas e . . .
'Us do b'aill leam fhaghail uait, Ossian nan ruaig nach tioma, [Fhinn?
Co an t-aon neach gun a luaidh, 's mo chuir de ghruaim an Fiannaibh
A chléirich a bhachuill bhric, bu mhòr am beachd dhuit ri d' linn,
A chur ann am briathraibh gnàthaichte, na bha a dh'agh air Fiannaibh
O na tharladh dhuit gun on, Ossian gun dol 'n an deidh, [Fhinn.
Bith-sa air chaithris gu bràth, thu'g aithris mu ghnàth nam Feinn.
Caogad bliadhna na 'm bithinn beo, ag éisdeachd ri d' cheòl 's a chill,
Ni h innisinn dhuit gu m' eug, a liuthad euchd 'rinn Fianna Fhinn.
Fearainne an domhain trein, bha againn féin air gach . . .
Cìs 'g a thogail gu Feinn Fhinn, air neo an teugbhail . . .
Ni robh anns an domhan mhòr, neach da 'm bu chòir
Ni robh ann an Almha nan lann breac, a gharbh . . .
Da 'n innisid dhoibh a nis, Ossian nan greas nach . .
Co an t-aon neach bu gheire lamh, bha . . .
Mòr a phéin a chuireas orm, a chléirich oide . . .
Ni h-innisinn gu la luain, na bha a luaidh . . .
O na tharladh thu 'n an déidh, Ossian da deanadh . . .
Co na laoich b' fhearr leat mu 'd sgéith, ri dol do 'n Fheinn anns a chath?
Osgar 'us Caoilt 'us Gall, us Mac Lughaidh nan lann maith,
Fa thimchioll Mhic Cumhail aille, buidheann do bu réidh 's a chath,
Fearghon fuileach mac an rìgh, 'us Caruill r'a 's nimhe gath,
Diarman dathta aluinn gun umhal, do fhuair sgiath chinn bu mhaith,
Collaidh mac Chaoilt air fleadh mìne, Corca curaidh nan geang maith,
Agus Roinn mac an rìgh, muirichinn nach mìn 'an cath,
Faolan folt-fhionn bu mhac Fhinn, agus Garaidh an dion nàmh,
Dearuinn mac Dobharain gun on, Aodh mac Garaidh bu mhaith làmh,
Mi fein 'us Garaidh mac Smail, 'us Daoire darrach mac Ronain,
Tri mic a Cheaird gun cheilg, ri 'r thionndadh do 'm b'arm dhearg.
Mar a dheanadh mi dhuit guth, a chléirich mhòr Phuirt na mionna,
Cha b' aithne dhomhsa de 'n Fheinn, ach gach fear dhiu bh' a breth a gheill
Suidh 'n ad chaithir 'us gabh do pheann, 'us gu faigheas an arm gu léir
Gach aon neach do 'm bu gheir làmh, thainig o chathaibh gus an Fheinn.
Thainig righ Lochlainn air lear, Daire donn sgiath bu mhor gné,

Di wraa keiss errin er koyne, fane deyryth r sloyg gyth ler
Hanyth ith chawr zar wane, twoa dey hug ass gi knok
Carbryth loaechr bi waath lawe, iiij chayth slane gow port
Vii caythin hanik in nane huggar in near o lea cuynni
Ne . . . sa nyth deacha rir gerrow, oo roe zein slane o zaryth dwnni
Is sai waa na chawlyth long, daryth deown syth hylych fene
xxx caath feit di loyith nath dea woyin dar der feine
Waa ga weeow er in trae, cown krer bi lawe gin locht
Ruk sloyg nyn hynea zeive, is di hog ea kenni reith er knok
Cown m'reith wllith nin eacht, agus dollir nan greath trom
Di zagamir er in traa er ym bayth fo zar tonni
iij mec doytith ga bi rane, yth toythit o lar yn long
Fer tenni is kerkil a flwk, a zaik sinni a gorp gi lommi
Oor armyth neyn reith grekga, agus forni nyn beyme trome
Di zagamir fa zaar byve, is ner aig synn in vyve fa bron
iiij mec reith lochlin bi a chasgr sein de neive arm
Ne tre balwe one vorrin or, neyn deacha sayd voyn ach marg
Re in doythin ga bi wor, Dare done skayth bi zall gnaa
Di zaig sinn sin a chorp er trae, er ni lot fo wail nyn nane
Di loyew in doythin trane neyn deacha woyn fene sin nar
Ach reith ni franki mir hea an lyn say brea er in nail
Er eggill in oskir wll, cha di leggi ay voyeni er lar
Gow glen baltan mir ta hest, is and di zawe ay foss is tawe
Er traye fintrath ni goyn fer in churri ni sloye in tar
Er reow in doythin trane, di zoil sein fene er sar
Di bimmi o reith r narm, leich a waa marve er in lar
Di bimmi clawe agus skayth na blaya har er in traye
Er traye fintraithin nyn port, di bimmi ann corp ferrane
Di bimmi leich fa zar byve, is di bimmi ann fyve ar
Phatrik V'Alpin ail, neyn danith zar wane wo rae
Ach da cath eggr gyn locht is ny roif in gorp slane
Cath di clanni bisskyni zeive, boein noch char vennyth in law
Cath di clanni mornyth nyn grath is in darne lay clannow smail
Er fr lawsyth ath halgin trane, say zaik sin dar wane sin nar
Coyk cathin eggr zar sloyig a legga woyn er in tra
xxxth ca feizit gin rath, deechcayd feithyit gith cath zeive
Zarremay loyg zar zoynn, nach dranik er toynn a reiss
A halgin da wreggrin clar, o baillait deym pen gych skail
Gow dukgai caa zawryth nyth glann, noch cha danik ken r lay
Di rynni sin a gawli long, agus argit trome in reith
In noor sin eydda sin neycht, in neirrin er gi lea dee
A Phatrik matha ny mynn an id keilli a waym bass
Cur feyn talla her mo knees oss aggit hay fiss mo skail

Do bhreith cis Eirinn air Chonn, fa 'n deurach ar sluagh gu léir.
Thainig de chobhar do 'r Feinn, sluagh do thug as gach cnoc,
Cairbar leobhar bu mhaith lamh, ceithir cathan slan gu port,
Seachd cathan thainig de 'n Fhéinn, thugar tri an car o leth Chuinn,
Ni mor nach deachaidh ghearradh na robh dhinn slàn o Dhaire donn.
Is e bha 'n a chabhlach long, Daire donn 's a theaghlach féin,
Deich cath fichead de shluagh, nach deachaidh uainn do 'n tìre féin,
Bha ga 'm feitheamh air an tràigh, Conn crithear bu làmh gun lochd,
Rug sluagh na h-Innia dhoibh, 'us do thog e ceann rìgh air cnoc,
Conn mac rìgh Ullaidh nan euchd, agus Dollar nan gniomh tròm,
Do dh' fhàgamair air an tràigh, air am bàthadh fo ghàir tonn.
Trì mic Dubhtaich dha 'm bu threun, a teachd o lar an long,
Feartan is Cearcul a phluic, do dh' fhàg sinn an cuirp gu lom.
Omhar armaicht nighean rìgh Greige, agus Forna nam beuman tròm,
Do dh' fhàgamar fo ghàire baoibh, is nior fhàg sin an aoibh fa bròn,
Ceithir mic rìgh Lochlainn, a chosgair sinn de nimh arm,
Na tri Balaidh o 'n Bhorruinn shoir, ni 'n deachaidh iad uainn ach mairg,
Rìgh an Domhain ge bu mhòr, Daire donn sgiath bu gheal gné,
Do dh' fhàg sinn a chorp air tràigh, air a lot fo bhuille na Feinn,
De shluaghaibh an domhain tréin, ni 'n deachaidh uainn féin 's an àir
Ach rìgh na Fraince mar e, ainlinn 's e breith air an àil,
Air eagal an Osgair oill, cha do leig e a bhuinn air làr,
Gu Gleannabaltan mar tha 'theisd, is ann do ghabh e fois 'us tàmh.
Air tràigh Fionntraigh a chuain, far na chuir na sloigh an t-àir,
Air righribh an domhain tréin, do dh' òl sinn féin ar sàr,
Do b' iomadh o fhraoich ar n' arm, laoich a bha marbh air an làr,
Do b' iomadh claidheamh 'us sgiath, 'n am bloighibh shear air an tràigh,
Air traigh Fionntraigh nam port, do b' iomadh ann corp fhearàn,
Do b' iomadh laoich fo ghàire baoibh, 'us do b' iomadh ann faoibh àir.
A Phadruig mhic Alpain àil, ni 'n d' thainig de 'r Feinn o thràigh,
Ach da chath eagar gun lochd, agus ni 'n robh an corp slàn.
Cath de chlannaibh Baoisgne dhiubh, buidheann noch char mhean an làmh,
Cath de chlannaibh Moirne nan grath, agus an darna le clannaibh Smàil.
Air bhur làmhsa a thailginn thréine, 's e dh' fhàg sinn de 'r Féinn 's an àir,
Coig cathan eagar de 'r sluagh, a leigeadh uainn air an tràigh,
Deich cath fichead gun rath, deich ceud fichead gach cath dhiubh,
De dh' àireimh sluaigh Dhaire dhuinn, nach d' rainig air tonn a rìs.
A thailginn da freagrann cléir, o b' aill leat uam féin gach sgeul,
Gu tugadh cath Ghabhra nan gleann, noch cha tainig ceann ar la
Do rinneadh sinn a gabhail long, agus airgiod trom an rìgh,
An t-òr, 's an eideadh, 's an ni, 'an Eirinn air gach leth di
A Phadruig mhaith nam mionna, ann ad chill am faigheam bàs ?
Cuir féin talamh air mo chneas, o 's agad tha fios mo sgeul.

Ossin o taa tow skeith, dane a noss di heith gou bass
Gau turnigin is ear tlws, is gew Dea mowch gi lay
Ar sleyve Seyane la luain, agus ni sloye er a lar
Meichall is mur is mac Dey, dy hoyrt fene er an law
In da espil deyk si wlay gi clerych may is gi faye
Edrwme agis effrin or di wi gi croy er my lay.
Lay.

Auctor hujus Osseane m'fynn.

Anvine in nocht nart mo lawe ne ell mi coozein er laar
Is nee enyth zof waa bronych ym zebil trog sennorych
Troyg gi neith cheddeyth doif scach gi dwn er twne talwon
Re tarring clach a hallinn gow relling hulchin talzing
It ta wrskal aggwme zut er ir zi wuntir phatrik
Estith re astenyth inn schal beg er tocht zin talgin
Brwin di rinnyth in swnn er sleywe quoalgein moelyth lwmm
Di churri er feanow phail ywir in ta hunwail
Da drane din wrwin wroyth chur finn er clan morn
Agus in trane elli zeit ormss is er clannow biskneith
Hugas fregryth nar choyr er m'cowle v'tranewoyr
Hurd nach bein fada fa smacht is nach danyth doo geilleicht
Di weit Finn fada na host in leich nac burras a cosga
Fer gin noyin gin eggill nor a quayl in doo regryth
Is sea coyrra di raa rwm flath eanyth ny vane finn
Bea tou schell a tarring clooch ma in deyt how in weit wronyth
Di zeyrris is sin ra erg soss o vak cowle a rinzerga
Sea lenn me din nane awnyth cathrow chath croychalm
Fastir miss ag in nane verrir royssa my wraa feyn
In lwcht a wa gim heit ann is da in deit id tame gi anvin
Faa meith in coythrlyth croo din nane in gath crwnvonyth Anvin
Ymyth nac gin anyth ann da in tallyth tame gyth anvin anvin
Anvin in nocht cley mo curp creddwm di wraer padrik
Eddir lawe is chass is chenn, it tame ullith gi anvin anvin
Anvin.

A houdir so Ossin.

In soo chonnich maa in nayne, di chonnich ma caynan is goole
Finni is oskir mi vacki rynith is art is dermit doone

Ossiain, o tha tu sgìth, dean a nis do shìth gu bàs,
Gabh d' ùrnuighean 'us iarr tlus, 'us guidh Dia moch gach la,
Air sliabh Sion la luain, agus na sluaigh air an làr,
Michal 'us Muire 'us mac Dhé' do thoirt féin air an laimh.
An da abstol deug 's a bhlaith, gach cleireach maith 's gach faidh,
Edaram agus Ifrionn, oir do bhi gu cruaidh air mo la.
La.

Is e ùghdair so Ossian mac Fhinn

Anmhunn an nochd neart mo laimh, ni bheil mo choimhghin er làr,
Is ni ioghnadh dhomh bhi brònach, 'am ghiobul truagh seanarach,
Truagh gach ni cheadaich domh, seach gach duine air tuinn talmhainn,
Bhi tarruing chlach a shallain, gu relig thulaich an tailghin,
Tha ursgeul agam dhuit, air ar dheadh mhuinntir, Phadruig,
Eisd ri fàistneachd Fhinn, seal beag air teachd do 'n tailginn.
Brughainn do rinn an sonn, air sliabh Chuailgne maola lom,
Do chuir air Fianaibh Fail, aobhair ann do thionail.
Da thrian de 'n bhrughainn bhreagh, chuir Fionn air Clanna Moirn,
Agus an trian eile dheth ormsa, agus air clannaibh Baoisgne.
Thugas freagradh nar choir, air mac Cumhail mhic Threunmhoir ;
Thubhairt nach bithinn fad fo a smachd, 's nach deanainn da géilleadh.
Do bha Fionn fada 'n a thosd an laoch, nach b' fhurasd a chosgadh,
Fear gun on gun eagal, 'n uair a chual an dubh-fhreagradh,
Is e an còmhradh do radh rium, flath ainbhtheach na Feinn, Fionn,
Bithidh tu seal a tarruing chlach, ma 'n d' theid thu 'na bhith bhrònach,
Do dh' eireas sin ri feirg suas, o mhac Cumhail rinn-dhearg,
Is e lean mi de 'n Fheinn ainbhtheach, an ceathramh cath cruaidh-chalm,
Fasdair mise aig an Fheinn, bheirear roimhse mo bhreth féin, [mhunn,
An luchd a bha ga 'm sheideadh, ann is do 'n teid, A ta 'm gu h-an-
Fa mi an comhairleach crodha, do 'n Fheinn an cath cruinnbheum.
Anmhunn,
Iomadh neach gun aithne ann, de' an talamh ta 'm gu h-anmhunn,
anmhunn,
Anmhunn an nochd chabh mo chuirp, creideam do bhriathra Phadruig,
Eadar làmh 'us chos 'us cheann, a ta 'm uile gu h-anmhunn anmhunn.
Anmhunn.

Is e ùghdair so Ossian.

An so chunnaic mi an Fheinn, do chunnaic mi Conan 'us Gall,
Fionn 'us Osgar mo mhac, Roinn, 'us Art, 'us Diarmad donn,

M'lowith kynkeith ni galge garrith derk is ey beg
Is ey m'carrith nor heyme ni tre finni is fed
Glass is gow is garri galwe nin gead is conane brass
Gole is cwin m'gwille sokkith m'fynni is bran
Keilt m'ronane ni gath doywn coylin is leym er glemm
Is caedith a fronith or is fer one woyne var by vinni
Baynith m'Brassil ni lanni m'chromchin tenni m'yn smail
Agus oskir m'carrith zerve ni tre balwa is ni tre skaill
Tre boyane zlinni schroill tre rwell o voynith reith
vii mic cheilt ni glass tre zlassni zlessra nyn ser
Tre beath chnoki durt be veddeis fa wurni znath
Deach m'eithit vorni vor oissi teacht er boie id tad
In soo a chonich ma in nane boyine eall di chenchyth koyll
In dimchill ossin is inn swle zlinni di fronfre or
Fer loo is kerrill croye di verdeis boye er gyth catht
Fay canym is felune feall di chonnik mi ead in soo
In soo chonni.

A houdir so ossin m'finn

Innis downe a phadrik nonor a leyvin
A wil neewa gi hayre ag mathew fane eyrrin
Veyriss zut a zayvin a ossinn ni glooyn
Nac wil neewa ag aythyr ag oskyr na ag goolle
Ach is troyg ni skayl channis tuss cleyrry
Mis danew chrawe is gin neewa ag fane eyrrin
Nac math lat a teneir vee tow si caythre
Gin keilt gin noskyr weith far zutt is taythyr
Beg a wath lwinsi wee ym hew si caythree
Gin keilt gin noskyr weith far rwm is maythir
Is farr gnwss vee neyve re agsin raa am lay
Na wil doyr si grwnnith vea aggit gi hymlane
Innis dwne a halgin skayli ni caythryth noya
Verinsi zut gi hayre scaylli cath gawrraa
Ma sea skayll ni cathrych zeawris tuss a hannor
Gin netow gin nagris gin nenkis gin nanehoyve
Ka id muntir neyve is oyssil fayne eyrrin
Vil kroyss na gree na deilli sead cleyrri
Ni heynin is ni fane ni cosswil eayd ree cheyll
Neir zlass glayrre wea geyrre sprey
Er zraw tenni phadrik na fagsi ni demyh
Gin nis di ree noya ber a steach ni fayni.

Mac Lughaidh geangach nan colg, Garaidh dearg, 'us Aodh beag,
'Us Aodh mac Garaidh nach tioma, na tri Fionna 'us Fead
Glas, agus Gobh agus Garaidh, Galabh nan gead 'us Conan bras,
Goll agus Crudhain mac Ghuill, Socach mac Fhinn agus Bran, [glinne,
Caoilte mac Ronain nan cath, deagh dhuine coimhlinn agus leum air
Is e a cheud a bhronnadh òir, 'us fear o 'n bhonn bharr bu bhinne,
Baithean mac Brasail nan lann, mac Croimchinn dein mic an Smaill,
Agus Osgar mac Garaidh ghairbh, na tri Balbh 'us na tri Sgeil,
Tri buidhinn Ghlinne Sròil, tri Ruaill o mhonadh Righ,
Seachd mic Chaoilt nan cleas, tri Glasa o Ghlasraidh nan saor,
Tri Beathach chnoic an Duird, do bhitheas fo mhuirn a ghnàth,
Deathach mac Fhichit a Bhoruinn mhoir, os a teachd air buaidh a taid.
An so chunnaic mi an Fheinn, buidheann fhiall do cheann 'chadh ceòl.
An timchioll Ossiain 'us Fhinn, siubhail ghleann do bhronnadh òir,
Fearluth 'us Caruil cruaidh, do bheireadh buaidh air gach cath,
Fa canaim 'us Faolan fiall, do chunnaic mi iad 'an so.
An so chunnaic.

Is e ùghdair so Ossian mac Fhinn

Innis duinn a Phadruig an onoir is leinn,
Am bheil neamh co h-aighear aig maithibh Feinn Eirinn ?
Bheirinnse dhuit a dheimhin, Ossian nan glonn,
Nach bheil neamh aig d' athair aig Osgar no aig Gall.
Ach is truagh an sgeul a chanas tusa chléirich,
Mise deanamh chràbhaidh 's gun neamh aig Feinn Eirinn.
Nach maith leat a d' aonar bhi d' shuidh 's a chaithir
Gun Chaoilt, gun Osgar bhi marriut 'us d' athair ?
Is beag am maith leamsa bhi am shuidh 's a chaithir,
Gun Chaoilt, gun Osgar, bhi marrium 'us m'athair
Is fearr gnuis mhic neimh ri fhaicinn réidh do la
No na bheil de dh' or 's a chruinne bhi agad gu h-iomlan
Innis duinn a Thailginn sgeul na cathrach naomha,
Bheirinnse dhuit co h-aighear sgeul catha Ghabhra
Ma 's e sgeul na cathrach, dh' iarras tusa a sheanair,
Gun iotadh gun ocras, gun airceas, gun aimeamh.
Ge iad muinntir néimh, is uasal Feinn Eirinn,
Am bheil cruas nan cridhe, na diolsa iad a chléirich
Ni h-ionann 'us na Feinn, ni cosmhuil iad ri cheile,
Ni air ghlas clàr a bhi ag iarraidh spéidh
Air ghràdh teann a Phadruig na fàgsa na daimhe,
Gun fhios do righ neimh beir a steach na Feinn.

A houdir soo Ossein.

Annit doif skayle beg er finn, ne skayle nach currein soym
Er v'cowle fay math golle, fa cowin sen rame ray
Di wamyn beggane sloyeg, ag essroyg nyn neggin mawle
Di chemyn fa holta yr trae, currych mor is ben ann
Keigit leich zownych mane leich, fa math er gneeit er gych gart
Fir rar ness is marg a cheith, di gowmist er gi ter nert
Derrymir wlli gi dane, ach finn no wane is gowlc
Dethow churrych fa hard keym wa na reym scoltyth nyn donn
Ne yarnyth tam in na techt gir zoywe calle si fòrt ynaa
Yth techt dey her in ness derre ass m'cayve mnaa
Gilli a darli no syth graanne, is ser mayne nossyth dalwee
In nynin hanyk in gane, di waymin feyn rompyth sorve
Heg thuggin gu pupaill finn, is banneis gi grin doyth
Reggir m'kowle na heiner, in bannow beinn gin toyth
Darrit in reith fa math drach, gi hard di neyn dath zlan
Ca trawe as danith in wan, toywr skaylli gi gar rowne
Neyn may re heir fa hwne, innosit gyth crwn my zayll
Ne elli trawe fa neyin grane nar caris feyn di leich feal
A reithyin hwlle gi royd a neyn oyk is math dalwe
In tosga fa daneis an gane tawiris doyth pen gi darve
Mi chomryth ort mass tow finn, di rae run in makayve mna
Daywis towr loyryth is di loye gave mi chomre gi loyth tra
Derrich in reith fa math fiss sloneit a niss ca ter a hei
Goym rayd chomre a wen er gi far za will in greit
Tay la feich a techt er murri leich is math gol er mi lorga
Mak re na Sorchir is geire erme is do fa anm in Dyr borb
Di churris gessi ne chenn gi berre fin may er saylle
Is nach bein aggi mir wnee gar wath a ynce is awgc
Di raye osgir gi glor mir far sin di chosk gi reith
Gin gar for finn di yess, ne rach tow less mir wneith
Di chemyn techt her stead leich si wayd oss gi far
Sowle ni farga gi dane si nwle chadni zoyve a wen
Clokgit tenn teygne ma chenni far nar heme is bi tien
Skaa yrwnnych you er a zess a drum lin cless era claa
Clawe trome tortoyl nac gann gi tenn er teive in ir vor
A gymirt class assi chind is a techt in genn tloye
Za voneis zasg gi moya a sessow in gawlow skay
Er nert er zask er zolle ne elle far mir achay
Naill flath is iosk reith in kenn in ir fa keive crow
Math in noyth fa gall a zayd is loayth a stayd ne gi srow

Is e ughdair so Ossian.

Aithnichte domh sgeul beag air Fionn, ni sgeul nach cuirear an suim,
Air Mac Cumhail fa maith goil, fa cuimhne sin ri 'm ré.
Do bha sinn beagan sluaigh, aig Easruadh nan eagan mall,
Do chi sinn fo sheòl air tràidh, currach mòr 'us bean ann.
Caogad laoch guineach mu 'n rìgh, fa maith air ghniomh air gach gart,
Fir d' ar n-eis is mairg a chite, do ghabhamaid air gach tìr neart.
Do eireamar uile gu dion, ach Fionn nam Fiann 'us Gall, [tonn.
Do fheitheamh a churraich fa h-airde ceum, bha 'n a reim a sgoltadh nan
Ni dheanadh tàmh ann a teachd, gu 'r ghabh cala 's a phort ghnàth.
Aig teachd do thìr an eas, do eirich as maca mnatha,
Gile a dealradh no sitheadh gréine, 'us is mìn nòs a deilbh ;
An ainnir a thainig an céin, do bhamaid féin roimpe soirbh.
Thig thugainn gu pubull Fhinn, 'us beannaicheas gu grinn doibh,
Fhreagair Mac Cumhail 'na aonar, am beannachd binn gun toigh,
Do fharraid an rìgh fa maith dreach, gu h-ard do nighean an dath ghloin,
Co 'n treabh as an d' thainig a bhean, thoir sgeul gu geur dhuinn.
Nighean mi rìgh thìr fo thuinn, innisid gu cruinn mo dhàil,
Ni bheil treabh fa 'n iadh grian, nar iarras féin do laoich fial,
A rioghan a shiubhail gach ròid, a nighean òig is maith dealbh,
An tosga fa thainigeas an cein, tabhaireas doibh féin gu dearbh
Mo chomraich ort ma 's tu Fionn, do ràdh ruinn am maca mnatha, [tràth.
D' fheabhas d' ùrlabhraidh 'us do shluaigh, gabh mo chomraich gu luath
Deir an rìgh fa maith fios, sloinn a nis co th' air do thi,
Gabham ri 'd chomraich, a bhean, air gach fear dha 'm bheil an cridhe
Tha le fioch a teachd thar muir, laoch is maith goil air mo lorg,
Mac rìgh na Sorcha is maith airm, 'us do 'n ainm an Daire Borb.
Do chuireas geasan 'n a chionn, gum beireadh Fionn mi air sàl,
'Us nach bithinn aige mar mhnaoi, ge 'r mhaith a ghniomh 'us 'àgh.
Do ràdh Osgar le gloir mhòar, am fear sin a chosg gach rìgh,
Gun ge 'r fòireadh Fionn do gheas, ni rachadh tu leis mar mhnaoi
Do chi sinn teachd thar steud, laoch 's a mheud os gach fear,
'Siubhal na fairge gu dian, 's an iùl cheudna 'ghabh a bhean,
Clogaid teann tighinn mu 'cheann, fa 'n fhear nar thioma 'us bu treun,
Sgiath chruinn dhubh air a dheas, a druim làn chleas air a cleibh,
Claidheamh trom toirteal nach gann, gu teann air taobh an fhir mhoir,
Ag imirt chleas os a chionn, 'us a teachd an connimh an t-sluaigh,
A dha mhanais gaisge le buaidh, a seasamh an gualainn a sgéith,
Air neart, air ghaisge, air ghoile, ni bheil fear mear ach e,
Neul flath 'us rosg rìgh, an ceann an fhir fa caomh cruth,
Maith a shnuadh 'us geal a dheud, is luaithe a steud no gach sruth,

Tanik in stead sin in deir sin far nar weine riss in nayne
Kegit leich wemir ann zonyth ra hynsyth gar nar
Er eggill in ir is a heyth ne royve leich zin gan zrane
Da twne mir hanik in deir darrit in reith fa math clu
In nathin tow feyn a wen in na sud in fer a der tow
Haneym a v'coulle a ynd is fowir linn a zi tane
Darg say miss wra less ga math di thress a inn aylle
Derre oskir agus Gowle bi worbe coskir lonn ni gath
Nanc sessow in gar in tloye eddir in far mor si flaath
Hanik in leich bi wath tlacht le feich is lay nart no genn
Aggis foddeis woyn in wen di we gar a zolin inn
Tuk m'Morn in turchir dane gi croy na zey din tleyg
Ner anni in turchir nar hay za sky gin darny da wli
Di crath oskir fa mor ferg a chrissi yerg za layve claa
Aggis marveis stayd in ir mor in teaach a rinyth lai
Nor hut in stayd er in lerg zimpoo la ferg is la feich
Agis fokgris borbe in teme corik er in kegit leich
In tewe moe zinsyth fene is dinn kegit leich nar heim no zall
Gar waat in tessow sid drost di zyle in gask la nyth lawe
Varrit da willi gi marri gi dane di gi far zew sin
De nemist wlli fa hur mir hu ac coryk fir
Chaywill tre nenor gi moy sin nirrill chroy solli di scur
Ga croy chaywill ni dre cheill er gi eine dew sin a churr
Di zrwt gowle in nagni vir gu leddirt in ir in gor roit
Ga bea chewic eads in sin bi zarve in gell sin gloe
Horchir m'Morn lai laive m're nyth sorchir skaylle mor
Is margk trave in danik in ven fa hut in far in gar roit
Is er tuttym in ir vor in gar zi choyn croye in ceme
Di we neyn re heir fa hwne bleygin ac finn ansyth nane
Flann m'Morn croy in cass hor bass fa mor in teacht
Ne reive leich a danik ass zeive gin a chneis lane di chrecht
Mathirsyth feine bi wath tlacht neach a wackyth reyve neir er
In nis ass derri dym zneith er inn is annit doth skayll.
Annit doth skayll

Do zawe sea churre no o skay leith na thraa zor royve ann
Na gin dug ayr mor er ir wane is gin dranik se a feyn fynn.

Mir wee kegit leich garwe in daall in narm zo gi loor
Wemist gin choywir fa smach da goyvys woyn in cor
Di weit in glywe gin tocht a cluyith chorp agus skay
Co math chorik pen a deiss ne aykyth reiss er mi ray
Eligir aggin ag in ess fer bi wath tressi is gneive

Thainig an steud sin air tìr, 's am fear nar mhìn ris an Fheinn.
Caogad laoch bhith'maid ann, a choinnich a dh' ionnsuidh an fhir,
Air eagal an fhir 'us a theachd, ni robh laoch gun ghrain.
De thuinn mar thainig air tìr, d' fharraid an rìgh fa maith cliù,
An aithnich thu féin a bhean, an e sud am fear a deir tu ?
Aithnicheam, Mhic Cumhail, a Fhinn, is pùdhar leam e do d' Fheinn,
Tairgidh se mise a bhreith leis, ge maith do threise, Fhinn aill,
Do eirich Osgar agus Gall, bu bhorb cosgair loun nan cath,
'N an seasamh an goire do 'n t-sloigh, eadar am fear mòr 's am flath,
Thainig an laoch bu mhaith tlachd, le fioch 'us le neart 'n a cheann,
Agus faigheas uainn a bhean, do bha 'n goire do ghualainn Fhinn,
Thug Mac Moirne an t-urchar dian, gu cruaidh 'n a dheigh do 'n t-sleigh,
Nior fann an t-urchar nior e, dhe 'sgéith gun d' rinneadh da bhloidh.
Do chrath Osgar fa mòir fheirg a chrios dhearg dhe 'laimh chlì,
Agus marbhas steud an fhir, mòr an t-euchd a rinneadh leatha.
'N uair thuit an steud air an leirg, dh' iompaich e le feirg 'us le fioch,
Agus fògras, borb an taom, comhrag air na caogad laoich. ['n a dhàil,
An taobh mo dh' ionnsuidh féin 'us d' Fhinn, caogad laoch nior thiom
Ge 'r mhaith an seasamh 's an trosd, do gheill an cosg le a laimh.
Bheireadh da bhuille gu mear, gu dian do gach fear dhiubh sin,
Do bhitheamaid uile fa h-ùir, mar h-ùmh ag comhrag fir.
Cheangail tri naoinear le buaidh, 's an iorghuill chruaidh sul do sguir,
Gu cruaidh ceangail nan tri chaoil, air gach aon diubh sin a chuir.
Do dhruid Gall an aigne mhir, gu leadairt an fhir an goire roimhe,
Cia b'e chitheadh iad an sin, bu gharbh an goile 's an gleò ;
Thorchair Mac Moirne le a laimh, Mac rìgh na Sorcha, sgeul mòr ;
Is mairg treabh o 'n d' thàinig a bhean, fa thuit am fear an goire romha.
'Us air tuiteam an fhir mhòir, an goire do 'n chuan, cruaidh an ceum,
Do bhi nighean rìgh thir fo thuinn, bliadhna aig Fionn anns an Fheinn.
Flann mac Moirne cruaidh 'an càs, fhuair bàs, bu mhòr an t-euchd,
Ni robh a thainig as dhiubh, gun a chneas làn de chreuchd .
M' athairse féin bu mhaith tlachd, neach am bochd riamh nior eur.
'Us nis is deireadh do 'n ghniomh, air Fionn is aithnichte domh sgeul.
Aithnichte domh sgeul.

Mar bha caogad laoch garbh, an dàil an arm dha gu leòr,
Bhitheamaid gun chobhar fo a smachd, do ghabhas uainn a chòir,
Do bhitheadh an claidheamh gun tochd, a claoidh chorp agus sgiath,
Co maith chomhrag air mo dheas ni fhaca mi ris air mo réidh.
Adhlacar againn aig an eas, fear bu mhaith treis 'us gniomh,

Currir fay wrayth gi moyer fane oyr in nonor mi reith
Deyth bleyin zoolle in narm naye in leith worb nar loyeth in reith
M'Morn fa deyiss lamm gai leygiss ag finn ni fleygh.

Actor hujus Ossane M'finn.

Sai la guss in dei oy nach vaga mai finn
Chanaka rem rai sai boo zar lym
Mak neyn oe heik ree nyth wollych trom
Meddi is mo raith mo cheyl is mo chon
Fa filla fa flaa fa ree er girre
Finn fla re no vane fa treach er gych ter
Fa meille mor marre fa lowor er lerg
Fa shawok glan geith fa seith er gi carde
Fa hillanich carda fa markyth nor verve
Fa hollow er zneith fa steith er gi scherm
Fa fer chart a wrai fa tawicht toye
Fa hynseith naige fa bratha er boye
Fa hai in techter ard er chalm is er keol
Fa dwlta nyn dawf o zaik graig ni glar
A kness mir a galk a zroie mir in ross
Bi zlan gorm a rosk a holt myr in tor
Fa dwle dawf is doonna fa haryth nyn aw
Fa hollow er znee fa meine ri mnawe
Fa hai meille mor mak mwrna gi mygh
Bar lynyth nyn land an cranna os gych ig
Fa saywar in rygh a vodla mor zlass nyth
Din zort zar zewe terf nocha thra . . .
. . . . brone bane
. . . er nyth tloye fa bi chroy cham
Fa chossnw in greit fa vanve ni bann
Gin dug in flath trechaid cath fa chann
Er scrattych o zea M'Cowle nor chail
Id deir fa zoo ne closs goo na vail
Ner earne er nach zor air voo ynd
Cha royve ach re grane re reyve vass a chynn
Neir aik pest in locht na arrych in noef
Neryn nyn neve ner varve in ser soyve
Ne hynasse zneve a beine gin de bra
Ner ynasse voym trane a voye si waa
Ach is olk id tam in dei ind ni vane
Di quhy less in flath gi math wa na zei

Cuirear fa bhràigh gach meur, fainne òir an onoir mo rìgh,
Deich bliadhna dhol an airm nimh, an laoch borb nior lughaich an rìgh,
Mac Moirne fa d' fhios leam, 'ga leigheas aig Fionn nam fleadh.

Auctor hujus Ossian Mac Fhinn.

Se la gus an dé, o nach fhaca mi Fionn,
Cha-n fhaca ri 'm ré, saoi bu gheire leam ;
Mac nighinn O' Theige, rìgh nam buillean tròm.
M' eud 's mo rath, mo chiall 's mo chon,
Fa filidh fa flath, fa rìgh air gheire,
Fionn flath, rìgh na Feinn, fa treabhach air gach tìr,
Fa miall mòr mara, fa leobhar air leirg,
Fa sheabhag glan gaoithe, fa sith air gach ceairde,
Fa oileanach ceart, fa mairg nior mhearbh,
Fa ullamh air ghniomh, fa steidh air gach seirm,
Fa fior ceart a bhreth, fa tàmhaiche tuaith,
Fa ionnsaichte 'n a aigh, fa brathach air buaidh,
Fa h-e an teachdair ard, air chalm 'us air cheol,
Fa diùltadh nan daimh, o dh' fhàg greagh na clàr,
A chneas mar an cailc, a ghruaidh mar an ròs,
Bu ghlan gorm a rosg, 'fholt mar an t-òr,
Fa dùil daimh 'us daoine, fa aireach nan àgh,
Fa ullamh air ghniomh, fa mìn ri mnathaibh,
Fa h-e am miall mòr, mac muirne gach magh,
B' fhear loinneadh nan lann, an crann os gach fiodh.
Fa saoibhir an rìgh, a bhotal mor glas,
D' fhion ghort ghear gharbh, tairbh noch char threa . . .
. . . . broinn bhàin,
. . . air an t-sluagh, fa bu chruaidh cheum,
Fa chosnadh an gniomh, fa Bhanbha bhain,
Gun d' thug am flath, tricheud cath fa a ceann,
Air sgraiteach dha, M'Cumhail nior cheil,
A deir fa a ghò, ni clos gò 'na bheul,
Ni euradh air ni, fhuair fear o Fhionn,
Cha robh aca ri grein, rìgh riamh as a chionn,
Nior dh' fhàg beist an loch, no nathair an nimh,
An Eirinn nan naomh, nar mharbh an saor seimh,
Ni h-innisinn a ghniomh, a bhithinn gu de bhràth,
Nior innisinn uam, trian a bhuaidh 's a mhaith,
Ach is olc a taim, an deigh Fhinn nam Féinn,
Do chaidh leis an fhlath, gach maith bha 'na dhéigh,

Gin angnow in vor gin annith glan geith
Gin nor in mne ree is gin wie ni leich
Is tursych id tam in dei chinni ni gaid
Is me in crann er creith is me keive er naik
Is me chnoo cheith is me in teach gin schiane
Achadane mi nor is me in toath gin treath
Is me ossin m'fynn er trane ym zneith
Nad be voa finn di bi lwm gi neith
Vii sliss er y hyg m'kowl gyn blygh
vii fythit skae cliss er gi sliss deu sen
Kegit ymme oole in dymchale mi ree
Kegit leich gin ymzwn syth gith ymme zeive
x^t pley bane na hallith re hoil
x^t urskir gorm x^t corn in noor
Ach bi wath in traive a wag finni ni vane
Gyn dochil gin drow gyn glw is gyn gley
Gyn talkis ind er in err za ayne
Ag dol er gi nae di weith cach za rar
Finn flath in tloye sothran er a lou
Re nyn wlle aig roy zwnni ni ner zwlt
Ner zwlt finn ree nath ga bi veg a lynn
Char churre ass i heach nach zor danyth ann
Math in donna finn math in donna ai
Noch char helic nath lai zor helic sai.
Sai.

A houdir so Allane M'Royree.

Glennschee in glenn so rame heive, a binn feig agus lon,
Menik redeis in nane, ar on trath so in dey agon
A glen so fa wenn Zwlbin zwrm, is haald tulchi fa zran
Ner wanew a roythi gi dark, in dey helga o Inn ni vane
Estith beg ma zalew leith a chuddycht cheive so woym
Er wenn Zwlbin is er inn fail, is er M'ezoynn skayl troyg
Gur lai finn fa troyg in shelga, er V'ezwn is derk lei
Zwll di wenn Zwlbin di helga, in turkgi nach fadin erm zei
Lai M'ezwnn narm ay, da bay gin dorchirre in tork
Gillir royth ba zoill finn, is sche assne rin do locht
Er fa harlow a zail, M'ozunn graw nin sgoll
Ach so in skayll fa tursych mnaan, gavr less di layve an tork
Zingywal di lach ni wane, da gurri ea assi gnok
In schenn tork schee bi garv, di vag ballerych na helve mok

Gun anghnath aoin mhòir, gun eineach glan gaoithe,
Gun òr 'us mnatha rìgh, 's gun bhreith nan laoch.
Is tuirseach a taim an deigh chinn nan ceud,
Is mi an crann air chrith, 's mo chiabh do m' fhàg,
Is mi a chno chith, is mi an t-each gun srian,
Achadan mi an uair, is mi an tuath gun treabh,
Is mi Ossian mac Fhinn, air trian de 'm ghniomh,
An fhad bu bheò Fionn, do bu leam gach ni,
Seachd slios air a thigh, M'Cumhail co fleadh
Seachd fichead sgiath chleas, air gach slios dhiubh sin,
Caogad uidheam olaidh an timchioll mo rìgh,
Caogad laoch gun iomagan, anns gach uidheam dhiubh,
Deich bleidh bàn, 'n a thalla ri òl,
Deich eascradh gorm, deich corn de 'n òr,
Ach bu mhaith an treabh, a bh' aig Fionn nam Feinn,
Gun doichioll gun druth, gun gleois gun gléidh,
Gun tarchuis ann, air aon fhear dh'a Fheinn,
Aig dol air gach ni, do bha càch d'a réir,
Fionn flath an t-sluaigh, sothran air a luaidh,
Rìgh nan uile aigh, roimh dhuine nior dhiult,
Nior dhiult Fionn roimh neach, ge bu bheag a loinn,
Char chuir as a theach, neach dha 'r thainig ann,
Maith an duine Fionn, maith an duine e,
Noch char thiodhlaic neach, le dha 'r thiodhlaic se.
Sé.

Is e ùghdair so Allan Mac Ruaridh.

Gleannsith an gleann so ri m'thaobh, 's am binne feidh agus loin,
Is minic a ruitheas an Fheinn, air an t-srath so an deidh an con,
An gleann so fo Bheinn Ghulbainn ghuirm, a's àillidh tulaich fo'n ghréin,
Na struthana a ruith gu dearg, an deidh shealg o Fhionn na Feinn.
Eisdibh beag mar dh' fhalbh laoch, a chuideachd chaoimh so uam,
Air Bheinn Ghulbain 'us air Fionn fial, 'us air Mac O'Dhuinn, sgeul truagh,
Gur le Fionn bu truagh an sealg, air Mhac O'Dhuinn a's deirge lith,
Dhol do Bheinn Ghulbain do shealg, an tuirc nach faodain arm a chaoidh.
Le Mac O'Dhuinn an airm àigh, do 'm b'e gun torchradh an torc,
Geillear roimhe bu dh' fhoill Fhinn, is e esan a rinn do lochd.
Fhear fa tharladh an gaol, Mac O'Dhuinn gràdh nan sgoil,
Ach so an sgeul fa tursach mnathan, gabhar leis do làimh an torc,
Dionghal do laoch na Feinn, do chuir e as a chnoc,
An seann torc, is e bu ghairbhe, do fhac ballardaich na h-alla-muic.

Soeyth finn is derk dreach, fa wenn Zwlbin zlass in telga
Di fre dimit less in tork, mor in tolga a rin a shelga
Di clastich cozar ni wane, nor si narm teach fa a cann
Ersi in a vest o swoyn, is glossis woyth er a glenn
Curris ri faggin nin leich, in shen tork schee er freich borb
Bi geyr no ganyth sleygh, bi traneiseygh na gath bolga
M'ozwnn ni narm geyr, fragor less in na vest olk
Wa teive reyll trom navynyth gay, currir sleygh in dayl in turk
Brissir an cran less fa thre, si chran fa reir er in mwk
In sleygh o wasi waryerka vlaye, rait less nochchar hay na corp
Targir in tan lann o troyle, di chossin mor loye in narm
Marviss M'ozunn fest, di hanyth feyn de hess slane
Tuttis sprocht er Inn ne wane, is soyis sea si gnok
Makozunn nar dult dayve, olk less a hecht slane o tork
Er weith zoyth faddi no host, a durt gar wolga ri ray
Tothiss a zermit o hocht, ga maid try sin tork so id taa
Char zult ay achonyth finn olk leinn gin a heacht da hygh
Toissi tork er a zrum, M'ozunn nach trome trygh
Toiss na ye reiss, a yermit gi meine a torc,
Fa lattis troygh ya chinn, a zil nin narm rind goit
Ymbeis bi hurrus goye, agus toissi zayve in tork
Gunne i freich neive garve, boonn in leich bi zarg in drod
Tuttis in sin er in rein, M'O'Zwne nar eyve fealle
Na la di heive in turk, ach sen ayd zut gi dorve
A ta schai iu swn fa creay, M'O'Zwne keawe in gleacht
Invakane fullich ni wane, sin tulli so chayme fa art
Saywic swlzorme essroye, far la berrit boye gi ayr
In dey a horchirt la tork, fa hulchin a chnokso a taa
Dermit M'O'Zwne oyill, huttom tra ead nin noor
Bi gil a wrai no grane, bu derk a wail no blai k . .
Fa boe innis a alt, fadda rosk barglan fa lesga
Gurme agus glassi na hwle, maissi is cassi gowl ni gleacht
Binnis is grinnis na zloyr, gil no zoid varzerk vlaa
Mayd agis evycht sin leich, seng is ser no kness bayn
Coythtyc is maaltor ban, M'O'Zwne bi vor boye
In turri char hog swle, o chorreich wr er a zroy
Immir deit eyde is each, fer in neygin creach nar charie
Gilli a bar gasga is seith, ach troyg mir a teich so glenn.

Glennschee.

Is subhach Fionn a's deirge dreach, fa Bheinn Ghulbain ghlais an t seilg,
Do frìth d'imich leis an torc, mòr an t-olc a rinn a shealg,
Ri clàisdeachd co-ghàir nam Feinn, 'us an airm teachd fa a cheann,
Eireas a bhéisd o 'shuain, 'us gluaiseas uath air a ghleann,
Cuireas ri fàgail nan laoch, an seann torc 'us e air friodh borb,
Bu ghéire no gath nan sleagh, bu treine a shaigh no gath bolga.
Mac O'Dhuinn nan arm geur, freagras leis a bhéisd olc,
O a thaobh thriall tròm nimhneach gath, cuirear sleagh an dàil an tuirc,
Brisear a crann leis fa thrì, 's i a crann fa réir air a mhuc,
An t-sleagh o bhos bhàrdhearg bhlaith, rait leis noch char e 'n a chorp
Tarruingear tan lann á truaill, do choisinn mòr bhuaidh nan arm,
Marbhas M'O'Dhuinn a bhéisd, do thainig e fhéin as slàn.
Tuiteas sprochd air Fionn na Feinn, 'us suidheas e 's a chnoc;
Mac O'Dhuinn nach do dhiult daimh, olc leis a thighinn slàn o'n torc.
Air bhi dha fada 'n a thosd, a dubhairt, ge b'olc ri ràdh,
Tomhais, a Dhiarmaid o 'shoc, cia meud troidh 's an torc a ta,
Char dhiult e achuinge Fhinn, olc leinn gun a theachd d'a thigh,
Tomhaisidh an torc air a dhruim, Mac O'Dhuinn nach tròm troidh.
Tomhais 'n a aghaidh a rìs, A Dhiarmaid gu mìn an torc,
Fa leat is truagh dha chinn, a ghille nan arm roinn ghoirt.
Imicheas, bu thurus goimh, agus tomhaisidh dhoibh an torc,
Guinidh a fhriogh nimh garbh, bonn an laoich bu gharbh 'an trod.
Tuiteas 'an sin air an raon, M'O'Dhuinn nior aoibh feall;
'N a luidh do thaobh an tuirc, ach sin e dhuit gu doirbh;
A ta se an sin fa chreuchd, M'O'Dhuinn caomh an gleachd;
Aon mhacan fulangach nam Fiann, 's an tulach so chì 'm fa ard,
Scabhag sùlghorm Easruaidh, fear le 'm beireadh buaidh gach air
An déigh a thorchairt le torc, fa thulchain a chnuic so a ta.
Diarmaid M'O'Dhuinn aibheil, a thuiteam troimh eud an òir.
Bu ghile a bhrù no grèin, bu deirg a bheul no blàth . . .
Fa buidhe innis a fholt fad, rosg bar ghlan fa liosg,
Guirm 'us glaise 'n a shùil, maise 'us caise cùl nan cleachd,
Binneas 'us grinneas 'n a ghlòir, gile 'n a dhòid bhàr-dhearg bhlàth,
Meud agus éifeachd 's an laoch, seang 'us saor fo a chneas bàn,
Cothaich 'us mealltair bhan, M'O'Dhuinn bu mhòr buaidh,
An tùr cha thog a shùl, o chorruich ùr air a ghruaidh,
Immirdich fhaoghaid 'us each, fear an éigin chreach nar char,
Gille b' fhearr gaisge 'us sith, ach truagh mar a theich 's a ghleann.

Gleannsith.

A houdir so seiss Allan M'Royre.

Mor in nocht my chow feyn a halgin a ta zim rair
Re smeinten a chaa chroy huggemir is carbryth cranroy
A maksen chormik ochwnni merga in nayn harlyth fa chung
Reith gin chass vin chaath di churri ris gin zrane royth boe
Kailswm gith ollith fame hwnni inni is clanni keive chwnn
Guss wyve sen charbre roye nir smeine seine olk na anweine
Di chan carbryth ranyth loyeth agus di be in nellith chroye
Gir bar less twttwm er mygh agus in nane la cheille
Nassyth reithre wea vir agus in nane a weith er nerrin
Di chan barrin gi prap cwneich mwkre agis art
Fir sinsir huttwm in sin di wreith fellith ni faynith
Cwneich a gessith chroye is cwneich in non oywir
Is nach reym cogeith rame linni ach na hoggeith vakkowle
Ba corle clonni cwne agus carbre a lay trome
Ead feyne a hawrt dar ginni agus sinni di zochin
Gow marreith na zey wleyg is gin nane a weith in nalwin
Is weadeist baiss fa zoem tra nach bedeis in mir zlee
Hug sen gi feich fergich in cathsin cacht zawraa
Di hut in nane bonni ri bonni is reithre olsa errin
Ne roygh o nynea nor gow fodleith earra in doythin
In reith nach roygh far smacht rar linni gwss a chaa sen a halgin.
O churre an sen r nar ner zoive rwneni keiss na kayn
Is ne roye ag dwn keith rwn ach far gwde di zea nerrin
Ymmi er fey in doyn worre nach lar wey in dey in tloye
Ni fonyeith la er lai a huttym la ny cheillith
Da deg feith awlwarreith in seu orrew in nerrin eazlyn
Ossin cred a zaneith finni agus ersemi far nerrin
Er a lave a cleyrre chaye ne royith si vanve vane
Beggane di leichre erse agus ogre gin darve
Ga bea reith heyssyth in sin zoive sai fodleith in nasgeith
Gin cath gin nirril gin nawg gin none gin achassen
Churr sin ir techta sorgow faa mayk v^c conni
Di hoith orrin nar genni di zowell reithreith errin
Mor in tysin dymith orweith a reith taureith fa mo torm
Twlleith owyr a tug gow dul di warwa er ollea
Ossin innis doive skail nor chorsew in nirril trane
Nor hutyth di waksi si chaa na drwg tow cr er lawryth
Oskin mi vec osgir ayen hanyth miss er curreith in nar a
Id tanik keiltyth er sen oskir a hechtir clynni
Hank in roze boa zar weane woskin in garrith dyth feyn

An t-ùghdair so sios, Allan Mac Ruaraidh.

Mòr an nochd mo chumha féin a thailginn a tha do 'm réir,
Ri smuaintinn a chatha chruaidh thugamar 'us Carbair crann ruaidh,
Am mac sin Chormaig O'Chuinn, mairg an fheadhan a tharladh fo 'chuing,
Rìgh gun chàs o 'n chath do chuireadh leis gun ghrain roimh beothaibh,
Cheangladh sinn gach uile Fiann, thun Fhinn 'us cloinne caoimh Chuinn,
Gus do bhi sin Carbair ruadh, nior smuaineich sinn olc no ainmhein.
Do chan Carbair ris an t-sluagh, agus do b 'e an ealaidh chruaidh,
Gur b' fhearr leis tuiteam air magh, agus an Fheinn le chéile,
No na righre bhi fa ùir, agus an Fheinn a bhi air Eirinn.
Do chan Barruinn gu prap, cuimhnich Mucraidh agus Art,
Bhur sinnsreadh thuiteam an sin, de bhreith foill na Feinn,
Cuimhnich na geasan chruaidh, 'us cuimhnich an on uamhor,
'Us nach robh aon chogadh ri 'm linn, ach na thog Mac Cumhail.
B'e comhairle chlanna Chuinn, agus Charbair na laimhe truime,
Iad féin a thabhairt do 'r cinn, agus sinne a dhochainneadh,
Gu maireadh 'n a dheidh fleadh, 'us gun Fheinn a bhi 'n Almhainn,
'Us bhitheas bàs fa dhiomb, an trath nach bitheas ann mar dhlighe.
Thug sinn gu fiadhaich feargach, an cath sin cath Ghabhra.
Do thuit an Fheinn bonn ri bonn 'us righre uasal Eirinn.
Ni robh o 'n Innia an ear, gu Fodla iar an domhain,
Aon righ nach robh fo 'r smachd, r 'ar linn gus a chath sin, a thailginn;
O chuireadh an sin ar n-àr nior ghabh dhuinn cìs no càin,
'Us ni robh aig duine cith ruinn ach far cuid de dh' iath an Eirinn,
Iomadh bhi air feadh an domhain mhoir nach làthair bhi an deigh an [t-sloidh,
Ni faoin lamh air laimh a thuiteam le na chéile,
Da tig fiadhaich almharaich an sin orra 'an Eirinn iath-ghlan.
Ossiain, creud a dheanadh Fionn, agus iarsma far an Eirinn?
Air a laimh a chléirich chaidh, ni robh 's a Bhanbha bhàin,
Beagan de laochraidh arsaidh agus oigridh gun dearbhadh;
Ge b' e rìgh a sheasadh an sin gheabhadh se Fodla an nasgaidh,
Gun chath, gun iorghuill, gun agh, gun on, gun achmhasan.
Chuir sinn ar teachta saor gu fàth Mac mhic Cuinn.
Do chaidh uainn 'n ar cinn do ghabhail righre Eirinn,
Mor an tigh sin d' imich oir bha rìgh Teamhra fa mòr toirm,
Tuilleadh aobhar a tug gu dol a mharbhadh ar n-uile.
Ossian, innis doibh sgeul 'n uair chuir sibh an iorghuill threun,
'N uair thuit do mhac-sa 's a chath, an do rug thu air a labhradh?
Os cionn mo mhic Osgair aine thàinig mis air cur an àir,
Do thainig Caoilte air sin oscionn a sheachdnar cloinne,
Thainig na robh beò de 'r Feinn os cionn an cairdean fein,

Drong zoe lawrrit or sin is weith drong ellith gin armyn
A cleyrreith na baichil bane ga bea zeith chewith in toyr
Byth vor in troye rar lin olsa errin di hwttim
Ymmeith caithraa codeith keive ymmi loereith heith her
Ymmeith skaith harsi si wygh agus a trea gin armin
Cha dewith sin din tloyg mirri baale er in roygh boye
Cha dwg sin lynni ass a chaa ach feve reith na ardlacht
Sanni a hor mo mi wag feyn na lea er a wllin claa
Is skaa nawriss er in layr agus a lanni na zess lawe
Donnwl allith er gith lea dea er bley a looreicha
Leggwm erla mi ley re lar is di bi rynis oss a chinni tawe
Sminum a healgin er sen cred a zanvin na zeye
Di hillith osgir rwmsyth soss agus bi lor lam a chross
Di hein a hwggwm a laave er wayn er ym choaailli
Di zoyve may lawe mi vec feyn is dyth hoeis ranyth crea
Is aon tw sin a lea char churreis caiss sin teil
Hurrt rwmsyth mi wak farryth agus a nar armyth
A woe riss ni dwllw sin di wesith slane a aythir
Ne zanwmsyth zewsytht gaeth ne roe aggwm fregreith zoe
Gin danik keilt worsin huggin a zeyzin oskir
A dowirt mak ronane in nawe ach keynis tazes a zrawg
A tame er oskir mir is dlee dul a gowar seil awzeive
Crachtea sley carbre roye fa ymlin oskir armroye
Lawe cheilt ga wllin doe reach in greachte nyth sley
Sirris keilta a knee er choyr id toyr a inni na zoee
It toyr a zrwme crechti kyn er a zerre din zorley
Skreddis makronane sin agus tuttis gow talwin
Id dowirt keiltyth ym meille trane er weith zoe er tryle in dyvenail
Feirane sen a oskir aile a skarris ranyth wane
Is skar raa caath ra fynni bae in keiss ag seil mor chwne
Gerrit a weith zone mir sin a vec alpin a chlerich
Gi waka a huggin wo nar ne roye boea zanew phail
Feichit keaid zonyth mir sin eddr ogre is arse
Ne roowe dwne slane dew sin aggin din neychit cadsin
Ach fer ix gonni gi reive fath low ag gin di chreactew
Togmir in tosgir arne er chrannew sley in nardew
Bermoyn e gu tullych zlin dyth howirt dea a heydyth
Lead nyth bossyth zane chorp cha royve slane wo na alt
Na gi ryg a wonyth lar ach a ygh na hynirrane
In nyith sin dwn sin naar geillingua churp gow laa
Gir hogsin clan v^c ne finni er chnokew ard evin
Neyr choneith neach a v^c fen nir chein a wrar fa zeyth
Re fegsin me vecsi mir sen kaach wllyth a kenyth oskir

Droing dhiubh labhradar sin 'us bhi droing eile gun anamain
A chleirich a bhachuil bhàin, ge bith do chitheadh an t-àr,
Bu mhòr an truaighe ri 'r linn uailse Eirinn do thuiteam.
Iomadh cobhra codat caomh, iomadh luireach shitheach shaor
Iomadh sgiath tharsna 's a mhagh, agus a triath gun anamain,
Cha dubhach sin do 'n t-sluaigh mar a b' àl air an robh buaidh,
Cha tug sinn leinn as a chath ach faoibh rìgh no ardlaoich.
'S ann a fhuair mi mo mhac féin 'n luidhe air 'uilinn clì,
A sgiath 'n a bhris air an làr, agus a lann 'n a dheas laimh,
De 'n fhuil aille air gach leth, d'iadh air blaghaibh a luirich,
Leigeam earrlinn mo shleidh ri làr agus rinneas os a chionn tàmh,
Smuaineam a thailginn air sin creud a deanainn 'n a dheigh,
Do thill Osgar riumsa suas agus bu leòr leam a chrois,
Do shìn e thugam a làmh air mhiann air mo chòmhdhail,
Do ghabh mi làmh mo mhic féin 'us do thugas ràn cruaidh,
'Us o an taobh sin a leth nior chuireas càs 's an t-saoghal,
Thubhairt riumsa mo mhac féin fear agus e an oir anamainn,
Fo ris na dùilibh sin do bhi-sa slàn a athair,
Ni dheanaimse innseadh ghò, ni robh agam freagradh dha,
Gu 'n tainig Caoilte mòr sin thugainn a dh' fhaicinn Osgar.
A dubhairt Mac Ronain an aigh, ach cionnus tathas, a ghràidh ;
A tathaim ar' Osgar mar is dlighe 'dol an comhar saoghail aighe,
Chreuchd sleadh Charbair ruaidh fa imlinn Osgair armruaidh,
Lamh Chaoilte gu 'uilinn do rach an creuchdaibh na sleigh,
Sireas Caoilte an cneadh air choir, do fhuair gach ni 'na dhoigh,
Do fhuair a dhruim creuchta glan air a ghearradh le 'gheur shleadh.
Sgreadas Mac Ronain an sin agus tuiteas gu talmhainn ;
Do thubhairt Caoilte am milidh treun air bhi dha air triall an dubh neul,
Fìrinn sin a Osgar ail a sgarras ri na Feinn,
'Us sgaraidh cath ri Fiannaibh, bithidh an cìs aig siol mòr Chuinn.
Goirid a bhi dhuinn mar sin a Mhic Alpain, a chléirich,
Gu facadh thugainn o 'n àr na robh beò de Fhiannaibh Fail,
Fichead ceud dhaoine mar sin eadar oigridh 'us àrsaidh ;
Ni robh duine slàn diubh sin againn de 'n fhichead ceud sin,
Ach fear naoi guine gu nimh, fath lugh aig gun de chreuchdadh.
Togamar an t-Osgar arnaidh, air chrannaibh sleidh an àirde,
Beirminn e gu tulach ghrinn, do thabhairt dheth 'éideadh ;
Leud a bhoise dhe 'n chorp cha robh slàn o 'fholt,
No gu ruig a bhuinn làr ach 'aghaidh 'n a h-aonaran ;
An inigh, 's an dùin, 's an àra, geilleachdainn d'a chorp gu la,
Gur thog sinn clann Mhic na Feinn, air chnocaibh ard aoibhinn,
Nior chaoin neach a mhac féin, nior chaoin a bhràthair fa dheoigh,
Ri faicsinn mo mhacsa mar sin, càch uile a caoineadh Osgair.

Gerrit a wee zown mir sin er curryth in a churp cheive zil
Gow vaka chuggin fa nona fin m'kowle vic tranevor
Gow dugsidir annsyth nar drane boe di zanew phal
Er fyail clynni boissni neyr fa chassil chroo sin nirril
Di bi roye baekeith ni werri agus skranil ni meillyth
Gow vaggi sin merga finni re cranni sley voss er gin
Hugsaid huggin assin nar di hug sin na goaill
Di vannych sinn ullyth zinni agis char reggir a sinni
Dulli er in tullych na rane far in rowe oskir armzar
Nor a wowych oskir finni er tocht daa voss a chinni
Togissa nye neachla is bannythchis da hanathir
Id dowirt in tosgir in sin re m'murnaith sin nor sin
Mi chin fest riss in naik er haggin a inni armzar
Troyg a oskir arne a zey v^c^ mo v^c^ syth fen
Miss er a zey is fanne is er dye fane errin
Mallych art in r gym moye sai sa dwe tanyth reym loyith
Di leon a orrwm a her na gi reach ma in noeneith
Slane wome a zirril is di zawe slane di gi keiss di hoikwail
Slane di gi math woym in nossa ach ne waym zin chomso
Re clastin kelwein nyth finni a arrwm a hosgir zi ling
Di hein a woa in dai lawe is di zea a rosga rinwlaa
Di hynta finni runna a chwle di hilla deara gow dour
Ach fa osgir is fa wranna cha drin sai dar er talvin
Ach missi wane agis fin ne royve a zayn woss a chin
Hug ait tree zayryth sin noyr a class fa errin awoyr
Coyk fichit kead x is deich kead er in goayrren zin fen
Wa din nam marve er a wygh gyn nane dwn za essen
A zaa urdill sin is ne goe is reith errin skail fa moe
Wa marve er in teive ellith di loyg errin armylin
Neyn roye finni swllor na saive o hen gow hyig a wass
Woyn zloossin ne far da less reithre wca zi werrin
Woyn chath sen cath zawryth noch cha drone ma tyn nawryth
Cha rowe in oor roea na loo nar leg maa ossni lan wor
Mor noch.

A houdir so seis Farris filli.

Ard agne zwlle, fer coggi finn
Leich loyvir loonn, owil ne timmi
Seir anich soss, ser snaig heive
Murrich er sloyg, goole crowich keive
Mak mornyth marri, fa croith in goll

Goirid a bhi dhuinn mar sin, air curaidh a chuirp chaoimh ghil,
Gu facadh thugain fa nòin, Fionn mac Cumhail mhic Threinmhoir
Gu tugsidear anns an àr trian beò de dh' Fhiannaibh Fail,
Air faighail clanna Boisgne an iuir fa chaiseal chrò 's an iorghuil;
Do bu ro bhacach na fir agus gràineil na milidh;
Gu faca sinn meirghe Fhinn, ri crann sleidh os ar cionn,
Thugsaid thugainn as an àr; do thug sinn 'n a comhdhail,
Do bheannaich sinn uile dh' Fhinn agus char fhreagair e sinn,
'Dol air tulach nan treun, far an robh Osgar armgheur,
'N uair a mhothaich Osgar Fionn air teachd da os a chionn,
Togas an aghaidh neochlaon, 'us beannaicheas d' a sheanathair.
A dubhairt an t-Osgar an sin, ri Mac Muirne 's an uair sin,
Mo chion feasd ris an eug air fhaicinn a Fhinn airmgheir,
Truagh, a Osgair arnaidh a dheadh mhic mo mhic-sa fein,
Mise air a dheigh is fann, 'us air deigh Feinn Eirinn,
Mallachd ort a fhir co 'm buaidh 's e is duibh thainig ri m' shluagh,
Do lean e orm o shear, na gu rachadh mi an aonach,
Slàn uam do iarghuil 's do àgh, slan do gach cìs a thogail,
Slan do gach maith uam a nis, ach na faigheam de 'n chom so,
Ri clàistinn caolmhuinn Fhinn, an arraing Osgar do ling,
Do shìn e uaith a dha làmh 'us do dh' iath a rosg roinnbhlath.
Do thionndadh Fionn ruinn a chùl, do shileadh dheur gu dùr;
Ach fa Osgar 'us fa Bhran, cha d' rinn se deur air talmhainn,
Ach mise mhain agus Fionn ni robh de dh' Fheinn os a chionn,
Thug iad tri ghàir 's an uair, a chlos fa Eirinn aghmhor.
Cuig fichead ceud, deich 'us deich ceud air an comhaireimh dhinn féin,
Bha de 'n Fheinn marbh air a mhagh, gun aon duine dheth easbhuidh,
A dha ùrdail sin 'us ni gò 'us Rìgh Eirinn sgeul fa mo,
Bha marbh air an taobh eile, do shluagh Eirinn arm-ghrinn,
Ni robh Fionn suilbhir no seimh, o sin gu theachd a bhàis;
O 'n ghleò sin ni fearda leis, righrean bhi a dhìth fearainn.
O 'n chath sin cath Ghabhra nocha d' rinn mi treun labhradh,
Cha robh an uair riamh no lo, nar leig mi osnadh lan mhòr.

Mòr an nochd.

Is e ùghdair so sios Ferghus Filidh.

Ard aigne Ghuill, fear cogaidh Fhinn,
Laoch leobhar lonn, 'fhoghail nach tioma
Saor cineach suas, saor snaidheach a thaobh,
Murrach air sluagh, Goll cruthach caomh,
Mac Moirne mear, fa crodha an goil,

A clew fa schen, far geinnoll sen
Reith finnith fayl, ne timmi glor
Ne seywe a chail, leich eyve mor
Noor heyd a gayth, rayme flath feich
Ga meine a chness, ne in tass in neith
A waid ne i myn, oosi geagi toiri
Say is glenny gen, eyddi ni skoll
Ooss barri benn, errir sen rynn
Fa heggill lenn, a hagri hecht rinn
Derrim rwt a inn, na drillis noonn
Di warr agli zwle, hagni gi tromm
Gin chur ra wath, si cath ne in doe
Inseich chayth, kinseleich sloe
A anich ne min, fullich in fer
Dossi ni skoll, ossil a zen
Wrrik a loeg, torvirdych fayll
A throst cayth is boyn, foss flath a chayl
Dwn na olt, á wrunni mir chelk
Wmlane mi chorp, lomlane da herk
Memnycht a weiss, dalweich a znwss
Ne elle re ooss gowle, ne chell ort a inn
Tress ni doon, a zasga zrin
Flaaoll foss, daytholl a kness
Er zoole ne cless, ne slim er hass
Broontych a zale, convych a royr
Ferriddi mein, melleddi moyr
Da rayth gi brayth, aw agis eich
Nawch ri cayth, lawch a leich
Claa chonis woyn, sonnis ni wayne
Monmurrycht coyn, illericht dane
Loyvin er aw, croyth na grewith
Loyvir a layve, royg ni reith
Sonnis ni rowd, sollis a zaid
Curris say layve, gych trayn da wayd
Boyn rowni a nir, boy corrik er
Leydwich a zolli, egni in sterr
Leich cwnych loonn, neawnych la lynn
Targissi goole, argissicht lynni
Leich arm mar, fargycht ra chin
Colg convych er, onchon er zoll
Fer zalle ni gonn, royt zraw ni ban
Beith dawe gin non, di znaa na zarr
La beowe rod, a rot ne in tlaa

A chliù fa sean, fear geanail sin
Rìgh feinnidh fial, ni tioma gloir,
Ni 'n saobh a chiall, laoch aoibhidh mòr,
'N uair theid an cath, reim flath fioch,
Ge mìn a chneas, ni 'n taise 'an ni,
A mheud ni mion, os geug an toradh,
'S e is gloinne gean, oide nan sgoil,
Os barraibh bheann, eirear 's an raoin.
Deirim riut a Fhinn, na triallas nunn,
Do fearr eagal Ghuill, aigne ge trom,
Gun chuireas ri mhaith, 's a chath ni 'n doigh,
Ionnsaidheach caidh, ceannsalach sloigh,
A eineach ni mion, fuileach am fear,
Toiseach nan sgoil, uasail a ghean,
Oirdhearc a shluagh, toirbheartach fiall,
A throsd cath is buan, os flath a chiall,
Donn 'n a fholt, a bhronn mar chailc,
Iomlan m'a chorp, lomlan de sheirc,
Eire fa chìs, bu choir dha chuis,
Meanmnach a bhitheas, dealbhach a ghnuis,
Ni bheil rìgh os Goll, ni cheil ort a Fhinn ;
Treise nan tonn, a ghaisge ghrinn,
Flathail fòs, dathail a chneas,
Air Gholl nan cleas, ni sliom air theas,
Bronntach a dhàil, confhadhach a threòir,
Fearanta mìn, mileanta mòr,
Do rait gu bràth, 'agh agus 'fhioch,
Nimheach ri càch, làmhach an laoch,
Cleith chonus bhuan, sonas 'na mhein,
Monamarrach cuain, iorghuileach dian,
Leomhan air agh, crodha 'n a ghniomh
Leobhar a làmh, roghadh nan rìgh,
Sonas 'n a ròd, solus a dheud,
Cuireas se leòn, gach treun dha mheud,
Buan reìm an fhir, buaidh comhraig air,
Leidmheach a ghoile, cagnaidh a stair,
Laoch guineach lonn, nimhneach fa lainn,
Tarchuiseach Goll, argaiseach leinn,
'Laoch arnaidh mear, feargach r'a chion,
Colg confhadhach air, onchu air ghoil,
Fearghail nan con, roghadh ghràidh nam ban,
Bithidh daimh gun on, do ghnàth 'n a ghoire,
Le 'm bitheadh an ròd, a ròd ni 'n tlàth,

Meith ni grayth, a zrayth fa blaa
Seyor a chrow, awzor a rath
Ne in tranith shrow, na reym in gayth
Math morn is dane, fa orryth a zoyl
Innoyr a zloyr, beith woyn a chrayn
Trayth marri mer, fayle ferri a chorri
Gin tayr na zerr, a zaille er forri
Mak teadis cheiwe, nach tregi dawe
Gin choggi reith, nar laggi a layve
Oowir a cholk, is borbe a zloa
Nor erris arg, trane shelga zea
A v^c cowle zrinn, coythwil ess gyle
See boynych di zoell, gin noa gin nawle
In ness rame lay, a zuayn zoo
Werrin gin chelga, trayn selga zoo
Ni twlli a ann, far nass i gor
Graw tenni inn, trane chon a zooll
Treg heich a zwle, be seichith ronn
Nad ray gin ving, trane feich finn
Zoywidsi sinni, arriss a ayll
Is skeil mi zroym, ne wor mi wane
Carri gin kelg, bail tanni derg
Anich si low, a clow oss ard.
Ard agni zwl.

A houdir so Farris Filli.

Innis donn a earris ille feynni errin
Kynis tarle zevin in gath zawrych ni beymin
Ne math v^ckowle mo skael o chath zawrich
Cha warr oskyr invin hug mor coskir calm
Cha warr seachta vec keilt na gasre fean alwe
Di hut oyk ni feani inn in eadyth arrych
Di marwe m^clowith si vi mek sin tathryth
Di hut oyk ni halvin di marwa feyn brettin
Di hut m^c re lochlin fa linnyth veith chonyth
Bi chre fael farri bi lawe chalma in gonyth
Innis doif a ille m^c mo vec is marrwm
Kynis di we oskyr scolta ni gathwarri
Bi zekkir a innis di bi vor in nobbir
Ne royve marve sin gath sen hut la armow oskyr
Ne loyth ess oyvin na seaywok re eltow

Meath 'n a ghruaidh, a ghruaidh fo bhlàth,
Seangmhor a chruth, aghmhor a rath,
Nin treine sruth, no 'reim an cath,
Mac Moirne is déine, fa orra a chuala,
Ionmhuinn a ghlòire, bu bhuan a ghreann,
Triath mòra mear, fiall fior a chor.
Gun tair 'n a ghoire, a dhàil air foir,
Mac teadaidh caomh, nach tréigeadh daimh,
An cogadh rìgh, nior lag a làmh,
Uamhor a cholg, is borb a ghleò,
'N uair dh' eireas 'fhearg trian sealga dha.
A Mhic Cumhail ghrinn, comhail 'us geall,
Sìth bhuan do Gholl, gun fhuath gun fheall.
An nis ri 'm là a gheibhinn dhomh,
Bheirinn gun chealg, trian sealga dha,
Ni tuilleadh dheth ann, fhir an taise a 'm ghoire
Gràdh teann Fhinn, trian chon do Gholl.
Treig fioch, a Ghuill, bi sìtheil ruinn,
'N ad ré gun mheang, trian fiodh o Fhionn,
Ghabhaidse sin, a Fherghuis aille,
Do sgaoil mo ghruaim, ni mair mo mhiann.
Charaid gun chealg, beul tana dearg,
'Eineach 's a lùgh, a chliù os aird.
Ard aigne Ghuill.

Is e ùghdair so Ferghus Filidh.

Innis duinn a Fherghuis, fhilidh Feinn Eirinn,
Cionnus tharladh dhuinn, an cath Ghabhra nam beuman,
Ni maith Mhic Cumhail, mo sgeul o chath Ghabhra,
Cha mhair Osgar ionmhuinn, thug mòr chosgar chalma,
Cha mhair seachd mhic Chaoilte, no gasraidh Fiann Almhuin,
Do thuit oige na Feinn, ann an eideadh airich,
Do marbh Mac Luighich, is sé mic sin d' athar,
Do thuit oige na h-Almhuin, do marbh Feinn Bhreatuin,
Do thuit Mac rìgh Lochlainn, fa leinne a bhi a còmhnadh,
Bha 'chridhe fial fearail, bha 'lamh calm an còmhnuidh,
Innis doibh, a fhilidh, mac mo mhic 'us mo rùn,
Cionnus do bhi Osgar, 'sgoltadh nan cathbharr.
Bu dheacair a innseadh, do bu mhòr an obair,
Na robh marbh 's a chath sin, a thuit le armaibh Osgair,
Ni luaithe eas aimhne no seabhag ri ealtaibh,

Na re vwnni sroyth na oskyr sin gath sin
Weith say ma zerri mir willith ra trane zeith
Na mir chran voass ewee si wew gi a nauetee
Hug oskyr na chonew mir harwe twnni traa
Mir chonnik sen carbre di chraa in tlye hantych
Gir chur treith a chinnbir gir bea in couva cadna
Ner impoo sin oskyr gin dranyth re errin
Gin dug beym gin deichill gir zoichin ay garlyn
Bollis art mac carbre er in darna bull
Sawle a weith in fer sin si winn reith um
Is mi ferris filli dar hwil gych innis
Troyg er essni feynith my skeall re innis.
Innis.

Gilcallum m'ynnollaig in turskail so seiss.

Di choala ma fad o hen skail di voneis re cowe
Is traa za haythris gow trome gata mir anneiss orrinn
Clanni rowre ni braa mawle fa chonchor is fa chonnil
Di bur low oyg err wyg er hurlar chogew ullytht
Ga hygh ne hanik ma genn fa ullyth leichre vanva
Cath ag waall innoyr ellyth dar zymone clannyth rowre
Hanik hukkith borbe a reith ir gurre croith connleich
A zis ni mur glarrith grinn oo zown skayth gow errinn
Di lawir conchowr re caach ca zoveniyn chon in naglath
Di wrea beacht nyn skaillith zaa gr teachta la harreith woa
Glossis connil nar lag lawe di wrea skailleith din vackein
Er darve torrin din leich cayvelir connil laa connleich
Ner zoive in leich ra lawyth connil freich forranych
Cayd dar sloyg di cawleith less aygnyth is bone ri haythris
Curreith teachtir canni ni conni woo hardre ayngneith ulleith
Gow down dalgin zranyth zlyin sen down gaylith ni geill
Woyn down sin di loyr linni di zangnowne neyn orginn
Teggowss gneive nyn serrith sange gow reith feiltyth ny warrinn
Dissrych sloyg ullith oynnyth teiggowss kow ni creive roye
Mak dettin o zoyg mir howe nar ettee teacht dor gowir
Faddeith or chonchowr riss in gon wayghiss gin teacht dar gowir
Is connil surrych nyn stead marryth in gwrych is keada dor sloygh
Deakir zoiss wee ym bred a ir churre er charrit
Ne in raith dole in ayngnyth a lanni si taa lar chawleith connil
Na smein gin dole na zye a re ni gormlann granole

No ruith buinne srutha, no Osgar 's a chath sin.
Bha se mu dheireadh, mar dhuille ri treun ghaoith,
No mar chrann uas eabhaidh, 's a bhitheadh 'g a shnaigheadh.
Mar chunnaic rìgh Eirinn, beò air làr a chath,
Thug Osgar 'n a choinnimh, mar gharbh tuinne traigh,
Mar chunnaic sin Cairbar, do chrath an t-sleagh shanntach,
Gur chuir troimhe a cheann bir, gur b'e an cumha ceudna.
Nior iompaich sin Osgar, gun d' ràinig Rìgh Eirinn,
Gun d' thug beum co 'n dichioll, gu 'r dhochainn e geurlann;
Bualas Art mac Charbair air an darna buille,
Is amhuil a bhi am fear sin, 's a bhinn rìgh uime.
Is mi Ferghus Filidh da 'r shiubhail gach innis,
Truagh tareis na Feinn, mo sgeul r'a innis.
Innis.

Gillecallum Mac an Ollaimh an t-ursgeul so sios.

Do chuala mi fad o shean, sgeul do bhuineas ri cumha,
Is tràth dha 'aithris gu trom, ge ta mar ainneas oirnne,
Clann Rughraidh nam breth mall fa Chonchoir 'us fa Chonnuil,
Do b'ùrlaimh oigfhir 's a mhagh air h-urlar Choige Ullaidh,
G'a thigh na thainig le gean fa uile laochraidh Bhanbha,
Cath aig faighail aon uair eile, de 'r dh' iomghuin clanna Rùghraidh.
Thainig thugainn, borb a fhraoch, an curaidh crodha Conlaoch,
A dh' fhios ni m 'ar claraibh grinn, o Dhunsgathaich gu Eirinn.
Do labhair Conchoir ri càch, Co a gheibheamar thun an oglaich,
Do bhreth beachd no sgeul dheth, gun teachd le curadh uaith ?
Gluaiseas Conull nior lag lamh do bhreth sgeul de 'n mhacan.
Air dearbhadh tarruing do'n laoch ceangailear Conull le Conlaoch,
Nior ghabh an laoch r'a tamhachd, Conlaoch fraochach furanach,
Ceud de'r sluagh do cheangladh leis, ioghnadh 'us buan ri aithris.
Cuirear teachdair gu ceann nan con o h-ardrigh eagnaidh Ullaidh,
Gu Dundealgain grianach glan seann dùn ciallach nan Gaidheal,
O'n dùn sin do leughar leinn do dh' eangnamh nighean Fhorgainn.
Thigeas gniomh nan saora seang gu rìgh faoilteach na fearainn,
Do fhiosrachadh sluaigh Ullaidh uaine, thigeas Cu na craoibhe ruaidh,
Mac deud-fhionn a ghruaidh mar shùgh nar eitich tighinn dh 'ar cobhar
Fad ars' Conchor ris a choin bhathas gun teachd d' ar cobhar,
Is Connuil suireach nan steud mear 'an cuibhreach 'us ceud d' ar sluagh.
Deacair dhomhsa bhi 'am bruid a fhir a chobharas air caraid,
Ni 'n reidh dol an eangnamh a lainn 's a ta le 'r cheangladh Conull.
Na smuanaich gun dol 'n a aghaidh, a rìgh nan gormlann gràineil,

A lawe croy gin lagga re nacht smoyn er heddyth is a gwreith
Cowchullin nyn sann lanni sleim noar a choala turyth connil
Di zlossa la trane a lawe di wraa skaille dyn wackawe
Innis downi er tocht id zailli a raig in tow nar ob tegwail
A liss raa in nawryth zoe fiss tarm ka di zowchiss
Dym zaissew er teacht wom hey gin skaili a zinsi zoew
Da ninsin di neach elli id zraith zinsin dare
Corrik rymsith is egin dud na skail ainsyth mir charrit
Gawsith zi royg a keyv lag ne gail tyigil vin chorrik
Ach na wea gne dighow nargenn a honchow aw ne herrin
A lawe zasga in dowss trot mo clow wea in nasge aggit
Heymon and dyr chon a chaill ni ta corrik a vanvaill
Na makan di tor a zwn in daltan croye layveith
Cowchullin is corrik croye di wee in lay sen fa zemoye
A invak di marwe less in ter lat chalm coive zlass
Innis downni er cowe ni glass o teith fest for naildeis
Tarm is di lonni gi lom na terg a zulchin orrin
Is me conleich m[c] nocon ir zleith zown dalgin
Is me rown dakgis ym bron is tow ag skay di tollwm
Vii bleyn di waa ma horri fylwm zasga wom war
Ni classi lcr horcher maa waa zessew a vylwum urma
Smenis cowchullin vor maik a v[c] ne in draich za chow
Gur smeine nar wraik feiltyth in ir a reyk a chwneith si chateive
A arrwm re corp no con di chow is beeg nor skarri
Re fagsin a cowlwoe a zlyn gasgeith zownyth dalgin
Mak sawalti mor a foyme ne low ym broin it ta orrin.

Di.

Auctor hujus in keich O Cloan.

Hossna charrit a cloan freich hossne leich a gassil chroa
Hossna zaneni tursyth far agus da gwllin ban oge
Ag so har in carn fane wil freich m'feich in ult woye
Fer a ryn bwychis byef is voe lontir carn freich
Gwl ein wna in crochin sor troe in skail fa wil a wan
Is say ver a hossna gyth trome Freich m'Feich nyn golk sen
Is see in nyn wan di neig in gwle ag dwle da eiss gow cloan freich
Fynowr in olt chass ail inne voyve ga bead leicht
Innen orle is our folt is freich in nocht teive er heive
Ga mor far za derge ee neir zrawig se far ach freich
Foyis mewe mwe foye cardiss freich fa far a gleye
Inchuss fa craichtyth a corp trai gin locht a zanew zee

A lamh chruaidh gun laige ri neach smuain air d' oide 'us e'n cuibhreach.
Cuchulain nan seang lann sliom, 'n uair a chual' e tuireadh Chonuil,
Do ghluais le treine a laimhe do bhreth sgeil de 'n mhacan.
Innis dhuinn air teachd a 'd dhàil a ghraidh an tu na 'r ob teugbhail,
A shlios reidh an abhraid dhuibh, fios d' ainm, co do dhùthchas ?
De 'm gheasaibh air teachd o'm thigh, gun sgeul a dh' innseadh dh' aoidh,
Da 'n innsinn do neach eile, a'd ghradhsa dh' innsinn d' àraidh.
Comhrag riumsa is éigin duit, no sgeul d' innseadh mar charaid,
Gabhsa do roghadh a chiabh lag, ni ciall tighinn gu 'm chomhrag.
Ach nior bhi gu tigeadh n'ar ceann a h-onchu agh na h-Eirinn,
A lamh ghaisge an tùs troid mo chliu bhi an nasgaidh agad.
Iomanadar thun a chéile ni ta comhrag a bhanamhuil ;
Am macan gun d' fhuair a ghuin, an daltan cruaidh lamhach.
Cuchullain is comhrag cruaidh do bhi an la sin fo dhiombuaidh,
A aon mhac do mharbhadh leis, an t-saor shlat chalm chaomhghlas.
Innis duinn ars' cù nan cleas o tathas feasd fo 'r n-ailleas,
D' ainm 'us do shloinneadh gu lom na teirig a dh' fholchainn oirnne.
Is mi Conlaoch mac na con oighre dligheach Dhuin dealgain,
Is mi an rùn d' fhagas 'am broinn 'us tu aig Sgiath 'g ad fhoghlum,
Seachd bliadhna do bha mi shoir foghlum ghaisge o'm mhathair,
Na cleasa le 'r thorchair mi bha dh' easbhuidh an fhoghluim orm
Smuaineas Cuchulain 'n uair a dh' eug, a mhac an dreach do chumhadh,
Gur smuain, ni breug, faoilte an fhir, do threig a chuimhne 's a cheudfaidh,
A urram ri corp na Con a chumha is beag nach do sgar,
Ri faicinn an culthaobh a ghlinn gaisgeach Dhun dealgain.
Mac samhailt mor a fuaim ni luaidh am bron a ta oirnne.

Do.

Is e ùghdair so an Caoch O'Cluain.

Osnadh charaid a Cluain Fraoich osnadh laoich a caiseal chrò,
Osnadh dheanadh tuirseach fear agus da an guilionn bean òg,
Ag so shear an carn far am bheil Fraoch mac Fithich an fhuilt mhaoith,
Fear a rinn buidheachas do Mhaoibh, 'us o 'n sloinntear carn Fraoich.
Gul aoin mhnath o 'n Chruachan shear, truagh an sgeul fa 'm bheil a bhean,
Is e bheir osnadh gu trom, trom, Fraoch mac Fithich nan colg sean.
Is i an aon bhean do ni an gul ag dol d'a fhios gu Cluain Fraoich,
Ainnir an fhuilt chaise aille, nighean Mhaoibh ri 'm bitheadh laoich.
Nighean Orla is òir folt 'us Fraoch an nochd taobh air thaobh,
Ge mòr fear dha 'n d'éirich e nior ghradhaich i fear ach Fraoch.
Faigheas Maoibh mo fuath cairdeas Fhraoich fa fearr a ghné,
A chuis fa creuchtadh a chorp troimh gun lochd a dheanamh rithe ;

Do churre ai gussyth vass teif re mrave ne tuk o nolk
Mor a foor a hoyt la meyf innossit gyn khelk in noss. Hossni.
Kerin di weith er loch maie de chemist in trath za hass
Gith rae gach mee torri abbe de we er
Sasse bee in kero sin fa millsyth na milli a ulae
De chonkfa a kerin derk far gin wey gi kend ix traa
Bleyn er heil gi ir di churri sin fa skail garve
Gi borin di lucht kneis froth a wess is e derk
Di wi ainsyth no zoi ga bea ley chawyr in tloye
Pest neif zo we no vonni vakki zi cath zol da woyn
Bein aslaynti throm throm ynnin ayith ni gorn seyr
Di curri lai fiss er freich feisrych kid hane ree
A durde meyve nach be slan mir woe lane i boss meith
Di cheyrew in loch oyr gin dwneni za woyna ach freich
Knossych reyve ne zarni mee er v'feich gi knai zerg
Ge ger darnis ai er freich rachsit di vonni ker a veyf
Glossis freich fa fer a naye voyne zi nave er in locht. Hossni.
For a fest is ee na soynna is a kenna soss ris in noss
Freich mac feich an erma zeiar hanik one fest gin is dee
Hug a houlti ker nark ferrin roif meyf zaa tee
Ach gai math in duggis latti i durt meyf is gal crow
Ne oyr mis a leith loayn ach slat a woyan as a bonni
Togris freich is ner zilli teymmi naf a riss er in ling vak
Is ner ead ach ga mor ayze hech one vass in roive chwd
Gawiss i kerin er varri targi a cran as i raif
Toyrt doe choss zo in der mogrziss zo riss in pest
Beris er agis ai er snawf is gavis a lawf no chrissyth
Di zave sessin is er chail trow gin a skayn ag freich
Fynowr in olt chass ail di ran chwggi skan din oyr
Leddryth a phest a kness bayn is teskith a lawe er looe
Di hudditeyr bone re bone er trae ni glach cor fo hass
Freich m'feich is in fest troy a zai mir hug in dress
Ga coyrik ne coyrik car di ruk lass a kanna na lave
Mar chonik in neyn ee di choy na nail er in trae
Eris in neyn one tave gavis in laive bi laive bak
Ga ta so na cwt nyn nane is mor in teach i rin a voss
Voyn vass sen di foar in far loch mai go len din loch
A ta in tarm sen dee gi loan ga zerma in noss guss in noss. Hossni.
Berrir in sen gu cloan freich corp in leich gow kassil chroyg
Er in glan tuggi a anm is mark varris da loo
Carn lawe in carn so raym heive a lave reyth di beast sonni
Fer ner ympoo in dress fer bo zawsi nert in drot
Invin im bail ner ob zawe ym beddeis mnan i torvirt fook

Do chuir i e gus a bhàs, taobh ri mnathaibh ni tug o 'n olc,
Mòr a phùdhar a thuit le Maoibh inniseam gun cheilg a nis. Osnadh
Caorthainn do bhi air Loch Maoibh do chimid an traigh do dheas,
Gach a ré 'us gach a mios toradh abuich do bhi air.
Seasamh bha an caora sin, fa millse no mil a bhlàth,
Do chumadh a caoran dearg fear gun bhiadh gu ceann naoi tràth,
Bliadhna air shaoghal gach fir do chuir sin is sgeul dearbh,
Gu 'm b' fhoirinn do luchd chneidh brìgh a mheas 'us e dearg.
Do bhi imcheist 'n a dheigh ge bith lighich a chobhradh an t-sloigh,
Béisd nimh do bhi 'n a bhun bh' aca do chath dhol g'a bhuain.
Bhitheann an euslaint throm, throm, nighean Athaich nan corn saor,
Do chuireadh leath fios air Fraoch ; dh' fhiosraich ciod 'thàinig rithe.
A dubhairt Maoibh nach bitheadh slàn mar bitheadh làn a boise maoith,
De chaoraibh an Loch fhuair, gun duine g'a bhuain ach Fraoch.
Cnuasachd riamh nior dheanadh mi ars' mac Fithich nan gruaidh dearga,
Ge gur dheanas e air Fraoch racham do bhuain caor do Mhaoibh.
Gluaiseas Fraoch fa fear an àigh uainn gu snàmh air an Loch,
Fhuair e a bheisd 'us i 'n a suain us a ceann suas ris an dos. Osnadh.
Fraoch mac Fithich nan arm geur, thainig o 'n Bhéisd gun fhios d'i,
Thug e ultach de chaora dearg far an robh Maoibh dh' a ti.
Ach ge maith na thugas leat, a dubhairt Maoibh is geal cruth,
Ni fhoghain dhomhsa, laoich luinn, ach slat a bhuain as a bhun.
Tugras Fraoch is nior gille tioma snàmh a rìs air an linn bhog,
'Us nior fhaod e ge mor 'agh, theachd o 'n bhàs 's an robh a chuid,
Gabhas an caorthuinn air bhàrr, tarruingidh an crann as a fhreumh,
Toirt a chosan dha air tìr mosglas da suas a Bhéisd.
Beireas air 'us e air snàmh 'us gabhas a làmh 'n a craos,
Do ghabh esan ise air ghial, truagh gun a scian bhi aig Fraoch.
Ainnir an fhuilt chaise aille do rainig thuige le sgian de 'n òir,
Leadair a bhéisd a chneas bàn 'us teasgadh a lamh air luath.
Do thuiteadar bonn ri bonn air traigh nan clacha corr fa dheas,
Fraoch mac Fithich 'us a bhéisd truagh a Dhé mar thug an treis.
Ge comhrag ni comhrag gearr do rug leis a ceann 'n a laimh,
Mar chunnaic an nighean e do chaidh i 'n a neul air an traigh,
Eireas an nighean o 'n tàmh gabhas an làmh bu làmh bog.
Ge ta so 'n a chuid nan eun, is mòr an t-euchd a rinn a bhos,
O 'n bhàs sin do fhuair am fear, Loch Maoibh do lean air an loch,
A ta an t-ainm d'i gu luain 'g a ghairm a nuas gus a nis. Osnadh.
Beirear an sin gu Cluain Fraoich corp an laoich gu caiseal chrò,
Air a ghleann thug e ainm, is mairg a mhaireas da éis beò.
Carn Laimh an carn so ri 'm thaobh is laimh rithe do bhitheas sona,
Fear nior iompaich an treise, fear a b' annsa neart an trod.
Ionmhuinn beul nar ob daimh do m' bitheadh mnathan a tabhairt phòg,

Invin tearn nyn sloye invin groye ner zerk in ross
Doigh no feach bar a olt derk a zroye no ful leicht
Fa meyni na kower schrowe gilli na in snacht kneas freicht
Cassi na in kaissnai olt gurm a rosg na yr lak
Derk na partain a wail gil a zaid na blai feich
Ard a ley na cranna swle beynni no teyd kwle a zow
Snawe di bar no freich cho di hene a heif re strow
Fa lannyth na koillith a skaith invin trae ve re drum
Coiffad a land is a lawe lanni cholk na clar zi long
Troye nach ann in gorik re leich di hut freich a fronni oyr
Durss sin a huttim la pest troe a zai nach marrin foss.
Hossni.

A houdir so Connil carnych m'eddirschol.

A chonnil cha salve no kinn devin lum gyr zergkis tierm
No kinn di chw er a zad slontir lat no fir foe fyve
A neyn orgil nyn nach a evir oik ne bree binn
Sanna in nerik chon ni gless hugis loym in ness no kinn
Ka in kenn mallych zow mor dergkyth nayn ross a zroy glan
Is sai is gir zin lee clea a kenn deive ne raa dait
Kenn ree mee nyn nach loait arse m'carbre nyn goith camm
In nerik mo zaltan fen hugis lwm in gayn a kenn
Kai in kenn oid er mye haale go volt fand gi malle sleime
Rosk mir erre dait mir vlait alda no cach crwth a kinn
Manne boe fir nyn nach makmeyf zi zrach gyth coyn
Dagis a chollin gyn kenna is di hwt wlle lum a loye
Ka in ken so zawis tow id laive a chonnil vor ne bae linn
O nach marrin kow nin gless keid verre how er less a kinn
Kann v'erris nyn nacht verreyth a ceith gyth gurt
Mac mo fayr in tur hang di skarris a khenn ra chwrp
Ka in kenn od hear in nolt inn da greddyth no kinn go laive
Hurris annith er a zow gyn roveddir sal da rar
Sess a sowd di hwt in kow di rad a chorp fa wrow dass
Cow mac conna re nyn rann hugis lam a kenn ter aiss
Ka in da ken so is fadde mach a chonnil vor a vraa byig vinn
Er zraigh tenne na kel orn anym no ver a zon ne herm
Kenn leyirre is clar cwlte in da kenn di hut lem zonna
Di zon swt cowchullin charn swn zergis merm na wulle
Kai in da kenn so is fadde sorre a chonnil vor gi gal znee
Ennyn dae er volt ni verr derk in groye na ful leych
Cwllin bray is cwnlit croye deiss di verre boye lai ferk

Ionmhuinn tighearn nan sluagh, ionmhuinn gruaidh nar deirge an ròs,
Duibhe no fiach barr a fhuilt, deirge a ghruaidh no fuil laoich,
Bu mhine no cobhar srutha, gile no sneachd cneas Fhraoich,
Caise no an caisein 'fholt, guirme a rosg na oidhre leac,
Deirge no partan a bheul, gile a dheud no blàth fiodh,
Ard a shleagh mar chrann siùil, binne no teud ciuil a ghuth,
Snamhaiche a b 'fhearr no Fraoch, cha do shìn a thaobh ri sruth,
Bu leathainn no comhla a sgiath, ionmhuinn tràth bhith ri druim,
Bu chomhfhad a lamh 'us a lann, leathainn a cholg no clar luinge,
Truagh nach b'ann 'an comhrag ri laoch do thuit Fraoch a bhronnadh oir,
Tuirse sin a thuiteam le Béisd, truagh a Dhe nach mairionn fòs.
Osnadh.

Is e ùghdair so Conull cearnach Mac Edarscoil.

A Chonuill, cha sealbh na cinn, deimhin leam gur dheargas d'airm,
Na cinn do chi'm air a ghad sloinntear leat na fir fo fhaoibh.
A nighean Fhorghuil nan each, A Eimhear oige na brigh binn,
Is ann an éiric Chon nan cleas, thugas leam an nios na cinn.
Co an ceann mullach donn mòr, deirge no'n ròs a ghruaidh glan,
Is e a 's goire do 'n leth chlì an ceann diubh nach d'atharraich dath?
Ceann rìgh mi nan each luath, ars' Mac Cairbair nan goith cam;
An éiric mo dhaltan féin thugas leam an cein an ceann.
Co an ceann ud air m' aghaidh thall, co folt fann gu mall sliom,
Rosg mar fheur, deud mar bhlàth, ailde no gach cruth a cheann?
Manadh b'e fear nan each, Mac an Aoife do chreachadh gach cuan,
Do fhàgas a choluinn gun cheann 'us do thuit uile leam a shluagh.
Co an ceann so ghabhas tu a'd laimh a Chonuill mhòir nam bàigh linn,
O nach marrainn Cu nan cleas ciod bheireadh tu air leas a chinn?
Ceann mac Fherghuis nan each, bheireadh e cith gach gurt,
Mac mo phcathar an tur sheang do sgaras a cheann r'a chorp.
Co an ceann ud shear an fhuilt fhinn d' an greadadh na cinn gu 'làimh,
Fhuaireas aithne air a ghuth gun robhadar seal d'a reir?
Sios an sud do thuit an Cu do rad a chorp fo bhrù deas,
Cu mac coin r'gh nan rann thugas leam a cheann tar éis.
Co an da cheann so is faide mach a Chonuill mhoir a bhreth bu bhinn,
Air ghràdh teann na ceil oirnn ainm nam fear a ghuin na h-airm?
Ceann Laoghaire 'us clar Chuilt an da cheann do thuit le'm ghuin,
Do ghuin sud Cuchullin ceairn, sonn dheargas m'airm 'n a fhuil.
Co an da cheann so is faide soir, a Chonuill mhoir gach geal ghniomh,
Ionnan dath air folt nam fear deirge an gruaidh no fuil laoich?
Cullain breagh 'us Cunnlaid cruaidh dithis bheireadh buaidh le feing,

A evyr seid sor a kinna dagis a gwrp fa linna derk
Ka ne vi kinn so solk maine de chewe feyn er mye hoyth
Gwrm in nye dwe a volt o hilla rosg connil croye
Sessir eascardin a chow chlann challidtein a mwe znaie
Is said sud in sessir leyve a hut lwm sin norm no laive
A chonnil vor aithr ree kayn in ken od da gallith catht
Gin or fai treilse wa keyand gyn codyth slem ghardyth vart
Kenna v'finn v'rosse roye v'necnee hor bas lam nert
A evir is se so a cheud ardree layyn nyn land brak
A chonnil vor mugh a skail creid a hut lad laive gin locht
Din tloe eignyth a veil sin a deiltiss kinn na con
Deachnor is seacht fychid kead derym peyn is awyr sloe
Di hut lomsa drwme er zrum di neve mo cwlk cunlaa rag
A chonnil kynis taidda mnae inssefail dessne ni con
Cowf v'hawalt haye na veil agga fein ar for
A evir keid di zarna mai gyn mo kowe ym rer san socht
Gyn mo zaltan fa mhaa crow a dol voym a mugh so n . . .
A chonnil tok me sa vert tok mo lacht oss lacht no con
Os da chowe rachfeu ayk cwr mo vail re bail no eon
Is mai evyr is keyn dalve ne feine sarve daylta zoive
Di zerr no cha nul mo spess troe murreich er eiss a chon.

A chonnil.

A howdir so Keilt m'ronane.

Heym tosk zoskla fynn gow tawri ni draive nevin
Gow hormy moyr mhorlat mhirr gow cormik m'art inir
Ner cleacht me meith my zloon orss afwllych fer eddrwme
Gi waldeis feynyth fail oss word locht a foyall
Warwemir in leich lan mir a warwemir in crayc
Di charmisdir leich fane lay mir a charssmir a ray
Hugssmir a cann gin cherri guss a gnok oss boyamir
Di rynis feyn boya tra di roynis fogryth owlay
Di warwiss mun er zlinn fer gi inwal in nerrin
Di roynissi boya tra di roynissi fogryth owlay
Di raddis mun er zlinu gwl gi inte in nerrin
Di roynissi boya tra di royniss fogryth owlay
Ni leith di legin fa boywa doybis sin nerrin awwor
Di roynissi boya tra di royniss fogryth owlay
Ni dorssa er a beith a zeith zark a dosslin ead gi hymard
Di roynissi boya traa di royniss fogry owlay
Ni gurt abbe um halvon di loskgin ead gu lassal

A Eimhear sud soir an cinn do fhagas an cuirp fo linne dearg.
Co na sé cinn so is olc méin do chitheam féin air m' aghaidh thuath,
Gorm an aghaidh, dubh am folt, o thilleadh rosg Chonuill chruaidh ?
Seisir eascairdean a Choin, clann Chaileidin nam buaidh ghnàth,
Is iad sud an seisir laoich a thuit leam 's an airm 'mo laimh.
A Chonuill mhòir athair rìgh co an ceann ud do 'n geilleadh cath,
Gur orbhuidh trillis o 'cheann co 'n comhdach sliom dh' airde bheart,
Ceann mhic Fhinn mhic Rois ruaidh mhic na Cneidh fhuair bàs le 'm [neart,
A Eimhear is e so a cheud, ardrìgh Laighein nan lann breac.
A Chonuill mhòir, mùgh an sgeul, creud a thuit le'd laimh gun lochd,
De 'n t-sluaigh eagnaidh a bheil sin a dioltas cinn na Con ?
Deichnear 'us seachd fichead ceud deiream féin is aireamh sluaigh,
Do thuit leamsa druim air dhruim, do nimh mo cholg conla rag,
A Chonuill, cionnus taid mnathan Innsefail an deigh na Con,
Cumha a mhic shamhailt tha na bheil aca féin air foir ?
A Eimhear ciod a dheanadh mi gun mo Chu a 'm reir s' an Soc
Gun mo dhaltan fa maith cruth a dol uam 'am mugh an nochd,
A Chonuill tog mi 's an fheart, tog mo leac os leac na Con,
Os d'a chumhadh racham eug, cuir mo bheul ri beul na Con.
Is mi Eimhear is caoine dealbh, ni faigheam searbh dioltadh dhomh,
Do dheur nocha n 'eil mo speis, truagh m' fhuireach air éis a Chon.
A Chonuill.

Is e ùghdair so Caoilte Mac Ronain.

Chaidheam tosg a dh' fhuasgladh Fhinn, gu Teamhra nan sreabh aoibhinn,
Go h-airm a 'm faighear' bhòrrshlat mhear, gu Cormaig Mac Airt aoin fhir,
Nior chleachd mi maidheamh mo ghlonn ger fuileach fior eutrom,
Gu bheildeis Fianna Fail os bhord Locha Feabhuil.
Mharbhamair an laoch làn, mar a mharbhamair an Cuireach,
Do chearbmasdair laoch fa liach, mar a chearbsamair an triath,
Thugsamair ceann gun choire, gus a chnoc os Buadhamair.
Do rinneas féin buaidh tràth, do rinneas fògradh ullamh,
Do mharbhais mun fhear ghrinn fear gach aon bhaile an Eirinn.
Do rinneas buaidh tràth do rinneas fògradh ullamh,
Do radas mu'n fhear ghrinn gul gach aon tigh 'an Eirinn,
Do rinneas buaidh tràth do rinneas fògradh ullamh.
Na laoigh do leigeann fa buaibh do bhitheas an Eirinn aghmhor.
Do rinneas buaidh tràth do rinneas fògradh ullamh.
Na dorsan air am bitheadh a ghaoth dhearg do fhosglann iad gu h-iom-[ard.
Do rinneas buaidh tràth do rinneas fògradh ullamh.
Na guirt abuich mu thalmhainn, do loisgeann iad gu lasail.

Di roynissi boya tra di royniss fogryth owlay
Noch char aggis reim linn aa na mullin in nerrin
Insin di leyggiddir rwm eech albin is errin
Teym boach er loyss mi chass gr ranegiss ross illirzlass
In sin glossimsi schear gow taura ni widdir chane
Ner harrin eine each zeive zea roym in dawra za essin
Tugis in dawra fa laa ben in ir chommi za cheilli
Is ben in r chomisso nach gwss in fer commisso ella
Tugis in dawri gi beach ben carbre zi cormik
Is ben chormik er sin di raddis ee zi charbre
Tugis lwm claywa in reith uch fa hay mor a wree
Mi clawe feyn fa gin gutti fagwm in droyl chulk chormik
In sin di quhoyis in nwnn is eaddi in dorsser owym
Inn nygyth sin doef ge beacht is me bi kyllor ze chormik
Is bert ooklachis is tei hawle a vaonissi reith errin
Ga zaynith leve raa mi zloor da hwle cheilt yn kyllnor
Na habbirsi sen er finn er ardre ny feyn voltynn
Ga tamsi in layve id tei na ber tar er my wntir
Ni hay sin agne cheilt far a will ay in vorwilty
Cha mir sen ay connil chynni er a wll dor er talvinn
In sin tarnik in toylli ag in re ro zast rawor
IIII choss geym in genn ni genn teym less a is tee cotkin
In sin chayis fa zass di bi wlyg ay di maylass
Aggis tuggis lwm ym zoyn kone esgin ard orwayll
Eynit lwm in nee riss a ben ers in re fati firzlinn
Balli kness cheilti za zoyn di chone essgin orwoyl
Na habbirsi sen a re er wiss in ryth a zillin
Brarryth broggodych a derri corsi hoich er orvidi
Er a layve a keilt chaylle mir woe finn flaa eyni
Gid tani ne hurfin gyle derrow albin no errin
Er maneach do gi beacht a deaffryth mis zi chormik
Gawa tow cow thlaa woyme zoskla mydda
Ne warrir fin lat id te er ane chowe er talwon
Ach ane chow a keilt chaye da bi toylling tow faywayll
Da waya a tow zoif re lay lawnon woada di gi feyane
Di zoyve tow hed er gi cart cowe cwnnvill
Di nasgis in brar mir er chormik m^c art inir
Gin leggi gi ray in re da waya ay ni feyweill
Mar nasgis in brar beynn er re errin ni nwlt inn
In deymsow gar zeggir royve heymsyth ze in dymf
Glossim turriss o hawre fa turriss fr gi mannee
Do hymsow ni heltin gar skeltyth a chwddychi
Tuggis lwm ii zelt zark is ii znew ignyth ym ard

Do rinneas buaidh tràth, do rinneas fògradh ullamh.
Noch char fhaiceas ri 'm linn àth no muileann an Eirinn.
An sin do leigeadar rium eich Albainn 'us Eirinn;
Teighim beò air luathas mo choise gur rainigeas Ros Iolair ghlais,
An sin gluaiseamsa siar gu Teamhra an fhidireachdainn,
Nior theàruinn aon each dhiubh dhe, romham in Teamhra do esan.
Tugas in Teamhra fa leth, bean an fhir choma dh' a chéile,
'Us bean an fhir choma so gun achd gus an fhear choma so eile.
Tugas an Teamhra gu beachd bean Chairbair do Chormaig,
'Us bean Chormaig an sin do radais i do Charbair.
Tugas leam claidheamh an Rìgh, Och ! fa h-e mòr a bhrìgh,
Mo chlaidheamh féin bha gun chuid fagaim an truaill chuilg Chormaig.
An sin do chaidheas a nunn 'us eideadh an dorsair faigheam,
An oidhche sin domh gu beachd is mi bu choinnleir do Chormaig,
Is beart oglachais 'us ti h-amhuil am fianuis rìgh Eirinn,
Ge iognadh leibh ràdh mo ghlòir, da shùil Chaoilte 'am choinnleir.
Na h-abairse sin ars' Fionn ars' ardrigh na Feinn folt-fhionn,
Ged thathamsa an làimh a'd tì na beir tàir air mo mhuinntir.
Ni h-e sin aigne Chaoilte fear a bheil e 'am mòralachd
Cha mar sin e coinneal chain air a bheil d'òr air talmhainn.
An sin tairngeadh an t-òl aig an rìgh ro ghasta ro mhòr,
Ceithir chois cheum an ceann nan ceann, teighim leis 'us ti an coitchionn,
An sin chaidheas fa dheas, do bu bhladh e de m' aimhleas,
Agus tugas leam a'm dheoin caoin éisginn ard fhuarail,
Iognadh leam an ni ris a bhean 'ars an rìgh fead fiorghriun,
Boladh cneas Chaoilte do gheibhean de' chaoin éisginn fhuarail.
Na h-abairse sin a rìgh, ars' mise an riochd a ghille,
Briathran bragaideach a deir thu, gur airidh air oirmhide.
Air do laimh a Chaoilte chàil mar bhi Fionn flath Fheinne,
Ged ta mi ni thoirinn geill d' fhearaibh Albainn no Eirinn.
Air m' aithneach' da gu beachd, do fheòraich mis de Chormaig,
An gabhadh tu cumha tlàth uam air fhuasgladh m' oide ?
Ni bheirear Fionn leat a'd thì air aon chumha air talmhainn,
Ach aon chumha, a Chaoilte chaidh, da bu thualainn duit fhaigheal;
Da 'm faigheadh tu dhomh re la, lanamhain uait de gach fiadhmhuin,
Do gheibheadh tu d' oide air gu ceart an cumha a chumail.
Do naisgeas am briathar mear air Cormag Mac Airt aoin fhir,
Gun leigeadh gu réidh an rìgh, da faigheadh e 'na fiadhmhil,
Mar a naisgeas am briathar binn air rìgh Eirinn an fhuilt fhinn,
An tiomsachadh ge dheacair riamh, thionnsgainn d'a dheanamh.
Gluaiseam turus o Theamhra, fa turus fir mu' n iath,
Do thiomsachadh na h-ealtainn ger sgaoilteach a chuideachd,
Tugas leam da gheilt gharg, 'us da ghriobh ioghnach iomard,

Aggis fey fy za won ii lach sin loch a seyllin
II hynnith sleyvecwllin ii zaw awlle a burrin
II zessivey zowrane zurm ii chellych fey a farzhram
II hyane kylty creive di latteve zrom zawrein
II zoyvrane o hen a mach o charri donnwane doyvr
II eillin o thrae leith lee ii rulli a port larga
IIII snekga on vrostna wane ii anoyk charga d . . .
II eachte one eachte ard ii smoyrych lettreth lom ard
II zroyllane downe yve ii cheinkych ni corywe
II chur one chorrin cleyth ii harreich mwe o foyall
II illir chargi ni glach ii hawik a keyndyth
II fess o locht melwa ii cherk ussga o locht erne
II cherk reich one vowna math ii zergin zow locha
II chreithrane mw cowlin ii wentane my foyllin
II cheythane a glenn awlle ii zalvon ni sen awle
II phedda oywrri a claa ii onchon o chroda claach
II zoyane o thrae za wan ii erboyk loychir yr
II chollum one chess chur ii lon a lettir fin chwle
II eddoyk letter roye ii thrudda tawrych teyve oyr
II choneyn a schee doe doynn ii wuk awlde cloyth chur
II choyag o zrom dave ii ane oywryth layn de
II yghrgane lanenyth furrith ii chreithir one chreive roye
II sperr hawk in swn o cleyve gla ii loch lay o lwnycht
II oyr ane one woyn ii ussock on vownych wor
II oynlayk a hon chnoyth ii brok a creich ollonych
II rynith strayth sinnyth ii zlassoyk o wroch urri
II chrottych o chonych zawlwe ii weil won wor hawni
II earrinnyth philloyrrych ii awllinnych seith boygh
II zassidi one wyg wylle ii cheith cheinekyche chnaw chyle
II woyok oo wrowych brn ii neiskin o zowdyr
II zerrin o leyve za ane da chyill wreane turle
II annan ar o wy walg ii chonlane zatta o zranard
II zrin zarrych o zruing ii vronargane on vor cheyyl
II wlyrrych o zowne ni barga ii elli zalle on zaltraach
II royin o challow charga ii wuk war on worarga
II eskar locht m'lanene ii zarzart my ni nellane
II ane vek o wess a chwle ii eggin ess v'mowrn
II ellit zlinni zlinn smoyl ii woyif o haach mow mor
II onchon loyath o loch conn ii eychat a hoyw chroychin
II chyraa schee zoyvlane zil ii vuk vwlcow vlyr
Rath is ker chorkrych chass tugis lwm o einnis
Tugis lum each agis lar di zrey vassych vanynane
Tarve is bo zarri o zrwm kein tugis lwn o wurn vunchane

Agus fithich Fiodh dha bheann, da lach sin Loch a Seillein,
Da shionnach Sleibh Chuilinn da dhamh allaidh a Burrainn,
Da cheis Fiodh dhobhrain ghuirm, da choilleach fiodha Faradhruim,
Da thaghan Coillte chraoibh, de lethtaobh Dhruim dha raoin,
Da dhobhrain o sin a mach, o charaig Donabhain dobhair,
Da fhaolan o thràigh Locha Léith, da Shruall a Port Lairge.
Ceithir snag o'n Bhrosna bhàn, da eanag Charga dàin,
Da eachta o'n Eachta àrd, da smeorach Leitir lom àrd,
Da dhreollan o'n Dùn aoibh, da chaingeach o'n Choire dhuibh,
Da chòr o'n Chorrainn cleibh, da earfhiach Magha Feabhuil,
Da iolar Chairge nan clach, da sheabhag Fiodh Chonnach,
Da fheis o Locha Meilghe, da chearc uisge o Loch Eirinn,
Da chearc fraoich o'n Mhonadh mhaith, da dhearcan Dhubh-locha,
Da chriochran Maigh Cuillin, da mhiontan Maigh Tuallainn,
Da chaochan o Ghleann Ghaibhle, da ghealbhan na sean Abhla,
Da pheata odhar Athcliath, da onchoin o Bhroit cliathach,
Da dhuibhean o Thraigh dha bhan, da earbag Luachair Ire
Da cholum o'n Cheas Chuir, da lon a Leitir Fionnchuil,
Da pheatag Leitir ruaidh, da thruid a Teamhra Taoibh uaine,
Da choinein a Sith dubh donn, da mhuc alta Cluaidh Chuir,
Da chuthag o Dhroma Daibh, da eun odhar o Lainde,
Da adharcan Leanain na Furraich, da chreabhair o'n Chraobh ruadh,
Da speirag an sin o Shliabh glé, da luch liath o Luimneach,
Da dhobhran o'n Bhuain, da uiseag o'n Mhonadh mhòr,
Da ialltag o uaimh Chnuadha, da bhroc o Chrioch Ullanach,
Da thraghna Srath Sinne, da ghlasag o Bhruach bhiora,
Da chrotach o chuain Ghailimh, da mhiol o'n Mhuirtheimhne,
Da fherain Fiodh luachraich, da thallan a Sith buidhe,
Da gheasadich o'n Mhagh mhall, da chlith cheangach a Chnamh choille,
Da bhuidheag o'n Bhruthach brugh, da neasgain o Dhubh dur,
Da dheargan o Shliabh dha eun, da chathail Bhraigh an Turla,
Da eun an àr o Mhagh bhuilg, da ghobhlan daithte o Ghranard,
Da ghriobh garrach o Ghruing, da bhroinndheargan o'n mhòr choille,
Da bhliorach o Dhun nam bàrc, da eala gheala o'n Ghealtraigh,
Da ruadhan o Chala Chairge, da mhuc mara o'n mhor fhairge,
Da easgair Loch M'Leanan, da ghearrghart Maigh nan eilean,
Da eun bheag o Mhios a Chuil, da eagan Eas Mhic Muirne,
Da eilid ghlan Ghlinne Smeoil, da bhuaibh o Achadh Maigh Moire,
Da onchon luath o Loch Con, da fhiadh-chat o h-Uaimh Chruachain,
Da chaora Sith Dhoibhlain ghil, da mhuc de mhucaibh M'Lir,
Reith 'us caora chorcrach chas tugas leam o Innis,
Tugas leam each agus làr de ghreidh mhaisich Mhananain,
Tarbh 'us bo dhàir o Dhruim Cain tugas leam o Mhuirn Mhuinchain,

Do chonni di chonnew ni wane di hir cormik orrum gi dane
Gi neith zar chursin ym chenn tugis lwm is teym [Teym
Er in dymsychyth ull doyf gow lar ane ew
Nor a baillwme a meyow zobbredir voyme ach skeillych
Di choy in feaych woym o zess di bi wlya dom awles
Di rukgis er in glenn da wan o orrir loch a lurgin
Di quhoy mi lach fa layve nach chussit faywail
Ter schroyow berwe brass gow aych inn zowlass
Di zowis e er wrawit gin ger walaa heach hanye
Tugis lwm ee lach gin wacht dosli fin o chormik
Ne fooris zolk roya heg rwm nyg ve me boa
Cha deyd ass mi chree chinn gin nawleggir may in dalvon
Lass ane nane beg lassane nane dolle a chass ymon
Er gi tullych er gi ay cor fa lawe ag lassyn ane
I chonwaille fynn ag in layve er seiltin gin ead wawne
Is vin zeyntyth ay sin de hoyrt er a gowe dinn fosslow zoywayl
In dymsychow sin mir sin ner toylling fir in doythin
Tugis ead gow taura lwm gow mowr a vor hyle
Doss gi zokkir a kin oppir ead in nyich sin
Caythir a wee si walli er ix dorss fossgillyth
Cormik hug zeyve in teacht mir zoy ym bea gi skei
Mir chonni may za gwryth sin wrow arsing ill wrunych
Legga brudlychyth gawe vin a guddichtyth greithane
Huggi ay brow slatzall sollis doyf er chegit fre zorre
Gi in dorris deyve downtyth ner way in soyve cond in . . .
Ead sin is tee gi bronych miss a mwe gi anoyith
Mi chree cowe connis fa la er gi in dorris
Ga mor nolk forris royth wonyth skeythow choolyth
Ner leigis ane deyve a mach gi tra erre in in varrich
Anmi ny hyrri skeiltyth a chorymryth keilta
Ach a wag sin teyve ra teyve ne dor chormik za soyve
Nor a leggi finn a mach di skeillidir gi skeiltytht
Cha deacha deis na trear wo hawra zeive er in . . .
Mi reith feyn agus reach fenn merrolta cheme wass mi chinn
Ni tre neachin fa darryth zoyve ni troyth sin di hymsichow.
We skay zoym er mi clow creddwm in crist is ow
Mimirche ass in ew inn gar vewwm lwm ne weym . . .
Gar wadda mi leymsi har in dawr lochra ni wayn,
Is fadda in laym rugis ter xx kead try in dawr
In sen fa lowwr mi leym wagis si viddircheyn
Gin ach bar mi choss a geill mawl gith tosk er deym
Teym tosk

Da chon de chonaibh na Fiann, do shir Cormaig orm gu dian,
Gach ni dha 'r chuir sin a 'm cheann, tugas leam a 's teigheam,
Air an tiomsachadh uile domh gu lar aon mhaigh,
'N uair a b'aill leam am maigheadh dh' obairidear uam gu sgaoilteach,
Do chaidh am fiach uam o dheas, do bu bhlagh do 'm aimhleas,
Do rugas air an Gleann da bhan, o oirthir Loch a Lurgain,
Do chaidh mo lach fa laimh, nach usa faighail,
Thar sruthaibh beirbh brais, gu Achainn dubh ghlais,
Do ghabhas i air bhraghaid, gun gur mhaith leath theachd thugam,
Tugas leam an lach gun achd, d' fhuasgladh Fhinn o Chormaig.
Na fhuaras a dh' olc roimh thig rium am feadh a thamhas mi beò,
Cha teid as mo chridhe chionn gun adhlaicear mi an talmhainn ;
Leis an eun bheag leis an eun, 'dol a chas ioman,
Air gach tulaich 'us gach feath, 'cur fa lamh aig leis an eun.
E 'cumail Fionn aig an laimh, air saoiltinn gun iad fhaighinn,
'Us o'n dh' aontaich sin do thoirt air a chumha d' Fhionn fhuasgladh,
An tiomsachadh sin mar sin nior tuallainn fir an domhain.
Tugas iad gu Teamhra leam gu maor a mhòr thalla.
Domhsa gu docair a chionn, obair fad na h-oidhche sin,
Caithir do bhi 's a bhaile air naoi dorsaibh fosgailteach ;
Cormaig thug dhoibh an teach mar gheibheam bhi gu sgìth.
Mar chunnaic mi g'an cur, s'a bhrugh fharsuinn uile bhreun,
Leigeadh bruaidleanachd garbh o'n a chuideachd grianach,
Thug e brugh slatgheal soluis domh air caogad fri dhorus,
Gach aon dorus diubh duinte nior bhi an saoibh . . .
Iad sin a 's tì gu brònach mis a muigh gu anaobhach ; .
Mo chridhe cumhadh connais fa leth air an dorus,
Ge mòr an t-olc fhuaras roimhe o na sgiathaibh chuallaidh
Nior leigeas a h-aon diubh a mach gu tràth éiridh a mharaich.
Ainm a chorra sgaoiltich "Corr imirce" Chaoilte,
Ach am faicinn taobh ri taobh ni 'n d'fhuair Cormaig de shoman.
'N uair a leigeadh Fionn a mach, do sgaoileadar gu sgaoilteach,
Cha deachaidh dithis no triar, o Thamhra dhoibh air aon rian.
Mo ruith féin agus rath Fhinn miorbhuil chitheam os mo chionn,
Na tri nithean fa d'éirich dhomh, an treud sin do thiomsachadh.
Bu sgiath dhomh air mo chliù, creideam an Criosd, 'us thu,
M'imirce as a mhagh, Fhinn, ge 'r bhitheam lom ni bhitheam fann,
Ge 'r fada mo leumsa shear, an Tamhra laochruidh na Feinn,
Is fad an leum thugas siar, fichead ceud troidh an Tamhra.
An sin bu leobhar mo leum, am facas 's a mheidir-chein
Gun ach bàr mo chois a geillt', mall gach tosg air an teigheam.
Chaitheam.

Gun ainm Ughdair.

Id ta fane tullych so toye m^c^ veckowle is groy colk
M'dadzail neyn in derk nach tug ra erk braeir borb
Id ta fane tullych so dess m'vec goyne kness mir wlay
Cha dor sai nach fa neith in gress noch char veine yth law
Id ta fa tullych horryth ossgyr bi vath gol is gnee
Clan morn gai math ni fir noch char chur sai sen im bree
Id ta fa tullych so har gillyth bi van less nyth mnawe
M'ronane dor weyth clar fane tallych soo har id ta
Id ta fane tullych so foyme innor vyth von groik is grane
Connan dyth zaf gyth murn fa tullych fume id ta.
Id ta

A ZORRI tryillmyt gow find ighilk ernacht sowch linn
Zarre kinn zulle er in ree gyn gurmist aye gai keive cleith
Is lesk lumsyth zwle anna onach clwnnwn gr fan chenna
Is nach feadmist a zeilt kenna v'morn vor znewe
Kail lusse ne is allwm pen id durd conan mor gyn keale
Marmy for mach gyth dunna in deilt zwle olt voe
Suyth in trur var mon din nane onach lamyt di zin fen
Abbir a zorre is lawr fayr sinni sin trom alle
Marvesyth ossin mor m'fyn marve mai in tosgir nach teymmi
Marve dyrre kilte kaye fayir sinni wlle er in lawe
Matht is aggwm ne veis anna cha dik linna movil er finn
Tuttmy ulle sin alle cha dikge gowle dr gowrne
Da byth inni byth le a nort dyth churmist finni za leacht
Is ferr nyth brar gyn nelle a derssi rwt a zorre.
A zorre.

A houdir so ——.

Laa zane deach Finn di zoill in nalwe is ner ymmit sloyg
Sessir bann is sessir far Iyn zhil is anneir ucht zaall
Finn fayn is Dermoit gin on keilt is ossain is oskir
Conan meithl gom maal er myg agus mnan nin vi leith scu
Mygin is ban einn bi zane is annir ucht zall mi wan feyn
Gormlay aolli is dow rosg neaof is neyn enneiss
Nor a zoyf meska no mnan tugsiddir in gussi raa

Gun ainm Ughdair.

A ta fo 'n tulach so tuath, Mac mhic Cumhail a's cruaidh colg,
Mac deudgheal nighinn an Deirg, nach tug r 'a fheirg briathar borb.
A ta fo 'n tulach so deas, Mac mhic Cuinn, cneas mar bhlàth,
Cha d' fhuair se neach fa ni, 'an greas nochar mhìn a làmh.
A ta fo 'n tulach so shoir, Osgar bu mhaith goil 'us gniomh,
Clann Moirn ged is maith na fir, nochar chuir e sin am brìgh.
A ta fo 'n tulach so shiar, gille bu mhiann leis na mnathaibh,
Mac Ronain do fhuair a bhith clàra, fo 'n tulach so shiar a ta.
A ta fo 'n tulach so fodham, am fear a bhi o 'n ghruaig is gràin,
Conan do gabh gach muirn, fo'n tulach fodham a ta.
A ta.

A Ghoraidh, triallamaid gu Fionn a ghilleachd air nach subhach leinn,
A dh'iarraidh cinn Ghuill air an rìgh gun cuirmaid e gu caomh clì.
Is leisg leamsa dhol ann o nach cluinneam gur fa 'n cheann,
Is nach faodmaid a dhiolt, ceann Mhic Moirn mhoir ghniomh.
Naile leatsa ni is aill leam féin a dubhairt Conan mòr gun chiall,
Marbhaidh mi air magh gach duine an diolt Ghuill fholt bhuidhe féin.
Suidhichidh an triùr armuin d'an Fheinn, o nach lamhamaid do Fhinn,
Abair a Ghoraidh 'us labhair faighear sinn 's an tròm aile,
Marbhais Ossian mòr M'Fhinn marbhaidh mi an t-Osgar nach tioma,
Marbhaidh Daoire Caoilte caidh, faighear sinn uile air an laimh.
Maitheas agam ni bhitheas ann, cha tig leinn modhail air Fionn,
Tuiteamaid uile 's an aile, cha tig Goll' gar cobharne.
Da beò Fhinn bithidh le a neart do chuirmaid Fionn d'a leac,
Is fior na briathran gun fhoill a deirsa ruit, a Ghoraidh.
A Ghoraidh.

An t-ùghdair so ——.

La dh' an deachaidh Fionn a dh' ol, an Almha 'us nior iomadh sluaigh,
Seisir bhan 'us seisir fhear inghin gheal 'us ainnir uchd-gheal,
Fionn féin 'us Diarmad gun on Caoilte 'us Oisian 'us Osgar,
Conan maol gu mall air magh, agus mnathan nan sé laoch sin,
Maigheaneas bean Fhinn bu dein, 'us ainnir uchd-gheal mo bhean féin,
Gormlaidh aoile is dubha rosg, Naoimh 'us nighean Aonghuis.
'N uair a ghabh misge na mnathan, tugsadar an cuis réidh,

Nach royf er in doythin teg sessir ban in goyth inrylk
A dowirt an nynnilt gyn on is Tulych carnich in doythin
Ga maath sewse is ymmith ban nach drynn fes ach re in ar
Gerrid er ve zawe mir sen tanik in van dar rochtin
Ein wrata wmpa gin alda agus e na iyn naygh
Tanik neyn a wrata inn an vaenissi v'kowle
Banichis din re gin non agis swis na arrygh
Fcafryth finn skail zyi din neyn lwchr lawzill
A wan a wrat gin alda keid a rad ow is tein naygh
As giss dym wrat gin alda ban ann ac na ennaygh
Nocht chay naygh dein fame wrat ach ben in ir gyn ralocht
Tawir ym brat dym wreith feyn do ter conane mor gyn chacle
Go westmist im brear mir a twg na mnawe wo chanew
Gawis ben chonnane ym brat is curris wmpa la rachta
Gom bea sen an loyth locht dar lek rys wlle a gall ocht
Mir a chonnik connan meil ym brat er cassyth fa teyf
Tawris in chreissyth gin neaf agis marveis in neyn
Gavis ben dermoit a zeil ym brat wo wrei chonnan meil
Noch char farr a wassi zyi cassi ym brat fa keiyf
Gawis ben oskyr na zey ym brad coo adda coyve ray
Ga loyvir skayth a wrat inn noch char ally a hymlyn
Gawis myghinis gi aal ym brad is di churri fa cann
Di chass is di chwar mir sen ym brat gi loa fa clossew
Tawir ym brata er m'raa dym wneissi is ne cwss clae
Go vestmist in ness gon non tres elli da hymlit dewe
Di warynsi brair riss agis ne brair eggiss
Nach darnis di weiss ri far ach dol dutsi in neiss lenew
Nochtis ben vek ree a teef curris umpi ym brat fer chei . .
A sayth eddir chass is lawe na gi ley er a lwdygnane
Ane phoik doaris in braed o wak o zwyne darmit
Di reissi ym brad owm laar mor wea see na hynnirrane
Tawrew mi wrat doyf a wnaa is me nein in derg zrana
Noch cha dernis di locht ach fess ri finn fyvir noch
Ber mo wallych is ymith woygin se der m'kowle gin boy
A dagis fa mhaalych er mnawe na tyr huggin ane lay.
Lay.

Coya lwm ymich ochtyr chor tocht er my venmyn
Cut da nymich cha chellwm gin gur wellwm gi calmi
Oskir is keilt crowith is m'lowith fa moltyr
Finn agis Dermit deadzale quogr leyttych zar nochtyr

Nach robh air an domhain tì seisir bhan ann cho ionraic,
A dubhairt an innilt gun on is tulach cearnach an domhain,
Ge maith sibhse is iomadh bean nach d' rinn fios ach ri aon fhear.
Goirid air bhi dhoibh mar sin thainig a bhean d' ar rochdain ;
Aon bhrat uimpe gun alt agus e 'n a aon fheadh,
Thainig nighean a bhrat fhinn am fianuis Mhic Cumhail,
Beannaicheas do 'n rìgh gun on agus suidheas 'n a fhaireadh,
Feòraicheas Fionn sgeul dhith, de 'n nighinn lùthor lamhghil,
A bhean a bhrat gun alt ciod a rad tu as d' aon fheadh ?
Is geas do 'm bhrat gun alt bean ann ach 'n a aon òigh
Noch cha-n fhaigh dion fo 'm bhrat ach bean an fhir gun ro lochd.
Tabhair am brat do 'm mhnaoi féin a deir Conan mòr gun chéill,
Gun éisdeamaid am briathar mear, a thug na mnathan a chianaimh,
Gabhas bean Chonain am brat, a chuireas uimpe le rachd,
Gum b'e sin an luath lochd, 'n uair leig ris uile a geal uchd.
Mar a chunnaic Conan maol, am brat air casadh f'a taobh,
Gabhas a chraoiseach gu nimh, agus marbhas an nighean,
Gabhas bean Dhiarmaid a ghaoil, am brat o mhnaoi Chonain mhaoil,
Noch char fearr a bhasa dhith, casaidh am brat f'a ciabh.
Gabhas bean Osgair 'n a déigh, am brat co fhada caomh réidh,
Ge leobhar sgiath am brat fionn, noch char fholaich a h-imlinn,
Gabhas Maigheanas gu h-aille, am brat 'us do chuireas f'a ceann,
Do chas us do chuair mar sin, am brat gu luath f'a cluaisibh.
Tabhair am brat ars' Mac Reith, do 'm mhnaoi-sa ni cuis cleith,
Gu éisdeamaid a nis gun on, treis eile d'a h-iomlaid domh.
Do bheirinnse briathar ris, agus ni briathar eigis,
Nach dearnas de fhios ri fear, ach dol duitse an aois leinibh,
Nochdas bean Mhic Reith a taobh, cuireas umpa am brat fionn,
A soigh eadar chos 'us làmh, na gu leth air a luideinean,
Aon phòg d' fhuaireas am braghad o Mhac O'Dhuine, Diarmad.
Do ruitheas am brat o um làr mar bhi si 'n a h-aonaran.
Tabhraibh mo bhrat domh a mhnathan, is mi nighean an Deirg ghraine,
Noch cha dearnas de lochd, ach fios ri Fionn faobhar nochta.
Beir mo mhallachd 'us imich uainn, is e deir Mac Cumhail gom buaidh,
A d' fhagas f'a mhallachd air mnathaibh, na d' eiridhse thugainn aon la.
Aon la.

Cuimhne leam imeachd ochdar, a chuir tochd air mo mheanmuin,
Cuid de'n imeachd cha cheileam, ged nach bheileam gu calma,
Osgar 'us Caoilte crodha 'us Mac Lughaidh a mholtar,
Fionn agus Diarmad deudgheal, cuigear laoich de'n n-ochdar.

Misse agis rynith is kerrill keyve in norrin gin lochti
Chinnimyr er chreith banwe gir wea anmyn nochtyr
Ymich orrin skaill darwe inni gi calm fane sottill,
Daggimir downe vec cowle cowin lwm ymich ochtyr
Zawrmir downe re albin bi chalme dwne a rochtin
Hut reith lay m'kowlle, cowin lwm ymich ochtyr
Er zorttymir zwle tagsin ymith class inta is corkir
Finni a wade gi brow cowin lwm ymich ochtyr
Huggymir cath sin neddall di fre tegwalle na porteiv
Rugimir boye is cowe cowin lwm ymich ochtyr
Hugimir caith ni frankgi o sann di fre gi doggir
Zowimir geylle is cowe cowin lwm ymich ochtyr
Hugimir cath ne spane a tantyn is a tochtyryn
Quhoye r my ray fane doyne cowin lwm ymich ochtyr
Hugimir caith brettin bi zeglich ay is be doggir
Hoggymır gayle doyne cowin lwm ymich ochtyr
Warrimir Crom ni carne er fargi is ay er ottill
Foyrrymir gi ter owille cowin lwm ymich ochtyr
Na rey harnik ni clossich a phatrik ossil hochmyn
Finni wayde er cowe cowin lwm ymich ochtyr
Noewe a manmsyth phadrik is hard crawe is sochyr
O phakgyth missi id coithr cowin lwm ymith ochtyr.
Cowin lwm.

NENOR a quhyme fa chyill, di woyn avr chenni cholin
Woyn avr chinni cholin chon ca mo dorin sin doyn
Zearemir my lenyth lerga is glen frethnich ni glawe nerg'
Is fer nach forrimir ann maddyth za damis cholin
Dearemir glen dorch dow glen zarve zorrith is gl clache
Is fer nach dorrimir ann maddyth za danmist cholin
Dearmir scheane zrwmmı clywe is finni wg leive na zei . . .
Is fer nach dorrimir ann maddyth za danmist cholin
Dearmir durlis war wail tawyr wry is down zawrane
Is fer nach dorrimır ann maddyth za danmist cholyn
Dearmir glen okoythyth fa forrais awr ossill
Is fer nach forrımir ann maddi za danmist cholin
Dearmir finni wy maye tawyr wry ıs kintaylle
Is fer nach dorrimir ann maddi za danmist cholin
Dearimir erri wllı eddir chonnith is donni
Is fer nach dorıimir ann maddi za danmist cholın

Mise agus Raoine 'us Caruil, caomh an fhoruinn gun lochda,
Chinneamar air chrich Bhanbha, gur b'e ainmean an ochdar.
Imeachd oinne, sgeul dearbh, fhine gu calm fo'n sotal,
Do fhàgamar Dùn Mhic Cumhail, cuimhne leam imeachd ochdar.
Ghabhamar duinn ri Albainn, bu chalm duinn a rochdainn,
Thuit righ le Mac Cumhail, cuimhne leam imeachd ochdar.
Air ghortamar dol a Shasunn, iomadh cleas ann 'us cosgradh,
Fionn gum faigheadh gach brugh, cuimhne leam imeachd ochdar.
Thugamar cath 's an Eadailt, do bhreth teagbhoil 'n a portaibh,
Rugamar buaidh 'us cumha, cuimhne leam imeachd ochdar.
Thugamar cath na Frainge o 's ann do bhreth gu docair,
Ghabhamar geill 'us cumha, cuimhne leam imeachd ochdar.
Thugamar cath na Spainn, a taintean 'us a tachdaran,
Chaidhear mo ré fa 'n domhain, cuimhne leam imeachd ochdar.
Thogamar cath Bhreatuin, b'eagalach e 'us bu dhocair,
Thogamar geall daoine, cuimhne leam imeachd ochdar.
Bheireamar Crom nan carn air fairge 'us e air oiteal,
Fhuaireamar gach tir umhal, cuimhne leam imeachd ochdar.
'N a dheigh thainig na toisich, a Phadruig uasail thochdmhuin,
Fionn gheibheadh air cumha, cuimhne leam imeachd ochdar.
Naomhaich m'anamasa a Phadruig, is airde cruth us sochair,
O pheacaich mise a'd chomhar, cuimhne leam imeachd ochdar.
Cuimhne leam.

NAOINEAR chaidheamaid fo cheangail do fhaighinn aobhar chinn chuilein,
Fhaighinn aobhar chinn chuilein chon, ged is mo doruinn 's an domhain,
Do shireamar Magh Leine leirge 'us Gleann freathnaich nan claidheamh [dearg,
Is fior nach d' fhuaireamar ann madadh, de 'n deanmaid chuilean.
Do shireamar gleann dorcha dubh, gleann ghairbh choire 'us gleann cloiche,
Is fior nach d' fhuaireamar ann madadh, de 'n deanamaid chuilean.
Do shireamar Sithean Dhruime Cleibh, is Fionn Mhagh Leibh 'n a dheigh;
Is fior nach d' fhuaireamar ann madadh, de 'n deanamaid chuilean.
Do shireamar Durlas nam fear fial, Tabhar Bhreagh 'us Dun dhobhran ;
Is fior nach d' fhuaireamar ann madadh, de 'n deanamaid chuilean.
Do shireamar Gleann a Cuaich fa forthais aobhar uasail,
Is fior nach d' fhuaireamar ann madadh, de 'n deanamaid chuilean.
Do shireamar Fionn mhagh mhaith, Tabhar Bhreagh 'us Ceanntaile;
Is fior nach d' fhuaireamar ann madadh, de 'n deanamaid chuilean.
Do shireamar Eire uile, eadar chon 'us duine ;
Is fior nach d' fhuaireamar ann madadh, de 'n deanamaid chuilean.

Gerrid downith mir sen sin feyn pupbill muntyr
Gin wakcamir tre cath nach di clanni reith ni roylayth
Cath catchennith de we ann is cath chonchennith na genn
Cath drumanich in dey in ney donn er chawyr in drom b . . .
In tley a soiltich gi hard er inni feyn in eingnyth zark
In nochtyr ske cheyttyth chay er we in tley . . . gead
In tleyg soyltich gi chert er inni feyn fa gall a zlak
Er layr skaye cheilt gyn wroyn weith in tly z in g.
In tley a soyltich gi heissil er inni feyn in nagnith eywie
In noythtyr skae chiwin charre we tley ac mak chrunchan
Leygis cheiltyth gallan gleith choylis e nalwin da reroiwe
Iss mygh lenyth nyn lanni in dawr is in down reillin
Reggir e goolle m'morn faynith kenard cion woyn
A zleyis felane m'fynni agis ni balwe a borrin
Reggir e za mhak mawoe breik is m'elle o noye brek
Scay bregh m'daythein dayn is keill croith in nerm rai zeyr
Reggir e keinkeith nith golg agis illin feywr zerg
Is keill croith a croyth zrinni nach estith goyth iywrin
Bi winni schenwrannyth sley agis mowr ni meillith
Agis rann wrattich schroill ag erri a maddin zeith ioeith
Di hoykgimir dalwe zreynith brattich inni vor ni faynith
Oyr chor sche tennal fa wor chanan cheintle rwe
Di hoykgimir fulling doyrith brattich zwlle wor v'morn
Menkith we gach troyle chroissich derryth agis tossyth foylith
Di hoykimir in menchenith oyrii brattich rynith gin nymig sloyeg
Sroill lay gonfee knaw is kenni, la leygis fwll gow fybrin
Di hoykimir kynill chath brattich eillane darre
Mak finni far flath ni waynith gilli lay gurre tromley
Di hoykimir down neive brattich ossin na grri
Laywe zarg brattich v'ronane is oarnay in deive elle
Di hoykimir skoyb zawe brattich oskyr in warffee
Re doll in gath na glaec menkith zarre skopbe zawe
Di hoykimir loith lynith brattich zarmit e zoenith awyissyth
Noar heyth in neanith wea sche awzissyth oeyrith a mach
Di hoykimir barne a reybgin brattich oskyr nar schanith
Danyth coyharme m'gar zlynni la garwe kinni is kenwr
Di hoykimir creiwe fowllith brattich clonni var v'lowich
Noar a heych in nane a mach is sche wea er in dossych
Di rimimir croith chath in dymchill inni oyrlach
Ma dudtych finni farri eddi ni wane worchalmith
Marwes ni catkenich linni agis di goyve ni chonchinnich
Hutti ni drumanich wlle in dymchall inn alwin
Munnich beg fa dassi zownith in nynwr wrow za zownith

Goirid duinne mar sin, sin féin, pobull, muinntir,
Gu facamar tri cath gun achd de chlann Rìgh na Ruadhleath
Cath catcheann do bhi ann 'us cath chonchcann 'n an ceann,
Cath drumanach an deigh an fheigh, donn air chobhar an drom . . .
An t-sleagh a soillseachadh gu h-ard, air Fionn féin an cangnaich ghairg,
An uachdar sgeith chailltich chaidh air bhith an t-sleagh . . .
An t-sleagh soillseach' gu ceart air Fionn féin fa geal a ghlac,
Air lathair sgeith Chaoilte gun bhròn, bhith an t-sleagh dhearg an cath,
An t-sleagh a soillscach' gu h-iosal air Fionn fein an aigne mhir.
An iochdar sgeith chruinn chàir bhi an t-sleagh aig mac Chruinchain.
Leigeas Caoilte gallan glé; chualas e an Almhuin de rìreadh,
'Us Magh Léine nan lann, an Tamhar 'us an Dun Reithlein,
Fhreagair e Gall Mac Moirn, Fiann ceannard Cronbhuain,
A ghleidheas Faolan Mac Fhinn, agus na Balbha a Borruinn.
Fhreagair e da mhac Maibh bhric, 'us Mac Ealaidh an aghaidh bhric,
Scaith breagh Mac Daithein deine, 'us Caol crodha an airm ro gheir.
Fhreagair e Geangach nan colg agus Iolunn faobhair dheirg,
'Us Caol crodha a chrutha ghrinn nach éisd guth ionbhruinn.
Bu bhinn seanmhoireachd sleigh agus meabhar nam milidh,
Agus ràn bhratach sròl ag eiridh am maduinn ghaoith reodhta.
Do thogamar Dealbh ghréine, bratach Fhinn mhòir na Feinn,
Or chuir se timchioll fa mhòr cana cinnealta ruadh.
Do thogamar Fulang Duaraidh, bratach Ghuill mhòir Mhic Moirn,
Minic bhi'n gach triall chraoisich, deireadh 'us toiseach falbh.
Do thogamar am Mincheann òir, bratach Raoine gon iomadh sluaigh,
Sròl le 'n gonadh cnàmh 'us cinn, le leigeas fuil gu aobruinnean.
Do thogamar Cineal chath, bratach Fhaolain daire,
Mac Fhinn fear flath na Feinn, gille le 'n cuireadh trom shleagh.
Do thogamar Dun Nimh, bratach Oisiain nan curaidh,
Lamh dhearg, bratach Mhic Ronain, is oirnidh an taobh eile.
Do thogamar Sguab ghàbhaidh, bratach Osgair am fear fioch,
Ri dol an cath nan gleo minic a dh' éireadh Sguab ghàbhaidh.
Do thogamar Liath loinneach, bratach Dhiarmaid aigeanaich aibheasaich,
'N uair a theich an aonach a mach, bhi se aibheasach oirdheirc.
Do thogamar Bearn Reubainn, bratach Osgair nar seanta,
Dheanadh cosheirm mac gair ghlinne le garbh cinne is ceannbhrat.
Do thogamar Craobh fhuileach bratach cloinn bhar Mhic Lughaidh;
'N uair theich an Fheinn a mach, is e bhitheadh air an toiseach.
Do rinneamar cruaidh chath, an timchioll Fhinn orfhlath,
Ma dhuda Fhinn fhearail, oide na Feinn mòir-chalma.
Marbhas na Caitcheannich leinn, agus do ghabh na Coincheannaich,
Thuit na Drumanaich uile an timchioll Fhinn Almhuin.
Monadh beag fa deas dhuinn, am faighear brugh dha dhùn;

Is math forrimir ann maddith za danmist cholin
Zearimir erre wlle eddir chonni agis donni
Is noech cha dorremir er a feyg cheaddi ferr o zarve na nenor.
Nenor a quhyme.

BINN gow duni in teyr in oyr binn a ghloyr chanyd nyth heoyn,
Bynn noaillane a nee a quhor bin in tonn a bwn da treoyr
Bynn in fygzir a ne zeye bin gow coyth oass cassyth conn
Alynn in delryth a ne greane byn in near feddyl nyth lon
Bynn gow illyr esse roye vass kynn coayne v'moyrnye mor
Bynn gow coythaa oyss barrye doss alynn in tost a nee in coir
Fynn mac cowil mayr fani sacht caa na eaynn gyth grynn
In oayr a lykeyst con ra feayn a garrye no zeye bye wynn
Bynn gow.

SKAILE oiknith er choyle cassil, gow cain wallir berrith mee
Na clwnnith dwnni za glwnnith gi glwnnith m'gweill ee
Makcowle di choill cossir er sliss alwin in nor weine
Essin oss in gend ne choll finni in cessew doyr reiwe
Ossin dein nichticht is dermit dey v'lowith leich nar zann
Deiss nar leyr cooza coskir conan feyn is oskir ann
Sloyne a zey leych zawsich di raye fin fer gyth eyth
Faikgen mir sin er oill inn ca coyll leiwe is binni er beith
Di raye conan yr we in nymirt eine choyll is binni hor feyn
Math lawe in ir re heygh enrwnith fer sen gr chwnith er cheyll
Foskgi zi chwlg in gaith nawit nach in gath ni choklit sa
A loywe in genn is in gossith koill a bar le oskir aye
Koill is mo ruggis zi iyin di rae deomit ni derk maal
A rozraw gin ga boa zawssith coraa ban is ansith ann
Sowd mi choilsi a v'murn er m'lowith ni narm glan
Leym in gleyw mi chon gow cre fey ga churri in derri zawe
Sowd in koill is koyle dowfsyth di rae fin fla in tloe
In neym zeith bayne ley biaddeiche raym finleich fa atteive oyr
In tra weime gin eggill nin neksith ossin a durt fa zoe
Mi zane is a zoissith in daskgi saif rame cloiss clastin a chole.

Is maith fhuaireamar ann madadh dhe 'n deanamaid chuilean.
Dhireamar Eire uile eadar chon 'us duine.
Is nocha d' fhuaireamar air a feadh, ceud fear a dhearbh na naoinear.
Naoinear.

Binn guth duine an tir an òir, binn a ghlòir a chanaid na h-eoin,
Binn an nuallan a ni a chorr, binn an tonn am Bun da treoir.
Binn am fabhar a ni a ghaoth, binn guth cuach os Cas a choin,
Aluinn an dealradh a ni grian, binn a nithear feadail nan lon,
Binn guth iolair Easruaidh, os cionn cuain Mhic Muirne moir,
Binn guth cuach os bàr dos, aluinn an tosd a ni an corr,
Fionn Mac Cumhail m'athair, fa 'n seachd cath Fhiann gu grinn,
An uair a leigeas con ri fiadhmhuin, ag éiridh 'n a dheidh bu bhinn.
Binn guth.

Sgeul oignidh air cheòl caislidh, gu Carn Bhalair beiridh mi,
Nan cluinneadh duine de 'n cluinneadh, gun cluinneadh Mac Cumhail e,
Mac Cumhail do cheal còisir, air slios Almhuin an oir mhìn,
Esan os an ceann 'sa cheòl Fionn an còisir d' fhaighear riamh,
Oisian dian euchdach, 'us Diarmad, deagh Mhic Lughaidh laoch nior [ghann,
Dithis na'r le'r cobhach cosgar, Conan féin 'us Osgar ann
Sloinn a dheagh laoich dhomhsa, do radh Fionn fior gach eadh,
'Faicinn mar sin air òl Fhinn, cia an ceòl leibh is binne air bith ?
Do radh Conan air bhi an imirt, aon cheòl is binne a fhuair mi féin.
Maith lamh an fhir ri aghaidh cruinnich' fior sin gun chuimhne air chéill.
Faosgadh a chuilg an cath namhaid, neach an cath ni choigleadh se,
A luaidh an ceann 'us an cos, ceol a b' fhearr le Osgar aigh.
Ceòl is mo a rugas de roghainn, do ràdh Diarmad nan dearc mall,
A ro ghràidh, gun ge beo dhomhsa, comhradh bhan is annsa ann.
Sud mo cheòlsa a Mhic Muirne, ars' Mac Lughaidh nan arm glan,
Leum an gleò mo chon gu cridhe feidh 'g an cur an deireadh dhoibh,
Sud an ceòl is ceòl dhomh féin do ràdh Fionn flath an t-slòigh,
An fheum ghaoith bhitheann le brataich, reim fionnlaoich fo a taobh òir.
An trath bhitheam gun eagal nan eigeas Oisian a dubhairt fadheoidh,
Mo Fheinn 'us i dhomhsa an tasgaidh, seimh le'm chluas claistinn a cheoil.

FLEYGH wor rinni lay finni innoiss dowt a halgin
Fa hymmi dwn we ann deanow albin is errin
Fearis m'morn mor din reane fa gall glor
A waktow fleywi zar o hanyth tow weanow errin
Di reggir sen finni wane fa math wle tor is tear
Dowrt gi wak fleywi zar na gi fley ane reywe in nerrin
Chongimir huggin won toun leich mor ayrrichtich foltinn
Gin ane dwn ag ach ay feyn fa math in toglach essane
Mir hanyth shay in gen ni wane a dowrt in toglach fa keyve keyll
Tarsyth lomsith noss inni is ber cayd leich id di hymchill
Deych mek eichit morne mor ber let in dowss di henoyll
Fer is ocht zet chlonn feyne ber is oskir di zane wane
Ber deachnor di clannith smoill is feichit di clanni ronanc
Ber di clanni mwin let deachnor olli gin dermit
Ber let dermit o dwnith bar ni swr is no schalge
A feyn is kerrill id lwng deychnor di zanith is di zorrin
Ber nenor do zillew let fa farda how ym bee aggit
Agis twss fen a inni a v'awasse erm zrinni
Ber C leich let er twnni di zna wnntir inn v'kowle
C skay gin m wi nor dinni m'kowle v'tranewor
Berssi let in nossa inni in da chonni is ferri in nerrin
Ber bran is skoillin let lowt di zorrin i gimicht
Na beith fadcheis ort a inni di ray in toglach ard evin
Tuggir fa woye id heith di we er ar sloye is soiche
Glor anwit hare id chenn ogle out hanik chwggin
Min fayin tow in weanoss inn di wea di chen gin chollin
Di choraa ni churffe in swm a chonane meill ni beymin
Is mest in sloye di wee ann id ta tow agrow anwin
Errissyth clanni biskni ann erss conane in nani
Gowis gi neach zeiwe erm leich tig ni feanith ass gi ane teiwe
Marwar in sen mak di zinn feani gall a zassgi zrinn
As mak a zillin m'morn fa math in gath chrwnwoynyth
Errissyth arriss ann is daniss a wurrill
Fearyth yn beinni cwt ag gowle di chonan in nani
Di wersi a wraa feyn di zinn di ray gowle mor nim beymin
War conan na mess a chinni na bonfeit ass in tinchin
Ferris koill D[r] eichid in glen er nach leyr rawe cheith in ferrin
Ay gin fiss nyth feanith ag finn troyg in skaill so halgin
Faddi lommi a halgin tranc nach wagga ma dunni zi nane
Ead a shelgi o zlenni gow glenn is nith aewlt no dymchol
Binvin lom ossin m'finni na hanich kenn nach deach zee
Ter gi dwni gar royve ann di binvin leom finni wley.

Fley.

FLEADH mhor a rinneadh le Fionn, innis dhuit a Thailgein,
Bu iomadh duine a bha ann, d' Fhianaibh Alba 'us Eirinn.
Feoraicheas Mac Moirne mòr de 'n rioghain bu gheal glòir,
Am faca tu fleadh ghara o thainig tu do Fhianaibh Eirinn?
Do fhreagair sin Fionn nam Fiann, bu mhaith uile soir 'us siar,
Dubhairt gum faca fleadh bu gharra no gach fleadh Fheinn riamh an
Chunnamar thugain o'n tonn laoch mor arachdach foltionn, [Eirinn.
Gun aon duine aig ach e féin, bu mhaith an t-oglach esan.
Mar thainig se an ceann nam Fiann a dubhairt an t-oglach bu chaomh
Tarsa leamsa nis, Fhinn, 'us beir ceud laoch a'd thimchioll, [ciall,
Deich mic fhichid Moirne moir, beir leat an tùs do thionaill,
Fear 'us ochd dhe'd chlann féin, beir us Osgar do dh' Fhiann Feinn,
Beir deichnear de chlannaibh Smoil, us fichead de chlannaibh Ronain,
Beir de chlann Mudhain leat, deichnear eile gun Diarmad,
Beir leat Diarmad o Duinn, b'fhear na suiridh 'us na seilg,
E féin 'us Caoruill 'ad long deichnear de dhaoine 'us de dh' fhoruinn.
Beir naoinear de ghillibh leat, a b'fheairde thu a bhi agad,
Agus tusa féin a Fhinn, a mhic aibheasaich, airmghrinn,
Beir ceud laoch leat air tonn de ghnàth mhuinntir Fhinn Mhic Cumhail,
Ceud sgiath gon mionna 'n òir, d' Fhionn Mac Cumhaill mhic Threin-
Beirse leat a nis, a Fhinn, an da chon is fearr 'an Eirinn, [mhoir,
Beir Bran 'us Sgoilean leat, luaithe de dh' fhoruinn ag imeachd.
Na bitheadh faitcheas oit, a Fhinn, do radh an t-oglach ard aoibhinn,
Tugar fo bhuaidh ad thì do bhi air ar sluaigh 'us soithichibh.
Glòir anmhaith tharladh 'ad cheann, oglaich ud a thainig thugainn,
Mum faigheann tu am fianuis Fhinn do bhitheadh do cheann gun choluinn,
Do chomhradh ni chuiream an suim a Chonain mhaoil nam beuman,
Is misd an sluagh do bhi ann, a ta tu aghara, anmhuinn,
Eiribhse chlanna Baoisgne ann, ars' Conan an anaithne.
Gabhas gach neach dhiubh arm laoich, thig na Fianna as gach aon taobh,
Marbhar an sin mac do Fhionn, Fiann geal a ghlaca ghrinn,
As mac de ghillibh Mic Moirne bu mhaith 'n cath Chruinnbhuain,
Eireas a Fhearghuis ann 'us deanas an iorghuill,
Feoraich am bi a chuid aig Goll do Chonan an anaithne,
Do bheirinnse a bhreith féin do Fhionn, do ràdh Goll mòr nam beuman,
Bheir Conan 'n a mise a cheann na buinid as an t-eanchain. [fearainn,
Ferghus, Caol, deich thar fhichead an gleann, air nach léir riamh chi
E gun fhios nam Fiann aig Fionn; truagh an sgeul so a Thailgein.
Fada leam a Thailgein threin, nach fhaic mi daoine de 'n Fheinn,
Iad a sealg o ghleann gu gleann, 'us mac eilde 'nan timchioll;
B'ionmhuinn leam Oisian Mac Fhinn, na h-aon cheann a chaidh dheth;
Thar gach duine de 'n robh ann, do b'ionmhuinn leam Fionn an fhleidh.
Fleadh.

TROYG lwm twllych ni faynith ag ni clerchew fa zeirse
Is danyth lucht ni billak in nynit clannyth beisknyth
Dayr missi raa croychin schell fada wroychow gi swgych
Beg a hellis gi tarfin in talgin er di wullych
Dayr meith skay is sley conn is gyir fad walle
Ga ta nocht knok ni fayni fa chleyrchew is fa wachlew
Da merra clanni morn ni wee fer nordsi seadtrach
Di zoyve schew fer grabbil a lwcht ni baychill breik
Da merra m'lowyth si vi curri chalma
Swl fowkweis in twllych di wee fer cowlyth garryth
Da merra clanni carda fir nachir chelggi bayssew
Ne weith fer glwkgi fer bachlaa nynit ni bradtych
Da merra clanni mayvin fer nach banvin in droddew
Ni weith di wuntir a phatrik gi laydyr er ni chnoken
Da merra clan in dew zerri da merra keilti croych
Ne weith gayr chloogi is chleyrri ga nestich in raa croychin
Da merra rynne roydda is keilcroy m'creyvin
Ne weith di loywr la cheyll ir a laywis a bebill
Is ni lwrga crwnni di ryn in swll doyne
Di weith di lorga na brossna da bea osgir er layr
Ir in trostane woye di ryn in swe swnda
Math dut nach marrin connan fa manach dorn duta
Da marrein swlzorm seir conan meil makave ni wane
A chleyrre ga mor di zorda di wonin zut dorn gi dane
Da marra m' o zoyni er ni lwrga crossi
Di weith di lorga sue mest a bresta fa chaythra clooch
Ir chlwga mir helim da weith dering na woye
Di weith di chlog na rabba woya fa edin a chaythre
Ner zarga shmor a cheyth er gayth geith m'roynan
Na be di chlog gi hannis ir a wanis a koyllan
Ni eddwm bi gi sowthych nc agkwm m'kowl si woe
Ne ekkym dearmit o doywn ne ekkym keilt m'cronan
Ne hynyth mi way gi dowyth er in tullych so phatrik
Ne ekkym m'lowth ne ekim in chwllych zrawcht
Ne ekkim far loo raym heive ne ekkim oskir na . . .
Ne ekkim in nymirt vor ne ckkim a choanirt cheyf
Ne ekkim clanni smoyl ne ekkim golli mor ni gneyf
Ne ekkim feillane fayill ne ekkim na zey in nayn
Ne ekkim ferris mi wrayir layr meyth layr woalta
Ne ekkim dyrri doynicht o woymist koyl gi noyrra
Ne ekkim fa kanyn nach beehow aggin er ayrre
Ne ekkim ane gar worrin di bi wor torrin a glar

Truagh leam tulach na Feinn, aig na cleirichibh fo dhaoirse,
'Us dana luchd nam billeag, an ionad clanna Baoisgne,
Do fhaighear mise a Rath Chruachain, seal fo do bhruachaibh gu sugach,
Is beag a shaoileas gun tarfainn an Tailgean air do mhullach.
Do fhaighear mo sgiath 'us sleagh, con 'us gadhair fa d' bhalla,
Ge'd tha an nochd cnoc na Feinn, fo chleirichibh 'us fo bhachlaibh.
Na 'm maireadh clanna Moirne, ni bhitheadh fear an ordsa seathardha,
Do gheibheadh sibh 'ur grabail, a luchd na bachuile brice.
Na 'm maireadh Mac Lughaidh, 's a sé cuiridh chalma,
Sol fhàgas an tulach, do bhi bhur culaidh gearr.
Na 'm maireadh clanna Ceairde, fir nach fir cheileadh basa,
Ni bhitheadh bhur cluig 's 'ur bachla, an ionad nam bratach.
Na 'm maireadh clanna Mudhain, fir nach b'anmhuinn an trodaibh,
Ni bhitheadh do mhuinntir a Phadruig, gu laidir 'n an cnocaibh.
Na 'm maireadh clann an deagh Ghoraidh, na 'm maireadh Caoilte cruadhach,
Ni bhitheadh gair chlog 'us chleireach, 'g an éisdeachd an Rath Chruachain.
Na 'm maireadh Raoine ruadha, 'us Caol crodha mac Reabhain,
Ni bhitheadh do leabhar r'a cheile, fhir a leughas am Biobul.
Agus na luirge cruinne, do rinn an siubhail domhain,
Do bhitheadh do lorg 'n a bhrosna, na 'm bitheadh Osgar air làr.
Fhir an trostain bhuidhe, do rinn an suidh sonda,
Is maith dhuit nach marruinn Conan, fa bhuineadh dorn duit.
Na 'm maireadh an Sulghorm saor, Conan maol macamh nam Fiann,
A chleirich ge mòr do dh' ord, do bhuineann duit dorn gu dian.
Na 'm maireadh Mac O'Dhuinn, fhir na luirge croise,
Do bhitheadh do lorga smiste, briste fo charragh cloiche.
Fhir a chluig mar shaoilim, na 'm bitheadh Daoruing 'n a bheatha,
Do bhitheadh do chlog 'n a reubach, uaith fa eudan a charraigh
An ior dhearg, a sheanair, da chitheadh air gath gaoith Mhic Ronain,
Ni bhitheadh do chlog gu h-ainnis, fhir a sheinneas an gòlan.
Ni fhaodam bhi gu subhach, ni fhaiceam Mac Cumhail 's a bheatha,
Ni fhaiceam Diarmad O'Duinn, ni fhaiceam Caoilte Mac Ronain;
Ni h-ioghnadh mi bhi gu dubhach, air an tulach so, Phadruig,
Ni fhaiceam Mac Lughaidh, ni fhaiceam an coileach gràdhaichte;
Ni fhaiceam Fear luath u'm thaobh, ni fhaiceam Osgar na Feinn;
Ni fhaiceam an imirt mhòr ni fhaiceam a chonairt chaomh,
Ni fhaiceam clanna Smoil, ni fhaiceam Gall mòr 'an gniomh.
Ni fhaiceam Faolan fiall, ni fhaiceam 'n a dheigh an Fheinn,
Ni fhaiceam Fearghus mo bhràthair, le 'r mithich le 'r mholta,
Ni fhaiceam Daoire duanach, o'm faigheamaid ceòl gach uaire,
Ni fhaiceam Fatha Canan, nach bi thu againn air uaire.
Ni fhaiceam aicme dhe 'r foruinn da bu mhòr torrun air clàr,

Ne ekkim evinis na hoyl ne clwnim in koyl di wee
Soll di curri mi mi hoo di fronfwn feyn or gi loyit
Inssim zwt a phadrik da bi zayllwm hecht harsta
Nach fayddwm a heillow a vacca may zeivinis agga
Missi is cleyrre ni bortwis nocha droyinum ra chaal
Ga ta mee nocht gi dowych, is troygh lwm tullych ni fayne.
Troyg lwm.

DYTH wylelyss myschi zraynnyth hwnggis nayrri w'cowle
Wee myr it tayme sin nagyn is bert nach fadyr a wllyng
Dyth zhagis clwycht is couzar er chompan zaw neyss tayr
Dyth zhagis mnan gin gillaa is dyth wilelis mischi a zraynna
Dyth zhagis murnd is meygzegr curme is greygzin is garae
Dyth zhagis clwithi fylli is dyth willis myschi a zraynnaa
Keiltaa mor is m'lowith deyss er nach drwngi taayraa
In feyth nayr roywaa rynnaa dyth wilelis mischi a zraynna
Gold is 'oskyr is osseyne acma nach corrith partaa
Dyth bynnwynne leo sen synnyth dyth wylelyss myschi a zraynna
Fynn fane in agnaa raawoyr is woygh zaifmost failtaa
Dyth zhagis murndnych hee is dyth wilelys mischi a zraynna
Myr aweyss in noyf chaythi zoyschi ne hewyr zayrraa
A coyad oywaa byggi dyth wilelis mischi a zraynnaa
It doll ter wennew borrifaa is er wollyth forynnych ban . . .
Ne mor nach tursych synnaa dyth willelis myschi a zraynnaa
It doll ter ess roygh roinyth is beg nar obyr my wayle
Faa rohwyr geltti glinni di villiss missi a zrannyth
Waym gi faddi is gi haazar a tastil eyrrin ani
Is trane di woyr sen sinni di williss mischi zrany.
Di williss missi.

LAY a royth in dundalgin cowchullin ni grow neynti
O taid ni gur er a gon gin sloig wlli na ochyr
Halli in noill erin nerre math si waggidir in nane wlli
Keltith fekkich fowich feine eltych laye za leetiwe
Gwr bei in nansych wllith mnan chogn clanni rowre
In cor sen bi degkir reyve cur ris in naltin dawail
In doychis lawee leich atte dr aythr chonleich
Ni hoynni giderring dalwe ser winn cholla in gallew
Gawis in crann tawill glan cowchullin gi . . .

Ni fhaiceam aoibhneas na òl, ni cluinneam an ceòl do bhi,
Sul do chuireadh mi am uaigh, do bhronnainn féin òr gu luath.
Inniseam dhuit, a Phadruig, nam b' ailleam theachd tharsta,
Nach faodam a fhileadh, na fhaca mi dh' aoibhneas aca.
Mise 'us Cleirich nam portos, nocha tarruingeam ri chéile,
Ge ta mi an nochd gu dubhach; is truagh leam tulach na Feinn.
Truagh leam.

Do fhileas mise a Ghrainne, chunnacas an goire Mhic Cumhail,
Bhi mar a taim 's an éigin is beart nach faodar fhulang.
Do fhàcas cluiche 'us coghair air chompan ghabh nise tàire,
Do fhacas mnathan gon gillibh, is do fhileas mise a Ghrainne.
Do fhacas muirn 'us meoghar, cuirm 'us greigh ghrinn 'us gàire,
Do fhacas cluiche fidhle, 'us do fhileas mise a Ghrainne.
Caoilte mor 'us Mac Lughaidh, dithis air nach d'rainig tàire,
Air fioch nior ro mhaith ruinne, do fhileas mise a Ghrainne.
Goll 'us Osgar 'us Oisian, aicme nach corra part,
Do b'ionmhuinn leo sin sinne, do fhileas mise a Ghrainne.
Fionn féin an aigne ro mhir, is uaith a gheibheamaid faillte,
Do fhacas muirneach e 'us do fhileas mise a Ghrainne.
Mar a bhitheas an naoi cathan, dhomhsa ni h-aobhar ghàire,
A coimhead uaimhe bhige do fhileas mise a Ghrainne.
A dol thar bheanntaibh borrafadh, 'us air mhullach fhormnach bhàn,
Ni mor nach tuirseach sinne, do fhileas mise a Ghrainne.
A triall tir eas ruaidh romhainn, is beag na'r obair mo fhàil,
Fa ruathar geillt glinne, do fhileas mise a Ghrainne.
Bhitheam gu fad 'us gu h-aithghearr a tasdail Eirinn àine.
Is treun do fhaighear sin sinne, do fhileas mise a Ghrainne.
Do fhileas mise.

La a robh an Dundealgain, Cuchulain nan cruth deanta,
O taid con cur air a ghean, gun sluagh uile 'n a fhochair;
O thall' an oil air an éiridh mach, gum facadar an Fheinn uile,
Ceilltach feacach fuathach fa'n ealta luidh dha shleitibh;
Gur b'e an annsachd uile, mnathan Choige clanna Rughraidh,
An cuir sin bu dheacair riamh, cur ris an ealtan d'fhaigheail;
An dochas laimh laoich; aiteadar athair Chonlaoich,
Na h-eoin go Daoirinn dealbhach, saor bhinn Cholla an gallaibh;
Gabhas an crann tabhaill glan Cuchulain gu . . .

In lawe bi wath troir er mor ni hoynene gr . . .
Ryntyr in neltych wo ner zarmit umpith ach awyr,
Gawis awyr racht fane rynn dayveine ner chart a cheive
Geltyr wee no errik sin ni kead oyne elli zayvir
Lar dorchrith er teive a chnok la creif ni norchr nerrik
In gen tryle hicgid gow caith za anee gin neigiss noynach
Ni roe fer gin oe orri wei slawre or datrych
Hug bancheill chongullin graw dinani di wllim
Din charrait eintych aynce hanik a ymill ollanith
Agris ayvr in nolt trwme a cu rith er chongullin
Ni hoyne mir gylle deith gin skail na hyi umpith
Da oyr no tre tilfer leis ni hoyne aldyth sner ammis
Gir leme couf mir a chur iii wrchir hor ni hannich
In hurchir reyve royve sen zoll di zaltane gawffee
Gin virn er wrane di wlyg ryef ach keym sin allane
Re bleygin ni deach zea ach twrss nin nane seach
Ne hay ymichtych nin nane is inleut ach in twrskail
Mass fer in dathris a woygr nach darn in cow on chref
Slat war zall di zrawhe mnaa laywith aig voye a
. . . . . myn fa reawrew beggane . . .
. . . . . feyne in tulg churr ay deis er gi . . .
Hw a feyne agus garri teive er heive in nane tr za
Gin darrith Finn di zarri er su zoith na arrith
Or is twss do wee ann kinnis di warve sew cowll
Di weyr si zwt mi wrarri er bee zwt orm za earre
Gir heith mi laive laytich lomm chur in kead za in gowll
For in caddrew zoiss sin a clanni morn mar zilli
Is wulling is reawor zoif zess dew mathr a varwi
Mass for in catdrew leat sin Inn vec cowill a halwin
Leig in carri dr bwnskinni is tog in nallydis chatchin
A dog mis zew lawe a clann morn is mor grane
Fa toylling missi wlle for gir gow deith eine dwn
Mass di zlassi tussi sin ymichtin er slycht haithr
Bith lemenor sinni er linni mir weith ein eillytin chowale
Gowal chor sinn in woyew cowle huc orn mor withwr
Gowal di zoichir a mach sinn a greithew ni geith
Chor dram zeine in nalbin inn is dram elle in dow lochlinn
In tress dram si zreyg zilli beddit woe cheyl r . . .
Wemir seableyn deyg a hagwss errin is ner wrag
Ner weg in smach downith sinni gin er dew zagkin
In kead lay choymir er teir zinse errin or weimin
Warveir dein is ner wraik a ray xvi c dein lay
Di warvis clanna morn dan leichew is . . .

'An laimh bu mhaith treoir air mor na h-eoin gur . . .
Roinntear an ealta uatha, nior dhearmaid umpa ach Eimhear,
Gabhas Eimhear rachd fa 'n roinn, deimhin nior cheart a chaoimh ,
Gealladar bhith 'n a éiric sin, na ceud eoin eile dh' Eimhear,
Le'r torchradh air taobh a chnuic le treibhe nan urchuir an éiric
An ceann triall thigead gu caithir da ni gon eigis dhuanach,
Ni robh fear gun e orra, bhi slabhraidh oir clatrach.
Thug bancheile Chonchulain gràdh do 'n Fhiann de bheileam,
Do 'n charaid aontach àine, a thainig a iomall Ullanaich.
Agras Eimhear an fhuilt truime a cunradh air Chonchulain,
Na h eoin mar gheall dith gun sgeul 'n a h-aghaidh umpa ,
Da uair no tri tillear leis na h-eoin ald 's nior amais,
Gur leum cobh mar a chuir tri urchuir thar na h-eunaibh;
An t-urchuir riamh roimh sin dhol da dhaltan gabhaidh,
Gun mhuirn air mhnathan de bhlagh, riamh ach caoine 's an allan ;
Ré bliadhna ni deachaidh dha ach tuirse an Fheinn seach,
Ni h-e imeachdaich nan Fheinn is ion leat ach an t-ursgeul ;
Ma 's fior an t-aithris a gheibhear nach tearuinn an Cu o'n chraoibh,
Slat bhar-gheal de ghràdh mhnatha, le bhi a bhuaidh ach . . .
. . . . . . min fa dheireadh beagan . . .
. . . . . . féin an t-sealg, chuir e dithis air gach aon . . .
Thu fein agus Garaidh, taobh air thaobh an Fheinn . . .
Gun d'fharraid Fionn de Gharaidh, air suidhe dha 'n a aire ;
O'n is tusa do bhi ann, Cionnus a mharbh sibh Cumhal ?
Do bheirse dhuit mo bhriathar, air bhi dhuit orm 'g a iarraidh,
Gur h-i mo lamh shleiteach lom, chur an ceud ghath 'an Cumhal ;
Fuar an caidreamh dhomhsa sin, a chlanna Moirne mar ghille,
Is fulangas ro mhor dhomh, dh' fhios duibh m'athair a mharbhadh.
Ma 's fuar an caidreamh leat sin, Fhinn Mhic Cumhail a h-Almhuin,
Leig an caradradh buinsgion, 'us tog an alltas choitchin.
An tog mise dhibh lamh, a chlanna Moirn is mòr grain,
Fa tualaing mise uile, fuair gur cuidich aon duine.
Mus do ghluais thusa sin, imeachdain air slighe d'athar,
Bu leimeanar sinn air linne mur bhi aon ealadhain Chumhail ;
Cumhal chuir sinn am buaidhibh, Cumhal thug oirnne mor ruathar,
Cumhal do dhiochuir a mach, sinn do chriochaibh nan coimheach,
Chuir dream dhinn an Albain fhinn, us dream eile 'an dubh Lochlainn,
An treas dream 's a Ghreig ghile, bithead o chéile air ioman.
Bhitheamar se bliadhna deug a h-eugmhais Eirinn 'us nior bhreug,
Nior bheag an smachd duinn, sinn gun fhear diubh fhaicinn,
An ceud la chaidheamar air tir dh' Innis Eirinn o'n bhitheamar,
Mharbhar dinn 'us nior bhreug, ré se deug ceud ri aon la ;
Do mharbhas clanna Moirn de 'n laochaibh . . .

Cha roif eine dwn zew sen nach cow caydi di v . . .
Gonith caslane da galnew clanni morn mor vanmnith
In ginni feyn bi leytich ann a weaniss far nerrin
Er a lawsi olach ni wane cha nakgis horri no har
Eine neith hug pask er mi hwle ach fagsin a choskir
Hug say teim fame chree re fagsin ni slintee
Huggimir nein teyg a crithew mowin mor zerg
A royth gasge in r bassid zown owin a warvi
Gyn deyve er in twlli hawle ymbi woa dwnni clann chwle
Ronimir reith nach royve maule guss in ty in roif cowl
Huggimir gwn zothin gr fr in goip chwall zor sleywe
Gir gar ruggi missi ann in nor a warve she cowall
Ne gneive roym scho ma haa dielmissi orr wa mer lay
Lay za roymir.

A houdir so Duncha mor voe lawenacht.

Mark dwnna a cayle a zoo agis ga vil schrow di zanna
Agus na ead gawal loa is nach ool wea no hawe
Agis nach synni corri na port is nach gawe gin locht leye
Agis nach skurre di chrwt veynni is nach synni mir is meynni
As marg nach skur da dryng drang agis di rann di ray
Agis na cluntyr a chrwt is nach tuggis a zayn
As marg na toyr toye da chael is nach cumi a feyn slan
As marg a ver trass gi trog ar a vess na rig a lawe
Da be mi vean annsyth vess neach foygin a zrab go hard
Di zoofin a cranni fa vonni ga bea neach er a cur merg
Mark.

A houdir so gilliecrist talzyr.

Bennycht di hylych a threnoite a ree pharris port nyn layk
Di hylych ner zann dit zoe how fan di zalve vlli ead
Is dutti di chommi seil nawzoe di zroy derk er da nyn sow
Ir a vennych port is pobbil malych di lwcht coggi cwlli
A ta chonurt curst chwllan danew wlk er clannow reicht
Gyn glwnnum ayr ni gonn gunnith is lane gi glenni dolli zeive
A lucht cogge er clanni awzoe o nach fadr vea nanc dost
Na geltow a chew ra chael ferten ree nyn grein a gosk
A lucht cogge er clan awzoe di fre lucifer nyn lube

Nochar robh aon duine dhiubh sin nach cumha ceud . . .
Gonadh caslain do ghalnaibh, clanna Moirne mòr mheanmnach
An cinneadh féin bu shleiteach ann am fianuis fhear an Eirinn.
Air do laimhse, olaich na Feinn, cha-n fhacas shoir no shiar,
Aon ni thug pasg air mo shuil, ach a faicinn a chosgraidh ;
Thug se tioma fa 'm chridhe ri faicsinn na slionachaidh,
Thugamar an aon tigh an criochaibh Mumhain mur dhearga ;
A ro ghaisge an fhir b' usaide dhuinn fhaighinn a mharbhadh,
Gun diubh air an tulaich thall, am bu bheo daoine chlann Chumhail ,
Rinneamar ruith nach robh mall, gus an tigh 's an robh Cumhal,
Thugamar guin dhomhain gach fear, an corp Chumhail dh' ar sleaghaibh ;
Ger ga 'r rugadh mise ann, an uair a mharbhadh Cumhal,
Na gniomharan so ma tha, diolamsa orra, bhamar là.
La dh' a robhamar.

Is e ùghdair so Dunchadh mòr o Leamhanach.

Mairg duine a chaill a ghuth, agus 'g a bheil sriuth r'a dheanamh,
Agus nach fhaod gabhail luath, is nach oil bhi 'n a thàmh,
Agus nach seinn cor no port agus nach gabh gun lochd laoidh,
Agus nach sguir de chruit bhinn, 'us nach seinn mar is miann,
Is mairg nach sguir dhe dring drang, agus de rann do ràdh,
Agus nach cluinntear a chruit, 'us nach tuigear a dhàn,
Is mairg nach toir toigh d'a chàil, 'us nach cinn e féin slàn,
Is mairg a bheir treis gu truagh air a mheas nach ruig a làmh, [h-àid,
Na 'm bitheadh mo mhiann anns a mheas nach fhaighinn a ghrabadh gu
Do ghearrainn an crann fa 'bhun, ge bith neach air an cuiream fearg
Mairg.

Is e ùghdair so Gillechriosd Tàillear.

Beannaich do theaghlach a Thrianaid, a Rìgh Pharrais port nan leug,
Do theaghlach nior dhean de'd dhubh, thu féin do dhealbh uile iad,
Is duit do chumadh siol Adhaimh, de ghruaidh dearg air dath nan sùgh,
Fhir a bheannaich port 'us pobull, malluich do luchd-cogaidh cùil.
A ta conairt cursta chuilean, 'deanamh uilc air clannaibh rìgh,
Gun cluinneam fabhar nan con guineach, is làn gach gleann dùile dhiubh.
A luchd cogaidh air clannaibh Adhaimh, o nach faodar bhi 'n an tosd,
'N an geall a chaoidh ri chéile, feartan Rìgh na grinne a chosg.
Luchd-cogaidh air clann Adhaimh, de frith Lucifeir nan lùb,

Na leg foiss na dein dyn drong soo losk a re nyth solsi sowd
Er deess eich chappil clawych nor is lane dyn choynnyth chwlle
Werrid wpe in nucht nyth selga leggi brucht a melga moe
Mallich nyth selga is a worloye deess eich keithryth is chrwe
Di chur drwme ra foyd ni foiche skeiltir kinni a zassre zoe
A ta gassre vaddi vasslaie er layr inche ald art
Lane truddyr ead treg a threnoit curseir ead a venoit valk
Ga zemmi crakkin chon alta agin wm clarsi is wm chrute
Cha terga clakin foyr fallwe aggin on chonni aalle wlk
Yr crisd dan sneicht seachin o loch chabbir gow ryn frewith
Loyth a gonnil da gorpe knawe orchis olk a raith rweith
Gon ga nerrik sen er scherchew di vak robert nyn royk tee
A lach venour ni glenni gust is lenonr kenn curst er claa
A vil o vinni zulbin zrenta di vaddrew sooss gu shrow tolve
Fissi er selgow sissi a soig derk ayr o christ ulli orve
Gi glwnnym is me in nynvr nissa meilchon skeilli nyn skonni
Marg ma nea balle ni bokneach gon dea gallyr tutmych trommi
Scawych connyth elsi is aggait er lucht varve nyn grey glass
Mak dey lai chre noy nawelych gyth sneach a choyn anvych ass
Loska gi sywe hay scheith chellin a oone stewart nyn stead braafe
Mas ber woym gir shreyth schranwoor a choyn zranith zranwor uigh
Er zarri oyone steadzil stewart cha learroith cabbir gyn chenn
Is ead er chollew cass corrych a choynnyth zlassi vongi hoenni.
Bennych di hylych.

A houdir so gilliecallum m'yn olle.

Ne heyvynis gin clyne donil ne coric veith nane naguss
In cland dyth bar sin gronevyth gir zeve gych done catew
Clann is ser zor zawe in rowe angnew is awziss
Clann zar woil ne terin in rowe creud is crawee
Clann chunlych chalmyth chroyth clann byth loyth in namm throd
Clann byth venyth in mesk beo is byth chalmyth in gogyth
Clann byth lenour orryth di oar anyth is ayrewe
Clann nar chattyth er egliss clann lor veggil in ganyth
Gythy ane albin oyn clann in croye zawe best
Gane royve tress gyth ter sawik eil er zasg
Clann bi vow is bi vir clann bi zrennis bi raith
Clann di barsingyth crei di bar fydin is feil
Mek rei nar hoyla in ner in royve dyntyth is trome
Fir alda olsai one nour in royve brontych is boke
Clann di bar feine is fasgyth clann di bar gasg lawe

Na leig fois, na dean do 'n droing so, loisg a Rìgh na soillse sùd.
Air dhithis eich, chapuill clamhach, 'n uair is làn de 'n chuainibh chùil,
Bheirid uaipe an uchd na seilg, leigeadh brùchd am meilge muigh.
Malluich na seilg 'us a mhortlath, dithis eich ciar 's a chruth,
Do chur druim ri foid na faiche, sgaoiltear cinn a ghasraidh dhuibh.
A ta gasradh mhadadh mhaslach, air lathair Innse Ald ard,
Lan trudair iad, treig a Thrianaid, cuirear iad a bhinnid bhalg.
Ge iomadh craicionn chon alda, againn um chlarsaich 'us um chruit,
Cha teirc claigionn fuar falamh, againn o'n chon alda uile.
Athair Chriosd dean snaigheadh seachuinn o Lochabair gu Raon Fraoich,
Luath an conuil do'n corp cnàmh, Oich ! is olc a radh ribh.
Gun gu'n éiric sin air saorchu, do Mhac Robaird nan gruaig tigh,
O Loch Mhenachoir nan gleann gusda, is lìonmhor ceann curst air clì.
A bheil o Bheinne Ghulbain ghrianta, de mhadraidh suas gu sruth Toilbh,
Fios air sealgaibh sios a soigh, dearc faighear o Chriosd uile oirbh.
Gu cluinneam 'us mi an Inbhirnise, miolchoin a sgaoileadh nan sgonn,
Mairg mu'n iadh boile nam boganach, gun d'iadh galar tuitmeach trom.
Sgiamhach con uailse a's agad, air luchd-marbhaidh nan greidh glas,
Mac Dé l'a chridhe naomh neamhaidh, gu snaigh a chuain ainbheach as.
Loisg gach saobhaidh tha 'n Sith Chailein, a Eoin Stiubhart nan steud breagh,
Mas beir uam gu'r sreith srannmhor, a chuain dhreunach ghreannar ribh.
Air Gharaidh Eoin steudghil Stiubhart, cha léir dhomh cabar gun cheann,
'Us iad air choillibh cas corrach, a chonairt ghlas mhuinge th 'ann.
Beannaich do theaghlach.

A h-Ughdair so Gillecallum Mac an Ollaimh.

Ni h-aoibhneas gun chlann Domhnuil, ni comhrag bhi 'n an eugmhais,
A chlann do b' fhearr 's a chruinne, gur dhiubh gach duine ceud,
Clann is saoire de 'r gheibh, an robh eangnath agus aghais,
Clann do 'r mhoil na tìrean an robh creidimh 'us cràbhadh.
Clann chunbhalach chalm chrodha, clann bu luaithe an am throd,
Clann bu mhìne am measg bheotha, 'us bu chalma a chog,
Clann bu lionmhor orra, do fhuair aithne 'us aireamh,
Clann nar chathaich air eaglais, clann le 'r am b'eagal an càineadh,
Gach aon an Albainn uaine, a chlann is cruaidh ghabh baisde.
Dh' an robh treas gach t're, seabhag fhial air ghaisge,
Clann bu mho 'us bu mhear, clann bu ghrinn 'us bu réidh,
Clann do 'm b'fharsuinn cridhe, do b'fhearr foighidin 's féile,
Mic rìgh nior thoill an aor an robh diontachd a's troma,
Fir allda uailse o'n uair, an robh bronntachd 'us bochda,
Clann do 'm b'fhearr fion 'us fasgath, clann do 'm b'fhearr gaisge laimh,

Olk lome gyrrit ernyth in ve lar sneyve in snaitht
Ner bait nyth drochir voyr na ni fir lowore lage
Re dol in nanit volc fir nach croye nyth cragi
Clann gin nouor gin naikgor-nar zove ach eddoil chogge
Gar vonnyth den olsai is gar vonyth boddi
Mark vor ruggi in nyin mark a zyil rane gaddrew
Gyn nyne clann mir clann donil ser clann byth chorit agna
Gyn arew er yth urdil gyn concta er in dossew
Gyn creich gyn tuss gyn derra er anyth ag in olscwe
In dossych clynnyth donil de vee folim ga faynyth
Is di wi nane derryth fein is anyth is nar
Er vrone is er hursa dyth reyggis twgss is folym
Gyth inne orcht reggis ne heyvenis gin chlynn donil
Bi trane geith in torrin, fan acmaa chrionda corit,
Ga tayd in dew fa zevis, ne hevynis gin chlynn donil
Na sloye vor is in grinne, ym murn si myr si wonyth
Ne gorith vi na vaguss, ne hevynis gin clynn donil
Makane lave na wymmyth dor seryth er gych dorin
Ga ta ai zone delis ne hevynis gin chlynn donil.
Ne heyvynis.

Ochagane is sai so in kenn di we er connil ny gormlane
In kenn za doaryth ein nwlli, di bossil ay is di binvin
Ochagane is sai so in towill di we in kenn connil knessi
In towle ma nea in narvryth di beale ee is boskirrych
Ochagane is a so in bail er nach doar filli fanskail
Bail tani is derkga na nwlle blass mallith er bail connil
Ochagane is a so in lawe we er connil mak skanlainn
Lawe firre bi chroeith in nymzwn lawe chonnil mi cheadinvin
Ochagane is a so in teive riss in seinmist ir sliss ser
Is sa maddi oo mwlli gow moil o laei ooyn er a heive
Ochagane is e so a chass nach teycha rooe leich za awivyf
Cass firri bi chroith in gaiew cass vec skanlane ska
Oych is sa in raa vee an connil gith traath mwcht
In nocht harrych nyth skail is sai balle nyn dear is ni noch
Ochagane.

A houdir so sayane chnoiddurt.

A chinn dernit a echarbre ga loyr harc agis toyill
Chay wor loymmi maid di zokgir ga teith i groith reith coyt

Olc leam giorrad earnaidh, a bhith le 'r sniomhadh an snàth,
Nior b'iad na droch fhir mhiodhar, no na fir liomhara laga,
Ri dol ann an ionadaibh olc, fir nach cruaidhe a chraig.
Clann gun uabhar, gun eucoir, 'n uair gheibh iad eudail chogaidh,
G'ar bhuineadh daoine uailse, agus 'g ar bhuineadh bodaich,
Muirg o 'r rug an dion mairg a dheilich r' an caidrimh,
Gun aon chlann mar chlann Domhnuil, saor chlann bu chomhrad aigne.
Gun aireamh air an urdail, gun chuntadh air an duaisibh,
Gun chrioch, gun tùs, gun deireadh, air eineach aig an uailsibh.
An toiseach chlann Domhnuil, do bhi foghlum 'ga àithneadh,
Agus do bhi 'n an deireadh, fion 'us eineach 'us nàire.
Air bhròn 'us air thursa, do ruigeas tuigse 'us foghlum,
Gach fhineadh orra ruigeas, ni h-aoibhneas gun chlann Domhnuil.
Bu treun gaoth an torrunn, fa 'n aicme chrionda chomhrad,
Ge taid an diugh fo dhimeas, ni h-aoibhneas gun chlann Domhnuil.
Na sloigh mhòr 'us an greann, am muirn, am meaghar s' am foghainteachd,
Ni còire bhi 'n an eugmhais, ni h-aoibhneas gun chlann Domhnuil.
Macan laimh a mhuime d'fhuair saoradh air gach doruinn,
Ge ta e dhuinne dìleas, ni h-aoibhneas gun chlann Domhnuil
Ni h-aoibhneas.

OCHAGAN ! is e so an ceann, do bhi air Conull nan gormlann,
An ceann dha 'n d'fhuaradh an iul, a b'uasail e 'us a b'ionmhuinn,
Ochagan ! is e so an t-suil do bhi an ceann Chonuill chneasda,
An t-suil mu'n iadh an fhabhrad, do b'fhialaidh i 's a b'osgarach.
Ochagan ! is e so am beul air nach d'fhuair filidh fannsgeul,
Beul tana a's deirge na 'n ubhal, blas meala air beul Chonuill,
Ochagan ! is e so an lamh, bha air Conull Mac Scannlain,
Lamh fir bu chruaidh an iomghuin, lamh Chonuill mo cheud ionmhuinn
Ochagan ! is e so an taobh, ris an sìneamaid ar slios saor,
Is e madadh o Muile gu maol o luidh Eoin air a thaobh.
Ochagan ! is i so a chos nach teicheadh roimh laoich dha bhitheadh,
Cas fir bu chruaidh an cathaibh, cas Mhic Scannlain sgiathach,
Oich ! is e an rath bha an Conull gach tràth an bhi moch
An nochd theirig mo sgeul is e baile nan deur 'us nan och.
Ochagan.

A h-Ughdair so Seathan Chnoideart.

A chinn Diarmaid O'Charbair, g'a leor airc agus tuaghal,
Cha mhòr leam meud do dhocair, ge ta e cruaidh ri chuadh.

Cha troyg lwmmi fad zroyk zrannicht, no geith glennich
Chay troyg lom gae id chaylow a chinn dermit echarbre
Mark a smein a veyym brayd nach bee nawa di chardis
Ocht is mark nar heilli teachta a chinn dermit echarbre
Di willi letti reith eillith far ymirt eine is argit
Ga tey in drillis wr eyrnich a chinn dermit echarbre
Reith eilli nin gorn coythoill na chur honor er chartin
Mark a chreachta a chness neafzall a chinn dermit echarbre
Invin loym a wass werri na zoythle oyr no argit
Is lar wansich fley is feyth a chinn dermit echarbre
Ea rom er reith nyn nestill in teith faskis la . . .
Duarrticht fest o feanon a chinn dermit echarbre.
A chinn dermit.

Auctor hujus Gormlyee nee lyne.

Dwrsin wr er hwcht a neill dursin dowyn ir toyth er hoye
Gin terf in nolsyth na neif oss marf reith toyskyrte toye
Drwme re seill ewin in nae mir a zonee a zae wee
Wye er lyneff go leyr o clyne naill tayfrith in ter
Daik mee m'cwlenane keif waa me ag mirogane mor
Di beyvin mo hell ag neell gall mo naeve go ner ag oill
Da zeywyn fleygh agus feine di verre crye di gi clar
Ma ta seyh in naeild neiwe keit nach beeow neif ag neell
Nocha naga fer mir neell di bi zale ae ach a zlownyth
Fa math a waysith si naewe tass a cheyve is glass a howle
Dass freich er in warga vor teik in zeith sin nart da nar
Di chrommi in neyl er a zlown logis gin scur erri gin naell
Ni warris sonis na schee ne skurris a zeith za glor
Gin nassith er chroymg na er chreif o wass re on wothirn wor
Tre wass v'key in neell inde fa dolle dreym riss in dronig
Re gai beith coyth agis cwrn di heill chwyne is toyle teynn
Da essi is follew gi rath is trome mo chrye za chrow
Beith no zey gin deith ymbraach tayvir gin ta mir a dow.
Dwrsin.

Gormlee nee Lyne.

Ber a vanne lett di choss tokg in ness di heyve naill
Is rawor churris di chree er in tee la leyvfin feynn
Ro adde a teith a vanne har a cur cree er naill nar

Cha truagh leam fo do ghruaidh ghreannaich, na gaoithe gleannaich,
Cha truagh leam 'gad cheangladh, a chinn Diarmaid O'Charbair.
Mairg an smuain a bha am braghad, nach bu naimhdeas do chairdeas,
Och is mairg 'n uair shaoileadh teachd, a chinn Diarmaid O'Charbair.
Do mhilleadh leat Rìgh Ile, fear imirt fhion 'us airgid,
Dha ta an trillis ùr earnach, a chinn Diarmaid O'Charbair.
Rìgh Ile nan corn cuachail, a chuireas onoir air chairdean,
Mairg a chreuchd a chneas neamhgheal, a chinn Diarmaid O'Charbair.
Ionmhuinn leam a bhos mhear nach doichleadh òr no argiod,
'Us le'r b'annsa fleadh 'us fiadhach, a chinn Diarmaid O'Charbair.
Iarram air Rìgh nan Abstol an ti a phaisgeas le a fheartaibh,
D'a fhurtachd am feasd o phianaibh, a chinn Diarmaid O'Charbair.
A chinn Diarmaid.

Auctor hujus Gormlaidh nic Fhlainn

Dursan ùir air uchd an Neill, dursan doimhne fhir tuaith air 'uaigh
Gun tairbhe an uailse na niamh, o's marbh rìgh tuaisgearta tuaith.
Druim ri saoghal aoibhin an aigh, mar a ghonadh dha a bhi,
Bhi air a shloinneadh gu léir o Chloinn Neill ta fri an tir.
Dh' fhàg mi Mac Cuilenain caomh do bha mi aig Muireagain mòr,
Do b'aoibhin mo shaoghal aig Niall, geal mo niamh gun eur ag òl.
Do gheibhinn fleagh agus fion, do bheireadh credh do gach cléir,
Ma tha se an dail n-aoin, ciod nach bitheadh neamh aig Niall ?
Nocha n'fhac mi fear mar Niall, do bu gheal e ach a ghlùn,
Fa maith a mhaise 's a niamh, taise a chiabh 'us glas a shùil.
Dh' fhàs fraoch air an fhairge mhoir, tig a ghaoth 's a neart de 'n ear,
Do chrom an Niall air a ghlùn leigeas gun sgur air gun eala ;
Ni bheireas sonas no sìth, ni sguireas a ghaoth dhe a gloir,
Gun easbhuidh air chronag no air chraoibh, o bhàs rìgh o'n mhuirn mhòr ;
Troimh bhàs Mhic Aoidh O'Neill an dé, fa duilich dream ris an droing,
Rìgh ge b'e cuach agus cuirn, do shiol Chuinn is tuaghal teann ;
D'a easbhuidh is falamh gach rath, is trom mo chridhe d'a chruth,
Bhi 'n a dheigh gun dìth am bràth, an t-aobhar gu tathamar dubh.
Dursan.

Gormlaidh nic Fhlainn.

Beir, a mhanaich, leat do chos, tog a nis de thaobh an Nèill,
Is ro mhor a chuireas do chré air an ti le 'n luidhinn féin ;
Ro fhada a ta a mhanaich shiar a'cur cré air Niall an àir,

Go kayn voyt a charre zonn na bonny di wonni re lay
Na dowin gi daein in noye oich a chleyrre troye di hoisg
Toygga di neyll zlowndow zall ber a wanne lat di choss
M'eneyll in noyr inn ne dyn zoyn a we fa chriss
Faykgir a lechta is a ert ber a wanne lat di choss
Is mee gormlay chummis ryne nee lyne chroith . . .
Na beith tessew er a lecht ber a wanne lett di choss.
Ber.

CREATHTITH sin a vakkeive vor ga bee sloye ler harli how
Ga ta tow gi tursich tinni is doe linni di weith fa clowth
X c long a greyg ni gayill is gin di weith ach trear sae
Di zayssi zoyve naew tarm is lea ymmirwe nassi ymboe
In sloyg sin gin nymit sleyg ne ymboe far weithe eicth.
Warwidir di hessir ser hugit id heive ymit caich
Zid turtich er neiw di zonni gwysyth ort agis gwe feynn
Er murrith waythr ni bocht mi pheddir lat is mo chre
Creathtih.

A houdir so so feylim m' dowle.

Ne math swille sin donich ga bee chongvis in ter
Ne math meith clowth a chenich ne math fammyth mnaei begh
Ne math screyve gin oylwme ne math coyrin gi gortyth
Ne math erle gin wearle ne math marrych na voddych
Ne math espic gin varrin ne math aneive er hanor
Ne math saggirt er laithwlli ne math parsone gith derrell
Ne math longfort gin nimirt ne math innilt gi roith lessga
Ne math earlow gin termin ne math tempill gin relik
Ne math ben gin weith narrich ne far clarsich gin tead
Ne math coggith gin chalmyth ne math gawle phort gin warrich
Ne math meydin gith kantich ne math deyvris ir aneich
Ne math caslane gin iyr ne math darmit chon teach
Ne math gin wrrwm daithyr ne math lawirt ne meshga
Ne math skaane gin yvir ne math cleynith ni bree
Ne math cardis nin newill did vak a reithin rath our
Ga zoyrsee seill aw ne math zawsin a chroichyth
Ne math leyor gin twsgsyth ne math dwnni gin charit
Ne math fillith gin yvir ne math eilcloth gin tallyth

Gu caoin uait a chara dhuinn, na buineadh do bhuinn ri làr ;
Na duin gu dion an uaigh och ! a chleirich truagh do thoisg,
Tog de Niall ghlundubh gheal, beir, a mhanaich, leat do chos ;
Mac O'Neill an oir fhinn, ni de'm dheoin e bhi fo chrios,
Fàgair a leachd 'us a fheart, beir a mhanaich leat do chos ;
Is mi Gormlaidh chumas rainn, nic Fhlainn chruaidh o Dhùn rois
Na bi ad sheasamh air a leachd, beir a mhanaich, leat do chos.
Beir a mhanaich.

CREUCHDADH sin, a mhaca mhoir, ge bith sluagh le'r tharladh thu,
Ge ta tu gu tuirseach tinn, is toil leinn do bhi fo chliù ;
Deich ceud long a Greig nan Gaidheal, is gun do bhi ach triar saor,
Do ghabhas dhoibh neimh d' arm, 'us le iomarbhaidh an fhad 's am beò ;
An sluagh sin gon iomadh sleagh, ni am beò fear bhi eachda,
Mharbhadar do sheisir saor, thug iad a 'd thaobh iomadh cath ;
Dh' ad fhurtachd air nimh do ghuinidh, guidheas ort agus guidh féin,
Air Muire mathair nam bochd, mo phaidear leat agus mo chreud.
Creuchdadh.

Is e ùghdair so Pheilim Mac Dhughaill.

Ni maith siubhal 's an domhnaich ; ge bith chumas an t-saor.
Ni maith michliu a chinnidh ; ni maith feamachd mnatha beith.
Ni maith sgriobhadh gun fhoghluim ; ni maith caoruinn gu goirt.
Ni maith Iarla gun bheurla ; ni maith maraich 'na bhodach.
Ni maith easpuig gun bharun ; ni maith ainimh air sheanair.
Ni maith sagairt air leth shùla ; ni maith parson gu dearoil.
Ni maith longphort gun imirt , ni maith mnilt gu ro leisg.
Ni maith earfhlaith gun tearmunn ; ni maith teampull gun reilig.
Ni maith bean gun bhi naireach ; no fear clarsaich gun teud.
Ni maith cogadh gun chalmachd ; ni maith gabhail phort gun mharaich.
Ni maith maighdean gu cainteach ; ni maith doibhreas fhir ainfheich.
Ni maith caslan gun oighre , ni maith dearmad chon teach.
Ni maith gun urram d 'athair ; ni maith labhairt na misge.
Ni maith sgian gun fhaobhar ; ni maith claonadh na breth.
Ni maith cairdeas nan diabhul ; do 'd mhac a rioghain rath oir,
Ge dh' fhoir se siol Adhaimh, ni maith dhasan a chroiche.
Ni maith leughair gun tuigse ; ni maith duine gun charaid.
Ni maith filidh gun aobhar ; ni maith aoilchludh gun talla.

Ne math eadyth gin owkkith ne math sowkgryth gin garrith
Ne math meizneive aworrith ne math poissith giu nanyth
Ne math corroyn giu warrith ne math traive sin neich
Ne math eyggiss gin chawis ne math craw gin nenich.
Ne math.

Di quhoye missi robert feyn di vanistir in ney nwnni
Agis neir leagow mee is steach o nach royth mo venni fer rum.

Foyach lam anit a treyl foach lam clar er ym beith ben
Foyach lam dobbroyn is doith neill foyach lam balle mor gin zann
Foyach lam droch weu ag far math foyach lam flath er ym be groyme
Foyach lam doech annin is he der foyach lam donyth ser gyn stoyme
Foyach lam a choggi na heith nach a leggir a neith mane seacht
Foyach lam kannort garwe chroy foyach lam sloge nach dany cacht
Foyach lam beith faddi ri port foyach lam weith gi holg fane weig
Foyach lam ben eaddor is ee drow foyach lam con nach marw in feygh
Lesk lam dol in nerrin schear o nach marrin brane na fonn
Foyach lam brantrych gin wea marri foyach lam far is agne tromm
Foyach lam caillicht is olk naill agis a tangyth gi bar loith
Ne ea dwm a chorri in geyll gith neith in duggis feyn foath.
Foath.

Gerroyd erle.

Marga a leymis herryth a each tuggi gi nach less in naaill
Gin dimeich mi chwddi orm feyn ne ell feym be riss nyth mnawe
Mi wallich a mesgi nyth banni ga di weym schalli no in daill
Mer rew hay gin cheyle ne ell feym be riss nyth mnawe
A zayg a zeyrris gi moch ne weith scheith gin locht no dale
Da ganfeit ne by leyr ne ell feym be riss nyth mnawe
Farre lay heine wneith weiss gin rath far nach math in dossith nawe
Na kead lollich a neith geym ne ell feym be riss nyth mnawe
A wennith a neith in testyth dowf a zestis re gow is re glaiw
Mar gi bi na clossew keyr ne ell feym be iiss nyth mnawe
Carit sche ferk er a fer keichlai genn riss gith dawe

Ni maith eididh gun fhucadh ; ni maith sùgradh gun ghàire.
Ni maith mighuiomh aghmhora ; ni maith pòsadh gun àithne ;
Ni maith coroin gun bhàr ; ni maith treabhadh 's an oidhche.
Ni maith eigeas gun chaomhas ; ni maith crabhadh gun aithne.
Ni maith.

Do chaidh mise Robart féin, do mhainisdear an dé a nunn,
Agus nior leigeadh mi a steach, o nach robh mo bhean marrium.

FUATHACH leam bhi annaid a triall ; fuathach leam clar air am bi bean ;
Fuathach leam dobhròn 'us dubhneul ; fuathach leam baile mòr gun ghean ;
Fuathach leam droch bhean aig fear maith ; fuathach leam flath air am bi gruaim ;
Fuathach leam deoch anmhuinn 'us e daor , fuathach leam duine saor gun
Fuathach leam a chogadh 'n a shìth ; nach leig a ni mu 'n seach ; [stuaim ;
Fuathach ceannard garbh cruaidh ; fuathach leam sluagh nach dean cath ;
Fuathach leam bhi fad ri port ; fuathach leam bhi gu h-olc mu 'n bhiadh ,
Fuathach leam bean eudmhor 'us i drùth ; fuathach leam cù nach marbh
Leasg leam dol an Eirinn siar, o nach marrainn Brian nam fonn ; [am fiadh ;
Fuathach leam bantrach gun bhi mear ; fuathach leam fear 'us 'aigne trom ;
Fuathach leam cailleach is olc neul, agus a teangaidh gu beur luath ,
Ni fhaodam a chur an ceill, gach ni dha 'n tugas féin fuath.
Fuathach.

Gearailt Iarla.

Mairg a leumas thar a each, tuigeadh gach neach leis an aill,
Gun d'imich mo chuid orm féin, ni bheil feum bhi ris na mnathaibh.
Mo mhallachd am measg nam ban, ge do bhitheam seall 'n an dàil,
M' fhearaibh tha gun chéile, ni bheil feum bhi ris na mnathaibh.
A gheug a dh' eireas gu moch, ni bhi sìth gun lochd n'a dàil,
Da canfaid ni bu léir, ni bheil feum bhi ris na mnathaibh. [nàmh,
Fear le h-aon mhnaoi bhitheas gun rath, fear gun mhaith an toiseach
Na ceud lullaich a ni geum, ni bheil feum bhi ris na mnathaibh.
A bhean a ni an t-éisdeachd domh, a dh' éisdeas ri guth 'us ri glaodh,
Mar gum bitheadh 'n a cluasaibh céir, ni bheil feum bhi ris na mnathaibh.
Cuiridh si fearg air a fear, caochladh gean ris gach daimh,

Curresceith nedrumi a keyme ne ell feym be riss nyth mnawe
Da wakgit sche schillith a sowllith di zillanyth or won. . . .
Ne zanic sche richt ach leym ne ell feym be riss na mnawe
Da wakkeith maedin or oygo za in durri poyk gith saive
Da ymbeith bayl deith weith er clar ne ell feym be riss nyth mnawe
Powysyth won altir is woyn cheill a laif in taggirt zrinn zrae
Dolle gi holgith is a mayn ne ell feym be riss nyth mnawe
Ne elli feym be riss nyth mnawe is eydde a glayf is a verg
Gi neach nach curri syn a geyll ne heddir nach d feyn is mark.
Marg.

Auctor hujus Andro tosschych.

Scoyd neyn dnnche a hayd eine scoyd is mow pleyd sloywg
Scoyd ag dae is a wreeith scoyd ni geith a harbill roy
Heill ni toythin mi vea balve is ni tre hoyvir gin ran woyme.

Auctor hujus im bard m'ynteir.

Cred eith in long soo er loch inchsyth na veadis a haithrynsyth
Cred hug in long er in loch is nach feadi ni fwnni a follych
Eaffre de bail lamm ka lar leggi in leythin
Er in locht fa lane fergith gith muth fa dail deveit
In garve zeith varri benni no in synteith serve schrowth zlen
Zoydith in cherwe won claddych er in choyne zarve zoyssidych
Ogleich chonnik in charve er in schrowth oyhorr ag garve
Keddey a heynyth na hynsyth na feyryth za forrinsyth
Senn long gin nearni gin derri ner iddir sinni a sawilt
Neyn lwng eith zi laythir lane gou twnni ni haythir imlane
Bwrdi zi skythew deilloik dowth o correw seiss na slissew
Tarni gin oyyme gai foyme er a woythchin ard inhor
Cred ee in lowht oyd sin lwg zoe ga torrin eddir honnew
An lwcht gin cheddrew gin cheyll baantrych in naknyth awree
Boein wroskgilyth wrewnych lot wr donnyth dechewnych
Scherryth connissych keikrych gyn nith donnith droch zentych
Droch lorg is laywryth fa linni coissryth cley nanyth cotchin
Flesk in goara gin choomn meskyth oyranith eddrwme
Coissryth tone zarve nin dolle tce ma za liss locha hynsith
Di boyl lit sin lwngi gi leyr cr zrwme oyrree in nagwaill
Ben waith ne lawyth sin lwng lyit a heagin aggin
Beith ni mnawen is melsith er a vurri fest gin chaich ga in gowr

Cuiridh si an cudruime a ceúm, ni bheil feum bhi ris na mnathaibh.
Da faiceadh si sileadh an sùla, do ghillean ùr o'n . . .
Ni dheanadh si ruith ach leum, ni bheil feum bhi ris na mnathaibh.
Da faiceadh maighdean ùr òg, dha'n toireadh pòg gu sèimh,
Da am bi beul do bhi air clàr, ni bheil feum bhi ris na mnathaibh.
Pòsadh o'n altar 'us o'n chill, á laimh an t-sagairt ghrinn ghràidh,
A dol gu h-olc 'us a mèin, ni bheil feum bhi ris na mnathaibh.
Ni bheil feum bhi ris na mnathaibh, is iad an glaodh 'us an fhearg,
Gach neach nach cuir sin an céill, ni h-eudar nach da féin is mairg.
Mairg.

Is e ùghdair so Anndradh Toiseach.

Sgoid nighinn Dunchaidh a Thaid, aon sgoid is mo pleid sluaigh,
Sgoid aig Daibhidh 'us a mhnaoi, sgoid na gaoith á h-earball ruaidh.
Shaoil na tuathan mi bhi balbh, 'us na trì aobhar gun ràn uam.

Is e ùghdair so am bard Mac an t saoir.

Creud i an long so air Loch Innse, na dh' fheudas a aithris,
Creud thug an long air an loch, nach faod na fuinn a folach.
Feòrach do b'aill leam, cia le 'r leigeadh an lion,
Air an loch fa làn feirge, gach mugha fa dàil do bhi.
An garbh ghaoth bhar beinne, no na sianta searbh sruth ghlinne,
Gheibhteadh a chairbh o'n chladach, air a chuan gharbh ghuaisideach.
Oglaich, a chunnaic a chairbh, air an t-sruth aghmhora gharbh,
Ciod e a h-ioghnadh 'n a innseadh na fhuaireadh d 'a foirinnse ?
Seann long gun iarna gun deireadh, nior idir sin a samhailt,
An aon long de leathar làn, gu tuinn ni thathar iomlan.
Buirde de sgiathaibh deileig dubh, o coiribh sios 'n a sliosaibh,
Tairgne gun fheum 'g a faitheam, air a fuath chinn ard eanchair.
Creud i an luchd oighe 's an long dhubh, 'g a tarruing eadar thonnaibh,
An luchd gun chaidrimh gun chiall, bantraich an aigne aibhrigh,
Buidhean bhrosgalach bhruidhneach, lod ùr dona deuchainneach,
Sior chonasach, ciocrach, guineach, dona, droch-dheantach ;
Droch lorg 'us labhradh fa leinn, coisridh cleamhanach coitchin,
Fleasg an comhradh gun chom, misgeach, oranach, eudrom ;
Coisridh ton-gharbh nan dollaidh, ta ma dha shlios Loch Innse,
Do buaileadh leatsa an long gu léir, air dhruim odhar an eugbhail ,
Bean mhaith ni lamhadh 's an luing, liuthad a h-éigin againn,
Bithidh na mnathan is miosa air a mhuir, feasd gun cach 'g an cobhar.

Royegir in long as in locht er in saill schrowth zarve swlich
Geith in lanvin ni lwg gow senn row nyth sanenych
Faik myn er in schrow seithnyth in long zonnicht zroithzenych
Si lanc di wantrych ni baid sin taaill gin salmmi gin saale chread.
Creaddyth.

TORRISKALLE tyllich zownnolle grass lag wo ni dimmon tread
Innin din wroid sin is din waddyth keithkr gow foill wradde ead.

A houdir so oone m'murreich.

Nawyth zoe in dane da in dwgi cach sowd
Na lig a vekzey mee si feane in dew
Beg a heyle in skol mi zayn a zoll fowm
A dayn tarle rinn is schea zi weill meith
Is moo wulle dim zeith riss fa thre na ee
A tegwaill doo zowf di weith clooch no skay
Air wen in dayn deim is mor meith is merg
Kness mir chow er tonn glak chor is . . .
Bail er dath nyn sowe trog mo chrow er schare
Od chotlysyth in ryir troyg a zea mo chorr
Di we sche far rowm er lwm kin gar royve
Gin ee ann o loo di choy er wroin doyth
Tin neach feicht coole russ is trom ri raye
Coyk fleska nin sneim it ta in nanm ni mna
Troyg gin cie fame wree er ni bree o cha . . .
Da wyginsyth feyne gi rar hor in daw
Slygh chonchwllin charn each teyg in teach bane
Skayth corkrych kin zayk fai meith head er chath
Schewle ceche v'erge ga mor sin ra raye
Owch is mo fa rer mo zeith riss in dane.

Duncha m^c^a pharsone.

Allex^r^ in di threig tw in zroyme na in vead schew a cur roeyve er layr,
In dan schewe in bliyn gin zey na ym beith scheve mir schen gi brach
Cheith nein doaris di zen o teith tow gi schen laeth
Maiss er zroyme veiss in rath is mor hoayr how zi wath o zea.

Ruagar an long as an loch air an t-sàil sruth gharbh siubhlach,
Gaoth an leanmhuinn na luinge, gu seann rubh nan Seananach.
Fàgaidh mi air an t-sruth seana, an long ghuineach dhroch-dheantach,
'S a làn de bhantraich nam beud, 's an t-sàil gun salma gun sal chreud.
Creud.

TUAIRISGEUL teaghlaich Dhunollaimh, gràs lag o na d'ioman treud;
Ionann do 'n bhrùid sin 'us do 'n mhadadh, ciocrach gu feoil bhradaidh iad

Is e ùghdair so Eoin Mac Mhuirich.

Nimheach dhomh an dàn, da an tuig cach sud,
Na leig a Mhic Dhé, mi 's a phéin an diugh.
Beag a shaoil an sgoil, mo dhàn a dhol fo bhinn
An dàn tarladh ruinn, is si do mhill mi,
Is mo a bheil de 'm ghaoth, ris fa thri na i,
A teugbhail dubh dhomh, do bhi cloch 'na sgeith.
Air bhean an dàin tiom, is mor m'fhioch 'us m'fhearg,
Cneas mar chobhar tonn, glac chorr is deirge.
Beul air dath nan sùgh, tug mo chruth air soirthe,
O'd chodladsa an raoir, truagh a Dhé mo chor.
Do bhi si far rium, air leam gun gàire robh,
Gun i ann o lò, do chaidh air bhuòn domh.
Duibh na fitheach a cul, ruis is trom a ràdh,
Coig fleasg 'n an snaim, a ta an ainm na mnath.
Truagh gun i fo 'm bhreith, air a breith o chach,
Da fhaighinnse féin, gu ri'r fhuair an daimh.
Sleagh Chonchulain charna, each Taoigh an eich bhain,
Sgiath chorcrach gun ghàig, fa maith h-iad air chath,
Siubhal eich Mhic Eirc, ge mor sin ri ràdh,
Och is mo fa réir, mo ghaoth ris an dàn.

Duncha Mac Phearsoin.

Alastair, an do threig thu a ghruaim, no am faod sibh a cur uaith air làr,
An d'fhan sibh am bliadhna gun Dhia, no 'm bi sibh mar sin gu bràth,
Chaoidh ni 'n d'fhuaireas do ghean, o ta tu gu sean liath, [o Dhia.
Ma 's ann air gruaim a bhithcas an rath, is mòr a fhuair thu a mhaith

Caithrir weith er oye in ir er fert allx[r] oye ree
Di chansit brayr reith gin wreyk osskanni ni flath finzreyk
Dowirt in kaid er zeyve di wemirin ncy fane reith
Sloye in doythin troyeg in dayll gay id taa in dew na anythrane
Di weith in ney dey reith in donane dwnne na warkkeich er tallwon truma
Ga zca in tallow id ta in newe na warkkeich er a wonsin
Id dowirt in tress owdir glik weith ym beith in ney ag m'phillip
In newe ag nocha nell a heacht troeith zin talwon
Allex[r] murnych mor allexandir hesgeith ergit is oyr
In newe erss in carrew far id ta in toyr gi hasgaissey
Mak phillip phelm oss crannew in ree oss ni readlainew
In toyr oss ni scheadew slane in meill moyr ossin braddane
In loyvin oss charrew gin blyi in nirwoye ossin nane laithe
Sleyw scheioyne oss gi sleywe slayne oss gi schrow schrow oyrrelane
In laik loyor oss ni cloichew in wurri oss minroythew
Sownirrich in warrith gin none ayne erri oss errow tallwon
Ayne err oss errew tallwon acht reith neyve is neyve hallwone
Reith teynni nin draid is nin dork kenni nin gaid agus nin garrith
Choyraa nin nowdir a beir er deacht er oye in nard reith
Ne chosswill ra beith zlar bainn er chansidir in caithrir.
Caithrir.

A howdir soo ooyne m'murreich.

Fir albin is ne eayd a wayne mir marrin m'gregar
Kay leine di chorreich a chossgir maiss olli er allestir.

Finlay ym bard royg say howird soo.

Gyllyth gith seith zin each oozr gylli di weithis issi
Fo hee woyichis si chossni gi neith loyis missi
Urrwme a loytha ga cossow gow roythir a wreiss
Notythseith neynyth a tressi si cheillith ga soiwe
Ne oonyn sayd da caythwe re yig a reiyth
Ne ym braik torriskall in eachsin stead loyildach gast
In dow seywlin is ray is coswil na iyr in lay macha
Ga zarrik ym maid sie gossnew ne hor eaid na ir nathna
Mir bi kithly geith di knokew roith ni seith in dachis
Mor cayd lor awsych a swil hed mir hawsyth scachew
Each in nee serrith ri sayid a gneiwroith is granta

CEATHRAR bhi air uaigh an fhir, air feart Alastair uaibhrich,
Do chansaid briathra gun bhréig, os cionn an fhlatha Fionnghréige.
Dubhairt an ceud fhear dhiubh, do bhitheamar an dé fa 'n rìgh,
Sluagh an domhain, truagh an dàil, ge a ta an diugh 'na aonaràn.
Do bhi an dé rìgh an domhain duinn, 'n a mharcach air talmhainn truime,
Gur e an talamh a ta an diugh, 'n a mharcach air a mhunsan.
A dubhairt an treas ughdair glic, bhi am bith an dé aig Mac Philip,
An diugh aige nocha 'n 'eil, ach seachd troidh dhe 'n talmhainn.
Alastair muirneach mòr, Alastair thasgadh airgiod 'us òr,
An diugh ars' an ceathramh fear, a ta an t-òr 'g a thasgadhsa.
Mac Philip a phailm os chrannaibh, an ré os na reultanaibh,
An t-òr os na seudaibh slàn, am mial mor os na bradanaibh.
An leoghan os chairbhe gun bhlagh, am fireun os na h'eunlaith,
Sliabh Shioin os gach sliabh slàn, os gach sruth sruth Iordain.
An leug liomharra os na clachaibh, a mhuir os na mìnshruthaibh,
Sonmharach am fear gun on, aon fhear os fearaibh talmhainn.
Aon fhear os fearaibh talmhainn ach rìgh neimh is neo thalmhaidh,
Rìgh tinne nan treud 's nan torc, ceann nan ceud 's nan garaidh.
Còmhradh nan ughdair a b 'fhior, air teachd air h-uaigh an airdrigh,
Ni cosmhuil ri baothghloir bhan, a'r chansadar an ceathrar.
Ceathrar.

Is e ùghdair so Eoin Mac Mhuirich.

Fir Albain 'us ni iad a mhàin, mar marrainn Mac Grigoir,
Cia lion do chorruich a chosgair, maise uile air Alastair

Fionnladh am bard ruadh is e thubhairt so.

Gaidhealach gach sith dhe 'n each odhar, gaidheal do bhitheas ise,
Fa h-i a bhuadhaicheas 's a chosnadh, gach ni a luaidheas mise,
Urram a luaithe dh' a cosaibh, gu ruathar a bhris.
Nodasach neimhneach a treise, 's a chill ge soitheamh,
Na h-eoin siad do chathadh ri aghaidh a ruith.
Ni breug tuairisgeul an eich sin, steud luailteach gasd,
An Dubh-seimhlin is rithe is cosmhuil, na aidhre an Lamacha.
Co ionraic am meud 's an cosnadh, ni fhuair iad r'a 'r n-eachne,
Mar bhi caochladh gaoithe de chnocaibh, ruith 'n a sith an t-each so
Mòi ceud le'r annsa a siubhal, theid mar amhas seachaibh,
Each a ni searrdha ri saighid, a gniomhara is grannta,

Leggis bann dossli a reith sin roythwr ma raithis
Ga fad in neachle rompyth ner anneith ym merkyth
Ga beg a wollich in neachsin a commis re altew
Coy zess a boy sa sowil in groyth syn laythith
Eggill in neych er gi donyth tegwe in gress chath
Ym weacht ym weayin in gomisk is each bray in teachsin
Grainyth er a vor each gi vasgill in genn chor wratty
Ver in stoyg ullingyth hogryth urrwme sloyg za in merkych
Hed one chorri di weith er hossi in mor each meine masklych
Berre boye reith agis choskir ga teith in nor eskir
Gow hassge oorchrissi wllew mor crith er faiche
Gow beithga cronni layvin crowich meine drumelayn dattyth
Each fa horriskail an neichsin di cholyth ma agga
Ca royve sessi reyve fa chommis ne vestyth in layth macha
M'gregor kennord in neichsin trane na zlan phort philli
Tigfeit one vanve gai wollith in nalbin ga hirri
Fer churris argnyth er zallew is arbsi ra zyllyth.

Finlay royg in bard.

Fad id tam gin woyg awghall doyth is meicht
Hanith teim hawyth as in ner zleicht
Is say connir a hayvin darre slat wir
Gow flath rane ni gaywill fer nar ayr lwth swill
Gow m'gregar denyth is kenn din nyth skollew
Na bea neweine fallew dleeir zom a wollith
Gow fer is trane coorri in dossyth gith sawie
Ni in sawth za wee be a nawch gith hawle
Ner heyrissaid ummyth gregorre na gadew
Bayh a chail ym vogryth gra traa ossni tradow
Oone is kenn din traitsen ri hoor creach a zawell
Heyris feynyth cooyll bail re bail syth chawar
Nor a chee tylych armezar v'gregar ym ballicht
Slee veine na chorrych ne berri rew in nalicht
Noor chinnidir a choyrk ga zerim in greith nawit
Is riss fene di heiwic in rycht gail is wrawit
Di waissew v'cregar toor chaach er a chowlaw
Gin dyill re denew is gith meyr na zownych
Nor zagwm mi woyg ym ess er lar trot
Me ginsith mi wwk sai is milsith la mydda
Ga zolk in locha wir mi zeillonis insith
Gin claa lani ni longsith say er lay caith is milsyth

Leigeas bann d'uailsibh a ruith, 's an ruathar mar rachas,
Ge fad an eachlaidh roimpe, nior aineimh a marcach,
Ge beag a mholadh an t-each sin, a coimeas ri ealtaibh.
Co dheas a buaidh 's a siubhal, an cruaidh 's an làthaich,
Eagal an eich air gach duine, tigeadh an greas catha.
Am feachd, am fiadhain, an coimeasg, is each breagh an t-each sin,
Greann air a mhor each sin, 'ga mhasguill an ceann chorr bhrataich.
Bheir an stuagh fhulaingeach thograch, urram sluaigh dh'a marcach,
Theid o 'n choire do bhi air thoiseach, am mor each mìn masgalach.
Beiridh luaidh ruith 'us chosgair, ge ta an uair fheasgair,
Gu thaisgeadh or-chrios ullamh, mor chrith air faiche.
Gu biodhgath, cruinn, leamhainn, crodhach, mìn, druim leathan, daite,
Each fa thuairisgeul an eich sin, do chuala mi aca,
Cia robh seis riamh fa choimeas, ni bheisd an Lamacha.
Mac Grigoir ceannard an eich sin, treun a ghlain phort filidh,
Tigead o 'n Bhanbha 'g a mholadh, an Albain 'g a shireadh.
Fear chuireas airgneadh air Ghallaibh, 'us earbsadh ri 'Ghaidhealaibh.

Fionnladh ruadh am bard.

Fad a taim gun bhuaidh, 'fhaigheal domh is mithich,
Thainig tìme thàmhach, as an aoradh dhligheach,
Is e conair a theighinn, d' iarraidh slait mhir,
Gu flath treun nan Gaidheal, far nar fhaighear luchd suaill.
Gu Mac Grigoir dion, is ceann air na sgoilibh,
Ni bhi neomhìn falamh, dlighear dhomh a mholadh.
Gu fear is treun còir, an toiseach gach samhradh,
Ni an samhach dha bhi, bithidh an amhaich gach h-amhuil.
'N uair theireas iad uime, Grigoir nan ceuda,
Bithidh a chail am fogradh, gu tràth os na treudaibh,
Eoin is ceann do 'n treud sin, rìgh fhuair creach a ghabhail,
Theireas féin ceol, beul ri beul 's a chamhar.
'N uair a chi teaghlach armgheur, Mhic Grigoir am Bealach,
Slighe mhin 'n a choire, ni b'eire riu an callach.
'N uair chinneadar a chomhrag 'g a ghairm an cridhe namhaid,
Is ris féin do theigheadh, an riochd goile 'us bhràghaid
De mhaisibh Mhic Grigoir, tothair chath r' a chulthaobh,
Gun diol ri daoinibh, 'us gach meodhar 'n a dhùna,
'N uair dh' fhàgam mo bhuaidh, am éis air làr trod,
Mi ag innseadh mo mhùc 's e is millse le 'm oide.
Ge h-olc an loch mhir mo dheileanas innseadh,
Gon cliath làn loingsich 's e air la cath is millse.

Cwne gym beym roythit v'gregar gin naga
Re yig gi troti a dail sayd fadda fadda
Allissaid ossill ympeich my weadda
A wen ni geyve bogga ga wanni a clar fadda.
Fadda.

A houdir soo duncha m'challin in riddiri math.

Kay din phleydda is ken oe o zi testa in dey zwni
Ta na deorri er ess in ir in phleydda gin tror ra fagsin
Ta na delicht ga zolk linn in pleyd er naik zi lochlyn
Is bayd sin er layr gith liss in pleyd er essew oliss
Ma hest ne choil mee layt lochlin er lay
O chrowich dea ni denith is cowe ee ear genyth
E gin wayr gin ayr in pleydd vocht er anffeine
Er nayk v'wretne vind a cretsin creyd nach keinfinn
Noch cho nel dwn er doythin do ne in pleyd a voerythchin
Er naik lochlin is layff linn olk in skailsen in nerrin
Ka zearis sporrane vegga ka zearis no snaydda
Ka zearis droch woynn gin dalf o testa lochlin layfherf
Ka zearis broik dowe ka zearis hi bowklin
Ka zearis breydda brawyd ka er kenn pleyd is fannayda
Ka zearis essit da wroiga ka zearis skayth feichok
Ka zearis ey za chriss ka neith leaf gi inliss
Ka zearis sen adda peillith ka zearis lowr leyin
Ka zearis deitta gow mowch ka er ym beith eyttow armycht
Ka zearis botin is spur ka zearis froygin aithchur
Ka zearis meskan is men ka zearis schesgane schoggill
Ka zearis spayn in sporrane ka in neith sollar gin nayr
O hest lochlin leywych ka ness ir neyvir zayr
Ka zearis leynte ban oyga er ess lochlin na senvroigga
Da eaksen is troyg in dail ka la nerrir in coarane
Ka zoyddis doss a zillith ka nach abir ferrine
Ka is leaf tryle a baada ka zearis no seucharda
Ka zearis cark le hoeow ka zearis leim keilwoe
Ka zearis corlycht in kerk in dey in dorlycht argit
Ka zearis prenyth gin chenn ka is fer layfin gomis cotchinn
Gin iyr er lochlin da ess dolli na eak re fassness
Ka zearis dowane is droif ka zearis dorssi dosklyth
Ka zearis binit gin wreith ka lay sirrir gith inneith
Ka nach doyr peyn di vocht ka zearis neith er ternocht
Ka zreisses gi groy oyd cheich ka weiss gi croy un v'neith

Cuimhnich gun bitheam romhad, Mhic Grigoir gun agadh,
Ri aghaidh gach trod an dail siad fada, fada.
Ealasaid uasail iompaich mo mheuda,
A bhean nan ciabh boga, dh' am buin an clàr fada.
Fada.

Is e ùghdair so Dunchadh Mac Chailein, an Ridir maith.

Co de 'n bhleid is ceann uidh, o do theasdadh an deagh dhuine,
Tha na deòir air éis an fhir, a bhleid gun treoir ri fhàgsainn.
Tha 'n a dileachd gu h-olc leinn, a bhleid air eugadh do Lachlainn,
'Us beud sin air làr gach lios, a bhleid air easbhuidh eòlais.
Ma theasd ni chuala mi, leithid Lachlainn air leth,
O chruthaich Dia na daoine, is cumha e air cinneadh,
E gun mhàthair, gun athair, a bhleid bhochd air anmhuinn,
Air n-eug Mhic Bhreatnaidh bhinn, a chreuchdsan creud nach caoininn.
Nocha-n 'eil duine air domhain, do ni a bhleid a mhuirichinn,
Air n-eug Lachlainn is leughadh leinn, olc an sgeul sin an Eirinn.
Co dh' iarras sporan bheag, co dh' iarras no snàthad ?
Co dh' iarras droch bhonn gun dealbh, o theasd Lachlainn laimh sheirbh ?
Co dh' iarras bròg dhubh, co dh' iarras na bucailean ?
Co dh' iarras bréid bràgbaid, co air ceann bleid is fanaide ?
Co dh' iarras asaichte de bhroig, co dh' iarras sgiath pheacoic ?
Co dh' iarras aedh dh' a chrios, co ni leibh gach ainleas ?
Co dh' iarras seann ada peillidh, co dh' iarras leabhar leighin ?
Co dh' iarras diota gu moch, co air am bith eideadh armach ?
Co dh' iarras botan 'us spuir, co dh' iarras fraoghan aithghearr ?
Co dh' iarras measgan 'us min, co dh' iarras seasgan seogaill ?
Co dh' iarras spain an sporran, co a ni solar gun naire ?
O theasd Lachlainn laochach, co nis ar n-aobhar ghaire ?
Co dh' iarras leinnte bhan òga, air éis Lachlainn na seanbhroige ?
Da eugsan is truagh an dàil, co le 'n iarrar an cuaran ?
Co ghoideas dos a ghille, co nach abair fìrinn ?
Co is leimh triall am bata, co dh' iarras na seana chairde ?
Co dh' iarras cearc le h-uibhibh co dh' iarras linn choileach ?
Co dh' iarras corlach na circe, an deigh an dorlach airgid ?
Co dh' iarras prin gun cheann co is fear leughainn coimeas coitchinn ?
Gun oighre air Lachlainn da éis, duilich a eug r' a fhaistneachd.
Co dh' iarras dubhan 'us droimh, co dh' iarras dorsa d'fhosgladh ?
Co dh' iarras binnid gun bhruidh, co le 'n sircar gach aon ni ?
Co nach toir peighinn do bhochd, co dh' iarras ni air tàrnochd ?
Co ghreasas gu cruaidh oidc elche, co bhitheas gu cruaidh um mhac nuaidh ?

Ka zearis ollin is ymmi chon a hee dess lochlin
Ka zearis collaryth banni ka lay mayne sollor sayllych
Ka zearis er mnaew oyga con vega agis nessoga
Ka zearis furssiñ oyd keich ka la in drussir gi marve neith
Ka zearis loist go wroit ka zearis truis tolwocht
Ka weiss gi tein is ay slayn ka zearis ymmi er vrochane
Dekrych lwn no eak in ir gin a iyr za essin
Deggil na pleyda zwll deyga issnach feadis ka neith coyvoyt
Ne zwme nine in ir danew a zenyth in doythin
Rann gith nach a chur na kann mallach din ner nach currin
Ma hest lachlin lay lon is swych a weiss gi downith
Da eak is bocith gi beith is ne cooyth gr eincheith.
Ka din.

Gormlay neyn lyne in ven watht.

Ochegane myth zallir feyn ochegane mi skarre reimi skaywe
In nocht is delis mo ladda o nach merrin m'eneall
Ochegane gin vak derwaill ochegane mo zail da ess
Noch char waill gayr naiss boylli fass erri zae essew
Ochegane re banich math gwss in nocht ner zani di chr . . .
Testoo vanmyn ess echaith ne abbrum ach och is oych.
Oche.

A houdir so duncha m'caybba.

A vec dowle toyr accane di loyt leich in lanvakcane
Hay mi zarve accane fer mon zalwe waccane wor wreith
Is ferri hik di chensi chew we riss na zoyss a vackeyve
Duncha carrych ga zerm zea is anm zoo a barryth boe
A dhuncha ni gor gassge cwneich anm do cheadwesti
A v'allen na twlle feyn tayweym noch char hoor allein
Wo tay schee in neiss in nenyth na hell yvyr ard wlyith
Gawe in cayd hoyr twss na ross woss tow eaddoill gi hawis
Davin gir a tow reiss fer zaywal ni gerve cheiss
Mir harve trodda agis tachir is darwe di hoggir a gayach
Is tow tastalych croychane i schelga sley fin vroychane
Di clow onchon ga inche is tow duncha durrinssi
Is tow chaskgeiss di nawe is to zergis di zallawe
Is tow zoiris vor skeiths sin is tow reiss doywnis aggin
Is sea fer da bi zussi a rinn di leyt camussi

Co dh' iarras oluinn 'us ìm, thun a thì d' éis Lachlainn ?
Co dh' iarras colaireach bhan, co le 'm miann solar salach ?
Co dh' iarras air mnathaibh oga, con bheaga 'us ncasagaibh ?
Co dh' iarras fursainn oide cìche, co le 'n trusar gach marbh ni ?
Co dh' iarras loisgt gu bhroit, co dh' iarras trùis tolbhochd !
Co bhitheas gu tinn 'us e slàn, co dh' iarras ìm air a bhrochan ?
Deacaire dhomh no eug, an fhir gun oighre bhi dha éisean,
D'eagal na bleid dhol eug, 'us nach faighideas co ni a coimhead.
Na dichuimhnichibh am fear, deanaibh, a dhaoine an domhain,
Raun gach neach a chur 'n a ceann mallachd do 'n fhear nach curainn,
Ma theasd Lachlainn a la luain, is subhach a bhitheas gach duine,
Da eug is bochda gu bith, 'us ni cumhar aon a chi.
Co de 'n bhleid.

Gormlaidh nighean Fhlainn, a bhean mhaith.

Ochagan mo ghalar féin, ochagan mo sgaradh ri' m sgéimh,
An nochd is dilis mo shlad, o nach mariainn Mac O'Néill,
Ochagan gun Mhac Diarbhaill, ochagan mo dhàil da éis,
Nochar fhéile Guaire an às, buaile fàs Eire da easbhuidh,
Ochagan rìgh Bhanbha maith, gus an nochd nior ghann do chruth,
O theasdadh m'anam 's a chath, ni abram ach och, agus och.
Och

Is e ùghdair so Dunchadh Mac Caibe.

A Mhic Dhughail a d'ùr achdmhuinn, do luath laoch a chlannmhacan,
Tha mo dhearbhachdainn fior mu 'n dhealbh mhacan mhoir bhrigh,
Is fearr thig do cheannsa chaomh, bhi ris na dhomhsa a mhacaimh,
Dunchadh carrach 'g a ghairm da, is ainm dha a b'fhearr buaidh.
A Dhunchaidh nan corr gaisge, cuimhnich ainm do cheud bhaisde,
A Mhic Allain na toill féin, toibheum noch char fhuair an linn,
O ta se nis an aithne na h-uile aobhar ard bhlagh,
Gu bhi an ceud fhuair tùs an arois, o 's tu eudail gu thathas.
Deimhin gur a tu rìs, fear ghabhail nan garbh chìs,
Mar tharbh trod agus tàchair, is dearbh do thogar an cathach
Is tu tasdaileach Chruachain, a sealg sleidh fo' bruachan,
Do chliù onchoin 'g a innseadh, is tu Dunchadh Diurinnse.
Is tu choisgeas do namh, is tu dheargas do dha lamh,
Is tu dh' fhoireas o'r sgios sinn, is tu rìs d'aoibhneas againn.
Is se fear do 'm b' usa, a rinn do luaidh cho musa,

Di neym eddir leich mır sin din dreggin cheive von chonnil
Is tayd agga di woeir kerd eili na coyllıfir
Gasga agis ennych errin gin nasga nyn lowveymnie
Gıth ınlycht zleis mak reich id tayd ag gin neyneyve
A zloyr zall zlan riss ga rec lor dı zarrı ın dy wec
A cheim gi wul a terri keıss lat ass gi inwalli
Rygh orricht ag gneith zlyn id tyicht ym chreif chosgir.
A vec.

Auctor hujus Ane m'eoin m'caychirn.

Daarych schayn er seil gwnn ne haarych in nochin
In dye oyne deive a zol seıth no zoye noch cha dantir
In sayn fa rowidir reyv finnich chwnn ner chleacht dewygh
In dey oyne gi arr er gowle da zoye ner an gin ympow
Da waass di reyggi in ter m'ir noyine wo allen
Mor ir schayn er gowl di chorri ner layn downyth na gi dear . .
In corsen lar olkyth zinn bass oyne is troyg in torrinym
Hanik braath o zwnn din chorri fa chung chaach dı quhyddir
Seil quhollych zoyss gow hayk oyne nar er adir gi ıntroyr
Faggis layn da heil wo henni in sayn ne in deive a zaith
Owr mrone a beıth mir sen clynn dowle di zeith in ır
Quhy barni nin sayn re schell sarwe in skail rı skeillych
A hechtich hug in skail huggin a zea di zroich zaal
Ni skailla di lawrit leive mawrit ner chayl in glwssin
Seır zail mi zar tree clawlt di von deim ryn mo ryirk
In dey oyne ne anvin a zulli cha naym doyr ra danew
Turri er in nane sin noe bass v'dowll downolle
Anna zye fa chrow chwnn ner zellı cnow ra croonith
Sein vorba brıssi no weig menich choyn ga cheynich
Er arda in trachta er ayk oyne ner ayd altaa won nayr
Loygh er evynis noch cha naıl in dye ayne ymzane
Nı sloygth ga braa dı wroon gin loyght er cryich na er coı
Id der riss in raythıd cayth id teacht wo toye gi intraa
Lay turre an nocchin nwll did chewe a var benchir
In neik monnor od tolt bog log aggwm na ynnit
Bei er hert fa zerryth doyf skaywolych mo zeık a zowe
Ne eddit mnae dolli zith woo toye la trwm in tuısi
Toggew fert dın wanyth wan layd lake cheılle croychin
Gar gır annychi orch di waas a laa laytromm
Finich did cowe ga ın gar dowe in cre nı codly
A chlyne dowle gow ayk oyne ne zaynith nach fir naw zoye

Do nitheam eadar laoich mar sin, do 'n dreagon chaomh o'n Chonuil,
A taid aige de bhuaidh air, ceaird eile na chuilbhr.
Gaisge agus eincach Eirinn, ga 'n nasgadh 'n a luath bheuman,
Gach innleachd ghleidheas mac Rìgh, a ta iad aig gun aineimh.
A ghloir gheal ghlan ris 'g a reic, le 'r do éirich an deagh mhac.
O chitheam gu bheil a toirt cìs, leat as gach aon bhaile,
Rìgh aireach aig gniomh ghrinn, a teachd um chraoibh chosgair.
A mhic.

Is e ùghdair so, Eoin Mac Eoghain Mhic Eachairn.

Deurach sian air siol Chuinn, ni eireach an dochainn,
In deigh Eoin doibh a dhol, sìth 'n a uaigh noch cha deantar,
An sian fa robhadar riamh, fine Chuinn nior chleachd dimhiodh,
In deigh Eoin gach fear air gul, da uaigh nior ann gun iompaidh.
Da 'bhàs do thruagh an tìr, Mac fhir a ghin o Allan.
Mòr ar sian air gul do chor, nior lion duine nach gu deurach,
An cor sin le'r olc dhuinn, bàs Eoin is truagh an torunn.
Thainig brath o Dhùn do 'n chor, fa chuing chàch do chaidhidear,
Saoghal caochlaideach dhomhsa gu h-eug Eoin, nior eireadar gu aintreòir.
Fagas làn do shìol o shean, an sian na an doibh a dhochainn,
Aobhar 'm broin a bhi mar sin, clann Dughail do dhìth an fhir.
Chaidh barn nan sian ré seal, searbh an sgeul ri sgeulachadh,
A theachdair a thug an sgeul, thugain a Dhé do dhroch dhàil
Na sgeul do labhairt leibh, m'amhra nior chaill an cluasan,
Saordhail mo gheire troimh chléibh uile, do bhuin diom roinn mo fhradarc.
An deigh Eoin ni anmhuinn a ghul, cha-n fhaigheam deoir ri dheanamh,
Tuireadh air an Fhian 's an uaigh, bàs Mhic Dhughaill Dhunollaimh.
Ann a aghaidh fa chruth Chuinn, nior ghile cno ri cruinne,
'S aon bhorb bhriseadh no bhith, mèin a chuain 'ga chaoineadh
Air ard an traigh air eug Eoin, nior fhaighead alt o'n athair,
Luaidh air aoibhneas noch cha-n 'aill, 'n deigh Eoin iomghain.
Na sloigh 'g am breith de bhròn, gun luaidh air creach no air còr,
A deir ris an rathad caidh, a teachd o d' uaigh gus an traigh,
Le tuireadh an dochainn null, do'd chumhadh a b'fhear banchaire.
An tig m'onoir o'd fholt bog, lochd agam 'n a ionad,
Bhi air 'fheart fa dheurach domh, sgiamhalach mo dhearc a ghabh.
Ni fhaotaid mnathan dol dhì, o d' uaigh le truime an tuirse,
Togaibh feart do 'n Fhian bhàn, leud laga chille Chruachain
Gu 'r gur aithnichte e orra, do bhàs a leth leatroma,
Fine do'd chumha go an gàir, dubh an cré ni codalaid.
A chloinn Dughail gu eug Eoin, ni dheanadh neach fear namh dhoibh,

Hanik di waass ir wllich sevif nach chass a chensyth
Ei oye oyne ne annit mnaw a dorta dear ge inlay
Kelle ban garri tra zoych troit er maye gin varrin
Ni henyth zoy turse throm in dey oyne di zallith orrwm
Nein deig lay nach lane cre in skail far taa ir tursine
Cwmmi lwm ca loo sin creid a zantyth za lesk lwmme
Da wass nach cha sokkir sinn degkir in gayss ner churrinn
Ym bessew tha melgwn er gin lay er ley e zaffere
Hug cre lwm na za laa sinn a lae er olwych
Cha darne reyve roye sen doy zein gow dowle e zaffre
Is yvir broyn gin ay ann is doy mee o nach merrin
Dess a chollyth nyth goyth noyr mir hay in ter troyg in tyrmno
Tra er durri noch cha nil syi in dwn sin dowchc
Lane marr techt har tulchew er naik oyne is da choythrrow
Oanych er in narga ne ull er ard choyn fa gonvell
Di chow owch reith raach chwnn si creich so clynni dowle
Blaa gal id zey er dowch bee ra heyg gin achroyeh
Eiss chwill ym clac zowill a egsi si ollonych
Lookir er teacht er oye oyne echtir waeth da nanoyn
Fadda in neyntoo neilla di chaith ga cwss tayweym
Nach spess deiv in noye zollyth dess oyne in neyntoo
Terk a hurri acmay chwnn wone lay nach mar m'dowlle
Breith in neyil noch cha null screive eyl na nessow
Onnor in neyl ne wae er testall di v'marae
Is beg a bail dawel deit di raye a honnor vayach
Na gi dacha drwm er zrwm voym za chenn clynni dowl
Re troyr ooyne ne zyil doyth in dyie oyne aythir
Gi lyi dea di zalwa neyf doyr in gligge in noid illeich
Voo eachree noch cha woyn baach za deache waach is ymza . . .
In dey in trur troyg in tolk mi chre ne for furtycht
Troyg na noyge gi chass di cheim di wass ii oyne is all . . .
Allex^r nach gavin gess in tra man deggir herris
Toycht er stoyg woynych bryi di royl oych mi nenin
Ni beit ga earre er dul dyr oyne gow hirrill
A beit er ter ni trodda ne beith naec fa noo adda

Auctor hujus finlay m'ynnab.

Doynirre nyn strakkirre da bi zail leif a screyve
Foyris din ni faggirre ne za weadir a leinyth
Ga zemmi ni ha deinnyth er teith milli ni toyth
Cha nayir na chomein in reid sin doyn boach

Thainig do bhàs fhir mhullaich scimh, noch chàs a cheannsachaidh.
Air uaigh Eoin ni ainnidh mnathan, a dortadh dheur gach aon la,
Càil bhan ag eiridh tràth dhoibh, troidh air mhagh gun bharran.
Ni h-ioghnadh dhoibh tuirse throm, an deigh Eoin do gheal urram,
Ni 'n tig la nach lion cridhe, an sgeul fa ta ar tuirsene.
Coma leam ge leo sin, creud a dheanadh do leisg leam,
D'a bhàs nocha socair sinn, deacair an càs 'na 'r chuireann.
A'm sheasamh tha melgthamh air, gun luaidh air laoidh a ghabhar,
Thug cridhe dhomh 'n a dha leth, sinn a luaidh air fhalbhaich.
Cha d'rinneadh riamh roimh sin, doighe dhuinn dhol d'a fharraid,
Is aobhar bròin gun e ann, is doighe mi o nach marrainn.
D'èis e chodladh na uaigh fhuair, mar tha an tir, truagh an toirm,
Traigheadh air deoir noch cha-n eil, saoth an Dùin 's an duthaich.
Làn mara 'teachd thar tulchaibh, air n-eug Eoin 's da choghairibh,
Onfhadh air an fhairg ni bheil, air ard chuan fa Chonnuill.
Do chumha och ! rìgh rathaich Chuinn, 's a chrioch so chloinn Dughaill,
Blath gal a'd dheigh air dùthaich, bithidh ri h-éigh gon eugchruas.
Aois chiuil um cliath Dhughaill, a eigse 's a ollamhan ;
Leachd air teachd air uaigh Eoin, eachdair a bhi de 'n aindeoin.
Fad an iontadh Neill, do chaidh gach cuis toibheim,
Nach spéis doibh an uaigh, dhol d'éis Eoin an iontadh.
Teirc a fhuaireadh aicme Chuinn, o'n la nach mair Mac Dhughaill,
Brìgh an fhiodhuill nocha n-'eil, scriobhadh fhilidh 'n a casbhuidh.
Onoir an fhileadh ni bhi, air teasdail do Mhac Mairidh,
Is beag am beul daimheil d'i, do radh a h-onoir bhuadhach.
Na gun deachaidh druim air dhruim, uam dha cheann chloinn Dughaill,
Ri treoir Eoin ni fhaghail domh, an deigh Eoin 'athair.
Gu gleidheadh Dia do dhealbh niamh, do fhuair innleachd an oide Ilich,
O eachraidh nocha bhitheann buaidh, dha deachaidh uath 'us imeachd.
An deigh an triur truagh an t-olc, mo chridhe ni fhuair furtachd,
Truagh nan oige go chàs do chitheam, de bhàs da Eoin 'us Alastair.
Alastair nach gabhann geis an trath mu 'n tigear thairis,
D'uchd air stuagh bhuaine brìgh do thruaill och ! mo nimhe.
Ni bhith 'g a iarraidh air dul d' oighre Eoin gu iorghuil,
A bhith air tir na troda, ni bhith nach fa'n uaigh fhada.

Is e ùghdair so Fionnladh Mac an Aba.

Duanair nan strangair, da b'aill leibh a sgriobhadh,
Fhuaireas de na fàgair, ni dhe faodar a lionadh.
Ge iomadh na tha daoine air ti millidh nan tuath,
Cha-n fhaighear 'n a choman an rud 's an duan buadhach.

Di wassew nin lorganych gan gir beith voach ach meile
In teigh gow be in goyalsi cho rik eayd ay gi heythe
A ta ossil anossil agki na chotti killi
Is ta wessew wca ray ayskey ga zeyg cha chlwni sinni
Quho we me ga slonissy cha null aggwmm za schenchas
Ach a be si choneskar agis no kon na lenvyn
A zowle a chompayne v'oyne nyn lann leyve
Ga will wlle ni lorganych dane in doynirre screyve
Screyve gi fessyth fer oylych in şchanchis is a gaer
Na ber doyni er weith heillyth ga leyve go m'challan
Cwne feyn in comyn so a zregar mir a choyle
Gi will aggwn orridsi di chwt a chur sin doynirre
Na bee ansin doyn so di haggirt na zi hoyctyth
Ga vil ne na coythrsi nach currir ay sin doynirre.
Doynirre.

A hujus Effric neyn corgitill.

A fadrin a zusk mi zair invin mar a weith ort
Invin cree faltyth faill gane royf reyve guss a nocht
Da eag is tursych a tam in lawe may bittee gi noyr
Nach clunnwm a bee in glee agis nach vaggum ee woyme
Mi creisi is tinn id taa o teic creich in lay zowin
Zerrid a zest ra zlor ra haggillow in noge wr
Bail ayssith di beive glor zaynti zoo si gi ter
Loyvin mwlle ni mour gall sawik eillith ni myg meine
Far bi zar moyvir er zane o nach deach dayve gin deill
Toissych dyghanich sork shawe ag a wayt mane v'reyth
Dawe a teach o zown noyr is dawe one voyn ga olt fay
Menik hanik ead fa hest ne menkyth na less in rar
Saywik schanglane sleyve geill far a chur a kenn re clar
Dreggin loyvis nin lerg gal ayg ag sannis nin schrawe sayth
A haguss ein donnyth wane amenir a tame za ess
Gin chlwich gin chorran kein gin awych gin yghe i geill
Gin dwnni ris tig mi wane er sleicht nin neaall o neal oog
Gin wurn gi weyr ag mnawe gin evinis in dane ym zoog
Mar hay geyaw in nwne wein down swenyth di chonne gin choill
Fayth longwrt ni war fayl aychwall ni neall in nawle
Cus ir loythirryth mane seach gwss a bemid a teach mawle
Is nach fulgwm in ness mi nor aggin woymo er gi ard
Ma wrissis a v'awce er baggit nin tre chnoo
Fa fer a zawis ir geyle di vonis in tranc bi woo

De fhiosaibh nan lorganach gun gur bu bhuadhach ach mìle,
An tigh gu bith an comhdhailse, cha ruig iad e go shìth,
A ta uasal, anuasal agc 'n a chota cille,
'Us ta 'fhiosa bhi ré acasa ge dh'eadh cha chluinn sinne,
Cha bhi mi 'g an sloinneadhsa, cha-n 'eil agam de sheanchas,
Ach a bhi 's a choinfheasgair, agus na con 'n an leanmhuinn.
A Dhughaill, a chompain, Mhic Eoin nan lann liobhta,
Ga bheil uile na lorganaich, dean an duanaire a sgriobhadh.
Sgriobh gu fiosach fior eolach, an seanchas 'us an gartha,
Na beir duan air bhith shaoghalach 'g a leughadh gu Mac Chailein
Cuimhnich féin an comunn so, a Ghrigoir mar a chuala,
Gu bheil agam ortasa do chuid a chur 's an duanair.
Na bitheadh anns an duan so de shagairt no de thuathach,
'G a bheil ni 'n an combairse nach cuirear e 's an duanair.
Duanair.

Ughdair so Eafraic nic Corcadail.

A phaidrein a dhuisg mo ghàir, ionmhuinn mar a bhi ort,
Ionmhuinn cridhe failteach fial, ga 'n robh riamh gus an nochd,
D'a eug is tuirseach a taim, an lamh mu 'm bithte gach uair,
Nach cluinneam e bhi an clì, agus nach facaim e uam;
Mo chridhse is tinn a ta, o tig creach an la dhuinn,
Goirid a dh' éisd r'a ghlòir, ri focalaibh an òige uir,
Beul aitheasach da 'm bu sheimh glòir, dh' aithnichteadh a ghuth 's gach tìr,
Leomhan Mhuile nam mùr geala, seabhag Ile nam magh mìne;
Fear a b'fhearr meodhar air dhaoine, o nach deachaidh daimh gun diol,
Toiseach deagh eanach suairc seimh, aig am faighteadh mèin mhic rìgh;
Daimh a teachd o Dhunanoir, 'us daimh o'n Bhoinn g 'a fholt fèidh,
Minic thainig iad fa theist, ni mince na leis an réir;
Seabhag seanglan Sliabh Ghaidheal, fear a chur a cheann ri cléir,
Dreagon Leodhais nan learg geal, agh aig sanas nan sreamh seimh,
A h-eugmhais aoin duine mhàin, a'm aonar a taim dha éis,
Gun chluich gun chanran caoin, gun àbhachd gun aoibh aig féill;
Gun duine ris an tig mo mhiann, air sliochd nan Nial o Nial òg,
Gun mhuirn gu bhithear aig mnaibh, gun aoibhneas an daoine um ghòig,
Mar tha gaoithe an ùine mhìn, Dun Suibhne do chunnaic gun cheòl,
Feuch longphort nam fear fial, aicheamhail nan Nial a nall.
Cuis ar luathghara mu seach, gus am bithmid an teach mall,
'Us no fuilgeam nis, mo nuar, againn uainne air gach aird;
Ma bhriseas, a Mhic Adhaimh, air bagaid nan tri chnò,
Fa fear a ghabhas ar gaoil, do bhuineas an trian bu mhò;

Knoo wullich a moggill feyn vonith di clyne neill gi noa
Is trig rynith nyth ver fail gow labbi ni neal in noyssa
In rygh fa derrig dewe say hug gin mi wreith in skayll
Di skar rwm mi la chwng rown a fadrin zusg mi zar
Is bristith my cree ym keith agis beith no gin dee mayg
Er ess in nawryth zoe wr a phadrin a zusg my zar
Mur wayir mumy in reith gin rowf gym zein er gi sayd
Is i mak a chrowich gi dowle a phadrin a zusg my zar.
Fadrin.

A howdir so Dowgall m'ille zlass.

Reicht zassge yricht ooyne is astrych za zoyn a zreyve
Nee nach illi nawrycht di chaych foyr in ny rych a saych reych
M'gregar ni greissi gar toissich is trane er gi ter
Eddir hoyr is creach zawle is doe a wee gi mawle meine
Eine rynn zaske zeyil greygga less nor meitht mayd clow
Fer is ferr aygh is eicht in lawa ter slicht in row
Shawik dayd zall nin dre zlann lass in leygr gaal gi gnew
Law is croith in gaaew kinith flaa is coryth zin tlicht reith
Er v'fadrik ni groygh derk nor assis ferg in nor aycht
Ni halych a ver no deygh nocha slane in loy caycht
Oyh vol challim nin derk corri ni skarri ra zor gin deith
Gilli dawych sothrych sang in law is ferri um gich neith
Acmich zregar tymchil oyne ne mir caylta in voal si wein
Drong wraych er nach leyr locht is grayth gort mir a hee
Clanni zregar in dramm nach trayth in namm nach bedis ray ra reith
Gyill ga fullichtych na fir ne churri schead sin ym bree
Ne mow loo geyl no gyill ni ser ir oo choynn in reith
Acmi zregar ni golga croy o worb sloye ne in gawe sneyve
Branane forna ni var faylla yr zregar nyn schiane oyr
Olk zi dwnc er in dane creach messit zi neach heyd na toyr
Flath zlinni leivin nin lann skayth wreour nach gann re clayr
Law mir oskir si gich cath is da is cosswill in flath feyn
Urrwm eincht da zroy zerg a hoyr gin chelg mir is coyr
Er zaill einenych zi gich nach er heilllgyth each is oyr
M'gregar in tylich zrinn ne henich linn na chwrt clayr
Ne el commis da ucht galle ach in fer ga royve in nane
Ag sen tri freccythchi finn braith a gilli ne vayccit reyve
Law bi wath inill in gress di binwin less fullich feyg
Cosslow a weine sa woywe riss in reith ga royve in nane
Re hawg v'gregar nin groach ver rawg gi nach a wane

Cno mhullaich a mhoguil féin bhuineadh do chloinn Nèil gun fhuath,
Is tric a roinn na fir fìala, gu leabaidh nan Nial a nuas,
An rìgh fa deireadh diubh, 's e thug gun mo bhrìgh an sgail,
Do sgar rium mo leth chunga ruin, a phaidrein a dhuisg mo ghàir,
Is briste mo chridhe a'm chioch 'us bithidh no gun dìth m'agh,
Air éis an amhra dhubh ùr, a phaidrein a dhuisg mo ghàir,
Mhuire, mhàthair, muime an rìgh, gu robh 'gam dhion air gach saighid,
'Us a mac a chruthaich gach dùile. A phaidrein a dhuisg mo ghàir.
A phaidrein.

Is e ùghdair so Dughall Mac Ghille ghlais.

Rìgh ghaisge eireachd Eoin, is asdaireach do dhuan a dhroing,
Ni nach bheil an amhra do chàch, fhuair an fhioradh an sàithe rìgh.
Mac Grigoir nan greas geur, toiseach is treine air gach tìr,
Eadar òr 'us creach a Ghall, is dòigh a bhi gu mall mìn; [chliù,
Aon roghainn ghaisge Ghaidheil Ghreige, leis nior meathaich meud a
Fear is fearr agh 'us iochd, an laimh an tir sliochd nan rìghe.
Seabhag deud gheal nan tri ghleann, leis an leughar goil gach gniomh,
Lamh is crodha an cathaibh cinnidh, flath a's còir dhe 'n t-sliochd rìgh,
Air Mac Phadruig nan gruaidh dearg, 'n uair athfhasas fearg an uair
Na h-alaich a bheir 'n a dheigh nocha slàn an luadh cath; [eachd,
Ogha Mhaoil Chaluim nan dearc corr, ni sgaradh ri òr gun dìth,
Gille daimheach, sothrach, seang, an lamh a 's fearr um gach ni,
Aicme Ghrigoir timchioll Eoin, ni mar chaillte a bhuille s'a mhèin,
Droing bhreagh air nach leughar lochd, is gnath gort mar a thì;
Clann Ghrigoir an dream nach treig, an àm nach bitheas réidh ri rìgh,
Gaidheil ge fulachdach na fir, ni chuireadh siad sin am br gh;
Ni mo leo Gaidheil no Goill, na saoir fhir o chuain an rìgh;
Aicme Ghrigoir nan colg cruaidh, o bhorb shluagh ni'n gabh sniomh.
Brainean foirne nam fear fiala, oighre Ghrigoir nan srian òr,
Olc do dhuine air an dean creach, miosad do neach theid 'nan toir;
Flath Ghlinne Liobhainn nan lann, sgiath bhrighmhor nach gann ri cléir,
Lamh mar Osgar anns gach cath, is da is cosmhuil am flath féin;
Urram eanaich d'a ghruaidh dheirg, a fhuair gun cheilg mar is coir,
Air ghabhail 'einich do gach neach, air thiolacadh each 'us òir;
Mac Grigoir an teaghlaich ghrinn, ni h-ioghnadh leinn 'n a chùirt cliar,
Ni bheil coimeas d'a uchd geal, ach am fear dhe 'n robh an Fhiann,
Aigesan tri freiceadan fionn, braigh a ghille ni facadh riamh,
Lamh bu mhaith iorghuil an greas, do b'ionmhuinn leis fuileach fiadh,
Cosmhuil a mhèin's a mhodh, ris an rìgh 'g a robh an Fhiann,
Ri h-agh Mhic Grigoir nan creach, bheir roghadh gach neach am miann,

Math is cowe a rosg gorm re m'cowle nin gorn far
Innin in nour fa din aggis in rownyth deil clayr
Innin in surri sin selga rew is cowe kerd ni wane
Id ta in rath er slicht in row is math in clow is a geyl
Enych is augnow is icht di cayvlyth er in slicht reyve
Fein is keyr agis milli a mayne sin la shelgow feygh
Finnyth oyne is gast gneyve eadda mir vackow re ni . . .
Aggis oyne mir in fin faye no chenn er gi dawe a . . .
Ga zurrik low flayis finn di cathyth ra linn na vane
Is er v'fadrik id ta in rath haryth schea gi matha . . .
M'gregar nin dochir tann cann sochir kawle agis clayr
Teyve sang er ym braith ben o zlann shraa ni ver fayle
Corrit zowne braa la oyne is nee ga zoyn di neith
A teillygyth each is oyr fayn scheach mir is coir i reith
Rey neive murr oe dlee mir is doe me zein
Mi wraa si cathir gin chelt a wull aythir v'in re
Reith.

Kellich zonith er ossil ga di choye schee re feith
Maggr mor a ze lonith weith garre zol lar reith
Estew zeym dar maggarich a heil boddich is serreith
Is a leive kennort baggantich less a beith lane vath meithtin
Fullul me clyne dowle boein is dowell corri
Ga tayd gi garga gast ne astith zane foynicht
Coythiltich me m'challane ver oyr gi rath rar clarrew
Cred fa im bein gi mwcknich ta mi zowch in nerli
Ta mi zowchess in nearli da ear o me clan donil
Innoo me clyne a layane wearri ne caith corrik
M'a ffeith cholfissay cha bea foryr mi loynti
Is m'neil a barray glan ossill a chwt slontich
M'onee tanik fame chwnith agis m'socnith faimyth
Clyne loyt is clyne rynilt ne kinn ignith von danic
Cattanich agis toissich ga taid zoissith na gardew
Camronaich is clyne zregar ni firsen a braid albin
Stewartich gai farssing eaid skeillit fane chrown chaw . . .
Sen skail kintich cassloyth is dew id ta senvaithir maithir
In bofuddir is in braid albin ta mi chardin gi lenor
Fir choyvil a teach ym chonew beaid sin mi loynnith
Clann lachlyn is clyne lymyn clyne nail ri foylwm zasg
Cardin doissi clyne tawssi er wwn is wrai zlassei

Maith is cumha a rosg gorm, ri Mac Cumhail nan corn fial,
Ionann an òr fa dhuinn, agus an rùn diolaidh cliar ;
Ionann an suiridh 's an sealg, riu 'us Cu ceaird nam Fiann,
A ta an rath air sliochd nan rìghe, is maith an cliù 'us an ciall ;
Eineach 'us eangnath 'us iochd, do cheangladh air an sliochd rìgh,
Fion 'us céir, agus mel, am miann sin le sealga fhiadh ;
Fine Eoin is gasda gniomh, iad mar mhacaibh rìgh na Feinn,
Agus Eoin mar am Fionn féin, 'n a cheann air gach daimh a . . . ;
Ge dhùrachd leo flaitheas Feinn, do chathaich ri linn na Feinn,
Is air Mhac Phadruig a ta an rath, shàruich se gu maith . . . ;
Mac Grigoir nan dochair a t'ann, ceann sochair ceall 'us cliar,
Taobh seang air am breith bean, o Ghleannsrath nam fear fial ;
Comhrad dhuinn breith le Eoin, is ni g'a dheòin do ni,
A tiodhlacadh each 'us òr, fa 'n seach mar is còir do rìgh ;
Rìgh neimh, Mhuire oigh, dlighe mar is doigh mo dhion,
Mo bhreith 's a chaithir gun cheilt, 's a bheil Athair Mhic an Rìgh.
Rìgh

CAIL dhuine air uasal, ge'd chaidh se ri feibh,
Magaireadh mòr do dhiolainich, bhi 'g iarraidh dhol làr rìgh ;
Eisdibh dhomh de 'r magairich, a shil bhodach 'us saoire,
'Us a liuthad ceannard bagainteach, leis am bu làn bha m'aoin ;
Fuileal mi' chlann Dughaill, buidhean is daimheile còir,
Ge taid gu garg gasda, ni asda a dheanainn foghainn.
Comhaltach mi do Mhac Chailein, bheir òr gu réidh ri'r cliaraibh,
Creud fa am bithinn gu mucnach, ta mo dhuthaich an Iarlaidh.
Tha mo dhuchas an Iarlaidh, do iar uam clann Domhnuil,
Iodhnaidh mi clann Ghilleathain, bheireadh an cath comhrag.
Mac a Phi Cholosaidh cha bu foirfhear mo shloinnte,
'Us Mac Neill a Baraidh, glan uasal a chuid sloinnidh.
Mac a Ni thainig fa 'm chuimhne, agus Mac Suibhne feudmhach,
Clann Leoid 'us clann Raghnailt, ni cinn fheadhna o'n d'thainig.
Catanaich 'us Toisich, gu ta iad dhomhsa 'n an cairdibh,
Camronaich 'us clann Ghrigoir, na fir sin a Breid Albainn.
Steuardaich ge farsuing iad, sgaoilte feadh a chruinne chearnach,
Sean sgeul cinnteach cas luath, is diubh ta seanmhathair m'athair.
Am Bochuidir 's am Breid Albainn ta mo chairdean gu lionmhor,
Fir chaomhal 'teachd am choinnidh, b'iad sin mo shloinneadh.
Clann Lachlain 'us clann Laomainn, clann an àill ri foghlum ghaisge,
Cairdean domhsa clann Tamhsa, air mhonadh 'us bhràigh glasa ;

Na fir veg vaggantich veiss er strath ni ter
Ty lwm m'cowle zraggin si carrit doth m'ewr
Gillane tanik a mwllith ben o choynith lwngiryraa
Cha di chortich in crwnith dunnith nach tugi . . .
A charri dangin delis maa is far re meil dwnyth
Si chalsi a fwoe in farsen far mor . . .
Kellich.

A houdir in barrone ewin m'comie.

Fadda zawf a loithsoo almirrich lwmmi my lan techt
Wearrin di loayith leyissith woyme da bi lwnn ni tantith
Tayn bach colgin caithrow trom tayn bo tart is boo fleyiss
Di wearrin is in tarrith trom da bi lwm in loyth leyis
Gregh is aithre vanynane clayve is cornc v'kowle
Doytdichy man allane wearoin is gath bolk chongwllin
Oar ewwir is errymone is a wea aggwm im choyrrith
Crwt curchoyll a chellith brone skayth reith ni gollnor
Long lymyn nar lwmmi leith si bee aggwm er gladdi
Di wearinse a hwlli cheith soll weyme mir so ra fadda
Fadda lwm gin Allex[r] m'yn tosscheach a hechta
Foddich schee in gallir so nach beith mir so re fad.
Fadda.

Er sleycht geil o zurt greyk ne el purt er in goe vait
Gan degow nach berda lat sleych geil di churre harrit
Stoe erre in nye gawle nach cha doye erre udwalli
Fyve er claif ranna gath coyr a gaif gi heyf
Ri gallew a derrum rwe sol zawiddir ir sowe
Na lekmit ir dowe deyn danmit ard chogga anmein
Ar aithris geil vano cathris er ir nayirnee
Di quhoyl mai gin royf sen oyr egin innis incin
Fa smacht ac finna fowrith rath le bil borowef
Salla di zallew mir sen a geik keiss as in dowe
Di zerna er eggil gych kin mor a ta teggow orrine
Gin danyk low terlynn mor veyn dau math derre
Ar marro ballir onaet bi sawle zoyn a laet
Ka ness er ayris in nir a zorfis geil er zallew
Rer linna mor a rin low tey a kin o angow

Na fir bhig bhagantich, bhitheas air srath na tìre,
Taghaileam Mac Dhughaill Chraignis, caraid domh Mac Iomhair,
Gillean a thainig a Muile bean o chuain longfhaire réidh,
Cha do chuartaich an cruinne, duine nach tugadh si breith.
A charaid daingean dìleas, maith is fearr ri Maol Domhnuich,
'Sa chàilsa a fhuair am fear sin, fear . . .
Càil.

Is e ùghdair so am Baron Eoghan Mac Comaidh.

Fada dhomh a luidh so, allamharach leam mo shlainte,
Bheirinn do luach leighis uam, nam bu leam na tainte;
Tain bo colgfhionn ceathraimh trom, tain bo tart 'us bo fleadhais,
Do bheirinn 'us an tarbh trom, da bu leam an luach leighis.
Greigh 'us aidhre Mhananain, claidheamh 'us corn Mhic Cumhail,
Dudaiche Manallain bheirinn, 'us gath-bolg Chonchulain.
Oir, Eimhear, 'us Eireamoin, 'us e bhi agam a choir,
Cruit Churcheoil a cheileadh bron, sgìath rìgh nan Gollnoir.
Long Laomain nar lom lith, 'us i bhi agam air cladaich,
Do bheirinnse a h-uile a chi, sol bhitheam mar so ré fada
Fadda leam gun Alasdair, Mac an Toisich a theachda,
Dh' fhuadach' an galar so, nach bi mar so ré fada
Fada.

Air sliochd Ghaidheal o ghurt Gréig, ni bheil purt air an gabh iad,
Gun teagamh nach beart leat, sliochd Ghaidheal a chur tharad,
Is tu an éiridh an aghaidh Ghall, nocha doigh éiridh udmhall.
Faigheadh ar claidheamh roinn gath, cuiribh na gathan gu thaobh,
Ri Gallaibh a deirim ribh, sol gheibheadar ar sùgh,
Na leigeamaid ar dùthaich dinn, deanamaid ard chogadh anmhìn,
Air aithris Gaidheil Bhanbha, caithris air ar n-athairne,
Do chualamaid gun robh sin, uaireigin Innis Ainghin,
Fo smachd aig fine Fomhoraich, rath le bheil boroimhe.
Seall do Ghallaibh mar sin, ag iochdadh cìs as an dùthaich,
Do dhearnadh air eagail gach cinne, mor a ta teagamh oirrnne.
Gun tainig luth tarlaidhinn, mòr feum do'n mhaith d' éiridh,
Ar marbh balair oinid, bu samhail dhuinn a leithid,
Cia nis air aithris an fhir, a dh' fhoireas Gaidheil air Ghallaibh ?
Ri'r linn mòr a rinn, luchd tì a chinnidh o eangaibh,

Annit doif da bi zail less donna zeaddeith ta aythris
Low er fey no banno cowe der a hynolle
Illespie na zette zar is tow in low fa zerre
A erle orreir zeil bey id currey a coysmeye
Cuwrre hurrogirre nor sin ner er zeillew o zurt zvyth . . .
Cur ser herre ardwir ni gyle nach bea er albin achryn
Chur low nar log trote lay chlaive gin chen ch . . .
Er fa smacht geill greyg ner beith cleacht . . .
Ne fraif o willit a faiss deye ead mor a vorshass
Is nach fagir gawle boe zit tess na gilsyth anna ra flath . . .
Losk a bantrych nach math man losk in glan vecna anfeinne
Is losk a dee dow is cosk zein in nangow
Bog le husk in lochre sen in dei losk zan dassew
Na dan deo chroy o boa gawle a vo vokinte anvin
Cwne feyn a zroe mir hoe gyn vill orrin ag gallew
An smacht rad linn agus pled nor chinna gawle smath
Cwnych callen ayr feyn cwneicht gillespik ansen
Cwnych duncha na nye in far conchur cardnel
Cwnych callen elly ann cwneich gillespik arrin
Is callen no keud mor a zle ler zawe gail in za . . .
Cwne nach dugit ni fyr wle er oyvne di zallew
Cai mowe fa dugga tussi owla voit in dullesoo
O nach marre ach fwil ayr di zeillew ym zurt ym zaif
Leggir le cheil na fir is chur hekgil fen er noydean
Saye er zallew nane draa feynna beit zusk v'callen
Derri coggi a olt mhir hor ne math in cotle rath mhor.
Mor.

A houdir so duncha m'dhulle voil.

Aythris raive rown oona makfadrik nar chred callwym
Na weym ga inni ner anna mane a kinne di charsin
Terka aythris inni anna zolsew geil nin glan zaale
Focht ni fraive ga ville zi lucht leava nyn lowr
Barrol deliss deive is doth fey ard eskar oorcht
In nulle rygh a goyve choyr in nyr zreve zreggar
Meith rai rad ross glass est oonna rad henchass
Rewe zi rave ta mest reygh sayve serhest
Padrik hayir annit dwt milchollum ayir phadrik
Makaynedoe nar zow braye dlwe a churre sa chraddane
Oone elle ayr oone doe m'gregar v'oone awyr
Ca trear farrycht fa feilla trear teawrycht ne throm cler

Aithnichte duibh da b'aill leis, duine a dh' fhaodta aithris,
Lùth air feadh na Banbha, cùmha daor a thional,
Ghillespuig a gheid gheir, is tu an lùth fa dh' éireadh,
A Iarla Oirthir Ghaidheal bith, a'd churaidh a chosnaidh.
Curaidh thuirigear 'n uair 's an eur, air Ghaidhealaibh o ghurt Gréige,
Curaidh saor ardmhir nan Gaidheal, noch bi air Albainn achruinn,
Chur lùth 'n ar luchd troda, le claidheamh gun cion chuid,
Air fath smachd Gaidheil Greige, 'n uair bu chleachdadh . . .
Na freumha o bheil iad a fàs, diogh iad, mòr a bhorrachas,
'Us nach fàgar Gall beo de d' éis, na geillse ann ri flaitheas ;
Loisg am bantraich nach maith méin, loisg an clannmhacne an sin,
'Us loisg an tighean dubh, 'us coisg dhuinn an eangnath ;
Bog le h-uisge an laochraidh sin, an deigh losgadh dh'an deisibh,
Na dean deochruaidh o beo Ghall, o bhogainte anmhuinn.
Cuimhnich féin a ghruaidh mar shùgh, gun bheil oirrne aig Gallaibh,
An smachd ri'd linn agus pleid, 'n uair chinnich gabhail smachd.
Cuimhnich Cailean d'athair féin, cuimhnich Gillespuig 'athair-san,
Cuimhnich Dunchadh an àigh, am fear conchobhar cairdeal,
Cuimhnich Cailean eile ann, cuimhnich Gillespuig araon,
Agus Cailean a cheud mhòr a ghlé le'r ghabh geill an gh . . .
Cuimhnich nach tugaid na fir, uladh air uamhainn do Ghallaibh,
Cia mo fa tugadh tusa, uile uait an t-uladh so.
O nach maireann ach fuidheall athar, do Ghaidheal o ghurt um ghabhaidh,
Leigear le chéile na fir, 'us cuir eagail feadh ar naimhdean,
Saghadh air Ghallaibh nan tràth féin, bi a'd dhuisg a Mhic Chailein,
D'eirich cogadh, a fhuilt mar òr, ni maith an codal ro mhòr.

Mor.

Is e ùghdair so Dunchadh Mac Dhughaill Mhaoil.

Aithris fhreumh rùna Eoin Mhic Phadruig, no'r creud cheileam,
Na bhitheann 'g a fhine nior fhanna, mu'm a chinnidh do char sinn,
Teirc ri aithris fhine fhanna dh' uailsibh Gaidheal nan glan dhàil,
Fochd na freumh gu bheil, do luchd leughaidh nan leabhar.
Barail dìleas doibh 'us domh, feadh ard an fheasgair orra,
An fhuil rìgh an caomh, chur an fhior dhream Ghrigoir ;
Mi réidh ri d'àros glas, eisd Eoin ri'd sheanchas,
Riamh de fhreumh tamaid, rìgh seimh saor-theist.
Padruig athair, aithne dhuit, Maolcholuim athair Phadruig,
Mac Eoin duibh na 'r dhubh bràigh, dligheach a chuire 's a chreadradh,
Eoin eile athair Eoin duibh, Mhic Grigoir, Mhic Eoin aghmhoir,
Ta triar feara fa feile, triar teamhaireach mu thromchleir,

Ayr in one sen oil nach milchollum nar cheil onyth
M'conzhe v'nor veg reym onchonna er nach deg taweim
Duncha el aythir sen m'gillelan orcilli
Da her lat nor zour re dave m'ey our o urquhay
Connane ni gorre gawe aythir ey urqhuay
O alpen in gargven glan ardre nyn balg veym breeor
Soo cathramh toaris is tug ummit a iyr phadrik
Cwnych cartweil faid chaive drom o alpen iyr dwilc
Far er eichit is tow zee one dow nach doe crei
Di chart hanchis is sai sen gow ferriss m'erk awyr
Id kinne nach crein ri foor sai lein di zave corron
Da eichit agis trur reyg dleyr in nuile sin ardreve
Tree toar tre dessirroe in dey vilchallum kennmor
Da choggyr chorrone a cheine o vilchollum gow alpen
O halpen soss is sai vess xiiii fir gow ferris
Di chart hanchis issi sen gow ferris m'eik awyr
Kai lein di hanchiss mir sen reve gow ferris is fedir
Immigh feinnoil fai twlle tais nach awrreymor nor arviss
Di bi skeith skol dan skealloe gi reyg vil fa terrawg
Fwlli artir fo terla fanna macht di chodych di chuslin
Fwlli choynna fwlli choonna fad kness da hoynna hothrin nin neg
Fwlli ghrantach maid zroy mir ulle fulle neil neveille nertur
Gargweine a geym si gi gress da reym ardre in naythris.
Aythris.

A houdir soo m'eachag.

Dymmych me zin zeith a deess o nach leggin in steach eoyn
Is ee er ni wraa mach er toytht doyth go m'cloyd
Mak soonayd nyn soill gal a bi zail less teach er choyn
Chan nasta zeith a deess oyne m'wllam nin naach loyth
Ni chotlwm eich no layth nach weggym o trayid so toycht
Long heithwl in twil zil long in ir la bristir royik
Ag so in torriskil hwg caith er m'wllam oo clar skeith
Gil denych deadzal dess far nach ayrryth nach ma neith
In toychtow lay oynyth faa oyne eiryth v'cloyd in rosg . . .
Cossloo in angnow sin nert re tylych morrith a vore chreith
Fer feiltych nach folchin soyd torriskail oyne nyn narm . . .
Fer heid sin tachchir er twss fer layr churryth a clw
M'wllam za dalter meyg v'soynoid er sleicht in reicht
A glwnym heacht a toyth di wea myth zroym er dol deim.

Athair an Eoin sin oileanaich, Maolcholuim na 'r cheil a nì,
Mac Dhunchaidh mhuiginir bhig reim, onchoin air nach tig toibheum.
Dunchadh eile athair-san Mac Gillfhaolain oirchill,
Do shaor leat 'n uair dh' fhoir ri daimh, Mac Aoidh ùr o Urchaidh.
Ceanan nan corr gatha, athair Aoidh Urchaidh,
O Alpain a gharg mhèin ghlan, ardrigh nam balg bheum brioghmhor.
So an ceathramh tuaraisg a's tug, umad a oighre Phadruig,
Cuimhnich ceart bheil fa'd chaomh, dream o Alpain oighre Dhughaill,
Fear air fhichead is tu fhéin, Eoin dubh nach dubh cré,
Do cheart sheanchas is e sin, gu Fearghus Mac Eirc aghmhoir.
A'd chinneadh nach crion ri fodhair, sé linn do ghabh coron,
Da fhichead agus triur rìgh, dlighear an fhuil 's an ardfhreumh,
Tri tuathruidh, tri deasruidh, an deigh Mhaolcholuim Chinnmhoir,
Da choigear choron a chinnidh, o Mhaolcholum gu Alpain,
O Alpain suas is e bhitheas, ceithir deug fir gu Ferghus,
Do cheart sheanchas is e sin, gu Fearghus Mac Eirc aghmhoir.
Cia lion de sheanchas mar sin, riamh gu Ferghus faighidir,
Iomadh fine oll fa d'fhuil tathas, nach àireamar n'uair àirmheas,
Do bu sgìth sgoil d' an sgeulaibh, gach rìgh a bheil fa d'ùr fhreumh.
Fuil Artuir fa d' urla fann, maith do chuid 'do chuislean ;
Fuil Chuain, fuil Chuinn fa'd chneas, da shuthain sothrain n'fhine,
Fuil Ghrantach ma'd ghruaidh mar ubhal, fuil Neil nimheil neart-mhoir,
Garg mhìn a ceum 's a gach greas, de reim ard rìgh an aithris.
Aithris.

Is e ùghdair so Mac Eachaig

Diombach mi dhe 'n ghaoith a deas, o nach leigionn a steach Eoin,
'Us e air a bhreith mach air tuath domh gu Mac Leoid ;
Mac Sheonaid nan seol geala, a b'aill leis teachd air chuan,
Cha-n éisd a ghaoth a deas, Eoin Mac Uilleaim nan each luath.
Ni chodaileam oidche no la, nach fhaiccam o thraigh so tuath,
Long shiubhail an t-siuil ghìl, long an fhir le'm bristear ruaig.
Aig so an tuairisgeul thug càch, air Mac Uilleaim o Clàr Sgìth,
Gille dian, deud-gheal, deas, fear nach euradh neach mu ni.
An t-ochdamh la uainn fa Eoin, oighre Mhic Leoid an ruisg . . .
Coslach an eangnath, 's an neart, ri teaghlach mòr a mhoir chridhe
Fear faoilteach nach folchainn sud, tuairisgeul Eoin nan arm . . .
Fear theid 's an tàchair air tùs, fear le'r chuireadh cliù . . .
Mac Uilleaim dha 'n daltair mi, Mac Sheonaid air sliochd an rìgh,
A chluinntinn a theachd a tuath, do bhitheadh mo ghruaim air dol diom.

A houdir soo m'gillindak in fardan.

Boye hearn er hoissichew itta voo huss in gyni
Ayrrewich zin ni okarrewich gych in ar a braa fisshe
Kead tearn in terre so duncha beg fa mor agne
Di zag mir chwt delippa ag clynna zreggar in gassga
Dunca mor za meillezow aythir vennych vilchollum
Sennor oone eynley ner zyil cwnrith nar chowil
Gregar deymhak duncha mak woo oone di bea iyr
Far awzissych one chontyth o locht heyve hollis tolve
Oonna dow in gal geilta m'ayrrewych oonna v'gregar
Salgre zawe dreyth twss gi coggi zi reythal
Mylcollum ga zei chowal annit oona doss a athyr
Dessgirt glinni gal urquhai maseith di chaith ma caga
Itta toisseich noymitin di clinni zregar oo zallew
Ga vil trey tearn boye graw sealga is boe gasga
In nimissir chooni chad chath di choala mi vaksawle
Finn ne zaif o zar lanew m'kowle nyn grat calm
Sealga errin si heyantis ag m'kule nyth guilley
Evy ni zoe no ternis er crechow clanni guil
Dey ra leyn dane lekfe o charre gow carn vallire
Royth zawf ne sessre veith ag no iye
O hawzone gow belten bonyth gi teith za eanew
In talga fa soyve sawke agga in nynnym in neye
Immyg keiss nach arfee ag finna no ag far a harffee
Feachw errin darrm er vakcwle no iye
Igh vorriddir zeyntew fa vroichew gi a boinna
Ag sen ne vil dennirgow voilchollum ag makmwin
Ne zernni finn feane sealga gyn sirreich a kedda
Sealga albin gin eafre ag milcollum si chreacht
Cunwallich ni coahalga ni gregar is gaig dennyth
Ner venkiche con croarga gow longwit clynni beskne
Leine trotdych di hoissichew erre less in lo caicht
Fir eydda er oyr leyow ga lucht tiy sin tachraa
Kennoss fynna is feyhonis chotkin is clwe zai kin
Er barn zasga zley zarvis m'gregar graigh ni vill
Immyg na chwrt coleyth selm cowdyth is colk ten
Ooyr derk er in dornerhew erm loyvin lochawe
Coyherm eddir clarsichow done in leicht nane lawow
A lucht tyi wo hayblissw dwl fa zowir gyr
Mak gregar boss bar chorkkir m'derwail boye a zallew
Ane charre nyth calmytht a lawe lar ranik gych raa boye

Is e ùghdair so Mac Gilliondaig am Fear dàn.

Buaidh thighearn air thoisichibh, a ta o thùs an cinne,
Airidheach de na h-oig fhearaibh, gach aon fhear a breith fios,
Ceud tighearn na tir-sa, Dunchadh beag fa mòr aigne,
Do dh' fhàg mar a chuid dilib, aig clann Ghrigoir an gaisge.
Dunchadh mòr de mhileadhaibh, athair beannaichte Mhaolcholuim,
Seanair Eoin aonfhlaith nior gheill, cunradh 'n uair a chunbhail
Grigoir deagh-mhac Dhunchaidh, mac o Eoin do b'e oighre,
Fear aibheasach o'n chontath, o Loch thaobh sholuis Tulaich.
Eoin dubh an goil geillte, mac aireadhach Eoin mhic Grigoir,
Sealgair dhamh dhreachach, tùs gach cogadh do fhritheal.
Maolcholum go dheagh chunbhal, aithnichte Eoin d'éis a athar,
Deisceart glinne geal Urchaidh, maiseach do chaidh m 'a cachta,
A ta toiseach an uibhireachd, do chloinne Ghrigoir o Ghallaibh,
'Ga bheil tri tighearn beò, gràdh sealga, 'us beò ghaisge
An aimsir Chuinn cheud chatha, do chuala mi a mhac samhail,
Fionn ni ghabh o gheur lannaibh, Mac Cumhail nan grath calm.
Sealg Eirinn 's a thighearnas aig Mac Cumhail 'n a coillibh
Aoibh dha no tighearnas, air criochaibh clanna Ghuill.
D'fhiodh r'a linn da 'n leigeadh, o Charaidh gu Carn Bhalair,
Roimhe ghabh na seisir, bha aig 'n a fhiodha.
O shamhainn gu bealltainn, bhuineadh gach tì d'a Fhianaibh,
An t-sealga fa soimheamh samhadh, aig an inbhe an fhiodha.
Iomadh cìs nach airmhear, aig Fionn no aig fear a àirmhidh,
Fiacha Eirinn da roinn, air Mhac Cumhail 'n a fhiodh.
Fiodh mhoir ridir dh' Fhiantaibh, air bruachaibh gach buinne,
Aig sin ni bheil diongairean, Mhaoilcholuim aig Mac Muirne.
Ni dheanadh Fionn féin sealg, gun sireadh a cheada,
Sealg Albainn gun fharraid aig Maolcholum 's a chreacha.
Cunbhalach 'n an coshealg Mac Grigoir is garg daoine,
Nior mhince coin cro-dhearg, gu longphort cloinne Bhaoisgne.
Linn trodach de thoisichibh, éiridh leis an la catha,
Fir iad air oirleachaibh, 'g a luchd tì 'san tàchair.
Ceannas fion 'us fiùdhantais, coitchinn is cliù dh'a chinneadh,
Air barn ghaisge ghlé dhearbhas, Mac Grigoir gràdh ni bheil.
Iomadh 'n a chuirt coluath, saolaim cuideachd a 's colg teann,
Or dearg air an dornairibh, airm leoghain Loch Abh.
Co sheirm eadar clàrsaichibh, na daoine an léich 'n an lamhaibh,
A luchd tì o thaibhlisibh a dol far gheibhear gadhar.
Mac Grigoir bos bàrr chorcuir, Mac Diarbhuil buaidh a Ghallaibh,
Aon chara na calmachd a lamh, le'r ràinig gach rath buaidh.

Boy feil re fillyth a ne v'clymont cossne
Di vaddee a clw kinnaze er heiliga a laif louye
Mare mwm ollone teyve menzail is math comma
Ni clar ga commol corgra groy na sowa.
Boye hearn.

A houdir so ym bard roygh finlay.

Hest ein doyll ni gcyll skailc is coyr a chomeith
Way ra der lot chaalle is crossimeil tork maale gin waas
A hewrin hanik er dwss ussit a skayle ymbuss
Mir haa wea reiss er ball in gae zreiss in dcoyll
Di naskiddir er fa rinn nor a zaig say teach eyffrin
Toycht din downe chadni er assi is cowle ra readli farris
Nayr hanik in tork dow bimmy dayvin ga chwnryth
Gerwe moeyr gi bestyth gir hein gow hanwe oyl eddyth
Er eggill a weith gin nee rinnith zi v'royre
A ckuycht gi honnarych ann an rycht chonna in neiffrin
Is coyr in nagryth hay in deewe ag allane er in deolew
Gar bee faa reit orrith er leym no heim etrycht
Is meith skurri ryth warwne hennwythick weicharne
Vek royre on wour a mach foyr nee gin low gin lawych
Fa chathram a chur in sinne dlewm conyth re collwm
O see cathram ter ulle allane weil wyonurre
Di rinn tussi is ne he wanenych creach y is rellig ooran
Is tow zochin gi borbe ann coychill nyn nord is nyn neiffrin
Is tow woyr olk inchezawle is tow vok a keiss si termyn
Is tow is geltee noss a mach la lentir foss di hossych
Ach ein wille er a law clee di wrayr a v'royree
Ne closs di zlo o sin machi si cross wee zid wallichyth
Math in deiss faa in will di lane dowsen foyss is dalwyth
Woo cheyd tossych di chogge a wrane clossich in abbe
Creach ellyth nach royth sin lygh er fenane in glen gar
Wallich di neive fertyth feyne di weill zalytth a allane
Id taa mir gith neiwe elli a deilt a orwrrych
Chur dowich la chwiss feyn in cowych in guwss allane
Di her zowich is di loyg di wonit deit a chraw hoygh
Leggit derri di wurn eddir selli is sowyrnni
Ne henyth a wee a banenych faddyth o bin chroich allane
Na looyewe er layr in ir quhoy ga wayr is ga fwyr
Meith in ness skurri zid ter a v'royre anmein
Ellein nach gress in gress cathrame tesgin is orchess.
Hest.

Buaidh feile ri filidhibh, a ni Mac Laomuinn a chosnadh,
Do mhadaidh a chliù ceann-aigh, air thiolacadh a lamh luath.
Mairidh muime ollamhan, mingheal is maith com,
Na cliar 'g a comoladh, corcra a gruaidh no sùgh.
Buaidh thighearn.

Is e ùghdair so am bard ruadh Fionnladh.

Theasd aon diabhul nan Gaidheal, sgeul is coir a chuimhneach,
Bha ri daor lot chille is chroise, maol torc mall gun mheas ;
A ifrionn thainig air tùs, usaide an sgeul iombus,
Mar tha bhi ris air ball, an gathaibh ghreas an diabhuil.
Do nasgaidear air faraon 'n uair a dh' fhàg se teach ifrinn,
Teachd do 'n dùn cheudna air ais, 'us cùl ri reulta Pharrais.
'N uair a thainig an torc dubh, b'iomadh deamhain 'ga chur,
Garbh meoghar gach béisd, gur h-aon guth sheanmh uile iad ;
Air eagail a bhi gun ni, roinneadh do Mhac Ruaraidh,
A chuid gu h-onoireach ann, an riochd chon ann an ifrionn
Is coir an agradh tha an diugh, aig Allan air na diabhlaibh,
Ge 'r bith fa ruig orra, ar leam ni tliom eadrochd,
Is mithich sgur ri foirionn, sheanmhadhach mhiochaireanach,
Mhic Ruaraidh o'n mhuir a mach, fhuair ni gun lùth gun lamhach.
Fa chaithream a chur an suim, dligheam coinnidh ri Calum,
O 's e caithream an tìr uile, Allan mhaoil a mhionoir,
Do rinn tusa 'us ni h-e mhàin, creach I 'us reilig Orain,
Is tu dhochainn gu borb ann, cochull nan ord 'us nan aifrionn;
Is tu mhòr olc Innse Ghall, is tu bhochd a cìs 's a tearmunn,
Is tu is geilte nòs a mach, le leantar fòs do thoiseach,
Ach aon bheil air a laimh chli, do bhrathair a Mhic Ruaraidh,
Ni clos do ghleò o sin a mach, 's a chrois bhi 'g ad mhallachadh,
Maith an dithis fa an bheil do lan, dubh sin fòs is dealbh,
O cheud thoiseach do chogaidh, a bhreun chlosaich an Aba,
Creach eile nach robh 's an lagh, air Finan an Gleann Garaidh.
Mhallaich do nimh fhearta féin, do mhaol dhealbh, a Allan,
A ta mar gach nimh eile, a diolt a oirbhireach ;
Chuir dùthaich le chuis féin, an cuthach an gnuis Allain.
Do shaor dhuthaich 'us do shluagh, do bhuineadh duit a chràdh thuath,
Leigeadh deireadh do mhuirn, eadar Seile, agus Subhairn.
Ni h-ioghnadh a bhi buininn, fada o binn chroiche, Allan,
Na luaidhe air lathair an fhir, chaidh 'g a mhathair 'us ga phiuthair,
Mithich a nis sguir dhe d'aoire, a Mhic Ruaraidh ainmhìne,
Oilean nach greasann greas, caithream d'éisgein is oircheas.
Theasd.

Hoaris mak mir in taayr mach er flathew ir neolyes
A areoll a eyg si agna is me ga chaddrew in looyss
Fess is agna flaa oyra raath la in deantir
Der lat in mak soo foyr mee gir a bea in royrce cadna
Is innyn in dy chooyll is monor za olt faymyth
Is innin woltyr in gaew torkild is ayir ayrrewich
Da deggew ra linn torkild ni hay lokgi din tromm zawe
Di ne za bert is boyn aythris zor v'colman
Immi carde er a moltyr torkill in awra chreive
Er low is er lawyth curre a tacht gow dull in c . . .
Is der me za halle dess ane si eolyss
Nach danik fer a eiss is farre no re so looyss
Da bi less a charga worwe schayd is sorve hor sal
Di wronna ni v'corkill da rochin ter a inna
Ag m'royere ne mercholl da ym beit in sann cholg sneith
No schayd elli a ber foynow di wronna so re ennycht
Skea chenzaik no schayd orryk far aiss formit ni wulle
Wssless ym brwnnych no elli ollew in sirri
Da ym bea in lea mor mathi zaithew no in dark drwtych
Ner wunyth farda clachlin gin weith fa eachrec dwltych
Da bi less in dow seillin m'leoda da in nythrin clarri
Less ni haksow in teachsin ga ba a racha da harre
Ta ag torkill ogeanych nach myghich namm choltke
Cosga gych terri zi hylych di loyg menych gow cokgi
Ne warri no eiss cachullin na torkill dwlling tentaa
Lawe is callma si is clista fer wreisse gi a bernna
Gar zinvin m'v^c corkill ne wollin ay er ansicht
Far is tress in noyr awza ewthir zraw zin wratycht
Ne elle ni re no flaa di wadda rath za goalla
No v'callen katreine boss weilli arla doilch . .
Inynn earla erzeill in neywen is farri hoaris
Horrimyr ben ir neille di zayk wor zreive zast
Ne v'callen crowich oykwla cowle mir in cornan cass.
Hoaris.

A houdir so gillecalum m'yn noollew.

Hanic yvyr mi hurss cha lamm quhoy in wlygin soo
Ne tugsi zi nach nacht tug mi hurss hecht mir hanic
Gai bee neach nach tuggi sin hecht coythlane dim chow
Ni lwtsi faich om chomm turssi na creachew royowm

FHUAIREAS mac mar an t-athair, mach thar flathaibh ar n eòlais,
A airill 'aghaidh 'us aigne, 'us mi 'g a chaidrimh an Leodhas ;
Fios agus aigne flath, uair rathach le an deantar,
Deirim leat am mac so fhuair mi, gur a b'e an Ruaraidh ceudna.
Is ionann an da chùl, is onoir athar dh' a 'fholt fainneach,
Is ionann a mholtar an cathaibh, Torcuil 'us 'athair airidheach.
De'n tigeadh ri linn Thorcuil, ni e lochda do'n trom dhaimh,
Do ni dha beart 'us buaidhean, aithris a fhuair Mac Colmain.
Iomadh ceaird air a mholtar, Torcuil an amhra chraoibh,
Air lùth 'us air làmhach, cuiridh a thaic gu dol an cathaibh
A deir mi dh' a thaobh, d'éis aithne 's a eòlas,
Nach tainig fear d'a aois is fearr, no rìgh so Leodhais.
Do bu leis a chairge mhordha, seud a's soirbhe a fhuair sàil,
De bhronnadh Mac Mhic Thorcuil, da rochdainn tir a fhineadh,
Aig Mac Ruaraidh nam mircheol, do'm bitheadh an seann cholg snaigh-
'N a seud eile a b'fhior fuanadh, do bhronnadh se rìgh Eanaich. [each,
Sgiath cheannghaig 'n a seud oirdheirc, fear is farumaich nimheil,
Usa leis am bronnadh, no a bheil ullamh an sireadh.
Da am bith an leth mòr maith, dh' eachaibh 'n an dearg druidhteach,
Nior bhuineadh fear a chleachdainn, gun bhith fo eachraidh diultach.
Do bu leis an Dubh Seibhlin, Mac Leoid do 'n iarraun cliara,
Leis na th' aigse an t-each sin, ge b'e a rachadh d' a iarraidh.
Tha aig Torcuil òganaich, nach meathaich an àm chogaidh,
Casgadh gach tir dh' a theaghlach, de shluagh miannach gu cogadh.
Ni b'fhearr 'n a aois Cuchullain, na Torcuil d'fhulang teanntachd,
Lamh is calma 's is clisde, fear a bhriseas gach a bearna.
Ge 'r ionmhuinn Mac Mhic Thorcuil, nior mholainn e air annsachd,
Fear is treise an uair agha, iuchar ghràidh do 'n bhantrachd.
Ni bheil mac rìgh no flath, do b'fhaide rath do chualas,
Ge minic leinn an rochdainn, is fearr no Torcuil a fhuaireas.
Ni Mhic Chailein, Caitriona, bos mhil earlamh dualchas,
Inghin Iarla Earaghaidheal, an aon bhean is fearr a fhuaireas
Fhuaireamar bean ar n-ìle, de gheug mhor dhream ghasda,
Ni Mhic Chailein chraobhach ògail, cùl mar an coirnean cas.
Fhuaireas

Is e ùghdair so Gilliecalum Mac an Ollaimh.

Thainig aobhar mo thuirse, cha leam chaidh a bhliadhna so,
Ni tuigse do neach nach tuig, mo thuirse theachd mar thainig,
Cia b'e neach nach tuigeadh sin, theachd comhlan do 'm chumha,
Na lotsa feuch o'm chom, tuirse na creuchda ro gheibheam.

Is hevin lamm ga degkir royf tegwaill er chort ni co . . .
It ta ym brone gym crayg fa claa is mor mi zrayg zin . .
Ha mi crei na za la cha neynith aa weith breista
Ha mi chorp gin noyill gin nwll mir wocht gin troyr ch . . .
Cha neynith kow za mayd orrwm in ney v'merraid
A beith cwnich er waath yn ir cha nwlmist flaath zaks . . .
Is trwmi zwnith na zwl anwon na zey sin seill
Mi craw is toyr er zwll ass in law foaris wo Eithnis
Ga dagkir lamm dellew riss m'oone a choarra will . .
Is messi ay gyn willi ass gin way tilli gow heinis
Ga fadda weithm woa mow is mi luch toayllis ym zei
Di bi zanith mi rayth rinn kenich cha nearrih orr . . .
Cha neynith magnith di waith re faggin tearn elli
Mi lane gin mi wreith gi tromm o ta mi re gin anw . . .
Di crawg mi crc za essi skaill is furris a assness
Cha nelli fwlich er mi wrone di wlygh cwrith mi . . .
Mor mi wrone is ne henith doith cha twrssi ta . . .
Zargin mi creith gi lomm gin sleith in albin aggwn
Nessi oss egin doif tryill mi wee ag caith f . . .
Ra luithsi di banith zwll a hinsoo ald a alb . . .
Ga di rylum is degkir lwm ga ta mir eahw orrwm
Mi rown di zlowe a mew cowle reim zowe ym zeyge
Is sai neit fa derri zoif er lamne cha vec in tyvir
Gin mi zeil a heacht er ass eill er a lechtisi enis
Is trwm na ayg sin a low tanic za amsir
A cnoo chre si craw cwip gin slee ag caich ga zeilt
Ner hellis dwnni er doithin a wayd a raith er chensichyth
Gyr falli orn agis ort malli lar horn a hygirt
O sai zonedir a zwll troyg nach awl di waamir
A v'mur wasszall vinn gin dwn tasgin aggin
In neau neach ra ygre zill na gar gin doll na zeyge
Noch rayey is feddi no sin din waid vag di wontyr
Luch catdrew a chowle gamm er nanich chach a gomun
A nagni di choye er assi troye gi caddrew ass taguss
Da bi zekgir commis rwmm is di we om hearn aggwm
Catdrew coychoill is tawf agni roywor gin an lawe
Nor hed caith za dy noyll is sea mi chwt da nonor
Weith fa wrone gin dein a mew ag goyll mi zeill di chowe
Tym anvin gin dol ter ayss cha nanin cowe ass magwss
. ach aggi din chowe mee is palte ni dowe elli
. ymith neach roythin reyvc di chur cowe fa zemeyg
. na wonso darvir loom wrskal nar zawe roythim
Di quhoala mee fad o hen—ut sequitur in alio loco etc.
Mac sowalti ni bree binn daltan chaiff is chonell.

Is aoibhinn leam ge deacair roimhe, teugbhail air ghoirt cna . .
A ta am bròn gu 'm chiadhadh fo 'm chlèibh, is mòr mo ghràdh do'n . . .
Tha mo chridhe 'na dha leth, cha-n ioghnadh e bhi briste,
Tha mo chorp gun fheol gun fhuil, mar bhochd gun treoir . . .
Cha-n ioghnadh cumha dh' à meud, orm an deigh Mhic Mairirid,
A bhi cuimhneach air mhaith an fhir, cha-n bheileamaid flath o dh' fhàg . . .
Is truime dhuinne na dhol, anmhuinn 'n a dheigh 's an t-saoghal,
Mo chràdh a's d'fhuair air dhol as, an làmhach fhuaireas o Aonghus,
Ge deacair leam dealach' ris, Mac Eoin a chomhraidh mhilis,
Is miosa e gun mhilleadh esa, gun bhi tilleadh gu 'innis.
Ge fada a bhitheam o m'àgh, us mo luchd tuaileis a'm dheigh,
Do bu dheanadh mo rath ruinn, ceannach cha-n iarradh orra . .
Cha-n ioghnadh m'aigne do bhaithte, ri faicsinn tighearn eile,
Mi làn gun mo bhrìgh gu trom, o ta mo rìgh gun anamain.
Do chràdhadh mo chridhe d'a éis, sgeul is furasd a fhaisneas,
Cha-n eil fulachd air mo bhròn, do bhlagh cuiridh . . .
Mor mo bhròn 'us ni h-ioghnadh dhomh, cha tuirse . . .
Dheargainn mo chridhe gu lom, gun sliochd an Albain againn
Nis o 's éigin domh triall, mo bhi aig càch fo . .
Ri luidhese do b'aithne dhol, á h-innse ald na h-Albainn.
Ge do thriallaim is deacair leam, ge ta mar fhiachaibh orm,
Mo rùn do dhlù a mùghadh, cùl re'm dhùthaich a 'm dheigh
Is e an ni fa d'éirich dhomh, ar leam cha bheag an t aobhar,
Gun mo ghaoil a theachd air ais, Ile air a leth taobh Innis.
Is trom na aghaidhsan, a lùth thainig dha aimsir,
A cnàmh' chridhe 's a cràdh' chorp, gun slighe aig càch d'a dhiolt
Nior shaoileas duine ar domhainn, a mheud a rath air cheansachadh,
Gur falamh oirnn agus ort, mala le'r h-oirnn a thigeadh.
O 's e ghuineadar a dhol, truagh nach amhuil a bhamar,
A Mhic Mhuire bhos-gheal bhinn, gun duine a d'asgainn againn
An aoin neach r'a aghaidh ghile, na gur gun dol 'n a dheigh,
Noch rath is fada no sin, de'n mheud bha aig do mhuinntir.
Luchd caidrimh a chuil caın, air n' aithnich càch an comunn,
An aigne do chaidh air ais, is truagh gach caidrimh as d'eugmhais.
Do bu dheacair coimeas rium, 'us do bhi o 'm thighearn agam,
Caidreamh cochaill 'us daimh, aigne ro mhòr gun a laimh.
'N uair theid càch dha do'n òl, is e mo chuid de'n onoir,
Bhith fo bhròn gun deanamh mùgh, ag òl mo dhiol de chumha.
Taim anmhuinn gun dol tar éis, cha-n anmhuinn cumha as m'eugmhais
Cach aig do'n chumha mi, is pailte na dubha eile,
Iomadh neach romhainn riamh, do chuir cumha fo dhimhiodh,
. na bhuin so dearbhar leam, ursgeul na'r ghabh romham,—
Do chuala mi fad o shean, etc.—Ut sequitur in alio loco.
Mac samhailt na brigh binn, daltan Chaoimh 'us Chonuil.

Artour dawle mak gurkych.

Dail chawle er chastel soyne swork in nathre in innisfail
Markeich yth rachtych nyth tonnyth glantyr barkyth done nyth zawe
Fir ardyth geggyr nyth longso er lome loyth lenis cort
Newe lawyth gin galzaith gast nare scarryth snast swork
Dyth chottonew is dew zegre yin nyth barg fa chrewe laig
Dyth chothrew in gress clar zone lochlynnych is armyn eaid
Dyth clyew gin or is ded eggyr vark nyth brad done
Narre claith dyth zaithew galzaith skaith re fraew lawrych long
Er skayth scai er scwddai brakith broo scarrych chorkrych cloch nor
Broythnyth ad keve agis collar er teve nyth slat ro zarrowe
Geyth gorm in golnew lowark long gai lenyth nare traith
Claith hend zai gohind dyth cholgew forrin skaith re bordew barg
Mnaew findmyth in grenanew longsyth lappyth ard ag naynyth vawle
Pyllyth vrakkyth zawe gane darryth lap ag mnaew ra hanelaith and
Pyllyth wrakith royl is tynoll is e sen lochr in long
Byve hwnenyth syth ror goth dwllych royl chorkir oss gych cran
Gin lawin chroy gin chreiss codyth nar gerve seiss gin chur la clar
Na said derrit and gyn nymirt dyth clarrew cland vyn ard vail
Ner cholis urdil in nane zor nynoss gyn chur re kard
Na said or o ermn aggyth dyn wrone var hang dattych derk
Ni low la long zane loigew ym baith na nach is nid boe
Gin ocht gin von dew gyn wronenyth snee el ter gyn lomyth loe
Ne heillssyth loa carve zai garrew in lane dynnoss hyntych voy
Ag ryne or er vardew ra hard zoive carve coyne
Ymit fer land is fer lorych ymit fer loith gyth lem caith
Ra sow monezone farg farzone ra hard in long banchar blaith
Ka so la soltyr in cawlych er chaslane soyne sleive trom
Fer srengych nach sechnit sedyth lai chryne schoiryth codeith coy
One m'soyne soil yth longsyth er drome yth choyne croy in kenn
Cryne yth long deine chor in nard dervit tone in varg . . .
Geith gyth derrych zove nane dye ag keil akkyth deryth trait
Soil vrakkyth zove na bolgew oyne id tech gow bordew barg
Gavis eine aggirsaid evin in nuch chnappiddil corg kow . . .
Nawra vartew donenyth dalvych lakrych crandyth lowyth is
Lynd ag ballichew albin fartych faltych ra hocht sliomis . .
Alin sin in gorkrych colane sillyth drochtych lomlane lynd
Faltych ag sroythew sleyve moone re m'soynyth sleve miss
Teggyth tantyth daksk nane nyrvr daltyr mir rask rinland riss
Leggyth gaiggyth in glownyth fow fartych failtych rar vlaith coil
Mest slantyth cowl gych callyth trome in valtyth nyc oyne

Artuir dall Mac Gurcaich.

Dail chabhlaich air Chaisteal Suibhne, suairc an eachdraidh an Innisfail,
Marcaich a rachadh nan tonn, glantair barc an tonn nior ghabh.
Fir arda ag eagar na luingse, air leam luath a leanas cuairt,
Ni bhith làmh gun ghalghath gasd, an aireamh sgarach, snasda, suairc.
Do chotanaibh is duibh dh' eagradh, do na bharc fa chraobh léig,
De choraighibh an crios clàr-dhaoine, Lochlanaich is armuinn iad.
De chleathaimh gon òr 'us deud, eagar bhàrc nam breid donn, [long.
An aireamh cliath de ghathaibh galghath, sgiath ri fraighibh lamhrach
Air sgiath sgiothach air sgud breac, brù sgarach chorcrach, chlothara,
Broin fhad caomh 'us comhlair, air taobh nan slat ro gharbh. [traigh,
Gaoth ghorm an guailnibh an luath bharc, long 'g a honadh an éiridh
Chabh theann do chochuinge de cholgaibh, foirionn sgéith ri bordaibh bàrc.
Mnathan fionn an grianaibh 'n longsa, leabaidh ard aig nigheanaibh mhall,
Pille bhreac dhoibh gun d'fhuaireadh, leap aig mnathaibh ri eanfhlaith
Pille bhreac de shroil is taithneal, is e sin lothar an long, [ann.
Baoibh, shonnanach, 's an ruathar gu dol, 'shroil chorcuir os gach crann.
Gun lamhan chruaidh gun chrios cuide, nar garbh sios gun chur ri cleir,
Na seoid d'eirich ann gun imirt, de chliaraibh, clann bhinn ard bhéil.
Nior chualas uidail an Fhian, dh 'ur n-innis gun chuir ri ceaird,
Na seoid ùr o Eirinn aca de'n bhroin bhar-sheang, dathta, dearg.
Ni luath leatha long dhe 'n longaibh, am bi na neach 'us ni 'd beo,
Gun och, gun lionn dubh, gun bhròn, 's ni bheil teirginn loma leo.
Ni shaoileadh si luath cairbh de chairbhibh, an làn de 'n nòs shinte
Aig roinn òr air bhàrdaibh, ri h-àrd dhoibh cairbhe cuain. [uaith,
Iomadh fear lann 'us fear luirich, iomadh fear luath gu leum catha,
Ri sùgh muinghin fairg fearghuin, ra h-ard an luing banchair blaith.
Cia so le soltar an cabhlach, air chaislean Suibhne Sleibh troma,
Fear sreangach nach seachnadh seideadh, le chroinn sireadh chuid còir.
Eoin Mac Suibhne, scol an longsa, air druim a chuain, cruaidh an ceann,
Croinn an luing dean chur an aird, dearbhaid tuinn a bharc sin. . . .
Gaoth gun d'éirich dhoibh 'n an deigh, aig Caol Aca deireadh tràigh,
Siuil bhreaca dhoibh 'n am bolgaibh, Eoin a teachd gu bord . . .
Gabhas an acarsaid aoibhin, an uchd Chnapadail coirce . . .
An amhra mhòr, tiugh, donn, dealbhach, lacharach, crannach, luath 'us . . .
Leinn aig ballachaibh Albainn, furtach failteach ri uchd sloimh . . .
Aluinn sin an corcradh comhlan, sileadh driuchd lomlan loinn.
Failteach aig sruthaibh Sleibh Muin, ri Mac Suibhne Sleibh Mis,
Tigidh caiuntich d'fhogus 'nan eirbhar, daltair mar rosg roinnlan ris
Leigidh geug an glùn fo fhàirtidh, faillteach ri 'r bhlaith goil,
Misde slainte cùl gach cala, trom am failte an aghaidh Eoin.

. . . . . .

Tegge eiss ellin albin yth fariit faltyth er one chone miss
Lwch canteith myr venour dychnir failtyth o renew riss
Grayth wee ymirwae ane ettryth feine in nan choil
Annyth mir doesyth dey hı mr haı tullyth hanyth oyne
Dyth neid caith in gasslane soyne fa hawik chroithin chryn vurb
Soyıt fa hymchil in scorsen fynvar neve luslaue lurk
Za ley hollis tewe nawit myr neve nathyr gone nyth grand
Keil clave o zress ezoyr meilnayr less golnyth gawle
Cellar mitt oil v'soyne ra solss ın nad clwk dyth choym
Is feyr nach deine din clok in cawor sie deine doltnych valklang vor
Nor nach deine dai lwrych thrawre er skaı chottone na skadow
Gavis rachlın sceinezar scarrych mevor clathwan calm cor
In tane clai is farryth sin norpe sai is lewıych lenis myne
Cai skaith sın doyn nach dıngsen treach gyn noyn clyne erm
One m'soyne ny sly godyth lai cholg tane teskbych vawle
Sar nach skaith wai skaı brak done taris treach dekhorn dawle.
Dail chawle.

Yssbell ne v'kellan

Margi za gallır ın grawg ga bee fa fane abbrum ee
Degkir skarrichtın ra phart troyg in chayss in vellum feyn
In grawg sen tuggis gin ness oss sai mi less gin a loyth
Mır hwe mı furtych traa beeth mı wlaa gi tannyth troyg
In fer sen za duggis graw ys nach feadis rawge oss nard
Da gurfee missa boyn gymi do feyn is kayd marg.
Margi.

A houdir so dunchaa ogga.

Seachta seyda ter mo hee ta gach sayada deıve gim lot
Teachta eddrim agis dea o say sin is mean lam chorp
Hein dew ta in near ym bey za in goo anmyth creiss
Menknit waal ay mee in boyt er ne hanyth foss yn neıss
In darnyth sayda in drwss sin a chwss da willum der
Woo lot nyth syda na zoo ne ellwm boa woa a rein
In tress dew id taa in naltew mi craw ıs steıth
Cha lega in lessga za doyn miss slee chor er beitht
An carıow sayd ın tant a zea mark in doyr ee gwn
Furtych cha naym rem ray gin reach crea or mo vwn
In cogew sayd din zlag chur demis a chur rwm gi holk

Tigidh aois Eilein Albainn, a farrach faillte air o'n thonn meise,
Luchd cainnte mar bhuinear, deichnear faillte o rannaibh ris.
Greath bhi iomarbhaidh ann, eadara féin ann an ceòl,
Aithne nithear doibh 's an deagh uair, mar tha tulach àine Eoin.
Do nithead cath an Caislean Suibhne, fa sheabhag chroidhein a chroinn
Suidhead fa thimchioll an sgor sin, fionnmhor nimh luslan luirg [bhuirb,
De shleigh thollas taobh namhaid, mar nimh nathair guineich grannd,
Caol chlaidheamh o ghreas a fhuair, meilnichear leis colna Ghall.
Ceilearmaid uile Mhic Suibhne, ri soillse an fhad ghlug d' an chuain, [mòr.
Is fior nach dean do 'n ghlug an cabhar, 's e dian, diultnach, balglan,
Ni'r nach dian doibh luireach threibheir air sgiath chotan na sgeith donn,
Gabhas Reachlinn sgian-gheur sgarach, meobhar claidhean calma corr.
An tan chlaidheamh is fearr 's an Eorpa, se is luireach le na 's miann,
Cia sgiath 's an domhain nach diongainn, treabhach gun on cloinn Eirinn.
Eoin Mac Suibhne na slighcadach, le 'cholg tan, teasgach, mhall, [ach, dall.
Fear noch 'sgiath bhi sgiath bhreac, dhonn, fhuaireas treabhach, deaghrun-
Dail chabhlaich.

Iseabail ni Mhic Chailein.

Mairg do 'n galar an gràdh, ge b'e fàth fa 'n abraim e,
Deacair sgarachdainn r'a phàirt, truagh an càs 's a bheileam féin,
An gràdh sin thugas gun fhios, o 's e mo leas gun a luaidh,
Mar fhaigh mi furtachd tràth, bithidh mo bhlàth gu tana truagh ;
Am fear sin do 'n tugas gràdh, 'us nach faodas ràdh os n-aird,
Da cuiridh mise am buan chioma, domh fein is ceud mairg.
Mairg.

Is e ùghdair so Dunchadh òg

Seachd saighid ta air mo thi, ta gach saighid diubh 'g am lot,
'Teachd edraim agus Dia, o 's e sin is miann le' m chorp ;
A h-aon diubh ta an t-uabhar, am bi dha an gath ann mo chrios,
Minic a mheall e mi am buaidh, air ni thainig fois a nis.
An dara saighead an drus, sin a chuis do bheileam daor,
O lot na saighid 'n a ghò, ni bheileam beò o a rian ;
An treas diubh a ta, an altaibh mo chré a stigh,
Cha leig an leisg dhe 'dheoin, mise slighe choir air bith ;
An ceathramh saighead an t-sannt, a Dhia mairg an d'fhuair e guin,
Furtachd cha-n fhaigheam ri m ré, gun riochd cré air mo mhuin
An cuigeamh saighead an glamair, dimeas a chuir rium gu h-olc,

Cut re marrum a chrawg agis o noch slane mi chorp
Zeiwe in tessow sayd garga churris ferga eddrwm is cayd
Mwrre chaska nyn nurchir reym o nath wewm dein gow brath
An seachtow sayd in tuil formit is tnow riss gi neith
Ni sayd gay in waymot kin inta sin cha nil er breith
Zlaksin ille nach choyr mor a wilter lessin narm
Char heilk dwn zeyve nar woyal char woul dwn reyve nor warve
Currwm peaddir ein v'dey is crea nyn nostil gyth beacht
Eddrwm agis gwn nyn arm is v psalm no vi no seacht.
Seachta.

Auctor murreich albanach.

Meich doth treyl gow teigh pharris nor a zone gon a sorve
Cossnome in teyg trane gin cherri gyn skail ag nach el orn
Dane dy struth rad haggirt scor cwne gi dlow ymit tolk
Na berra a hy reith gyn ag skail is preve ra akre ort
Na dan folchan id fekgith ga grane re ynnis a holk
Legga did chwt a clath davr mar be angre zayvil ort
Dane di he ris in luchd drach ga din ga avezon lad cor
Scur rid locht di zul dyn doyn ma ym be olk ri oyn ort
Marg a threig teyg in ardre er zray phekke troy in nee
In tolk in ne donna gi devyr ymmi in sin feyzin mon zneve
Ag so sermon di heil nawzeve mir helim nath vil sche in brek
Fulling a vaissyth schal gow sathin in fer noch dothe gin ded
Ar a chenych seil nawzeve dwl a cholle agis da chree
Er a reir gi dany salke gyr ga deine ra ym begca mee.
Meich.

Murreich *ut supra*

Baith yn cie vec zey pekkich mir a mee mor in skail
Meissit dith di dor in neiss cross eiss crist er my vail
A cissi crist sayn ditvoss mayth za choss is mo za lave
Agis saynsi mis id zone a eddir ulli is sal is chnave
Ner scurris danew ulk di chin voyr mi churp an . . .
A choissvoyg gyn rove hawle er mi chenn is er mi chree
Raith mis a voyr vor vin gi brone a ma dor li mai
Sol fan dachaa mee fan nod gin rove roym gych rod raa.
Baith.

Cuide ri m'urram a chràdhadh, agus o nach slan mo chorp ,
Dhiubh an t-seathamh saighead gharg, chuireas fearg eadraim 'us càch,
Muire 'chasgadh nan urchair rium, o nach fhaigheam dion gu bràth ;
An t-seachdamh saighead an t-sùil, farmad 'us tnù ris gach ni,
Na saighid 'g am faigheamaid cion, annta sin cha-n 'eil ar brìgh ,
Ghlac sin gille nach còir, mòr a mhiltear leis an arm,
Char thilg duine dhoibh nar bhuail, char bhuail duine riamh nar mharbh.
Cuiream paidear aoin mhic Dhé, 'us creud nan Abstol gu beachd,
Eadraim agus guin nan arm, 'us cuig salm no sé no seachd.
Seachd.

An t-ùghdair Muireadhach Albanach.

Mithich domh triall gu tigh Pharais, 'n uair a ghuin gun e soirbh,
Cosnaim an tigh treun gun choire, gun sgeul aig neach eile oirnn,
Dean do sriuth ri 'd shagairt, 's coir cuimhneach gu dlù mu d' olc,
Na beir do thigh rìgh gun agh, sgeul is priomh ri agradh ort
Na dean folchainn a'd pheacadh, ge grain ri innseadh a h-olc,
Leigeadh do chuid an cleith diomhair, mun bi angair gabhail ort,
Dean do shìth ris an luchd dreuchd, ge dona, ge anbhuan le'd chor,
Sguir ri'd lochd, do ghul dean domhain, mu 'm bi olc ri fhaighinn ort
Mairg a threigeadh tigh an Ardrigh, air ghràdh peacaidh, truagh an ni,
An t-olc ni duine gu diomhair, iomadh an sin fiachan mu'n ghniomh.
Aig so searmon do shiol an Adhaimh, mar shaoilim nach bheil se am
Fulang a bhàis seal gu seachainn, is fior nach deth gun d'theid, [breug,
Fhir a cheannaich siol an Adhaimh, d' fhuil, a cholla, 'us da chridhe,
Air a réir gun deanadh sealga, ge'r ge dian ri'm bitheadh mi.
Mithich.

Am Muireadhach ceudna.

A bhi an cridhe Mhic Dhe, peacach mar mi mòr an sgeul,
Mise d'a gun d'fhuair a nis, crois Iosa Criosd air mo bheul ;
A Iosa Criosd sean de'd mhos, mo dha chos 'us mo dha làmh,
Agus seansa mise de'd dheòin, eadar fhuil, 'us shal, 'us chnàmh.
Nior sguireas deanamh uilc, do chion mhòr mo chuirp a ni,
A chaisrig gun robh thall, air mo cheann 'us air mo chridhe.
Rath mis a mhoir fhir bhinn, gach bròn mu'n d'fhuair le mi,
Sul fa 'n deachaidh mi fo 'n fhoid, gun robh romham gach ròd reidh.
A bhi.

A houdir soo murreich albanych.

Dane mi heggissk a threnoit a hearn in deit in choyl
Ling er mi hange a threnot bennych inn id venot wor
A threnot new er ni neyve nert marm neyve in noss
Ling agis coddill ym chree a chinn phopbill neywe in noss
Stur my layve teggisk mi chree teggisk mi roskg reith nyn skayle
Ling er mi zouth gloss ym henge skouth reim chloos benne mi wayl
Soo ym bayl leddri leive chaskis cayth chwneiss gi neith
Soo yn tange nach terg lawryth benne a herk manmi ee
Ort a threnoit ocht a threnoit ter yn leyghis lawyr rwmm
Id ta a will zal chrann darrych cree pekkych sallych yn sown
Gar zolk maa nar willis denyth ne zarni merlee a v'zey
Mi law nochar leddar dwnyth fregir er zraw wur mee
Fer gin danynsi dane breyga er wrega ella awra gorm
Ne zin wreyga er wreyga ella re in deyd er ormmae
Hwss a hug elle in nwm ne hagoyr zoiss zwll reay
Noch cha lawe in rik no aalsi helic dane dawsi ach dea
Ne dwni er talwun dim heggisk a hearn ach hwss feyn
Ne far a ne rann ach re neiwe di ne hawle si chre cheyll
Ma si licht fer er a willum caythe ay mayd moyd iun
Mass er a wreyg a taym a threnot leyg er layr ner royd inn
Ner choyr crea na tallow harrum ach tonn wraye beg in nerg
Ner choyr ne elli dim allich a reith ach tennyth zarrych zerga
Di zalvesi in teyve soo a threnot di hallow is di henni wee
Dwnni di henni is hallown fwnni zy r awli ee.

THE following fragment is continued from pages 12 and 13 of the Gaelic, where the first twenty-two lines of the composition will be found. Having been misplaced in the MS., the leaf containing the following lines was only discovered after the rest had been printed off :—

Ga beg a chwle chronanych ni in dad one zat zryme
Gin nis din re woralych ne rey fa wil a skaye
Ne hay sin di v'cowle re math we sin ne faynow,
Rachteis fir in doythin 'n a thigh wle gin nearri
Is troygh lwm a henor is how in derri teissi
Cha chorymich a wia sin ver how er mi reissi

Is e ùghdair so Muireadhach Albanach.

Dean mo theagasg a Thrianaid, a Thighearna d' an teid an ceòl,
Ling air mo theangaidh a Thrianaid, beannaich ann ad bhinne mhòir,
A Thrianaid naoimh air na neamhaibh, neartaich m' arm naomh a nis,
Ling agus codail a'm chridhe, a chinn phobuill neimh an nois
Stiuir mo làmh, teagaisg mo chridhe, teagaisg mo rosg, rìgh nan sgeul,
Ling air mo ghuth, gluais a'm theangaidh, sguth ri m chluais, beannaich mo
So am beul leadradh leibh, chaisgeas cath, chuimhn 'eas gach ni, [bheul,
So an teangaidh nach tearc labhradh, beannaich a sheirce m 'anamain
Ort a Thrianaid, och ! a Thrianaid, toir mo leigheas, labhair rium,
A ta amhail gheal chrann daraich, cridhe peacach salach an sunn.
Ge h-olc mi nior mhilleas daoine, ni dheanadh mearla, 'Mhic Dhé,
Mo lamh noch char leadar duine, freagair air ghràdh Mhuire mi.
Fior gun deanainnse dion breige, air bhreug eile amhra gorm,
Ni dhe 'n bhreug air bhreug eile, a rìgh an teid air orm ;
Thusa a thug eile annam, ni h-eucoir dhomhsa dhol réidh,
Noch cha lamh ionraic no uasal, thiodhlaic dion dhomhsa ach Dia.
Ni duine air thalmhainn do 'm theagasg, a Thighearna ach thusa féin,
Ni fear a ni rann ach Rìgh neimh, do ni h-amhail 's a chré cheill.
Ma 's e slighe fhior air a bheil eam, gabhaidh e meud moid inn,
Ma 's air a bhreug a taim a Thrianaid, leig air lathair an fhior roid fhinn.
Nior chuireas cré na talamh tharam, ach tonn bhraigh, beag an fhearg,
Nior chuireas ni eile do 'm fholach, a Rìgh ach teine gàireach dearg;
Do dhealbhassa an taobh so, a Thrianaid, do thalamh 'us de theine bhi,
Duine de theine 'us thalmhainn, fuine gheibhear amhlaidh e.

Ge beag a chul chronanach, ni 'n teid aon ghath gréine,
Gun fhios do 'n rìgh mhoralach 'n a ré fo bhil a sgéith.
Ni tha sin do Mhac Cumhail, rìgh maith bhi sin na Fianna,
Rachadas fir an domhain 'n a thigh uile gun iarraidh.
Is truagh leam a sheanair 'us thu an deireadh d' aoise,
Cha chothromach a bhreith sin bheir thu air mo righse.

Barr in chath layddir verri fenni ny fayni
Na di hearnyth crawe is tow feyn lay cheill
Bog sin a henor a ne an coyra bolla
Is far dea re hynlay na fayne errin olla
Ga taring mi layis is me derri meissi
Phadrik na toythr ayhis er mathew clynni beiskni
Ne hurrinn zwt aythris ossin v^c in reayne
Ach nath innyn far mathis agis flathis mi heyarni
Di marra aggwm conane far mewlass ni fayni
Ne legfe layd wnnill di chomis a cleyrri
Na habbir sen a ossin is anmein di wrayrri
Be fest gi fostynich is gawe hugit me ryilt
Da wacca ni catha is ni braddiche grast
Ne wee ane reid id ter ter ach moyir ni fayni
Ossin v^c ni flaa mest tanmyn a beithyll
Na cwne ni cath cha nil ag asling sin seill
Da glun ni gyir is meith ni shealga
Bar lat wee na warri na wea si chaythir noya
Troyg sin a henor is meithur ni schelga
Faychin gi honnor za wil si chaythir noa
Na habbir sin a phadrik is fallow di wrayrri
In deggow sin daynyth barr finn is no fayni
Er a lawe v^c eweissni ne fallow mi wrarri
Is farr angil din di hanglew na finn is ni faynyth
Da beanyth mir a weissith a gath zawryth ni beymin
Di zelin in demis ver tow er ayne errin
Dimmyth di wor zail er cath di heill
Ni warrin did choyth lawyth ach how neiss a tenour
Da marri mi zenissi ne estin di choyllane
Is zoywo di hemoo in narrik di choyrra
Da mardeis sin ulli si goynith ra cheilli
Ne wea mi holli lwe re vii caithe ni fayni
Vii fegthit urrit urrit vil tuss zi cleyrrew
Di huttideis sin ulli lay oskir na henyr
Ta tou in der di heill a henor gin cheyll
Scur a neiss id wreysrow is be fest zim rayr
Da wacca in lwcht cogthoill a v^cfin in alvin
Ne raacha za gomor re muntir ni caythre noya
Aggis ner low ir dynoyll nor heg most gow tawri
Sanossil ni braythryth fane woory zi rynis
Mathwm zwt a cleyrre di sgeul na hynnis
Innis down

B' fhearr an cath laidir bheireadh Fionn na Feinn,
No do Thighearn cràbhaidh 'us tu fhéin le chéile
Bochd sin a sheanair a ni an còmhradh boile,
Is fearr Dia re h-aon la no Feinn Eirinn uile.
Ge teirce mo laithese 'us mi an deireadh m' aoise,
Phadruig na toir aitheas air maithibh Cloinne Baoisgne.
Ni h-urrainn dhuit aithris Ossiain Mhic an Rioghain,
Ach nach ionann ar maithese 'us flaitheas mo Thighearna.
Da marrainn agam Conan fear mi-bhlasd na Feinn,
Ni leigeadh le d' mhuineal do chomas a chleirich.
Na h-abair sin a Ossiain 'us ainmeine do bhriathran,
Bi feasd gu foistinneach 'us gabh thugad mo riaghailt.
Da facadh na catha 'us na brataichean greasda,
Ni bhi aon rud ann d' aire ach meoghair na Feinn
Oisiain, mhic na flath misd d' anamain a bicheanta,
Na cuimhne na cath cha-n eil aig aisling 's an t-saoghail.
Da cluinnteadh na gadhair us meoghair na seilge,
B' fhearr leat bhi 'n a ghoire na bhi 's a chaithir naoimhe.
Truagh sin a sheanair is meoghair na seilge,
Fa chionn gach onoir dha bheil 's a chaithir naoimh.
Na h-abair sin a Phadruig, is falamh do bhriathra,
An deugaidh 's an deimhin, b' fhearr Fionn 's na Fianna.
Air a laimh Mhic Baoisgne, ni falamh mo bhriathra,
Is fearr aingeal do na h-ainglibh na Fionn 'us na Fianna
Da bithinn mar a bhitheas an cath Ghabhra nam beuman,
Do dhiolainn an dimeas bheir tu air Feinn Eirinn.
Do imich do mhòrdhail air càch de d' shaoghal,
Ni marrainn de d' chomhlamhaich ach thu nis a'd aonar.
Da maireadh mo dhaoinese ni éisdinn do ghòlan,
'Us gheibheadh tu do iompaidh an éiric do chòmhradh.
Da mhairdeas sinn uile 's sinn coinneachadh r' a chéile,
Ni bhi mo h-uile luaidh, ri seachd cathan na Feinn.
Seachd fichead uiread uiread am bheil tusa di chleirichibh
Do thuiteadas sin uile le Osgar 'n a aonar.
Tha thu an deireadh do shaoghail a sheanair gun cheill,
Sguir a nis de'd bhriathraibh 'us bi feasd do 'm réir.
Da fhacadh an luchd cochaill a Mhic Fhinn an Almhuinn,
Ni rachadh do chomoradh muinntir na cathrach naoimhe,
Agus nior lugha ar tionoil 'n uair thigeamaid gu Tabhra
Is anuasail na briathran fa 'n mhòr righ a rinneas,
Maitheam dhuit a chléirich, do sgeul 'n a h-innis.

Innis duinn.

EONE makphadrik vec voylchollum v'eoin doif vec eone v'gregor v'eone v'weillchollum vec conquhy veg v'conquly a strwlee v'illelane v'ey urquhaych v'kennane vec alpen agis in kennan seu bee ardree albin gi daywin ansi norsin agis in teone soo au in tean dwn deyk von kennan so id dowirt me—agis duncha deyroclych m'dowle v'oyne reywych di skreyve so a lowrow shenchyth nyn reig, agis roo zenyth anno dni millesimo quinmo duodecimo.

Eoin Mac Phadruig, mhic Mhaoilcholuim, mhic Eoin duibh, mhic Eoin, mhic Grigoir, mhic Eoin, mhic Mhaolcholuim, mhic Dhunchaidh bhig, mhic Dhunchaidh a Sruileadh, mhic Ghillfhaolain, mhic Aoidh Urchaidh, mhic Coinnich, mhic Alpain; agus an Coinneach sin b'e ard-rìgh Albain gu deimhin 's an uair sin; agus an t-Eoin so an t-aon duine deug o'n Choinneach so a dubhairt mi.—Agus Dunchadh daor-oglach Mac Dhughaill, mhic Eoin Riabhaich, do sgriobh so á leabhraibh seanachaidh nan rìgh; agus ro dheanadh Anno Domini Millesimo Quingentesimo duodecimo.

NOTE BY TRANSLATOR.

THE Dean's MS. was put into the hands of the present translator a few years ago by Mr. Cosmo Innes, with a view to a correct account being given of its contents. After a considerable time spent on deciphering the difficult handwriting, and resolving the strange and irregular orthography, he gave a fuller account of it than had been given before, in a paper read before the Society of Scottish Antiquaries. He was aware that a transcript of the MS. had been made by a Gaelic scholar of the highest reputation, the late Mr. M'Lachlan of Aberdeen; but that transcript was altogether unknown save by one or two individuals, and was at the time thought to be lost. In December 1860, the publishers proposed to the writer that he should undertake transcribing and translating the MS. with notes, Mr. Skene undertaking to write a historical introduction, with additional notes. There was good reason for reluctance in undertaking such a work. There was immense difficulty in the task itself, consisting very much in an exercise of ingenuity, the results to be tested by comparison, in guessing the meaning of words phonetically spelled; there was the labour of writing the same thing in three different forms; and there was in all this large demands upon time otherwise engrossed by the duties of a profession, whose calls the keeping of a good conscience, and duty to a Divine Master, would not admit of being neglected or postponed. The work itself, however, was very congenial, as contributing somewhat t the literature of the Celtic countrymen of the writer, th literature of a period, too, of which few other literary remain of theirs exist. He therefore undertook to devote his spa hours for a season to the work, which is now laid before th public.

The difficulties did not become less than was anticipate when they came to be practically dealt with. There was first th transcription of the original. A facsimile specimen of the writin is given in this volume, from which some idea may be forme of its character. The handwriting is the current English han of the fifteenth century, with a few additional peculiariti borrowed from the Gaelic writing of the same period, practised both in Scotland and Ireland. As is common i the writing of the period, the same sign is used both for *c* an *t*. There is often no distinction between *o* and *e*, *u* and *n*, or and *s*; and in the hurry of writing the Dean often wrote *m* f *n*, and *vice versâ*; and the letter *z* stands for all the soun resembling the consonant *y*. Besides, there are numerous co tractions, the same sign being often used for *in*, *im*, and *ir*, a the Irish dot (·) is often used as a substitute for *h*. The MS. in many places much decayed, and the writing in consequen much obscured, while the orthography is by no means qui regular. The transcript has, however, been carefully made fro the original, and compared again in proof, and the reader, wi the allowance necessary in the circumstances already describe may feel assured that in the original, as printed, he has a corre copy of the Dean's work.

The work, however, was not beyond the threshold when t transcription was complete. It was in interpreting the Dea phonetic Gaelic, so as to form the modern Gaelic edition, th the chief difficulty arose; and here the translator was left alt gether without guide to lead the way, except in the case of a fe of the Ossianic poems. There were three peculiar difficulties to be encountered here,—first, the frequent occurrence of obsolete words,—words not to be found in any dictionary of the Scottish Gaelic,—and the meaning of which could only be learned from some acquaintance with the ancient MS. writings of Scottish and Irish scribes; secondly, there was the introduction into the Dean's grammar of the Irish eclipsis, turning in his orthography *f* into *w*, *c* into *g*, *b* into *m*, and *d* into *n*, without any hyphen; and there was, last of all, the accentuation, which, in a number of the pieces, lays the emphasis on the latter syllable of dissyllabic words, and thus alters to a Scotch reader the whole rhythm of the lines. Many of these pieces will not read as poetry at all, unless read in accordance with the Irish method of accentuation. It was known to all acquainted with early Gaelic literature, how much there was that was common to the literature of Scotland and Ireland. This miscellany fully establishes the fact, while it also shows that, in the fifteenth century, Scottish Gaelic, as exemplified in some of these compositions, especially those of Finlay M'Nab, had its own distinctive features. There is nothing more interesting than the weight given in the allusions in these poems to the existence and influence of the Bardic schools at the period, and the large prizes usually conferred by the wealthy on successful poets.

The translation into English was, upon the whole, a less arduous process than the previous one. It might have been otherwise had the attempt been made to translate into English poetry. This, however, has been carefully avoided. The rendering has been made so literal as that the meaning of every sentence in Gaelic is conveyed in English, so far as the editor has been able to do it; and the translation is merely somewhat lightened, and the reading made more agreeable, by having the baldness of mere literality removed, and the lines made somewhat smooth and flowing.

In some cases the spelling and handwriting together have so obscured the words, that the editor has been quite unable to give anything like a satisfactory rendering; hence there will be found, in a very few instances, what are apparently different words in the original and modern version. Some instances will also be found of words written in the modern version according to the analogy of the Dean's orthography, while the precise word intended has not been identified. The editor has only to say regarding these and any other cases of doubtful rendering which in such a work must be numerous, that he will be happy to receive through the publishers any suggestions from Gaelic scholars which may help to secure greater accuracy.

It is only necessary to say farther, that in extending the modern Gaelic version of these poems, it was perfectly impossible to exclude all the older forms of the language. In many places to do so would have been to destroy the whole poetical structure of the composition. It was essential to retain the "da," *if*, the "fa," *on*, or *under*, and the "co" or "go," *with* besides numerous forms of the verb, which it is the practice now to call Irish, but which were common at an early period to the literature of both countries. It was perfectly impossible, with anything like justice to these compositions, to bring them into exact conformity with the rules of modern Scottish Gaelic.

The present volume contains every line of Ossianic or Fenian poetry in the Dean's MS. It also contains every composition having reference to Scotland, with the exception of five; two of these being so much defaced, and so many of the words obscured by time and exposure, that it is impossible to give anything like an accurate version of them. The other three are eulogies on the clan Gregor chiefs, so much of a piece with those already given, that they would not contribute to the literary value of the work. The purely Irish poems of the O'Huggins, the O'Dalys, etc., are not given in this work, whose object is to illustrate the language and literature of the Scottish Highlands at an early period. A few specimens, such as the laments of Gormlay, wife of Nial Glundubh, and daughter of Flann Sionna, Queen of Ireland, have been transcribed as specimens, which may be not uninteresting either to the Scottish or Irish reader. The Irish compositions are, with few exceptions, of a religious character.

T. M'L.

EDINBURGH, *December* 1861

In a note at p. 43, it is said that an edition of the poem by Allan M'Rory, there translated, would be given at the close of the work, as taken down from the recitation of an old woman, Christina Sutherland, in Caithness, in the year 1854. It is now given, but without a translation, which is not thought necessary

DUAN CATHA GHABHRA.

Is trom an nochd mo chumha féin, guilgeantach mo rian,
Smuaineachadh a chatha chruaidh, chuir mise 'us Cairbar claon-ruadh.
A mhic 's a Chormaig shuinn, is mairg sin fhuaireadh fo a laimh,
Laoch gun ghràin cha do chuir, ann a dha laimh iuthaidh.
Labhairidh Baranta gu prap, cuimhnich Mucanais, cuimhnich fathasd,
Cuimhnich 'ur sinnsreadh, 's 'ur linn, cuimhnich na clsean bhitheadh
cruaidh,
Bha aca an Eirinn ri'r linn, gu 'n bhi ag iocadh do Mhac Cumhail.
Gu 'm b'fhearr tuiteam air a mhagh, sinn 'us an Fheinn le chéile,
No bhi air barr a mhaigh, bhi an Fheinn air a mhòr thir.
Chuir sinn ar comhairle chruaidh, sinn 'us an Fheinn ri aon uair,
Feuchainn an cuireadh gach òg aghach, ceangal air . . .
An oidhche sin duinn gu lò, eadar mhnathan Fhiann 's na Feinn og òl,
An la sin gu 'm bitheamaid muigh, 'g oillt air Chairbar 'na liath-theach.

Chuir sinn sin Cath Ghabhra, 'us chuir gu fuathach, fuileach, feargach,
Thuit an Fheinn bonn ri bonn, 'us feara uasal Eirinn.
Deich fichead agus fichead ceud, sgeul fior, ni abraim breug,
Gun robh sinte an la sin, air a mhagh gun anamain,
Dha uiread eile 'us sin bha ann, aig rìgh Eirinn, sgeul bu mho,
Gun robh sinte air an taobh eile, de uaislibh Eirinn airm-ghloin.
Chuir sinn ar teachdair saor, gu Fathacanain mac a Choin,
Rachad an teachdair o ar cinn, gu ard thulach Eirinn.
Ciod e sin a phlòdh a bhuail oirbh, ars' an rìgh le meud a thoirm,
Is e mheud 's a bha annaibhse d'an uabhar, sin a mhill na fir eile.
Ach innis duinn Oisiain fheile, 'n uair chuir thu gach iorghuill treun,
An d'fhuair thu do mhac anns a chath, no an d'rug air 'ard labhradh.
Thainig mi an deigh cur an àir, os cionn mo mhic Osgair àigh,
Gun d'fhuair mise a sgiath ri làr, 's 's a lann 'n a dheas laimh ;
Chuir mi bonn mo shleagh ri làr, 'us rinn mi os a chionn tàmh,
Phadruig, smuainich mise an sin, ciod a dheanainn ri mo shaoghal ;
Gum b'e freagairt mo mhicse féin, 'n uair bha e an deireadh anamain,
" Fo ris na duilibh, thusa a bhi lathair, athar."
Ach nior their mise a ghò, freagairt cha robh agam dhò,
Ach an d' thainig Caoilte cain, thugamsa dh' fheuchainn Osgair.
'N uair dh' fheuch Caoilte gach cneadh air chòir, fhuair e gach aon ni c
dhòigh,
Fhuair e 'chorp creuchdach, glan, air a sgaradh le geur shleaghan ,
Sleagh chrithinn a Chairbair ruaidh, an innibh Osgair, mo thruaighe !
Bha lamh Chaoilte gu uileann deas, ann an àite na sleagha,
Leud na coise bhàn air 'fholt, cha robh sin slàn 'n a chorp,
Ach an ruigeadh e 'bhonn làr, ach 'eudan 'n a h-aonai.
Mar bhuinne aimhne bha a shnuagh, no sruth reothairt bha ro luath,
Gun robh e 'cuir 'fhola dheth, 'am blaghaibh a luirich.
Thog sinn an t-Osgar suas, chunnacas tochdair mu 'r coinnimh,
Fionn mac Cumhail is e treunmhor, 'us e 'g imeachd feadh an t-sloigh
Ag iarraidh mo chorpsa 's a chath, 'us corp Osgair an aird fhlatha,
Corp Chaoilte nach tinn, deagh mhic a pheathair ionmhuinn.
Chunnaic sinn nis Fionn, 'us e 'g imeachd feadh an t-sloigh,
Thog sinn ar sleagha os ar cionn, 'us ruith sinn uile 'n a chomhdhail.
Bheannaich sinn an sin do Fhionn, 'us cha d'fhreagair esan sinn,
Ach ruith gu tulach nan treun, far am bith Osgar nan arm geur.
'N uair chunnaic an t-Osgar Fionn, 'us e tamuil os a chionn,
Thog e air an aghaidh aluinn, 'us bheannaich e d'a sheanair,
Beagan bu mhiosa thu na sin, an la Chab-an-eudainn,
Chiteadh na neoil troimh do shlios, 'us dh'fheudar do leigheas,
Rachad na coirean air luathainn, troimh do cholainn chraobh uallaich,
D'fhuaigheal dh' iarr thu le goid, nach d'rinneas air laoch romhad.

Mo leigheas cha-n 'eil aig fàil, nocha-n fhaighear e gu bràth,
Tuilleadh cha-n 'eil agaibh do 'm thoirbheirt, ach an t-sreangsa do 'm ard labhradh,
Sleadh Charbair chràdh mo chridhe 's gur i sgar mi o mo chairdibh,
Chuir e sleadh nan naoi slinn, eadar m'imleag 'us m'airnean,
Mo thruaighe sin! Osgair fhéile, 's a dheagh mhic mo mhicse féin,
Bha sgaradh na sleagh o do dhruim, 'n am togail cis o shliochd mhòr Chuinn,
D'eisdeachd ri briathraibh Fhinn, an ainm an Osgair dhuinn,
Shin e uaith a dha laimh, 'us dhùn e an rosg bha ro mhall.
Thionndadh Fionn ruinn a chùl, 'us shil a dheura gu dlù;
An taobh muigh de Osgar 'us de Bhran, gun chaoineadh air neach bh'air thalamh.
Cha chaoineadh duine a mhac féin, 's cha chaoineadh e brathair 'n a dhèigh,
Bha sinn mar sin uile, 's gach neach a caoineadh Osgair.
A mhain ach mi féin 'us Fionn, cha robh aon neach os a chionn,
Nach tug tri glaodhan mu'n uaigh, chuir clos air Eirinn ri aon uair.
D'éisdeachd ri beucaich nam fear, 'us sgreadail nan comh-mhilidh,
Ri faicinn an oig-fhir thrcin, 'us e 'n a luidh 'n a bhaoth-neul,
Ge b'e righ thigeadh an sin, gheibheadh e foide gun aoidh,
Gun fhuathach, gun umhladh, gun dail, gun achmhasan, gun iomadan.
O'n la chuir mi cath Ghabhra, gu dearbh mi gun trom labhradh,
'Us oidhche cha robh mi no lo, gun osnadh bha gu lionmhor.

T. M'L.

ADDITIONAL NOTES.

(*Introduction*, p. xv.)

DIFFERENCES BETWEEN IRISH AND SCOTCH GAELIC.

DR. O'DONOVAN, in his Irish Grammar, gives a statement of these differences, which is somewhat meagre. He appears, however, to have had little knowledge of Scotch Gaelic, except what he gathered from Stewart's Grammar; and this statement of the differences between the two dialects is taken almost *verbatim* from a prior statement of them by P. M'Eligott, in the Transactions of the Gaelic Society, published in 1808, p. 15.

Dr. O'Donovan, in his account of grammars previously published, gives Stewart very just praise for the excellence of his Grammar; but throughout his own work he never loses an opportunity of carping at him, and is especially indignant at him for daring to state that the Scotch Gaelic wants the present tense of the verb, and very disingenuously quotes Shaw's Grammar as a superior authority. He likewise attacks Stewart for not producing ancient MSS. to prove it, and for not seeing that the present tense is used by Bishop Carsewell, in 1564. Stewart, however, was not undertaking a grammar of the *ancient* Scotch Gaelic, but of the dialect *then* spoken by the people; and most unquestionably, in the spoken dialect of Stewart's time, the present tense was not used. Dr. O'Donovan denies this fact, and even charges Stewart with dishonesty. His theory is, "that Stewart was induced to reject this tense, in order to establish a striking point of resemblance between the Erse and the Hebrew, which the Irish, supposed to be the mother tongue, had not,"—a most unworthy insinuation, and most unphilosophical, for O'Donovan ought to have known that the changes which take place in the structure of spoken languages proceed from organic laws which cannot be influenced or directed by grammarians. The will of any single man is powerless to alter the minutest particle in the language; and the fact that the inflected present tense is not used in Scotch Gaelic, is evident to any one acquainted with the language, or who has come in contact with those who speak it.

Dr. O'Donovan also finds fault with Stewart for expressing an opinion that, "as the Erse dialect has not the inflections in the termination of its verbs, which characterize the Irish, it is therefore more original than the Irish." This is, no doubt, an erroneous view; and O'Donovan correctly states "that the mode of inflection, by varying the termination, is more ancient than the use of particles;" but he might have recollected that the contrary opinion was very generally held when Stewart wrote; that the sounder principles of philology, in this respect, were not known or understood till after the publication of his Grammar; and that he could not, with any candour, impute it to him as a fault that he had not anticipated the conclusions of a science which had, so to speak, been created subsequently to his time. That the same peculiarities existed in the language in the last century, is proved by the fact that the Gaelic colonists in Canada, who have been separated from the mother country since that period, speak a form of Scotch Gaelic precisely similar to that now spoken in the Highlands, and possessing all those dialectic peculiarities which distinguish it from Irish. Although the present tense of the verb is usually expressed by the auxiliary, the Highlanders also use the future tense to express the present.

The leading differences between Irish and Scotch Gaelic may be stated generally as follows:—

SOUNDS OF THE LANGUAGE.

1. The initial consonants are not affected to the same extent as in Irish and Welsh; and in pure Scotch Gaelic the eclipsis is unknown, except in the case of the letter *S*.

The following table will show their relative position in this respect:—

TABLE SHOWING THE CHANGE IN THE INITIAL CONSONANT IN WELSH, IRISH, AND SCOTCH GAELIC.

Initial Consonants	Welsh			Irish		Scotch Gaelic	
	Eclipsis.	Aspiration	Nasal	Eclipsis	Aspiration	Eclipsis	Aspiration.
P	B	Ph	Mh	B	Ph		Ph
C	G	Ch	Ngh	G	Ch		Ch
T	D	Th	Nh	D	Th		Th
B	M	Bh or F		M	Bh		Bh
G	NG	—		NG	Gh	Wanting.	Gh
D	N	Dd or Dh		N	Dh		Dh
Ll		L			L		L
M		Mh or F			Mh		Mh
Rh		'R			R		R
F.				Bh	Fh		Fh
S				T	Sh	T	Sh

2. In Irish, words beginning with *A* may take the digamma *F*, as *aill, faill*, a rock; *ata, fata*, a plain; *iolair, fiolair*, an eagle, etc. The digamma never appears in Scotch Gaelic.

3. The vowel sounds *O* and *U* in Irish, pass into *A* in Scotch Gaelic; as, *oir*, Ir., *air*, Sc. G.; *og*, Ir., *ag*, Sc. G.; *ugadh*, Ir., *achadh*, Sc. G.; *chuaidh*, Ir., *chaidh*, Sc. G.

4. The vowel at the end of nouns in Irish, is dropped in Scotch Gaelic; as, *tigherna*, Ir., *tighearn*, Sc. G.

5. In the consonants the older form is often retained in Scotch Gaelic; thus, the initial *S* in Irish, is often *D* in Scotch Gaelic, which is the older form, as *suil*, Ir., *duil*, Sc. G.,—hope. *S* is sometimes changed to *P*, as *siuthar*, Ir., *piuthar*, Sc. G.,—sister.

6. The accentuation in Scotch Gaelic in dissyllables is on the first syllable; in Irish, on the last.

GRAMMAR.

1. *Article.*

The genitive plural before a labial is *nam.*

2. *Noun.*

The nominative plural frequently ends like Welsh and Manx in *an;* as, *Slatan,* rods; *Maithean,* chiefs.

3. *Verbs.*

The analytic form is alone used, there being no inflections for persons or numbers.

The Irish present is used as the future, and there is no present tense.[1]

The past-participle is invariably *te* hard, and is not varied as in Irish.

There are no consuetudinary tenses.

4. *Adverb.*

The negative is *Cha,* instead of *Ni,* in Irish.

VOCABULARY.

There is a considerable difference in the vocabulary words being now used in Irish, which are unknown in Scotch Gaelic, and *vice versa,* and a comparison of the lists of idiomatic phrases in Irish or Scotch Gaelic shows a very great difference in the mode of expressing familiar phrases.[2]

[1] In the old form of the verb, in German, the present tense exercised likewise the function of the future.

[2] Since this note was written, the writer has learned with great regret of the death of Dr. O'Donovan, and hesitated whether these strictures on some opinions in his able Irish Grammar ought to be retained, but justice to an equally able Scotch grammarian seemed to require them; and he may be allowed this opportunity of expressing his sincere admiration of the great learning and knowledge of that distinguished Irish scholar, and his sense of the loss which Celtic philology has sustained by his lamented death.

(*Introduction*, p. lxxxiv.)

The Welsh poem alluded to is contained in the Welsh Archæology, vol. i. p. 168. The text is, however, very corrupt. It has been translated by Mr. Stephen in the *Archæologia Cambrensis*, new Series, vol. ii. p. 150, who did not, however, see its real character, and very strangely supposes it to refer to the actions of Cuichelm, one of the West Saxon kings, who died in 636, and whom he identifies with the Chocholyn of the poem, while of Corroi, son of Dairy, he can give no account.

The poem is in reality an Ossianic poem referring to the death of Curoi, son of Daire, by Cuchullin, the celebrated Fenian hero of Ulster.

Keating gives the following account of the death of Curoi:— "The heroes of the red branch united to plunder an island near Alban, called Manann, where there was a great quantity of gold, silver, jewels, and many other valuable articles, and a lovely marriageable young lady, who surpassed all the women of her time in exquisite figure and beauty, the daughter of the governor of the island, and her name was Blanaid. When Curigh was informed that the heroes were setting out on this expedition, he transformed himself by magic into a disguised shape, and joined the party; but when they were on the point of plundering the island, disguised like jugglers, they judged that there would be great difficulty in taking the fortress in the island, in which were secured Blanaid and the valuable treasures of the whole island, on account of its strength and the number of men who defended it. Then Curigh, who was attired in a coarse grey habit, engaged, if he were to get his choice of the treasures, that he would himself take possession of the fort. Cuchullin promises this, and immediately they attacked the castle with the man in the grey habit at their head, who stopped the motion of an enchanted wheel that was placed at the castle gate, and let in all the troops, by whom the fortress was sacked, and Blanaid and all the treasure borne away. They then set out for Ireland, and arrived at Evan; and on dividing the treasure, the man in the grey habit demands his choice of the jewels, as was promised to him. 'You shall have it,' says Cuchullin. 'Well, then,' says he, 'Blanaid is the jewel I choose.' 'Take your choice of all the jewels except Blanaid alone,' replies Cuchullin. 'I will not exchange her,' says Curigh, and thereupon he seeks to carry her off by force; and having surprised her unperceived, took her away concealed under an enchanted mask. When Cuchullin perceived that the lady was missing, he suspected that it was Curigh that stole her off, and pursued them directly to Munster, and overtook them at Sulchoid. The champions engage, and a brave and well-fought contest ensues; but at length Cuchullin was overcome by Curigh, who tied him neck and heels, and left him shackled like a captive, after cutting off his hair with his sword, and then carried away Blanaid into the west of Munster. Then, however, came up Laogh mac Riain of Gabhra, and unbound Cuchullin, and they set out for the north of Ulster, where they resided near the peaks of Boirche for the space of a year, without appearing in the Council of Ulster, until Cuchullin's hair grew again; and at the expiration of the year, happening to be on the peaks of Boirche, he saw a great flight of birds coming on the sea to the north, and on their landing upon the shore, he pursues them, and by a feat called *Taveim*, killed one of them with his sling in every district he passed through, until the last of them fell at Sruv Bron, in the west of Munster. On his return from the west, he found Blanaid in solitude near the Finglass, in Kerry, where Curigh had a palace at that time. A conversation ensued between them, in which she declared to him that there was not on the face of the earth a man she loved more, and entreated him to come near Allhallow tide with an armed band, and carry her off with him by force; and that he might the more easily accomplish his design, she would take care that Curigh should, at that time, have but few soldiers or attendants. Cuchullin promises to come to her at the appointed time, and then takes his leave, and sets out for Ulster, and relates the adventure to Choncubar.

In the meantime Blanaid told Curigh that he ought to erect a palace for himself that should exceed all the royal palaces in the kingdom, and that he might do so by sending the Clanna

Deaguid to gather and collect all the large upright stones in the kingdom to form this palace. Blanaid's reason for this was, that the Clanna Deaguid might be dispersed in distant parts of Ireland, far from Curigh, at the time that Cuchullin should come to carry her off. Cuchullin, being informed that the Clanna Deaguid were scattered over the kingdom, sets out privately, and soon arrived at a wood near the seat of Curigh, and sends secretly to inform Blanaid of his arrival with a large body of troops along with him. She sends him word that she would steal Curigh's sword; and then, as a sign of attack, that she would spill a large vessel of new milk that was in the house into the rivulet which flowed from the castle through the wood where Cuchullin was concealed. Having heard this, in a short time he perceived the stream white with the milk, when, sallying out, they forced into the palace, and slew Curigh, who was alone and unarmed, and took Blanaid away with them to Ulster."

WELSH POEM.

MARWNAD CORROI MAB DAIRY.

Dy ffynhawn lydan dyleinw aches
Dyddaw dyhepcyr dybris dybrys
Marwnad Corroy am Cyffroes.

Ordyviwr garw ei anwydeu
A oedd mwy ei ddrwg nis mawr gigleu
Mab Dairy dalei lyw ar for deheu
Dathl oedd ei glod cyn noi adneu.

Dy ffynhawn lydan deleinw nonneu
Dyddaw dyhepcyr dybrys dybreu
Marwnad Corroy genhyf inheu.

Dy ffynhawn lydan dyleinw dyllyr
Dy saeth dychyrch draeth diwg dybyr
Gwr a werescyn mawr ei faranrhes.
(*Line wanting.*)
A wedy mynaw myned trefydd
A ant wy ffres ffra wynyonydd
Tra fu vuddugre vorc ddugrawr
Chwedleu amgwyddir o wir hyd law
Cyfranc Corroy a Chocholyn.

Lliaws eu terfysg am eu terfyn
Tarddei pen amwern gwerin goadd fwyn
Caer y su gulwydd ni gwydd ni gryn
Gwyn ai fyd yr enaid ui harobryn.

TRANSLATION.

THE DEATH-SONG OF CORROY, SON OF DAIRY.

I.

Thy large fountain fills the river,
Thy coming will make thy value of little worth,
The death-song of Corroy agitates me.

II.

If the warrior will come, rough his temper.
And his evil was greater than its renown was great,
To seize the son of Dairy, lord of the Southern Sea.
Celebrated was his praise before she was intrusted to him.

III.

Thy large fountain fills the stream.
Thy coming will cause saddling without haste.
The death-song of Corroi is with me now.

IV.

Thy large fountain fills the deep;
Thy arrows traverse the strand, not frowning or depressed
The warrior conquers, great his rank of soldiers,
(*Line wanting.*)
And after penetrating, enters the towns,
And . . . the pure stream was promptly whitened.
Whilst the victorious one in the morning heaps carnage,
Tales will be known to me from the sky to earth,
Of the encounter of Corroi and Chocholyn.
Numerous their tumults about their borders,
Springs the chief o'er the surrounding mead of the somewhat gentle wood.
A city there was, love—diffusing, not paling, not trembling.
Happy is he whose soul is rewarded.

The allusions in this poem are to Cuchullin's expedition to attack Curroi, to Blanaid's giving the signal by filling the stream with milk from a large vessel, and to the encounter between Curroi and Cuchullin, in which the former fell.

It may not be out of place to insert here a few stanzas of an old Manx historical poem, written between 1504 and 1522, to show the relation of the Manx orthography to the Welsh and to that of the Dean of the same age.

I.

Dy neaishtagh shin aghrish my skeayll
As dy ving lhiclu ayns my chant
Myr share dy voddyms lesh my veeal,
Yinnin diu geill da 'n Ellan Sheeant.

II.

Quoi yn chied er ee row rieau ee
Ny kys eisht myr haghyr da
Ny kys hug Parick ayns Creestiaght
Ny kys myr haink ee gys Stanlaa.

III.

Manannan beg va Mac y Leirr,
Shen yn chied er ee row rieau ee,
Agh myr share oddyms cur my ner,
Cea row eh hene agh an chreestee.

TRANSLATION.

If you would listen to my story,
I will pronounce my chant
As best I can. I will with my mouth
Give you notice of the Holy Island,
Who he was that had it first,
And then what happened to him;
And how Patrick brought in Christianity,
And how it came to Stanley.
Manannan beg was son of Leirr,
He was the first that ever had it;
But as I can best conceive,
He himself was not a Christian.

10

Poems, p. 3.

This poem has a strong resemblance in its character and sentiment to the oldest poems in the Cymmrian dialect.

The oldest known poem in this dialect which has been preserved in its original orthography is a short poem of three stanzas, written in the Irish character in a parchment MS. at Cambridge, containing a paraphrase of the Gospels by Iuvencus, a Latin poet. The writing of this MS. is anterior to the year 700.

The poem is as follows :—

I.

Ni guorcosam nemheunaur henoid,
Mi telu nit gurmaur.
Mi am franc dam an calaur.

II.

Ni canu ni guardam ni cusam henoid,
Cet iben med nouel
Mi am franc dam an patel.

III.

Na mereit im nepleguenit henoid
Is diszur mi coueidid
Donn am riceur im guetid.

It is the song of a warrior mourning his fate and his solitude, and may be thus translated :—

Neither repose nor sleep for me this night,
My house is no longer great.
For me and my servant no caldron more,
No songs, no smiles, no kisses this night,
As when I drank the fortifying mead.
For me and my servant no goblet more,
No longer joy for me this night.
My supporter is discouraged;
No one aids me in my distress.

The Irish character, in which this poem is written, is of the eighth century, and Villemarqué has remarked upon its resemblance in sentiment and character to a poem of Llywarch Hen, a Cumbrian bard of the sixth or seventh century, whose poems are universally admitted to be genuine, the orthography of which is much more modern. The poem is in triplets, the first line also ending with "heno," and a single stanza or two will show the resemblance :—

Y stafel Kyndylan nis esmwyth-heno
Ar benn karec Hydwyth
Heb ner, Heb nifer, Heb ammwyth.

Istafel kyndylan ys tywyll—heno
Heb dan, Heb gerddau
Dygystudd deurudd dagrau.

The following are a few of the verses :—

The hall of Kyndylan is not joyous this night,
On the top of the rock of Hydwyth,
Without its lord, without company, without feasts.
The hall of Kyndylan is gloomy this night,
Without fire, without songs,
Tears afflict the cheeks.

The poem, attributed to Ossian in the Dean's MS., is of the same character :—

Long are the clouds this night above me,
The last was a long night to me
This day, although I find it long,
Yesterday was longer still.

. . . .

Long are the clouds this night above me.
No rising up to noble feats;
No mirthful sport as we would wish,
No swimming heroes on our lakes.
Long are the clouds this night above me, etc.

Poem, p. 4.

This is a well-known poem, termed Sliabh nam ban Fionn. A copy almost identic with this is published by the Ossianic Society of Dublin in their sixth volume, and a comparison of the first stanza with that of the Dean will show the relation the orthography of it bears to his :—

DEAN.

La zay deacha finn mo rayth
Di helg er sleyve ny ban finn
Tri meillith wathyon ny wayn
Ne zeaath skaow vass in ginn.

IRISH.

La da n-deachaidh Fionn na bhfiann
Do sheilg ar shliabh na m-ban fionn
Tri mhile do mhaithibh na bhfiann
Sul n-deachaidh grian os ar g-cionn.

It will be observed that the Irish eclipsis is only partially recognised by the Dean.

There is a copy of this poem in Kennedy's Collection, p. 29. The number of verses is the same, but some variation occurs in the reading of several of them.

Dr. Smith remarks, in the Highland Society's Report, that an edition of this poem, under the title of La mor Seilg na Feinne, occurs in the oral recitations communicated by the Rev. Francis Stewart of Craignish, and another was written from memory by Archibald M'Callum.

Poem, p 20.

The King of Sorcha is here opposed to the daughter of the King of the Tir fo thuinn, or land beneath the waves; and in this respect it resembles the Welsh poems, where the King of Annwn and his daughter play so great a part.

Sorcha is light, in opposition to Dorcha, dark; and there seems to be a poetic contrast between the kingdom of light and the kingdom under the waves.

Historically the land under the waves was the low-lying coast of Holland and Germany, extending from the Rhine to the Elbe.

Dr. Smith remarks that this poem differs little from Kennedy's and other oral editions in the possession of the Society.

Poem, p. 26.

There is an edition of this poem in one of M'Vurich's MSS. in the collection deposited in the Faculty Library. The lan guage is more Irish than the Dean's. The first verse may be given for the purpose of comparison:—

DEAN.

Sai la guss in dei
Oy nach vaga mai finn
Chanaka rem rai
Sai boo yar lym.

M'VURICH

Se la gus an de
Nach faca me fionn
Ni fhaca re mo re
Se budh faide leam.

It will be observed that the Dean uses the Scotch negative *Cha*, while M'Vurich has the Irish *Ni*.

Poem, p. 30.

Dr. Smith states that this poem corresponds in a great measure with one taken down from oral recitation in Sutherland and another in Isla.

Poems, p. 35 and p. 48.

This poem is one of the editions of the Cath Gabhra, and, along with the poem by Feargus Filidh on the same subject, forms part of the long poem called Cath Gabhra, printed by the Ossianic Society of Dublin in their first volume.

In this poem it is said—

Eastward we sent ambassadors,
To Fatha of Conn's great son,

Or more literally—

To Fatha, son of Maccon.

The expression east or eastward always refers to Alba or Scotland, in contradistinction to west, which was Sire, and the allusion here is to one of the mythic colonies from Ireland to Scotland

In addition to the historic colony of Dalriada in the sixth century, the Irish historians record four colonies in pre-historic times.

These were—

1. Dalriads under Cairbre Riada, in the third century.
2. The Clanna Breogan, under the Fathads, sons of Lugad Mac Con, King of Ireland, in the third century, from whom the Campbells are said to be descended.
3. Eremonians, under Colla Uais, King of Ireland, in the fourth century, from whom the M'Donalds are said to be descended.
4. Eberians, under Cairbre Cruithnechan and Maine Leamhna, sons of Corc mac Lughadh, in the fourth century, from whom the Maormers of Marr and Lennox are said to be descended.

The second of these colonies, under Fatha Canann, is here connected with the legends of the Feinne.

Dr. Smith states that this poem agrees, with some variation in words and arrangement, with one transmitted by Mr. Maclagan from oral recital.

The poem on the battle of Gabhra, attributed to Fergus, is obviously the older piece, and some of the stanzas are the same with those in the Irish poems. It also refers to the Feinne of Britain and of Lochlan.

There is an edition of this poem in Kennedy's Collection, p. 148; and another, taken down from recitation, was communicated to the Highland Society by Mr. Malcolm M'Donald.

The first stanza of this poem, with the corresponding stanza in the Irish poem, is given for the purpose of comparison:—

DEAN.

Innis donn a earris
Ille feynni errin
Kynis tarle zevin
In gath zawrych ni beymin.

IRISH.

Innis duinn a Oisin
Re h'anam Fhianna Eirionn
Cia agaibh ba threise
I g-cath Gabhra na m-beimionn.

It will be again observed that the eclipsis is only partially recognised. The Dean seems rarely to employ it in the genitive plural, where it is rigorously demanded by the rules of Irish grammar.

Poem, p. 50.

Dr. Smith remarks that this poem agrees very much with one got from Isla by recitation, and communicated to the Society by Robert Campbell, Esq., Advocate.

Poem, p 54

Dr Smith states that this poem, on the death of Fraoch, differs very little from Mr. Jerome Stone's edition, and still less from Mr. Gillies' Collection, page 107.

Poem, p. 58.

Dr. Smith remarks that this poem nearly agrees with one in Kennedy's Collection, p. 69. Some of the names are different, and the stanzas not all in the same order.

The same poem appears, with a few lines more or less, and a slight variation of words and arrangement, in one of the MSS. deposited in the Faculty Library; and two editions were communicated to the Highland Society taken down from oral recitation, one from an old man in Isla, the other from Donald M'Callum in Kilcalmonell, in Kintyre.

Poem, p 72.

The idea which forms the subject of this poem is common to the Gael and the Welsh.

Poem by Gilchrist Taylor, p. 93.

This poem certainly refers to the taking of the murderers of James I., by Robert Reoch Duncanson of Strowan, and John Gorme Stewart of Garth. Robert Reoch bears on his seal two greyhounds, and on 15th August 1451 received a charter from James II. of the barony of Strowan "pro zelo, favore et amore quos gerimus erga dictum Robertum Duncanson pro captione iniquissimi proditoris quondam Roberti de Graham."

John Gorme Stewart receives in the Exchequer Rolls a payment "pro arrestatione Roberti Grahame traditoris et suorum complicium."

Poem by John of Knoydart, p. 99.

In the Annals of Ulster there is the following notice of the murder of Angus Og, son of John, Lord of the Isles :—

Aois Criost 1490, Mac mic Domnaill na h-Alpan, .i. Aengus, .i. nec da n-gairti an Tigerna Aacc do marbad a fill le ferted Erennac, .i. Diarmidt h-ua Cairpri, 7 a n Inhernis do marbad h-e. That is,—Year of Christ 1490, Angus, son of Macdonald of Scotland, who was called the young Lord, was murdered by his Irish harper, Dermed O'Cairbre, and at Inverness he was slain.

The Annals of Ulster are cotemporary authority for the event.

Poem by Finlay M'Nab, p. 125.

The Dougall, son of John, who is here reproached as a sluggard, and exhorted to write in the Book of Poems, was no doubt the Dean's father, Dougall Johnson. It would appear from this that the taste for collecting Gaelic poetry was a family quality.

The genealogical poems relating to the M'Gregors, M'Dougalls, and M'Donalds, are curious, but it would be out of place to enter here upon the family history of these clans.

W. F. S.

INDEX.

NOTE.—The numerals refer to the Introduction; the common figures to the English Translation; and the ancient figures to the corresponding Original Gaelic.

EDINBURGH: T. CONSTABLE,
PRINTER TO THE QUEEN, AND TO THE UNIVERSITY.

Printed in the USA
CPSIA information can be obtained
at www.ICGtesting.com
LVHW010142290224
772895LV00019B/25